THE PAPERS OF
THE ORDER OF INDIAN WARS

THE PAPERS OF
THE ORDER OF INDIAN WARS

Introduction by John M. Carroll

Preface by Col. George S. Pappas (Ret.)

THE OLD ARMY PRESS

1513 WELCH
FORT COLLINS, CO. 80521

CONTENTS

Acknowledgements

I wish to thank the following persons and organizations for their great cooperation in getting this material re-assembled and allowing me to help get it back into print for all to use and enjoy:

Colonel George S. Pappas, Director of the U.S. Army Military History Research Collection at Carlisle Barracks, Pennsylvania. It is here that the complete files for the Order of Indian Wars have been preserved.

Dr. Richard J. Sommers, Supervisor of the Manuscript Division of the U.S. Army Military History Research Collection. Dr. Sommers is directly responsible for the order and safety of these invaluable documents.

Dr. Pogue, President of AMI, who extended the necessary permission to use these documents.

and

The staff of the U.S. Army Military History Research Collection for their many hours of helping hands — everything from reams of xeroxing to just listening patiently to my requests for additional help. And to the center itself for being the fantastic resource center that it is. I pray it continues to exist and grow, and I urge all interested scholars to turn to this repository for expected and unexpected rewards in military history.

For

"Chickie" and Byron Price

Preface

Histories are unusual writings. Unlike the scientific treatise which is based upon formulae, experiment, and derivation and equally unlike the novel which is the product of its author's fabrication, the history reflects the events of the past based upon the interpretation and opinions of its author. The historian seeks all possible sources of information for his work: official documents, private writings, art works, photographs, and — in this modern period — oral recorded interviews. The depth of his research and the quality of the research source materials he has used contribute directly to the validity, opinion, interpretations, and concepts the historian builds into his discussion of past events.

Great reliance is placed on the official records, for these are — at least in theory — the most valid account of what has taken place. Here can be found the who, the what, the when, and the where related to any specific event. Unfortunately, all too often all too little of the how and the why is to be found in the official report. In many ways, the official account must be termed to be a sterile bone lacking meat or marrow — the flavor provided by the more intimate and personal account of the participant.

Today this need can be met by personal interviews — oral history — of individuals who have participated in events of interest to the historian. But it is obviously impossible to personally talk to those who have passed on. Such being the case, the historian must then look to other sources for the intimate and personal account of events so important if he is to add flavor to the bone he may find in the official record. The personal writings of the individual — diaries, letters, books, articles, speeches — all help provide some of the color and the flavor needed for the historian's research. Admittedly, materials written shortly after an event has taken place are in most instances more accurate than those written years later. Man, being man, often has the tendency to "remember" what took place at a certain time, subconsciously and unintentionally using the knowledge gained subsequently to add to his recollections. Nevertheless, papers written at much later dates are still an excellent research source.

Secondary sources — books and other published materials — cannot be completely ignored by the research historian. One cannot completely digest and absorb everything read as being complete truth, for if such were done the legend of Washington chopping down his father's cherry tree would still be accepted as fact. Secondary sources must be used with the full realization that each is but one man's interpretation of his subject, one man's opinion based on his own research and study.

When all of these source materials are used by the research historian, he is better able to provide a factual yet flavorful description to his reader and to the student of history. Research cannot be restricted to a single source or to a single type of source material. Official reports, personal writings, oral interviews, photographs, periodicals, and secondary source materials all contribute to varying degrees to the knowledge required by an historian in his research of the events of the past.

The papers and proceedings of the Order of the Indian Wars are but one group of source materials to be found in the US Army Military History Research Collection. This institution is unique for here in one location has been assembled an outstanding collection of research materials relating to a single discipline, military history. The Military History Research Collection was established in 1967 at the personal direction of the then Chief of Staff of the Army, General Harold K. Johnson. The mission assigned the institution was to preserve materials of historical significance relating to the US Army and to make these materials available for research and study by all scholars, civilian and military alike.

In the six years since its establishment, the Research Collection has grown at an amazing rate. Today the research historian has access to over 300,000 books on military history, more than 30,000 bound volumes of periodicals, over 2,500 document boxes of manuscripts and diaries, several thousand rolls of microfilm, and thousands of photographs. More than 30,000 official documents are available for scholarly study. The Research Collection sponsors an active oral history program which in its first three years has generated nearly 500 hours of taped interviews with distinguished Army officers. Although not fully cataloged, all of these materials are shelved and immediately available for use by the research historian, the student, and the history buff.

The research historian and the student using the facilities of the Military History Research Collection is enabled to do his research using a variety of media. In many cases, he can immediately compare the official record to the personal accounts of individuals, both written and oral, as well as making additional comparisons with accounts in secondary sources. This is an advantage available only when major source materials have been gathered in one location. Maximum research and study can thus be accomplished in a single visit, a decided contrast when added time is required for travel from one source to another to accomplish the same amount of research.

Although preservation is in itself important to a certain degree, the costs involved — in both funds and personnel — cannot be justified unless the primary and secondary source materials thus preserved are made available for use. The Research Collection welcomes — and encourages — the use of its facilities by all scholars and historians. Reference assistance is provided whenever possible.

The "discovery" of new facts brings excitement and enjoyment to the scholar and to the history buff alike. John Carroll found this to be true in screening the Order of the Indian Wars papers at the Military History Research Collection for he found included *Proceedings* not elsewhere available as well as other accounts by members of the Order. Mr. Carroll is a very dedicated historian who has as a personal objective locating and making available for others to use those rare source materials not normally available to the student and scholar. This is accomplished through the reprint capability so fortunately available today. By consolidating scattered writings in single volumes and by adding explanatory and illustrative materials to the original texts, Mr. Carroll is performing an outstanding service to the scholar and historian of today and the future. The US Army Military History Research Collection congratulates him for his contribution in furthering the study of American history.

GEORGE S. PAPPAS
Colonel, US Army
Director, US Army Military History
Research Collection

Introduction

Just "how" the Order of Indian Wars began is not known; neither is the "why." We do know that during the early part of the summer of 1896, Colonel B. J. D. Irwin, Assistant Surgeon General, U.S. Army Retired, in several conversations with officers on duty in Chicago and at Fort Sheridan, offered a proposal to organize "a Society that should stand related to the Indian Wars of the United States as the Society of Cincinnati stands related to the Wars of the Revolution and the Military Order of the Loyal Legion of the United States to the War of the Rebellion." This much was found in the 1914 *Proceedings* published by the Order of Indian Wars (hereafter referred to as OIW). There was nothing unusual in this desire to congregate; man is a very social and aggressive animal, and it was only natural that men who had shared some exciting moments in our history would want to band together into an organization for the purpose of collecting historical information and for camaraderie.

But unlike the Society of Cincinnati and the Military Order of the Loyal Legion of the United States, the resulting Society would not commemorate a single struggle nor a single moment of history. Instead, it would commemorate a loosely defined period in our history especially, but not exclusively, devoted to westward movement.

Several meetings were held at which the question of the name, the statement of the objectives and the conditions of membership were considered. It was eventually decided that the new organization would be called *The Order of Indian Wars of the United States,* and that a charter should be obtained from the State of Illinois. This was done.

The Charter Members were B. J. D. Irwin, Colonel, U.S.A.; G. W. Baird, Major and Paymaster, U.S.A.; Ruben F. Bernard, Lieutenant Colonel, U.S.A.; C. H. Conrad, Captain, 15th Infantry, U.S.A.; J. W. Clous, D. J. A. General, U.S.A.; F. H. Hathaway, Major and Q.M.U.S.A.; and Allyn Capron, Captain, 1st U.S. Artillery. The charter was granted on June 10, 1896. Their original decision on conditions of membership was to have only two classes on Companion:

FIRST CLASS — Commissioned Officers of the Army, Navy or Marine Corps and of State and Territorial Military Organizations who had been, or who probably could and would be engaged in the service of the United States in any military grade whatsoever, *in conflicts, battles or actual field service against hostile Indians* within the jurisdiction of the United States; also the male descendents of those above specified who would have been eligible to membership but who died without such membership.

SECOND CLASS — Sons of living members of the first class.

Over the years the standards and qualifications for admission were amended several times as will be reflected in the reading of the final configuration of the complete Constitution and By-Laws which precede the text of this volume.

One item which did not undergo alteration, however, was the main objective of the organization, i.e., To perpetuate the history of the services rendered by the American military forces in their conflicts and wars within the territory of the United States and to collect and secure for publication historical data relating to the instances of "brave deeds and personal devotion" by which Indian warfare had at that time been depicted. This is the thrust of this volume, to preserve that historical data which the IOW collected and published in very limited printings and distribution.

The Order met informally from 1896 to 1910; this is an assumption for it wasn't until 1911 that their official publication, *The Proceedings of the Order of Indian Wars of the United States,* was first issued. By 1911, they met at the Army and Navy Club in Washington, D.C., most usually in the late spring or early summer of each year. At all the meetings the membership enjoyed a business session, and then a dinner after which one member or invited guest spoke informally or formally of experiences in Indian battles or on some phase of the history related to that subject. Talks often dealt with the subect of the Order's organization and purposes. But the bulk of the meetings between 1911 and 1916 were devoted to organizational matters relating to either the Constitution or By-Laws, or membership, finances and/or a combination of these. Unlike the years subsequent to 1916, the texts of the speeches were not recorded, an unforgivable oversight for an organization supposedly devoted to the perpetuation of historical data relating to their area of interest and knowledge. Then, in 1917, the first publication of the papers delivered at the year's meeting was released. After that, almost every year's publication contained that year's presentation(s) before the assembled membership at dinner. The exceptions were 1918, 1920, 1922-25, 1934-35 and 1942. In 1919 and 1927 the IOW did not meet. It is suspected that World War I influenced the decision in 1919 not to meet, but there is no officially published reason. The no meeting in 1927 is another matter. It seems as if at the 1926 meeting some member suggested the Society meet in the fall or winter instead of the spring or summer thereby assuring more membership attendance. It was agreed to, but by the time a schedule meeting was announced the year 1927 was over. They did meet in January, 1928. In 1920, the main speaker, Walter M. Camp, gave a general review and survey of the Indian wars and battle sites which was eventually published in the *Winners of the West,* a newspaper published in St. Joseph, Missouri, and devoted to lobbying for the needs of the Veterans of Indian Wars. The particular issue was October, 1933, hence its preservation today. It was not published in the *Proceedings.*

As one reviews the *Proceedings'* contents it becomes rather obvious that other papers were delivered at specific meetings of the IOW, but unfortunately were not published in their official periodical. Many of these unrecorded speeches must be considered irretrievably lost as they probably were impromptu; though many were not. Recent discoveries have uncovered the original texts of some of these unrecorded presentations, and they are presently under study and are being edited for possible publication in the near future. Some of these date back to 1915, two years before the first officially published presentations. To date none of the papers prior to 1915 have surfaced, even though careful search has been made of the only known (contrary to the Union List of Serials) complete collection of the *Proceedings* and related papers. It was not until this recent search that it was discovered that 1941 was not the last year in which the IOW met, nor was it the last year which saw their publication. The last for both of these was 1942, but that *Proceedings* was not published in the regular format so readily identifiable. Instead of the usual white booklet, it was mimeographed on very few sheets unlike the twenty-five or thirty pages ordinarily expected. For the very reason of its rarity and the unliklihood of its ever appearing in the holdings of other institutions who do have interrupted runs of the *Proceedings,* it is reproduced in this volume as Appendix A.

Then, somewhere in the late thirties, the IOW went into high gear, and began collecting historical data in an effort to fulfill their main objective as originally stated in 1896. In many of the folders from the IOW files recently discovered and reviewed were found several manuscripts prepared by members. These represent eyewitness accounts to, or first person recordings of many of the exciting events which transpired during the period of the Indian Wars. These accounts were never presented to the assemblage either orally or in printed form. They will also be included in that possible publication mentioned above.

Much serious consideration was given to the best method of presenting this important material from the IOW *Proceedings.* One way might have been by grouping the papers according to subject such as Apache Wars. Or it could have been organized according to special interests such as Custeriana, etc. Both were discarded in favor of the chronological approach which is both simpler and more meaningful in terms of history and orderliness. Consequently, each paper, or group of papers, delivered in a specific year and published in that's *Proceedings* will be prefaced in this publication with a short introduction capsulating as much as possible the items of primary interest also reported in that particular issue of the *Proceedings.*

It is hoped that in this way everything of major historical value will be preserved for students of this period of American History, since a complete collection of the *Proceedings* is something which exists only at the U.S. Army Military History Research Library, Carlisle Barracks, Pennsylvania, and is therefore, for all practical purposes, inaccessible to researchers and special interest groups who would want to study them on a moment's notice.

JOHN M. CARROLL
New Brunswick, N.J.

Constitution and By-Laws

OF

THE ORDER

of

INDIAN WARS

OF THE

UNITED STATES

———————

CHARTERED JUNE 10, 1896

WASHINGTON, D.C.

1925

Constitution

Article I.

This Society shall be known as The Order of Indian Wars of the United States.

Article II.
Objects.

The objects of this Society shall be to perpetuate the memories of the services rendered by the military forces of the United States in their conflicts and wars against hostile Indians within the territory or jurisdiction of the United States, and to collect and secure for publication historical data relating to the instances of heroic service and personal devotion by which Indian warfare has been illustrated.

Article III.
Organization.

SECTION 1. The Society shall have its headquarters in Washington, D.C., and shall consist of one body in which shall reside all the authority for admissions to membership, and which shall be the custodian of all historical data, the records of the Society and the Companions thereof, seal, property and funds.

SEC. 2. Upon the application of ten or more members of the Society, branch societies may be authorized by the Official Board or by the Society at any annual meeting. Each such branch society shall be known by its local name, and may provide such organization and impose such duties as are not inconsistent with the provisions of the Constitution and By-Laws of the Society.

SEC. 3. Companions transferred to branches of the Society shall not be relieved thereby from any duty or obligation imposed upon them by the Constitution and By-Laws of the Society.

Article IV.
Members.

SECTION 1. Companions of the Society shall be elected as herein provided and for the two classes specified, and shall be designated as Original and Hereditary Companions; and who alone shall have the right to vote and be eligible to office. Under the qualifications set out in this Article there may also be elected Honorary and Associate Companions whose membership shall be for their own lives only.

Original Companions.

Commissioned officers and honorably discharged commissioned officers of the U.S. Army, Navy and Marine Corps, and of State and Territorial Military Organizations, and Acting Assistant Surgeons, U.S. Army, of the Caucasian race, who have been or who hereafter may be engaged in the service of the United States in any military grade whatsoever, in conflicts, battles or actual field service against hostile Indians within the jurisdiction of the United States, or whose service was under the authority or by the approval of the United States or any State or Territory in any Indian War or Campaign, or in connection with, or in

VIII

the zone of any active Indian hostilities in any of the States or Territories of the United States. Those becoming Companions under any of the foregoing qualifications shall be designated as Original Companions.

Hereditary Companions.

The male descendants of Original Companions and the male descendants of those eligible for membership as Original Companions, such descendants having attained the age of twenty-one years, shall be eligible for membership and shall, when duly elected, be designated as Hereditary Companions.

Commissioned officers of the Army, Navy and Marine Corps of the United States, Commissioned officers of the National Guard and persons holding commissions in the Officers' Reserve Corps, descendants of honorably discharged enlisted men who had the qualifications requisite for eligibility for membership as Original Companions save that of having been commissioned, are also eligible and may be elected as Hereditary Companions.

Junior Companions.

Original and Hereditary Companions may propose for membership as Junior Companions a minor who fulfills as to descent, direct or collateral, the qualifications, except as to age, for membership as Hereditary Companion as set forth in this Article. Upon such Junior Companion becoming of age, if deemed worthy by the Investigating Committee, he shall become automatically an Hereditary Companion for life, with all the privileges pertaining thereto.

Honorary and Associate Companions.

As there are, and will be at all times, men eminent for their abilities and patriotism whose personal interests as manifested by their researches, investigations, and reports, and whose views or efforts shall be or may have been directed to the accomplishment of the objects of the Society, or men who have rendered, in a civil capacity, direct and exceptional service with troops in conflicts, battles, or in actual field service against hostile Indians, such men shall be eligible as Honorary or Associate Companions as the Official Board shall determine in each case, provided, however, that in any case such men shall not be eligible as Original or Hereditary Companions.

Sec. 2. Any Original Companion, or any Hereditary Companion having no direct male descendant, may, by writing filed with the Recorder, nominate an Hereditary Companion or Companions descending from his own brother or sister, if any there be, or failing such immediate collateral line may nominate from a more remote collateral line, and the person so nominated shall, upon attaining the age of twenty-one years, be eligible as an Hereditary Companion. If any such Original or Hereditary Companion for any reason fails to so nominate an Hereditary Companion or Companions the Official Board may make the nomination, which then to all intents and purposes shall be considered as having been made by such Original or Hereditary Companion.

The Official Board is authorized to nominate an Hereditary Companion in all cases where both the direct lineal and immediate collateral lines fail, taking the nominee from the nearest male relative deemed desirable and worthy of becoming supporters and companions of the Society, the Board being guided in their selections by the principles of this article. Persons nominated under the provisions of this paragraph, upon attaining the age of twenty-one years, shall be eligible as Hereditary Companions.

The Official Board shall take no action under this section until after the death of the Original or Hereditary Companion whose successor is unprovided for.

Persons elected as Hereditary Companions from other lines of descent than the direct lineal shall have all the rights and privileges inhering or granted herein to Original Companions or Hereditary Companions in direct line of descent.

SEC. 3. No person shall be deemed eligible for membership in the Society who has not maintained a good moral character and reputation.

SEC. 4. The eligibility of any person to be an Hereditary Companion shall not lapse by reason of any person in the line of descent either failing to become a Companion of the Society or forfeiting, for any cause, his membership or eligibility

Article V.

SECTION 1. Applications for membership as Original or Hereditary Companions shall be made to the Recorder or through a Branch Society in the form required by the Society and shall be accompanied by the entrance fee. The application must be signed by the applicant, bear the recommendation of two Companions, Original or Hereditary, and should show the rank, residence and military history of the applicant so far as it relates to service in Indian Wars; this history to include the names of battles, campaigns or field service participated in by the applicant or participated in by the person upom whom is based the eligibility of the applicant. An applicant for Hereditary Companionship based upon direct descent shall also trace his descent from the original founder of the membership in the Society or from a deceased ancestor who was eligible for such original membership, if based on collateral descent shall trace his relationship to such original founder of the membership or to such relative as was eligible for such original membership.

Proposals for membership as Junior Companions shall be in writing, shall embody all the information required in applications for membership as Hereditary Companions, and shall be accompanied by the life membership fee of twenty-five dollars, or the initiation fee of five dollars without annual dues and the candidate to elect, when he becomes of age, whether he will pay annual dues or the life membership fee.

SEC. 2. Nominations for membership as Honorary Companions, and nominations or applications for membership as Associate Companions shall show one or more of the following: 1st. Distinguished or faithful service in furthering the objects of the Society. 2nd. Have conferred or by their positions or influence may confer a lasting benefit upon the Society. 3d. Eminence for abilities and patriotism, and whose views and efforts have been directed to the same objects as those of the Society. 4th. Direct field service with troops in campaigns, conflicts or battles with hostile Indians.

SEC. 3. Each application for membership as Original or Hereditary Companions shall be referred to a Committee of Investigation consisting of three Companions. This Committee shall, after due consideration, make recommendation in writing as to the worthiness of the applicant. If this recommendation is favorable the committee shall so report to the Recorder, who shall immediately enroll the applicant as a Companion of the Society. Should the recommendation of the Committee be unfavorable to the applicant, the reasons for which will be stated in the report, he will be notified, and may either appeal to the Society for a hearing at its next annual meeting, or withdraw his application. The appeal will be forwarded to the Recorder, who will present it at the next annual meeting with such papers as the applicant may desire to have considered. The applicant may appear in person to present his case.

The Recorder will enroll the nominee for membership as a Junior Companion immediately upon approval of the Committee of Investigation and receipt of life membership fee.

Each nomination for membership as an Honorary Companion and each nomination or application for membership as Associate Companion shall be seconded by two Companions — Original or Hereditary — and then shall be referred to the Official Board for consideration and recommendation. If the recommendation is favorable, joined in by not less than a two-thirds vote of the whole Board, the Recorder shall make the enrollment accordingly.

The Recorder will report at each annual meeting of the Society a list of all Companions favorably acted upon by the Committee of Investigation and the Official Board since the last meeting, the Society to take such action on each such new Companion as it may deem proper.

SEC. 4. A second application for membership as Original or Hereditary Companions shall not be considered except at the annual meeting of the Society and such application shall not receive favorable action unless by a two-thirds vote of the Companions of the Society present at the meeting.

Article VI.
Resignation.

SECTION 1. Resignations shall be submitted in writing at an annual meeting of the Society, and must be accompanied by a statement of the Recorder that the person resigning is not in arrears, and that the badge, rosette, and Certificate of the Society have been returned, the number of which shall remain unassigned; in the case of the reinstatement of any such Companion to membership in the Society, these shall be reassigned to him.

The acceptance of the resignation of any Companion shall require the votes of the majority of the Companions of the Society present at an annual meeting. The reinstatement of such Companion shall be made only by the votes of the majority of the Companions of the Society present at an annual meeting, after an application in writing has been made and reported on by the Committee of Investigation.

Article VII.
Expulsion of Members.

SECTION 1. Any Companion may be expelled by the Society for gross disregard of its rules, or for disgraceful conduct, or upon conviction of crime by Civil, Military or Naval Court.

SEC. 2. A Companion against whom charges involving good character and conduct shall be preferred by a brother Companion shall be brought before a Board composed of five Companions convened to investigate the same, and shall be allowed to defend himself by the introduction of testimony and, if found guilty, as charged, shall suffer expulsion or suspension as may be determined by the said Board.

SEC. 3. Any companion expelled from the Society must return the badge, rosette, and Certificate of Membership. In the case of the reinstatement of such a Companion in the Society these shall be reassigned to him.

SEC. 4. Any companion who has been expelled may be restored to membership by a three-fourths vote of the Companions of the Society present at an annual meeting of the Society, after an application in writing has been made and reported on by the Committee of Investigation.

Article VIII.
Certificate of Membership.

SECTION 1. A certificate of membership shall be furnished to all Original and Hereditary Companions. It shall be signed by the Commander, have the seal of the Society appended, be attested by the Recorder, and have the following form:

ORDER OF INDIAN WARS OF THE UNITED STATES.

To all who shall see these Presents, Greeting:

KNOW YE, that _____ was duly received as an _____ Companion in the Order of Indian Wars of the United states, on the _____ day of _____ Anno Domini one thousand, nine hundred and _____ in recognition of the fact that _____ (In this space, for an Original Companion — insert a statement of services against hostile Indians. For an Hereditary Companion — insert the name of the person upon whom the eligibility for membership is based together with the statement of his services against hostile Indians. For other Companions — insert a statement of the qualifications upon which the membership is based.) _____ especially distinguished for services in Indian warfare in maintaining the supremacy of the United States of America.

In witness whereof the names of the Authorized Officers and the Seal of the Society are hereto affixed.

Given at Washington, this _____ day of _____ in the year of our Lord one thousand, nine hundred and _____ and of the Independence of the United States of America the _____ and of the Society Society the _____

L.S.

Attest:

Recorder.   Commander.

SEC. 2. A certificate of membership shall be given to all Honorary and Associate Companions, signed, sealed, attested, and in form as prescribed in Section 1 of this Article, except that the words, "especially distinguished for services in Indian warfare in maintaining the supremacy of the United States of America" shall be omitted.

Article IX.
Officers.

SECTION 1. The officers of the Society shall be a Commander, a Senior Vice-Commander, a Junior Vice-Commander, a Recorder, a Treasurer, an Historian, a Chaplain, and a Council of Seven Companions, all of whom shall comprise the Official Board. The officers shall be elected annually, and by ballot. The candidate receiving the majority of votes cast shall be declared elected. Officers elected shall be installed in person or by acceptance in writing, and shall enter upon their duties at once and perform the same until their successors are elected and quality. The offices of the Recorder and Treasurer may be consolidated and the duties performed by one Companion.

Article X.
Duties and Authority of Officers.

SECTION 1. The Commander shall preside at all meetings of the Society and of the

Official Board, require a rigid observance of the Constitution and By-Laws and execute such duties as may be required under parliamentary usage.

SEC. 2. The Vice-Commanders shall, when necessary, assist the Commander in his duties, and when he is absent, shall assume, in succession, his duties.

They shall likewise, in order, succeed to office in case of vacancy.

SEC. 3. The Recorder shall record the proceedings of the meetings of the Society and of the Official Board; he shall receive all moneys due and transfer the same to the Treasurer. He shall have custody of the badges, rosettes, Certificates of Membership, seals, dies, and Society property, and hold them in accordance with the rules of the Society. He shall also keep a record of the Companions and embody therein all substantial facts concerning eligibility of membership, whether derived from personal services or inheritance. In the absence of the Recorder the Treasurer shall perform his duties. In the absence of both Recorder and Treasurer the Commander shall designate a member of the Official Board to act *ad interim.*

SEC. 4. The Treasurer shall receive all moneys transferred to him by the Recorder, properly account for the same, and give bond if required.

SEC. 5. The Historian shall be especially charged with the attainments of the objects of the Society as indicated in Article II of the Constitution and, to this end, shall prepare or secure historical data, especially in the form of narratives and descriptions of eye witnesses of and participants in Indian warfare, biographical sketches of noted white and Indian commanders and warriors, and, in general, whatever best illustrates the varying phases of the prolonged conflict and best makes record of its influence upon our history.

SEC. 6. The Chaplain shall open formal meetings of the Society with prayer, and officiate, if required, at the obsequies of deceased Companions; he shall also perform such clerical duties as may be assigned him.

SEC. 7. The Official Board shall have general charge of and exercise the proper control over all Society property. It shall be required to fill all vacancies below and including that of Commander, until the next election occurs. The presence of five members of the Official Board shall constitute a quorum for the transaction of business and a majority vote of those present shall be decisive upon any question.

Article XI.
Removal of Officers.

An officer who fails to perform his duty properly may be removed by a majority vote of the Society at an annual meeting.

Article XII.
Meetings.

SECTION 1. Meetings of the Society shall be held at such time as may be practicable but not oftener than once a month. The time of the annual meeting for the election of officers shall be determined by the Commander. Wherever it is provided in this Constitution that action shall be taken at the annual meeting it shall be held to refer to the annual meeting for the election of officers.

SEC. 2. Extra meetings of the Society shall be held at the call of the Commander on his own motion or at the request, in writing, of five Companions.

SEC. 3. Twelve Companions of the Society shall constitute a quorum competent to transact business at any meeting. A majority vote shall, unless otherwise provided herein, be decisive on all questions. Only Companions of the Society shall be present during the transaction of business.

Sec. 4. The Official Board shall meet at the call of the Commander.

Article XIII.
Arrearages.

Section 1. A Companion in arrears shall not be allowed to vote at the annual election and shall not be nominated for or elected to any office.

Sec. 2. A Companion who on the first day of January is in arrears shall be notified of the fact, and unless the indebtedness is paid within six months he shall be liable to suspension by the Society at any regular meeting. A Companion thus suspended shall not enjoy the privileges of the Society during such suspension, but may be restored to full membership upon the payment or remission of dues as may be determined by the Official Board or upon appeal by the Society.

Sec. 3. A Companion who shall wilfully defer or decline to pay dues may be deprived of membership by a majority vote at any annual meeting of the Society. In cases where it can be shown that such arrearages occurred beyond the control of the persons involved, the Society may, by a majority vote, cancel a part or the whole.

Upon his written request, any Companion dropped for non-payment of dues may, upon payment of such arrearages, be restored to membership by the Official Board or at any annual meeting.

Article XIV.
Members of Societies No Longer Existing.

Section 1. Persons who have been members of certain societies no longer existing, whose objects and aims have been similar to those of this Society, and whose qualifications for membership were, in substantial respects, similar to those of this Society, may be admitted to membership without the payment of the regular initiation fee.

Any such person making application for membership must show evidence, in writing, of his previous membership in such organization, and must render a full statement of the qualifications which rendered him eligible for membership therein.

All such applications are to be passed upon by the Committee of Investigation in the same manner provided in Article V, Section 3.

Sec. 2. Any such applicant who has been admitted to membership in this Society, and who was a member of such other society by reason of his own record of service in military or naval operations against hostile Indians within the territory or jurisdiction of the United States, shall be designated as an Original Companion.

Sec. 3. Any such applicant who has been admitted to membership to this Society, who was a member of such other society by reason of the eligibility of an ancestor and not as a result of his own military or naval service against hostile Indians within the territory or jurisdiction of the United States shall be designated as an Hereditary Companion.

Sec. 4. The Certificate of Membership of the Society and the rosette may be furnished such Companions upon the payment of them of the actual cost price thereof.

Article XV.
Seal of the Order.

The Seal of the Society shall be circular, two inches in diameter. On two concentric circles the following shall be engraved, namely: Next the border of the seal, the words, Order of Indian Wars of the United States; on the inner circle the words, *Patriam Tuens Civilitatem Ducens*. Across the central part of the Seal in two lines, equally distant from the center, Chartered June 10, 1896.

Article XVI.
Badge of the Order.

Observe: A star of seven points, measuring one and three-quarters inches from opposite points, enameled gules, edged or, charged in the center with a circular disc one-half inch in diameter. Thereon, gules, an Indian chief, habited. In his dexter hand a musket in pale, the butt resting on the ground. In the dexter background the setting sun and in the sinister, a wigwam, all or. Surrounding the disc a circular band one-eighth of an inch wide azure, edged or, thereon the inscription: "Order of Indian Wars of the United States," argent. This band enclosed by a wreath of laurel leaves or. Above the star an arrow and sword in saltire or, points downwards. The whole suspended from a ribbon one and seven-sixteenth inches wide paly of five azure, gules, argent and tenne.

Reverse: A star of seven points azure, edged or. Upon each point, the name of an Indian tribe, respectively: "Cherokees, Seminoles, Comanches, Sioux, Apaches, Nez Perces, Miamis," argent. In the center a plain circular disc or, nine-sixteenths of an inch in diameter (thereon the name and number of Companion to be engraved), surrounded by a circular band one-eighth of an inch wide gules, edged or; thereon the motto: *"Patriam Tuens Civilitatem Ducens,"* argent. Above the star a sword and arrow in saltire, points downwards.

Rosette of the Order.

The Rosette of the Society shall be circular, one-half of an inch in diameter, of watered silk; the rim and a point in the center dark blue, three sector-shaped sections of white, scarlet and orange, respectively.

Article XVII.

The badge of the Society shall be worn on the left breast, except the officers of the Society shall wear the badge suspended by a ribbon from the neck. Companions must not display the badge and rosette at the same time. The badge may or may not be purchased by Companions.

Article XVIII.

The Constitution shall not be deemed adopted until not less than two-thirds of the membership of date of March 6, 1915, shall have approved it in writing, and the fact that it has been approved by such a vote has been certified by the Commander and published in orders, and thereafter it shall constitute the supreme law of the Order and no amendment shall be made unless it shall be proposed at the annual meeting and adopted by a two-thirds vote of those present at the meeting and ratified by a three-fourths vote of all the members of the Society, such vote to be taken within six months after its adoption at such meeting. The vote upon the ratification of an amendment shall be taken, if necessary, by submitting it through the mails to all Companions.

BY-LAWS

OF

THE ORDER

OF

INDIAN WARS

OF THE

UNITED STATES

———————

Chartered June 10, 1896

———————

By-Laws

Sec. 1. At the annual meeting of the Society, which may take place on an historical or ceremonial date, the senior officer of the Society shall preside and business shall be presented in the following order, viz.:—

1. The call to order.
2. Entrance of the colors.
3. Prayer by the Chaplain.
4. Roll call by the Recorder. (This may be omitted.)
5. Proceedings of the last meeting shall be read and passed upon.
6. Report of the Recorder on action take by the Committee of Investigation.
7. Recorder's report on appeals taken from action of the Committee of Investigation.
8. Unfinished business may be considered and acted upon.
9. Official reports of officers and committees shall be read.
10. Communications in writing shall be presented.
11. Introduction of new business.
12. Necrology.
13. Installation of Companions-elect.
14. Installation of officers.
15. Removal of colors.
16. Adjournment.

The business of the annual meeting may precede the ceremonies, in which case numbers 2 and 3 of Sec. 1 will immediately precede number 12 of Sec. 1. The annual meeting may be followed by a banquet, in which case the ceremonies may take place in connection therewith and immediately preceding the banquet.

At called meetings the senior officer of the Society present shall preside and only the business for which the meeting was called shall be considered.

Sec. 2. Parliamentary law in general usage in legislative bodies shall be used in the transaction of business of the Society and Branches of the Society.

Sec. 3. All official records, papers, etc., shall conform, as nearly as may be practicable, to the rules and customs obtaining in the military service.

Sec. 4. Companions elected to the office before entering upon the duties of the same shall take the following oath, orally if present or in writing if absent, viz: "I do solemnly swear (or affirm) that I will perform in good faith and to the best of my ability the duties entrusted to me as an officer of this Society and that I will support and maintain its constitution, by-laws and regulations, so help me God".

Sec. 5. The Commander shall appoint all officers and committees not otherwise provided for by the Constitution. He shall appoint an Auditing Committee who shall examine the accounts of the Recorder and Treasurer at a time specified by the Commander and shall report, in writing, at the next annual meeting of the Society.

Sec. 6. The Recorder shall keep the following records:

(a) A complete file of all applications for membership; with all of the correspondence relating thereto.

(b) A complete file of all correspondence of the Society, retaining carbon copies of all letters written by him.

(c) A cash book showing the receipts from all sources, itemized, and the expenditures for all causes, itemized.

(d) Separate vouchers for all payments made by him.

(e) A complete record of the issuance of Certificates of Membership.

SEC. 7. On the first of January of each year the Recorder shall mail to each Companion a full statement of his account. He shall communicate to persons desiring it, such information concerning eligibility, membership, etc., as may be required. At the annual meeting he shall render a full report of all money received since his last annual report, make a statement as to the general condition and membership of the Society, new members, deaths, resignations, and expulsions.

SEC. 8. The Treasurer shall be the custodian of all moneys received by the Society. He shall invest the funds of the Society in securities approved by the Official Board.

He shall render receipt to the Recorder for all funds which that officer turns over to him, and shall approve such expenditures of the Recorder as are required by him in the fulfillment of his duties.

SEC. 9. Companions-elect when installed shall, orally if present or in writing if absent, taking the following oath, viz: "I do solemnly swear (or affirm) that I will perform in good faith and to the best of my ability the duties and obligations of a Companions of the Order and that I will support and maintain its constitution, by-laws and regulations, so help me God".

SEC. 10. The fiscal year of the Society shall commence on the first day of January.

SEC. 11. All expenses of the Society shall be met by funds raised by annual assessment of at least $2.00 paid in advance. Companions elected in the first quarter shall pay full annual dues for the year of the election. Companions elected in subsequent quarters shall pay three-fourths, one-half and one-fourth of the dues of that year, according as they may be elected in the second, third and fourth quarters. Honorary Companions shall be exempt from payment of all fees and dues.

SEC. 12. The initiation fee for admission to the Society shall be $5.00 payable in advance. This sum includes the cost of Certificate of Membership and one rosette.

SEC. 13. A Companion paying $25.00 at one time in addition to his fee of admission shall be exempt from the payment of further dues.

SEC. 14. Changes in or amendments to the By-Laws, if not otherwise provided for, shall be made only when agreed to at the annual meeting of the Society.

SEC. 15. The colors of the Order shall be the National Color and a color of the same dimensions as the National Color, four feet four inches on the pike, five feet six inches fly, and similarly mounted on a pike. The Color of the Order shall be of silk, the stripes being of equal width and of the number (5) and the colors of the Order and embroidered thereon the insignia of the Order. The National Color and the Color of the Order will be displayed at all ceremonial meetings and ceremonial banquets. Two Companions will be designated by the Commander as color bearers and at "the entrance of the colors," will carry them to and place them in stands provided for them at the right and left of the Commander and in front of and near the corners of the Ceremonial tables. The color bearers will be seated near the colors. All Companions will stand until the colors are placed.

SEC. 16. In the ceremony of necrology, installation of Companions-elect and installation of officers, the four Original Companions of the Order, senior in Indian War service, will sit with the Commander as a Ceremonial Council. The tables for the ceremony will be so arranged that the Recorder of the Order may sit at a separate table placed in front of and to one side of the Commander and facing him. The Commander will wear the Badge of the Order suspended from a ribbon of the colors of the Order, to be worn around the neck. He shall have as a badge of office a coup stick of black walnut or other suitable American wood, about 24 inches long and one inch in diameter, one end of which will be shaped so as to receive the eagle feathers, and the other end to be provided with a ferule of appropriate metal suitable for engraving. To the coup stick shall be attached an appropriate number of eagle feathers — the feathers being symbolical of Indian Wars, and on the ferule shall be engraved the names of the principal tribes of Indians engaged in these wars. The four Companions of the Ceremonial Council may each wear an appropriate necklace of bear claws, or elk teeth, or rattle snake rattles, or bird wings, or bead work, suitably made, and will sit to the right and left of the Commander in the order of seniority. The Chaplain may wear at all ceremonies a stole of wampum, or bead work (white), of suitable length and width. The Recorder may wear a stole of same as that of the Chaplain except that it will be blue in color. The ceremonial tables may be decorated with Indian blankets and Indian trophies may be displayed.

SEC. 17. In the ceremony of necrology (order No. 12), a number of candles, corresponding to the number of Companions who have died during the past year, will be placed in a suitable candlestick on a table to the left of the Commander. A Companion of the Order will be designated to light and extinguish the candles at the proper time. The Commander will call on the Recorder for the names of those that have died. The Recorder will read the names in order of the dates of their death. He will give a brief account of the service of the deceased, or he may call upon a Companion, who has been designated for the purpose, to give such an account. As each name is called a candle will be lighted. This will be continued until all names have been called and accounts given. All of the candles will then be extinguished. The Commander will then call on the Chaplain for prayer and the Companions will all stand. The Chaplain, raising both hands, may then repeat the ceremonial prayer of the Order, viz:—

There the Father comes,
There the Father comes
Speaking as he flied,
Calling as he comes, this joyous word,
"You shall live again," he calls,
"You shall live beyond the grave."
He is calling as he comes,
Help us, O Father,
Hear us Great Spirit.
At the close of the prayer the Companions will be seated.

SEC. 18. In the installation of Companions-elect (order No. 13), each Companion-elect will be provided with a coup stick to which is attached three eagle feathers. The Companions to be installed will assemble outside the ceremonial hall. As each name is called the Companion will enter, carrying his coup stick in his right hand. He will take position directly in front of the Commander and after the Recorder has read the service for which he was elected, will present to the Commander his coup stick. The coup stick will be passed by the Commander to each member of the Ceremonial Council and as each examines it he will nod assent. The Commander will then pass the stick back to the Companion-elect and direct him to stand aside to his left. This procedure will be followed for each Companion-elect. Original Companions-elect should be called first, followed by Hereditary Companions-elect. As soon as all names have been called the Companions-elect will take position in line in front of the Commander. The officer of the Ceremonial Council with seniority of Indian War service will then present the Certificate of Membership to each Companion-elect who will then take his place in line as before. The Commander will then administer the oath (Sec. 9). The Council will then rise and all Companions will stand and will join with the Ceremonial Council in giving the salute of the Order which will be returned by the Companions just installed. At the fall of the gavel all will be seated.

The Certificates of Membership properly prepared will be placed by the Recorder previous to the ceremony, in front of the senior Companion of the Ceremonial Council.

Sec. 19. In the election of officers the election will be by written ballot. The nominations will be made by a Nominating Committee appointed by the Commander. The Recorder will canvass the votes and certify to the election of the nominees. This election should take place at least a month before the Annual Meeting and all officers-elect should be notified to be present for installation. As their names are called by the Recorder, the officers-elect will form in line in front of the Ceremonial Council. The Commander will then administer the oath (Sec. 4). Upon completion of the oath, all Companions will rise and the senior officer of the Ceremonial Council will take the insignia of office from the old Commander and place on the Commander-elect. The Ceremonial Council and the Companions will then salute the officers-elect with the salute of the Order and the officers-elect will return the salute. Then the old will let the gavel fall for adjournment.

Sec. 20. All flags, colors, regalia and property pertaining to ceremonials shall be the property of the Order and the Recorder shall be the custodian for all such property above mentioned.

Sec. 21. At all banquets the colors should be properly displayed and appropriately placed. The Commander and Ceremonial Council, in full regalia, should be appropriately seated in such order as may be deemed expedient.

Sec. 22. The Commander may attend and may designate Companions to attend the funeral service of a Companion. Services at the grave may be held by the Order at the appropriate time. At least a Chaplain and four members should be present if the burial ceremony is to be carried out. The Chaplain should wear the stole and the Companions the insignia of the Order. At the appropriate time the Chaplain should approach the grave and the four Companions should station themselves near the four corners of the grave. The Companion nearest the head of the grave should have a garland or wreath of white flowers. The Chaplain then should raise his hands and may repeat after saying, "The Great Spirit has taken from us our brother and Companion", the following ceremonial prayer:

The Father says so,
He has promised surely,
You shall see your dead once more,
They will come to life again,
You shall see your kindred
Of the Spirit land.
This the Father saith
To His faithful ones.
The flowers are then placed on the casket and the Chaplain repeats the ceremonial prayer

of the Order (Sec. 17).

All Companions will then give the salute of the Order and retire from the grave. Ceremonies at statues of heroes of Indian Wars should be made ceremonious, the colors being carried, regalia being worn and white flowers being used. After the eulogy, the flowers should be placed, the ceremonial prayer of the Order repeated by the chaplain, and the salute of the Order given.

SEC. 23. A Junior Foundation Fund may be established by donations of units of cash, stock or bonds from members or friends of the Order. When the interest on the unit amounts to five dollars the donor will nominate a Junior who is eligible for membership whether his ancestors were members of the Order or not. If the donor fails to make the nomination within one year then the Official Board shall make it. The interest will be transferred to the general fund. The unit may be reinvested if necessary but used for no other purpose.

XXII

1917

Until this year no papers delivered before the annual meeting of the Order of Indian Wars had been published; indeed, no meeting had been published until 1911. All of the *Proceedings* from 1911 through 1916 contained nothing more than the minutes of the previous meetings, discussions on the contents of their Constitution and By-Laws and the membership list as of that particular meeting. Sometimes the dinner guests were mentioned, the subjects of whatever talks to be heard were announced, frequently the menu, often the financial status and that was about all. The *Proceedings* for 1917 was to change the norm.

Brigadier General Edward S. Godfrey, the presiding Commander for 1917, called the meeting into session at which time the standard reports were heard, moved for acceptance, seconded and then voted upon. That meeting, when adjourned to attend the annual dinner at the Army Navy Club in Washington, D.C., had 25 Companions and 20 guests present.

After the banquet General Anson Mills delivered a paper on the "Battle of the Rosebud," which was later recorded in the *Proceedings*. His address was supplemented by remarks by General George F. Chase and Colonel J. H. Patzki, remarks which were not officially recorded in the same issue. Two other addresses were made but also not recorded. They were by General Nelson A. Miles and General Hugh L. Scott on the subject of Indian Wars and the "part played by the American Army officers and soldiers in blazing the pathway for civilization."

Oddly enough, Captain H. R. Lemly's article, "The Fight On The Rosebud," was printed in the *Proceedings* along with General Mills' presentation, but it was not identified in the minutes of the meeting as having been delivered. He was listed, however, as a Companion present for the meeting and it is safe to assume he did make those comments about the Rosebud conflict.

Address by General Anson Mills, U.S. Army Ret., On "The Battle of the Rosebud."

Mr. Commander, companions and guests: I have been requested to describe to you my recollections this evening of the Battle of the Rosebud. General Godfrey last year gave you a description of the Battle of the Little Big Horn most excellently. I hope I can approach him in my efforts tonight.

I speak without notes from memory only, after a lapse of forty years, and will doubtless be incorrect in many things, but several officers of my Regiment who engaged in the battle are present and may correct me, particularly Colonel Lemly, then a Lieutenant, who wrote a detailed account immediately after the battle which I have never seen; it would be interesting if he would read it so you may compare it with my recollection after forty years.

As the Battle of the Rosebud was so different, although second in importance in the Sioux war to the Battle of the Little Big Horn (in that it only occupied about four and a half hours), I am going to ask you to indulge me a few minutes to tell you some of the happenings which led up to this fight with the Sioux Indians.

First I want to say I have had a great deal of experience with wild animals and wild Indians, and so far as I know the buffalo were the only wild animals wholly nomadic, having no habitation or home, and their companions, the Sioux Indians, are the only humans that were entirely nomadic.

Coronado tells us of his great explorations through Northern "New Spain," of the movement of the Indian cows, as the Spaniards calls them, and their companions the Indians, in his marches northward from the Pecos River (where the Indians had never before seen horses, they using dogs for their pack animals, and the Spaniards had never before seen buffalo and so called them cows), with the Buffalo and Indians to the Platte River near what is now McPherson, Nebraska, so that to understand our discussion, with the relations that the Army had to the Sioux, we ought to understand that they were confirmed nomads as much as the buffalo that furnished their supplies. I have seen the whole face of the earth covered with buffalo moving at from four to six miles an hour.

In 1856-58 I traveled twice back and forth through Kansas, Indian Territory and Texas to the Pecos River (the buffalo never went west or south of the Pecos River), and encountered the buffalo and Indians moving back and forth; the buffalo in such great numbers that I felt the earth tremble under their movement, and we were obliged to stop our vehicles and turn the animals' heads in the direction of the buffaloes' flight, firing our pistols to scare them away.

In 1865, after the surrender of Appomatox, my Regiment, the 18th U.S. Infantry, was ordered from Fort Leavenworth to Fort McPherson, Nebr. The Union Pacific R.R. was just then being commenced from Omaha, and it was not known then what route we ought to take to the Pacific, so the Government ordered Colonel Carrington (in my reference to officers to avoid confusion with higher brevet rank, I will use only their actual rank at the time) to open a road through the Northwestern Territory, and he proceeded to obey that order with his twenty-four company regiment, building the new forts of Fetterman, Reno, Phil. Kearny and C. F. Smith, a march of about fifteen hundred miles through the then

State of Nebraska and territories of Wyoming, Dakota and Montana.

Colonel Carrington established these posts with the greatest expense, carrying all kinds of necessary material, saw mills, hardware, and everything essential to building first-class posts.

This was done without the consent of the Indians, who then generally occupied the wild country. After the establishment of the posts the Indians immediately began to annoy and harass them, and finally after they had assaulted the forts several times, the largest, Phil. Kearny, was unsuccessfully attacked, and a detachment of over one hundred men under Captain Fetterman was sent out by Colonel Carrington to attack the Indians, who after their manner ambushed and surrounded them, and kills all the officers and men before any rescue could be made from the post.

Finally the Government became alarmed and withdrew the soldiers from these posts so suddenly that they were unable to take with them the valuable stores, munitions, furniture and supplies, leaving everything to be destroyed by the Indians. I was one of the captains of that Regiment.

The Indians then demanded that all the troops be permanently withdrawn from their country, and a Commission was organized consisting of Generals Harney, Sherman, Terry and others, they formulating a treaty of 1868 by which they gave the Sioux in perpetuity all these lands, and agreed that they would never be dispossessed without the agreement of three-fourths of the Indians.

Time passed on. I was transferred to the Cavalry, and strangely enough in 1872, I was ordered back to the command of North Platte Station, a sub-post of Fort McPherson, where my Regiment, under Carrington, was in '65.

The Union Pacific R.R. had then been completed, though the Indians and buffalo were making their annual pilgrimage across the road as before, to the north in the summer, and the south in the winter, accompanied by the nine confederated tribes of the Sioux — Brules, Ogalallas, Minneconjous, Uncapapas, Two Kettle, San Arcs, Lower Brules, Yanktons and Santees, associated with them were also the Northern Cheyennes and Northern Arapahoes.

As the Indians were entirely dependent upon the buffalo for subsistence, the buffalo became the controlling factor in the change that then took place, by refusing to no longer cross the road, and the buffalo took up their permanent abode north of the Platte River, the last of the buffalo passing in 1874.

There were different ideas as to what impelled the buffalo to come to this conclusion, but most probably the smoke and noise, and the terrible appearance of the engine, resembling huge monster animals, prevented the buffalo from attempting to cross, and consequently they never returned south after their northern trip in '74. The Indians, of course, for obvious reasons following permanently.

There can be no reasonable doubt that the fore-bears of these Indians and these buffalo were the companions of Coronado in his wonderful exploration (for that day), from the Pecos to the Platte (over four hundred years ago) at the great forks near the present city of North Platte and these Indians were the adversaries we were to meet at Rosebud.

Here at North Platte, while the buffalo were hesitating to go north permanently, I often met and became well acquainted with Spotted Tail, Chief of the Ogalallas, the greatest and best chief I ever knew.

Spotted Tail, with a great portion of his Ogalallas, remained around North Platte until some time in 1873, when his agency was established on the head waters of the White River,

4

on a branch called Bear Creek, near the boundary between Nebraska and Dakota. Here he assembled all his tribe, some four thousand.

In the winter of 1874-5 General Crook directed me to follow Spotted Tail and build at his agency a five-company post to be called Camp Sheridan (three cavalry and two infantry companies), in which Lieutenant Lemly assisted.

Like Carrington, we were furnished with everything necessary: soldier labor, saw, shingle and lath mills, hardware and some thirty skilled artisans, and as we were in a pine forest many trees were felled, and the lumber from them placed in the building on the same day. There were no contracts, no delays in construction, and it was probably the cheapest, most satisfactory, and most rapidly constructed post ever built by the Army.

Shortly before this Lieutenant-Colonel Custer, with an expedition including engineers, mining experts, and geologists, had been ordered to make an exploration of the Black Hills. Custer returned reporting gold in the hills, which excited the western people so they began to move in from all directions.

This again aroused the Indians, and it became apparent that there would be trouble. General Sheridan issued ordered to myself and adjacent commanders to prevent the whites from violating the Indian non-intercourse law by arresting and destroying outfits for that purpose.

I, together with a co-operative detachment from Fort Randall, commanded by Captain Fergus Walker, on May 21st destroyed by fire a wagon train with mining equipment destined for the Black Hills, under the command of one Major Gordon, at a point now known as Gordon City, returning the party which numbered about 75 people, to Fort Randall, confining Gordon at Camp Sheridan.

The Indians at my agency, and I presume at the others, were constantly forming war parties to go out against these trespassing miners, and Spotted Tail, realizing the critical status, made a confidant of me, and frequently reported as near as he could the probable time and number of warriors that were leaving his agency, suggesting that I intercept them by sending out soldiers to head them off, which I often did.

As they were acting in violation of his orders it was difficult for him and the other Sioux chiefs to know where they went, and for what purpose, but he did his very best to suppress the insurrection which was then before him.

The War Department has kindly furnished us with two large photographic maps to which I call your attention. The first represents a portion of the States of Colorado and Nebraska, and the territories of Wyoming, Dakota and Montana. On this map I have indicated Carrington's route from Kearny to C. F. Smith in green ink, and underscored Forts McPherson, Laramie, Fetterman, Reno, Phil. Kearny and C. F. Smith, the last four being built by Carrington. I have also indicated in red squares the seven principal engagements during the Sioux war, Powder River, Little Big Horn, Tongue River, Rosebud, Slim Buttes, McKenzie's Fight, and later Miles' Battle of Wolfe Mountain. The Camp on Goose Creek is marked with a red circle.

The other map covers the Rosebud battlefield, enlarged from one in Cyrus Townsend Brady's book. In my further remarks I will refer to those maps by names and letters.

The roving bands of Indians from the nine Sioux agencies continued their resentful depredations during the fall of '75 and finally a hostile party attacked Fort Fred Steele in considerable numbers, entering the parade ground and killing five or six soldiers right in the presence of the officers and men of the command. About the same time a similar attack was

5

made on Fort Fetterman, and the Indians pinned one of the soldiers they had killed to the ground with sticks in sight of the troops.

In March of '76 the War Department ordered General Crook to send a force from Fort Fetterman to chastise any of these roving bands wherever found. General Crook commanded this expedition which left Fort Fetterman, and proceeded by the Carrington route to the Tongue River, then down the Tongue River, crossing over and attacking a large force of Indians at Powder River. Through some misunderstanding it did not turn out very favorably, and it was considered advisable for the troops to return to the vicinity of Fort Fetterman.

The War Department and the Interior Department then concluded to make general war on these hostile Indians in the field, and General Terry and General Crook were directed to organize armies, the former at the mouth of Powder River, and the latter at Fort Fetterman.

The aggregate number of the nine Sioux agencies was supposed to be about sixty to sixty-five thousand souls, the Minneconjous being the greatest in number, and the most hostile, but it was not known by any one how many Indians had left each of the agencies, or where they had gone; however, it was supposed that they would follow the buffalo wherever they might be, so Terry was to assail them from the north and Crook from the south.

Crook had to do everything hastily, and a more incongruous army could hardly be conceived of; packers, guides, teamsters, and camp followers of all kinds, were assembled together with regular troops from different parts of the country.

Finally we started from Fort Fetterman on May 29th, with twenty companies of regular troops, fifteen of cavalry and five of infantry, amounting to over one thousand soldiers. We followed Carrington's route but before we reached Fort Reno, communication with our base was forbidden because of the danger from the surrounding hostile Indians, and we could neither receive supplies nor return our sick and disabled.

It might add a little spice to my story to relate some of the humorous incidents that occurred on this very somber and serious expedition.

In organizing the wagon train at Fort Fetterman, the wagon master had unintentionally employed a female teamster, but she was not discovered until we neared Fort Reno, when she was suddenly arrested, and placed in improvised female attire under guard. I knew nothing of this, but being the senior captain of Cavalry, having served as a Captain for 16 years, and being of an inquisitive turn of mind, I had become somewhat notorious (for better or worse).

The day she was discovered and placed under guard, unconscious of the fact, I was going through the wagon master's outfit when she sprang up calling out "There is Colonel Mills, he knows me," when everybody began to laugh, much to my astonishment and chagrin, being married.

It was not many hours until every man in the camp knew of the professed familiarity of "Calamity Jane" (as she was known) with me, and for several days my particular friends pulled me aside, and asked me "who is 'Calamity Jane'?" I denied any knowledge of her or her calling, but no one believed me, and I doubt whether they all do yet.

We carried her along until a force was organized to carry our helpless back, with which she was sent, but she afterwards turned out to be a national character, and was a woman of no mean ability and force even from the standard of men. I learned later that she had been a resident of North Platte, and that she knew many of my soldiers, some of whom had probably betrayed her. Later she had employed herself as a cook for my next door neighbor,

6

Lieutenant Johnson, and had seen me often in his house, I presume.

When we arrived at Fort Phil. Kearny, the whole command went into camp near the ruined post on the headwaters of Goose Creek, between its two forks, almost under the shadow of Cloud Peak of the Big Horn Mountains, where General Crook had made arrangements to meet 250 friendly Indians, Shoshones, Crows and Snakes.

The wagons, supplies, and animals, were parked for defense by the teamsters and civilian employees and we made ready to proceed against the Sioux as soon as joined by the Indians.

The friendly Indians having arrived on the morning of June 16th, we started out to find the Sioux. I did not think that General Crook knew where they were, and I did not think our friendly Indians knew where they were, and no one conceived we would find them in the great force we did.

General Crook ordered his classmate, Major Chambers, to select from the one thousand mules a sufficient number on which to mount his infantry soldiers. Chambers and his officers protested, but Crook was obdurate and compelled him to do so suddenly but very reluctantly.

Captain Stanton was our engineer officer, and in order to make good in his scientific profession, equipped himself with a two-wheeled gig, drawn by a mule, which he ornamented with odometers, thermometers, barometers, and other meters, not forgetting some creature comforts visible to the men as they passed and repassed. The road was extremely rough even for the cavalry, there being no trail and as the soldiers were required to carry, each one on his person, four days' simple rations, the sight of his wheeled conveyance aroused their jealousy and envy, and whenever he appeared they would cry out "Mother's Pies, Mother's Cakes," etc., making life a burden to him. After he had progressed a few miles the gig broke down and he reluctantly abandoned it where I presume it lies today (but for illness he would be here), and I have promised to explain that he did not ride the gig but a horse.

We marched 35 miles the first day until we came to a lake or swamp of about 500 yards diameter, the headwaters of the Rosebud, which I have marked on the small map. We left Chambers' command several miles in the rear, and when we had bivouacked our camps on three sides of the lake, leaving the fourth side of the rectangle for Chambers when he arrived, the officers and many of the men walked over to observe the military movements of the "mule brigade" as it was called.

Chambers was proud and ambitious to do his duty, however humiliating and disagreeable, as well as he could, so when the leading company came near the line designated, he gave the command "Left front into line" in military style, and the first company came into line, but no sooner had the mules halted when, after their custom, they began to bray as loud as they could, making extra effort in accord with the extra effort they had made to carry their strange burden into camp. The cavalry officers began to laugh and roar. As the other companies began to halt Chambers lost courage and with oaths and every evidence of anger threw his sword down on the ground and left the command to take care of itself as best it could.

We remained there that night. There were no buffalo, and we could not learn anything from the friendlies about the enemy. The next morning, the 17th, at sunrise we started on our March down the Rosebud, without any indication of danger. General Crook had previously to do only with the semi-nomadic tribes, and from conversations with him I felt

7

he did not realize the prowess of the Sioux, though it was hard to think that he was not well informed by his numerous guides, scouts and especially the 250 friendly Indians.

About 9:30 or 10 o'clock, General Crook, being with Captain Henry's squadron marked "C" on the left bank, signalled a halt. Van Vliet's squadron "D" was in the rear of Henry, and Chambers' battalion marked "E" was in the rear of Van Vliet, and the packers were in the rear of Chambers. My squadron of four troops of the Third was in the advance on the right bank marked "A," followed by Captain Noyes with five companies of the Fifth marked "B." Everything was quiet, the day was beautiful, clear, calm and very warm. All had unbridled and were grazing for perhaps half to three-quarters of an hour, when my colored servant observed he heard shouting, and knowing that his ears were better than mine, I advanced up the hill towards "D" until I got to a high piece of ground, when looking north I saw on the crest of the horizon about two miles distant, great numbers of moving objects, looking somewhat like distant crows silhouetted on the clear sky above the horizon. I soon came to the conclusion that they were Indians in great numbers.

The friendly Indians were supposed to be in advance to find the enemy for us. General Crook and the troops on the left bank of the river were prevented from seeing anything to the north by the rising bluffs between them and the approaching Indians. I am satisfied that I was the first person to observe the coming hostiles.

They were, when I first saw them, from two to three miles distant, coming at full speed towards us and cheering. I immediately sounded the alarm, directing some of my squadron to mount, and calling out to General Crook, who was playing cards with some of his officers, that the Sioux were rapidly approaching.

He ordered me to report to him with my squadron at once. When I met him after crossing the stream, which was very boggy, I told him we were about to be attacked by a large force, and that the Indians were coming from due north. He told me to march rapidly and as soon as I got to higher ground to take the bluffs and hold them. I did so. What orders he gave to others I have never known. There are members of the Third Cavalry here, and they would probably correct me if I made mistakes. In all of this fight I do not remember to have received a single order except from General Crook personally or his Adjutant, Major Nickerson.

I marched as rapidly as I could through the rough and broken rocks, and as soon as I got on smoother ground gave the command "front into line," and sounded the charge.

There were two prominent rocky ridges, the first about a half mile from where I met General Crook, and the second probably about a half mile further on. When I reached the first ridge the leading Indians were there but gave way. There were large boulders at its foot, some large enough to cover the sets of four horses. I dismounted and directed the horse holders to protect them behind these rocks, advancing the men to the top of the ridge where the boulders were smaller but of a size to protect one or two soldiers, and appeared to be just what we wanted to fight behind. We met the Indians at the foot of this ridge, and charged right in and through them, driving them back to the top of the ridge. These Indians were most hideous, every one being painted in most hideous colors and designs, stark naked, except their moccasins, breech clouts and head gear, the latter consisting of feathers and horns, some of the horses being also painted, and the Indians proved then and there that they were the best cavalry soldiers on earth. In charging up towards us they exposed little of their person, hanging on with one arm around the neck and one leg over the horse firing and lancing from undernearth the horses' necks, so that there was no part

8

of the Indian at which to aim.

Their shouting and personal appearance was so hideous that it terrified the horses more than our men and rendered them almost uncontrollable before we dismounted and placed them behind the rocks.

The Indians came not in a line but in flocks or herds like buffalo, and they piled upon us until I think there must have been one thousand or fifteen hundred in our immediate front, but they refused fight when they found us secured behind the rocks, and bore off to our left. I then charged the second ridge, and took it in the same manner and fortified myself with the horses protected behind the larger boulders and the men behind the smaller ones.

These Indians lived with their horses, were unsurfeited with food, shelter, raiment or equipment, then the best cavalry in the world; their like will never be seen again. Our friendlies were worthless against them; we would have been better off without them.

In the second charge my trumpeter, Elmer Snow's horse became unmanageable, and he could not halt him but continued through the Indians receiving a wound shattering the bones of both forearms, but guiding his horse with legs only he described a circle of several hundred yards, returning to us and throwing himself on the ground.

On our right we were absolutely protected by the jagged and rough places down to the Rosebud Canyon, so we were most fortunate in securing this position.

On examining my front after taking the first ridge, I found that one of my troops, Captain Andrews, was missing, and learned that Colonel Royal had cut him off and directed that he report to him, as he was moving to the left with Captain Henry's squadron. We could see little of the left, as the ground depressed and the rough rocks obscured vision of what was going on by either the Indians or Henry's, Van Vliet's and Royal's commands.

I observed about this time two troops which I afterwards learned were Van Vliet's, going to "D" on the South Bluff, and later saw them proceed in a northwesterly direction towards where we could hear firing from Henry's and Royal's commands.

Soon after I took the first bluff the infantry took position on my left and Captain Noyes with his five troops arrived and was placed in reserve by General Crook in our rear and left, and the infantry joined on the ground lying on my left. General Crook held his position near my squadron, between my squadron and Noyes', during the entire battle, but I had little communication with him save when he came to me to give orders, and I knew little of what was going on until finally most of the Indians left my front. About 12.30 he ordered me to take my command of three troops and ordered Captain Noyes with his five troops to report to me, and proceed with the eight down the canyon and take the village which he said he had been reliably informed was about six miles down the canyon.

Henry, who was one of the best cavalry officers I ever knew, moved off here (indicating on the map).

This canyon was about six miles long. I was directed to follow it until I came to the village, and take it, and hold it until he came to my support with the rest of the command. I obeyed the order until I reached the vicinity of the village when I heard a voice calling me to halt, and Major Nickerson, the Adjutant General, directed me to return at once to General Crook. Some of the officers advised not. "We have the village," they said, "and can hold it." Nickerson then came across the stream. I asked him "are you sure he wants me to go back," he replied he was.

The canyon had opened here so I found I could climb the rocks and get out here (indicating on the map).

I returned about 2.30 and found General Crook in about the same position I had left him and said "General, why did you recall me? I had the village and could have held it." I never saw a man more dejected. He replied, "Well, Colonel, I found it a more serious engagement than I thought. We have lost about fifty killed and wounded, and the doctors refused to remain with the wounded unless I left the infantry and one of the squadrons with them." He said, "I knew I could not keep my promise to support you with the remainder of the force."

The General had assembled the hospital around him and the infantry, also two battalions near him. In visiting my wounded Captain Henry heard my voice and called me. I did not know until then that he had been wounded, and going to him found his breast all covered with clotted blood, his eyes swollen so he could not see and a ghastly wound through both cheeks under the eyes. I said, "Henry, are you badly wounded?" and he replied, "The doctor's have just told me that I must die, but I will not," and he did not, although nine out of ten under such circumstances would have died. Henry and I were rival captains in the same regiment but always friends.

Though the Third Cavalry had less than one-half of the soldiers engaged, their loss in killed and wounded was about four-fifths, principally of Henry's and Van Vliet's squadrons and Andrews' company of mine, that of Vroom's company being the greatest in proportion, this owing to their isolated exposure on level ground where the Indians could pass through them.

The officers then mingled and talked over the fight. I learned that Royal with Henry's and Van Vliet's squadrons and my troop E had gone to the extreme left where the ground was open, and that when the 1,000 or 1,500 Indians had refused to fight in the rocks they had swung around and overwhelmed them, charging bodily and rapidly through the soldiers, knocking them from their horses with lances and knives, dismounting and killing them, cutting the arms of several off at the elbows in the midst of the fight and carrying them away.

They then swung around and passed over the halting ground we had made at 9:30 in the morning, capturing some horses and killing an Indian boy left there. We then all realized for the first time that while we were lucky not to have been entirely vanquished, we had been most humiliatingly defeated, and that the village which Custer was to meet only seven days later, 14 miles west on the Little Big Horn, contained probably 15,000 or 20,000 souls, perhaps 4,000 or 5,000 warriors, and that perhaps only half of them had met us in battle, and that had my command remained at the village not one of us would have returned.

In fact I, with General Crook, visited this village site in our fall campaign, and he told me I ought to have been thankful to him for returning me from that canyon as they were as well or better equipped to destroy me as they were to destroy Custer and his command, and here I want to pay tribute to both Colonel Custer and Captain Henry. I knew both as long as they lived, and have been acquainted with nearly all prominent cavalry officers during my service, and they were always in my mind typical cavalry soldiers of the U.S. Army. I always resented criticisms that were made against Custer by men from General Terry down, who had little or no knowledge of Indian warfare. While a good man, Terry was not familiar with Indian warfare.

The next day we returned to our camp on Goose Creek where General Crook and all of

10

us made very brief reports of the battle, having little pride in our achievement. General Crook asked for reinforcements, and went into camp awaiting them, meanwhile we amused ourselves by hunting and fishing in the Big Horn Mountains, both General Crook and I being very fond of hunting we spent much time in the mountains and some two days later, after the Custer engagement, I and my Lieutenant Schwatka, went to the peak of the Big Horn Mountains, the northernmost point, thinking we might observe something in that direction, it being about 35 or 40 miles to the Rosebud. About 2 p.m. we observed a great smoke and realized that there had been a fight. Returning to camp in the night we reported to General Crook. About June 30th I with my squadron being the outpost on the lower Goose Creek observed at sunrise some smokes which created suspicion, and looking down the valley I saw three mounted men coming towards me which I first thought were Indians, but later discovered that they were white men on mules, Private James Bell, William Evans, and Benj. F. Stewart, Company "E," 7th Infantry (who were awarded medals on December 2, 1876), and I rode to them. They handed me a dispatch from General Terry to General Crook stating that Custer and his command had been massacred and that they had been sent by General Terry to carry his message to General Crook. Crook was in the mountains hunting. I carried the dispatch to Colonel Royal, commanding the camp, who opened it and read the dispatch, which horrified the assembled officers.

He ordered me with my full company to carry it as rapidly as I could to General Crook, and after climbing about 18 miles in the mountains I found him returning with his pack mules loaded down with elk, deer and big horn sheep. He read the dispatch and while all of us were horrified and suppressed with mortification and sympathy for the dead and wounded there was with all, particulary in General Crook's expression, a feeling that the country would realize that there were others who had underrated the valor and numbers of the Sioux.

While Gen. Crook was a cold, gray-eyed and somewhat cold-blooded warrior, treating his men perhaps too practically in war time, there yet ran through us a feeling of profound sympathy for his great misfortune, while at the same time we had a still more profound sympathy for the other gallant, more sympathetic Custer — at least, most of us. There were some there, I regret to say, who had ranked him and over whom he was promoted, that would insinuate, "I told you so," and for these sentiments the majority of us had no respect.

Finally, we were joined by General Merritt and the entire Fifth Cavalry, and the fall campaign ensued. After its termination I was returned to the command of Camp Sheridan, my former post, and was directed by General Crook to enter into communication with Chief Touch the Clouds of the Minneconjous, whose tribe still remained hostile, and I proposed to approach him through Spotted Tail and try to induce him to surrender. He approved, and I fitted up Spotted Tail with about thirty of his friendly Indians, rations and pack mules, and he proceeded to the camp of Touch the Clouds, and after some protracted negotiations induced him to return and surrender at a given time, about thirty days in advance, stipulating, however, that he was to be received with honors when he joined Spotted Tail's band. This reception, according to Indian tradition, consisted of the following program:

When a hostile band agrees to return to peace and join its former friends, the hosts are supposed to be captured by them; the tribe to be joined is notified when the tribe joining will approach; the approaching tribe is drawn up in war paint in apparent hostile array, and with great shouts and whooping, charge through the receiving village, who stand out receiving them with cheers, apparently of joy; the charging Indians firing their pieces in every direction save towards their supposed make-believe enemies. After charging fully through the village they return again, dismounting, and shake hands with their newly-made friends, and direct their squaws to pitch their tepees around those of the village. Chief Touch the Clouds sent in word that he would like to make a formal surrender, and if Gen. Crook and his staff would appear on the parade ground of the military post, he, with his principal chiefs — about thirty in number — would gallop in mounted as with hostile intent and when arrived within a few yards of the General, would cast their arms on the ground. And this ceremony was actually gone through by Gen. Crook and his staff officers. The arms they threw down were pieces of no value.

It will be observed that the ethics of the North American Indians did not differ materially from the ethics of the barbarians now fighting in Europe, in that they wanted no peace without victory.

Touch the Clouds surrendered about 1,500 Minneconjous, which increased Spotted Tail's tribe to nearly 6,000.

I thank you for your attention and manifested interest.

The Fight on The Rosebud*

By Capt. H. R. Lemly, U.S. Army

Big Horn and Yellowstone Expedition, Camp Bloud Peak, W. T., June 20, 1876

On the morning of the 16th inst., this entire command under Brigadier General Crook, comprising fifteen companies of cavalry under Lieutenant Colonel Royall, Third Cavalry, to-wit: ten companies of the Third Cavalry, commanded by Major Evans, the separate battalions thereof consisting of five companies each under Captain Mills and Henry, respectively, and five companies of the Second Cavalry under Captain Noyes; five companies of the Fourth and Ninth Infantry, commanded by Major Chambers, of the latter regiment; a party of packers under Chief Packer Moore, and 250 Crow and Shoshone or Snake Indians under Chief Washakie, of the latter tribe — in all, about 1,500 men broke permanent camp on Goose Creek and marched north in the direction of the Yellowstone River.

The infantry, with the exception of the camp guard that remained with the wagon train under command of Major Furey, quartermaster, were mounted upon pack mules, an improvisation by General Crook not wholly to the taste of Major Chambers. We were provided with four days' cooked rations and saddle blankets had to serve as bedding, since there was no transportation. Of course, there were no tents. Consequently, we were without *impedimenta* and free to go and come as we pleased.

After following the Tongue River Valley for some miles, we marched a little west of north and struck the source of the Rosebud River. The ground had been extremely rugged, and in character was not unlike those sections, in the vicinity of the Black Hills, denominated *Mauvaises Terres*. When we approached the Rosebud, however, we encountered a beautiful region. It is called, indeed, the Indian Paradise. The appellation "Rosebud" may have been given on this account, or derisively, perhaps, because there are no rosebuds there. "Red as a rose was she" the next day, however, as we shall presently find. While on the march, a few buffalo were seen and killed; and as they appeared to be driven, our friendly Indians concluded that were being hunted by the Sioux. Hence, they immediately halted and began their war dance and song, while several braves were dispatched to scout and ascertain the whereabouts of the enemy. When they returned, they reported signs of a *tipi* or lodge, so fresh as to indicate that our approach had been discovered by its occupants and that they had fled precipitately. Buffalo meat was upon the fire, burnt to a crisp. Upon receipt of this news a song and dance were again in order, and the mettle of war ponies was tested before we could persuade our allies to resume the march. As nothing further occurred, however, we bivouacked near the Rosebud, in the form of a hollow square, with the animals picketed inside. The night was very cold.

Early on the morning of the 17th, the march was resumed down the Rosebud, with General Crook and the mounted infantry and Second Cavalry upon the left bank and Colonel Royall with the Third Cavalry, Captain Mills' battalion in front, upon the right

---

*This account was written by Second Lieutenant H. R. Lemly, Third Cavalry, A.A.A.G. of Cavalry, a few days after the occurrence of the events it describes. The ranks of officers and designations of units are those which obtained at the time.

bank, of the river. The command was probably divided in order to shorten the column, and the stream was supposed to be readily fordable. About 8 o'clock our Crow scouts in advance returned rapidly to General Crook and reported the proximity of the Sioux. Immediately all the Indians began to strip themselves and their ponies and, amid great excitement, to dance and sing. Meanwhile, the command was halted and dismounted, and as nothing further happened for some time, even saddle girths were loosened, while the horses nibbled at the grass. In this state, not wholly one of expectancy (because we were getting accustomed to such demonstrations upon the part of our Indian allies), we were suddenly surprised by the sound of shots from in front and the whistling of bullets falling in our midst. With yells of defiance the Crows and Snakes dashed wildly up the adjacent slopes, but retired as quickly, being hard pressed by the Sioux, who fairly swarmed over the ridge. The Third Cavalry was promptly ordered to the left bank of the Rosebud, and Captain Mills, being in advance, succeeded in getting across with his battalion and thereafter was under the immediate orders of General Crook, who directed him and Captain Noyes to deploy and support our retreating Indians, which maneuver they executed in gallant style. Meanwhile, Colonel Royall, with Captain Henry's battalion, succeeded with difficulty in effecting a crossing in his vicinity; and your correspondent saw young Sioux braves ride into our temporarily disorganized ranks and strike at the soldiers with their *quirts* or riding whips, before they were shot down. The position of Captain Henry's battalion, the last to cross the Rosebud, threw him upon the extreme left of the line, where he deployed and charged; consequently, the writer, who accompanied Colonel Royall personally, witnessed only this part of the fight. The battalion engaged here comprised Captains Henry's, Meinhold's, Van Vliet's, Crawford's, Vroom's and Andrews' companies, the last-mentioned having become separated from Captain Mills' battalion, to which it rightfully belonged. The infantry under Major Chambers was held in reserve by General Crook, near the center. Our entire line was now under fire from the Sioux, who occupied the highest ridge in our front, but shot rather wildly. As we advanced, they retired successively to ridges in their rear and, throwing themselves prone upon the ground, reopened fire while their well-trained ponies grazed or stood fast at the extremity of their lariats, upon the reverse of the slope. The country presented, in fact, a succession of small hills, covered with grass and occasional boulders, but rarely with trees. At first the fighting was most severe upon the right and in the center, but the Sioux, in giving way, retired by our left, where they occupied a high and wooded crest, from which point of vantage Captain Henry's battalion was soon exposed to a heavy enfilading fire that was only checked by a brilliant charge made by Lieutenant Foster, Third Cavalry, at the head of his platoon. He was, however, forced to retire by overwhelming numbers, a line of skirmishers being rapidly deployed to cover his retreat.

Meanwhile, General Crook had conceived the idea that an Indian village existed at no great distance in the valley of the Rosebud, and Captain Mills and Noyes were dispatched to find and attack it, while the infantry and friendly Indians were held in check in the center, to which point Captain Henry's battalion was ordered to withdraw. Evidently the intention was to march the entire command upon the supposed site of the village. Nothing had been accomplished by our repeated charges except to drive the Sioux from one crest, to immediately reappear upon the next. Casualties occurred among them, of course, as with us, but beyond their indefinite equalization, nothing tangible seemed to be gained by prolonging the contest. When we took a crest, no especial advantage accrued by occupying it, and the Sioux ponies always outdistanced our grain-fed American horses in the race for

14

the next one.

In obedience to instructions, Colonel Royall now ordered Captain Henry's battalion to withdraw, and it was during this movement that the most of our casualties occurred. The men were dismounted and deployed in line of skirmishers, which constantly covered the led-horses as they slowly retired from one ridge to another. Captain Henry, himself, was in immediate command. But the instant this retrograde movement began, the Sioux appeared to construe it as a retreat and doubtless believed they had inflicted a severe loss upon us. From every ridge, rock and sagebrush, they poured a galling fire upon the retiring battalion, encumbered with its led-horses. They seemed, indeed, to spring up instantaneously as if by magic, in front, in rear and upon both flanks. Our casualties, compartively slight until now, were quickly quadrupled. The ground to be traversed was such that it was difficult to retire and protect the movement. Seeing this, Colonel Royall sent Adjutant Lemly to ask General Crook to station two companies of infantry with their longer range rifles upon the crest in front, from which to cover his withdrawal up the exposed slope; and Captains Burt and Burroughs, of the Ninth Infantry, with their respective companies, were promptly posted for this purpose. At the foot of the hill there was a wide ravine, deep and difficult of passage; and here in the confusion of mounting, quickly as commands were given and obeyed, five men fell dead and as many more were wounded. Some of the led-horses unfortunately escaped and galloped madly away, leaving their troopers at the mercy of the savage Sioux, who now swarmed in the ravine. Many of them appeared to be without firearms, for they used bows and arrows or spears. One of our wounded, who was subsequently recovered, relates a sad story. Separated from their horses and saddle pouches, in which they carried extra ammunition and that in their cartridge boxes having become exhausted, several of our men, led by Sergeant Marshall, of Troop "F," Third Cavalry, clubbed their carbines and fought bravely to the last. One poor lad, a recruit, with an insane idea of surrender or because he preferred a fatal bullet from his own piece to the torture of being transfixed by spear and arrows, calmly gave up his carbine, handing it to the nearest Sioux, and was brained instead by a blow from its butt. Captain Guy V. Henry, who had fearlessly exposed his life during the preceding fight and had been brevetted brigadier general for gallantry during our civil war, now fell from a terrible wound through his jaw and the roof of his mouth. He was assisted to mount his horse by two Crow Indians who had been conspicuous for their bravery; and with remonstrances against leaving his men, he was hurried to the field hospital. The last to come up the slope was Colonel Royall, an old soldier of the Mexican War, who had seen hard and constant service in our army, principally upon the plains and frontier. He ascended the hill calmly and without precipitation, the bullets whistling near him and raising a cloud of dust about him and his horse. Naturally he was chagrined at such an unfortunate issue to his withdrawal, but he had obeyed his instructions under very difficult circumstances, and those instructions were doubtless the only ones that should have been given at the time. The Sioux had evidently made every exertion to cut off and, if possible, annihilate Captain Henry's battalion and, after witnessing its escape from such fate, they silently disappeared.

Captains Mills and Noyes, meanwhile, had likewise received orders to return to the main body, as General Crook feared that they, too, might be attacked and overwhelmed by superior numbers. The Sioux had not been believed until then to be in such large force; but the command having once more assembled, the march upon the supposed site of the village was resumed, General Crook and our allied Indians marching in advance, while the troops of Captains Van Vliet and Crawford served as flankers, the only time during the entire campaign when such disposition was made. The trail of the retiring Sioux now entered the canyon of the Rosebud not unlike a muskrat slide in a pond. It was narrow and precipitous. Beyond, there appeared to be a veritable gorge with timbered cliffs and lateral ravines, in which the entire Sioux tribe might have been concealed. When our Crow and Snake Indians reached this point, they refused to proceed farther, and when urged by General Crook, some of them replied in the few English words of their vocabulary, which were more emphatic than polite. They were, in fact, unquotable. Our Kanaka scout and interpreter, Frank Gruard, who had lived many years among the Indians, now explained their reluctance to proceed, while the entire column halted. The Crows, it seems, had once been enticed into this very defile, which is several miles in length, and they had been massacred almost to a man by the wily Sioux, who literally lined its almost perpendicular sides. They called it the "Valley of Death." Finding further exhortations useless, General Crook now recalled his flankers and returned to the scene of our morning's combat, where the infantry was still guarding the field hospital. Here we bivouacked for the night, without incident.

An enumeration of our casualties is now in order and a painful but necessary task it is.

ROLL OF HONOR

Killed

Third Cavalry—Sergeants: Marshall, Newkirken; Privates: Roe, Allen, Flynn, Bennett, Potts, Connors, Mitchell.

Snake Indians—One.

Total killed, 10.

Wounded

Third Cavalry—Captain Henry; Sergeants O'Donnell, Mayher, Groesh, Crook; Corporal Carty; Trumpeters Edwards, Snow; Privates: Steiner, Herold, Broderson, Featherly, Smith, Stewart, O'Brien, Lorskyborsky, Kramer.

Fourth Infantry—Corporals Dennis, Ferry, Flynn.

Crow Indians—Four.

Snake Indians—Two.

Total wounded, 26.

Grand total, killed and wounded, 36.

None of our dead or wounded were mutilated, and the former were buried upon the field of combat, fires being kindled over the places of interment in order to conceal them.

The casualties among the Sioux were certainly much greater than our own. Many times they were observed lassoing their dead and wounded and withdrawing them from the ridge upon the reverse slope, within reach of their waiting ponies. Their conduct upon the field was admirable, and their riding superb, especially when they first approached and charged, entirely naked with the exception of a breech clout, hideously painted and yelling frightfully. No finer irregular cavalry ever existed.

At dusk, General Crook held a council with the Crow and Snake Indians, to whom he proposed a night march with a daylight attack upon the Sioux village, but they resolutely refused to accompany him. They had taken thirteen scalps during the day, and they were satisfied. A Shoshone was seen to drag a Sioux from his pony, disarm him and scalp him alive, afterwards killing him. One of our difficulties in the fight had been the impossibility of distinguishing the foe from our friendly Indians. General Crook had, indeed, ordered the latter to wear red about their heads, but this, as is well known, is a favorite color among all

16

our Western tribes. Its unfortunate adoption only added to the confusion. During the night the writer visited Captain Henry at the field hospital and found him suffering from an intolerable thirst, although no word of complaint escaped his lips. There were no invalid stores at hand, but finally Lieutenant Rawolle, of the Second Cavalry, produced some red currant jelly (probably the only delicacy among the fifteen hundred men present), which, although almost insoluble, was partially disintegrated in water and furnished a grateful relief to the wounded officer. Otherwise, the night passed without incident, although we had expected that the Sioux would attempt to stampede our animals. Not a shot was fired.

The next morning General Crook, handicapped by short rations and ammunition, and the necessity of caring for the wounded, determined to return to our permanent camp and await reinforcements. The Sioux had proved more numerous than he expected.

Litters and *travois* (adopted by the Indians from the French *voyageurs*) were therefore improvised for the wounded and we were soon en route. The former were suspended between two mules, while one end of the poles of the latter traveled upon the ground. The locomotion was uncomfortable in the extreme and, despite all precautions, Captain Henry was once or twice thrown out bodily.

On the night of the 18th inst., we bivouacked in sight of the Little Big Horn River, the proximity of which was too much for our valorous Crows, and shortly after dark they left us for their agency. Yesterday we reached our former camp, where we found everything in *statu quo;* and today, it was transferred to this spot, near which the Tongue River issues from the Big Horn mountains. Here we are to await the return of the wagon train with rations from Fort Fetterman, whither it is now marching, accompanied by the wounded in ambulances and guarded by three companies of infantry. The Snake Indians will remain with us, but will depart in a few days for their villages, near Camp Brown.

The "Fight on the Rosebud" is still the all-absorbing topic of conversation, and some of its incidents are rather severely commented upon. It is not my business or purpose to criticise. General Crook has shown great energy in the inception and progress of the campaign. He hoped to surprise and certainly destroy the Sioux village, and is doubtless deeply disappointed at the frustration of his plans. His enemies say that he was outgeneraled. That his success was incomplete, must be admitted, but his timely caution may have prevented a great catastrophe. He has chiefly become famous as an Indian fighter among the Apaches in Arizona, but the mounted and nomadic Sioux are a more difficult proposition. No doubt he will eventually solve the problem. He has much of the Indian in his composition, for he is as taciturn and abstemious and is, moreover, a thorough backwoodsman, an admirable scout and a wonderful hunter. One who knows him well says he could live on acorns and slippery elm bark!

The number of Sioux taking part in the engagement is variously estimated at from two to five thousand, but the writer believes the former figure is more nearly correct.

Crazy Horse and Sitting Bull are thought to have been in command. Both have proved wily diplomatists in council, and in this fight they showed themselves tacticians, if not strategists, quick to observe and prompt to take advantage of everything that favored or strengthened their position. Their scouts had doubtless been eagerly watching our advance, while the main body was quietly awaiting our arrival with the intention of entrapping us, as the Crows contended, in the gruesome yet beautiful "Valley of Death." The position selected was admirable. The canyon of the Rosebud is said to be fourteen miles in length, and a similar gorge exists in the Tongue River. Now, the general theory of both our attacks is this:

17

the Sioux were determined to give us battle, provided we permitted them to choose their own ground, and they had selected either of these defiles. Both are surrounded by country remarkable for its defensive qualities. While we were on Tongue River, becoming impatient and misapprehending our delay, they attacked us with the design of leading us into the defile on that stream. In this they were disappointed; but the Rosebud, our other available avenue to the Yellowstone, furnished them an equally good opportunity. Our scouting Crows, however, discovered their presence and misconstruing our halt, probably alarmed at our force and the number of our Indians, or fearful of a night attack, they concluded to force the issue immediately. General Crook appears to think our advance was unexpected and that the fight was but a demonstration to enable them to remove, if not the village itself, their families and principal effects, which is not improbable. I repeat, his prudence may have saved us from a great disaster.

It is also thought that the disappearance of the Sioux from the field may have been due to lack of ammunition. Our own friendly Indians almost exhausted the forty cartridges per man issued to them, that is, they fired nearly 10,000 rounds, which is not saying much for their marksmanship. One fact was clearly demonstrated during the engagement — the superiority of the Indians as skirmishers.

An unfortunate feature of the fight, already alluded to, was the impossibility of distinguishing between the Sioux and our friendly Indians. We fired many shots at the latter, no doubt, while the former as frequently escaped us. This was one of the causes of the dissatisfaction of the Crows and Snakes.

The officers of General Crook's staff, Captain Nickerson and Lieutenants Bourke and Schuyler, as well as the adjutants of the subordinate commands, were much exposed while carrying orders, and several had their horses wounded. Lieutenant Bourke gallantly rescued Trumpeter Snow, who was shot through both wrists, by catching his runaway mount and bringing both helpless rider and animal back to our lines. In England, this act would have been rewarded with the Victoria Cross!

It is understood that General Crook has sent for the Fifth Cavalry, five more companies of infantry and a battery of mountain guns — a weapon never before used in our Indian warfare, and that may go far to solve the problem. Meanwhile, we can not complain of our surroundings. Cloud Peak towers nearly 13,000 feet above us. Fed by its melting snows, the Tongue or Talking River (*Degi-agie*, of the Indians) has cut a deep gorge, through which its waters, clear as crystal, pure and cold, find their way to the plain in a thousand leaping cascades and foaming pools. Myriads of brook trout disport in its rocky depths or poised and alert, watch eagerly the rippling surface for floating fly or bait. The almost perpendicular canyon walls admit deep and timbered ravines, which give shelter to deer, elk, bear, and occasionally buffalo. The mountain sheep make their home beyond, among jutting peaks and projecting crags, where human footsteps have never trod. Here grows a hardy laurel, at a less altitude flourishes the birch and pine, while still lower are cottonwood groves. Upon the banks of the stream are found numerous varieties of ferns and beautiful and verdant moss. In close proximity to our camp, there are many ponds, formed by beaver dams and filled with fine salmon or rainbow trout. Already the soldiers are making nets of commissary twine. Just fancy seining for trout!

1918

The regular meeting of 1918 as published in the *Proceedings* did nothing but talk of the Constitution and By-Laws and have dinner. There is no record of any papers being delivered at the session, and there certainly is no record in print.

1919

There was no meeting held for this year and no reason was ever given — at least none which was recorded.

1920

At this year's meeting, the major address before the group was delivered by Mr. W. M. Camp, a noted historian of the day. Although not titled, the subject was a general survey of the Indian Wars touching upon some notable battles. It was not recorded in the *Proceedings* for that year, but thirteen years later it did reach print, but this time it was in the October, 1933, edition of *Winners Of The West,* a newspaper devoted to news of, for and by veterans of Indian Wars and their widows. It is because of this newspaper's alertness this address has been preserved.

Address by Mr. W. M. Camp

*Before The Annual Meeting And Dinner Of
The Order Of Indian Wars, Of The United States*

Washington, D.C. January 17th, 1920
Brigadier General Edward S. Godfrey, presiding

Note: This address having been delivered in January 1920, several of the sites mentioned by Mr. Camp have been marked since, notably Summit Springs, Adobe Walls, Buffalo Wallow, Grattan Massacre, Red Buttes Fight, Connor Engagement on Tongue River, Fort Reno, Fetterman Massacre, Redwater, White Bird Canyon and Wounded Knee.

I consider it much of a courtesy as well as an opportunity, to again be a guest of the Order of Indian Wars at one of its annual banquets. Being requested to address you, I have to regret that I am not able to talk of any of the events of which I am to speak from experience, for I have never seen a "wild" Indian except in the "pacified" condition. To be invited into the atmosphere of a meeting like this is, indeed, a rare privilege for one who is only a student of western history instead of one of the makers of it, such as you veterans are.

Not having participated in any of the events of the frontier days of the West, the nearest approach I have been able to make to the realities of those times has been as a student and as a trail hunter. In days gone by you often followed hot on the trail of dragging lodge poles, only to be baffled when the trail split up and scattered in all directions. Of course the trails that I have tried to follow in these later years were not discernible by scratched earth, nor by downtrodden grass, nor by pony droppings; but I have had to take for guidance official reports and maps, often roughly drawn; and the reminiscences of survivors; and, nearly always, there are local traditions as to the landmarks; and I can tell you truly that these various sources of information often diverge, and sometimes they mislead, or they may leave one in about as much of a perplexity as did the wily Indians their pursuers whenever they took it into their heads to split up and throw following troops off their track. And another source of difficulty is the extent to which settlers have gone in changing the names of streams and other geographical features, for the names which were official in the day of your campaigns are usually the translated Indian names.

But there were any number of times when you did overtake them, or when they overtook you, or laid in wait for you; and you fought many engagements — a battle here, or a skirmish there; or, in the small hours of morning you "jumped" a village by some stream, in a valley or canyon; and in these days it is the problem of the historical investigators to hunt up and identify the sites where the more important of these events transpired. Some of

21

these are well known; a very few of them are marked in some shape, and many of them have been lost as far as public knowledge is concerned. The sod over the graves of many of the soldiers killed in these Indian wars had remained unbroken save by the plow of the rancher, for, by necessity, identification marks had to be dispensed with to prevent exhumation by the foe. More than once did it happen that the final resting place of the brave soldier was, prudently, trampled under the hoofs of the animals ridden by the survivors, in order that all trace of burials might be obliterated. Thus, often has it occured that identification of the resting places of the dead as well as of the site of the engagement, was lost.

During frontier times the great highways across the plains and into the mountains were by way of the Arkansas, the Platte and the Missouri rivers. The last named, only, was navigated, but in the wide valleys of the other two streams were the historic Santa Fe trail, following, generally, the course of the Arkansas until it reached the mountains and along the Platte and its northern branch went the Overland trail, from which, well into the mountains, the Oregon trail branched off. Along both of these trails were numerous forts and supply depots, and many battles were fought right on the trails, particularly so in the case of the trail along the North Platte, but there were hundreds of engagements at long distances from lines of communication. As resourceful as was the Indian, he was, in the end, at a disadvantage when pursued by the indomitable men of the Regular Army under determined commanders. On good grazing the tough and hardy Indian pony was not easily to be overtaken, but when, in deep snows and the blasts of winter, he had to be put on forage of cottonwood bark, he stood a poor chance of getting away from the grain-fed, long-legged "American" horse and the Missouri mule. Even civilized war is hell, so we had been told by the best of authority, but war on Indians was certainly hell on horse flesh. In civilized warfare the contestants usually "dig in" or "hole up" for winter, but experience taught that the way to hit an Indian "under the belt" was to fight him in winter time; and the tactics of Custer and Crook and Miles, not to mention others, was planned to that advantage.

Battle of the Washita, Nov. 27, 1868

The first severe blow struck the Indians after the Civil War was the destruction of the Cheyenne Chief Black Kettle and his camp on the Washita, November 27, 1868. This was a village of peaceable Indians, but no investigation could be made in advance of the attack, and the Indian custom of shedding the blood of the other race for the sake of revenge, without respect to who the individuals might be, was imitated here. The stroke did have the intended effect, as events afterward proved, and General Sheridan always insisted that Custer made no mistake. The site of that historic fight has not yet been marked. It is in Roger Mills County, Oklahoma, nor far from the county seat town of Cheyenne. That part of the country is thickly settled and the land whereon the village stood is under cultivation.

Battle of Sand Creek, 1864

Four years previous to this the unfortunate Black Kettle, while encamped on Sand Creek, in Colorado, in obedience to the request of the Governor of the territory that all peaceable Indians assemble at designated places, was attacked by Colorado militia, under Colonel Chivington, as you will remember. His village was destroyed; a large number of his people — women and children and old men — were massacred, and the survivors were scattered over the country. At the moment of attack the American flag was flying over the lodge of Black Kettle.

The site of that historic affair has not been marked. If it were possible we, as a nation, doubtless had rather the event could be forgotten. But, while Black Kettle and his own band remained peaceable after this outrage, there were other Cheyennes and Arapahoes, who did not forget it, and the toll of life exacted by them on defenseless settlers of Kansas and Nebraska during the next few years must have exceeded, by ten times, the number of Indians that Chivington and his men had laid low, with shots and bayonets, on Sand Creek.

Battle of Beechers Island

Now, I shall not proceed chronologically in going over the list of battlefields which I have in mind, because to do so would keep me jumping all around the plains country, from one stream to another and from Texas to the Canadian border. But, going forward now to 1868, in September, or a couple of months earlier than the Battle of Washita, with which I started, we have the very gallant and determined defense made by Lieut. Col. George A. Forsyth and his little command of fifty enlisted scouts on the Arickaree fork of the Republican, in eastern Colorado. While these men were without military training, or largely so, they were plainsmen who had seen much service in that kind of country, and how efficiently they did their duty has gone down into history. The point is 17 miles south of Wray, Colorado, on the Burlington Railroad, and it is marked by a splendid monument, the money for erecting it being appropriated jointly by the States of Colorado and Kansas. The site was not identified until 1898, or thirty years after the fight, when three of the survivors came out looking for it, and actually passed it unaware. They would have given up the hunt as a failure had it not been, quite by accident, too, that a rancher who had settled there some twenty years previous had noticed horse bones and rope halters on what is commonly known as the "Island" (but actually it is not such,) and directed them to a spot, which, after some reflection and exchange of recollections, they finally recognized as the scene of the battle.

Tall Bull Killed

In July of the year following, 1869, General Carr, then Major of the 5th U.S. Cavalry, with part of his regiment and some Pawnee Indian scouts, attacked the village of Tall Bull and his Cheyennes, not far from where this fight of Forsyth's occurred, destroyed the camp, killed a number of Indians and scattered the rest of them. Tall Bull was among the slain. The spot is on a divide between the Republican and the South Platte, in eastern Colorado, and the place is not marked.

Battle of Adobe Walls

Before leaving the south let us go back to Oklahoma and Texas where, in 1874, General Miles, with the 5th Infantry and part of the 6th Cavalry, and Colonel Mackenzie, with the 4th Cavalry, fought several engagement each, in the fall of that year, and greatly discouraged the Southern Cheyennes, Arapahoes, Kiowas and Comanches, who had left their reservations to resent the wholesale slaughter of buffaloes by white hunters, who were killing them solely for their hides. The fight began with the famous battle of Adobe Walls, in the latter part of June. The site of that fight is still far from a railroad, and is not marked. There were two battles there — first, as already noted by buffalo hunters who

23

defended themselves inside of stone buildings for cover, with but small loss, while inflicting severe punishment upon the Indians; and later in the year a minor engagement was fought in the same vicinity by some of General Miles' scouts against a party of Indian raiders.

Buffalo Wallow Fight

The site of the famous Buffalo Wallow fight, of Sept. 12th between Indians and 4 soldiers and 2 civilians (Chapman and Dixon) has not been discovered. The site of Captain Wyllys Lyman's fight, while corralled with a wagon train and surrounded by a big band of Indians for three days, about the same time, is known but not marked. The rifle pits which he dug, with plenty of "45-70" empty cartridge shell lying about are still clearly in evidence.

On August 30th, and again in November, other troops of General Miles fought important engagements farther south, in the Panhandle of Texas, but I have been unable to get any information as to the exact location of these events and I therefore infer that they have not been marked. The points where Colonel Mackenzie fought his battles have been identified, so I am advised, but have not been marked.

Julesburg Fight

Along the main Platte and the South Platte there were many engagements of a minor character, but a great deal of bloodshed principally through attacks on ranches and wagon trains and small detachments that were doing escort duty. In December, 1864, Indians attacked the stage station, about a mile from Julesburg where there was a post, and a relief party of soldiers of the 7th Iowa Cavalry who were sent out were cut off and about fifteen of them were killed. This was a running fight and I do not think that any marker has been placed for it.

Grattan Massacre

Below the forks of the Platte there were two noted posts; Forts McPherson and Kearny, and these were needed supply and refuse points on the old Overland trail. The first conflict with the Sioux was on the North Platte, some distance below the renowned Fort Laramie. Everyone has heard of the Grattan "Massacre," where Lieut. Grattan, with some 28 or 29 soldiers of the 6th Infantry from Fort Laramie, while trying to arrest some Indians, was attacked and all killed. He was in a big Indian village and showed poor discretion in the use of threatening and abusive language over a matter of no consequence and for which the Indians were hardly blamable at all. The place where this encounter occurred is not marked.

Ash Hollow Fight

This fight took place in August 1854, and the next year General Harney went out to take revenge, and he got it by attacking a band of Sioux, at Ash Hallow, between the two Plattes, in western Nebraska. Some eighty or more women and children were killed while trying to run away, and Harney made a reputation; but the revenge which the Indians afterward took on emigrant trains and settlers, as usual, brought great hardship and terror upon the people of the frontier. Some ten years later, in 1865, some 7th Iowa troops were attacked near the mouth of Horse Creek, farther up the North Platte, and an officer and one or two men were killed. These troops were escorting Indians on their way to some point near the forks of the Platte, when the Sioux decided they did not want to go further and killed the officer, waded or swam the Platte and escaped. The site is not marked.

Fights Around Platte Bridge

This year was notorious for desperate fighting up in the vicinity of Platte Bridge, which was just above there the city of Casper now is. The city was named for Lieut. Caspar Collins, of the 11th Ohio Cavalry, who was killed in the battle of Platte Bridge, in the latter part of July, 1865. On the same day Sergeant Amos J. Custard, with some 18 men, while escorting a wagon train, was surrounded and all of the men with him were killed. This fight took place a few miles above the bridge, while Lieut. Collins' battle began within a mile of the north end of the bridge and continued right up to the bridge. The site of neither battle is marked. From Deer Creek, below, to Red Buttes, above Platte Bridge, there were numerous engagements between small parties of soldiers and bands of Indians with considerable loss of life to the troops.

Conner's Fight on Tongue River

A few weeks later General Conner, with quite a force of California, Kansas, Nebraska, Missouri and other volunteer troops of the Civil War organizations, left Fort Laramie for a campaign against the northern Indians. His command was in two columns, he, personally, conducted one part of it north or northwest to the Powder River country, and thence over to the Tongue, while another large force started from Omaha and marched north passing to the east of the Black Hills, thence northwest to the Little Missouri, and on west to the lower Powder River. Conner's column struck an Arapahoe village on the Tongue, pretty well up toward the Bighorn mountains. He attacked and destroyed the camp and killed a few Indians, capturing some women, among whom was the wife of the leader, Black Bear. This fight was on the main Tongue River, and the site is not marked.

Conner's plan was to meet Colonel Cole, the commander of the eastern column, at or near the mouth of the Tongue, on the Yellowstone. Cole followed down the Powder nearly to its confluence with the Yellowstone, when he was attacked by Sioux in large force, and harassed continually for many days. For lack of grazing the horses fell off in flesh and in a big snow storm, during September, more than half of them died. Although both he and Conner had plenty of Indian scouts, they missed each other and failed to connect. Cole's command ran entirely out of supplies, nearly the whole force were set afoot, they wore out their shoe leather, and the expedition came near ending up in disaster.

Fort Conner and Fort Reno

On the march northward General Conner had built a supply station which he named Fort Conner, on the west side of the Powder, near the mouth of Dry Fork. Here, fortunately, he had left men and supplies, but the fact was unknown to Cole, and the men of the latter, very hungry and footsore, had made their way up the Powder to within two days' march of Fort Conner before they became aware that relief was nearer than Fort Laramie. A day or two later Conner was much disappointed at the way things had turned out, and, greatly to his chagrin, here received dispatches directing him to march to Fort Laramie and hand over the command of the district to a Regular Army officer. This was done, the volunteer troops were sent east and mustered out of the service, and this was the last of Indian fighting by volunteer State troops on the plains.

Conner's losses in killed amounted to only one man, but a number with Cole's

25

command were killed and buried, no one, at this day knows where. Neither are the sites of his engagement known. Some of his artillery was rolled into deep water, in the Powder, and abandoned; and in recent years settlers have picked up rusty gun barrels and sabers, on sand bars and at other places along the river, that are supposed to have been some of the abandoned property of this command.

Fort Phil Kearny

During the next year, 1866, General Henry B. Carrington, with a battalion of the 18th U.S. Infantry, went out on the Bozeman trail, on essentially the same route that had been traveled by Conner, and built three forts. The first of these was at the site of Fort Conner, which was only a ramshackle affair and tumbled down, so a new post was built and named Fort Reno. Carrington went on to the forks of the Pineys and built a fort which he named after himself, but later this was changed, by official order, to Fort Phil Kearny. Still further on, at the point where the Bozeman trail (commonly known in those days as the Virginia City trail) crossed the Bighorn River, Fort C. F. Smith was built and garrisoned. These were among the historic army posts of the West, although garrisoned less than two years, being abandoned in the spring of 1868. The site of Fort Reno is marked only by debris, principally fallen chimneys of the buildings. It was filed on by a homesteader in 1918, and now is probably a plowed field, as the land is level and the soil fertile. Ten miles distant on a main automobile route, a pretentious granite monument has been erected, with the simple inscription "Fort Reno." The site of Fort Phil Kearny is a cultivated field and is not marked. The site of Fort C. F. Smith is still identified by portions of the adobe walls of some of the barracks.

Fight of Crazy Woman Creek

During the less than two years that these three posts were occupied there was almost incessant fighting, and, on the whole, the troops suffered many losses from the Indians, who lay in wait to cut off detachments and to attack supply trains. A few days after Carrington had reached the Piney's a party of officers and their families, with a small escort of soldiers, was attacked at the crossing of Crazy Woman Creek, and Lieut. Napoleon H. Daniels was killed. On December 6th there was a skirmish some miles north of Fort Phil. Kearny in which Lieut. H. S. Bingham was killed and two weeks later the historic Fetterman disaster occurred, in which three commissioned officers (Fetterman, Brown and Grummond), 76 enlisted men and 2 civilians were killed, no man getting away to tell the tale. The site of this battle has been marked by a well-constructed monument of granite boulders 6 feet in diameter and 18 feet high.

Fetterman Massacre

Other soldiers and civilians had been surprised in the vicinity of the fort from time to time and killed. Wood for fuel had to be hauled from the mountain canyons, about six or seven miles distant and, during the summer of 1867, the wood trains were attacked almost daily and compelled to corral and make a stand until reinforcements could be sent out from the post to drive off the Indians. On a high butte near the fort from the top of which they could overlook the whole country, a non-commissioned officer and squad of men were kept constantly on guard during day time to signal the fort whenever a wood train in the direction of the mountains or a supply train on the main trail was attacked by Indians. On

26

the morning of August 2nd the Indians appeared in large force, about 1,500 of them, as I have learned from their own accounts, with the intention of cutting off the wood trains in the mountains. Fortunately for the main train, it had proceeded nearly to the fort before the Indians showed up, but the guard for the wood camps and roads into the fort, consisting of part of Company C, 27th U.S. Infantry, commanded by Captain James Powell and Lieutenant John C. Jenness, had to leave their camp and take refuge, on short notice, within a corral of empty wagon boxes that had been used to hold cattle during night time. These two officers and 25 enlisted men (there were no civilians at this corral) made a most gallant defense for more than three hours, until relief could be sent out from the fort. The Indians, who were very poorly armed, had planned to rush on the corral afoot, but, greatly to their surprise, they, for the first time in fighting infantry, encountered breechloading rifles. Lieut. Jenness and two soldiers were killed and several others wounded.

Wagon Box Fight

The loss to the Indians in killed was surprisingly small, according to their own authentic accounts, and I want to say that I have generally found them to be reliable on such matters. Captain Powell estimated that he had killed as many as 60 of them, but the Indians report a much smaller number, although they say that more than a hundred of wounded had to be hauled off on travois. A significant fact which has a bearing on the number of Indians killed is that only one Indian body fell into the hands of the defenders, although it is a fact that many Indians had charged up within a hundred feet of the corral. A clear-headed old man who survived this fight has told me that he never saw such poor shooting by soldiers in his many years of experience at Indian fighting. Anyhow, the shooting was sufficient to keep the Indians out of the corral, and the event has passed into history as one of the most hotly contested engagements with Indians that occurred in all of the fighting of the plains, and such it undoubtedly was. It is commonly referred to as the "Wagon Box" fight.

A survivor of this battle, Max Littman, who visited the place in 1916, pointed out a spot which seemed clear to him as the site of the battle, and an iron post, with an inscribed brass cap, has been planted there. However, another survivor came along three years later and disagreed with his location, and thus the matter stands. There are still five more survivors known to be living, and these, or some of them, ought to be consulted before proceeding with the erection of the monument that is now provided for. Contentions over such questions in the West often run to partisan extremes. When I first visited this locality nine years ago I found five conjectural locations for the supposed site of the corral where this fight occurred, each clique of settlers being confident in their selection of the site, yet none of them had ever met a survivor of the battle.

Battle of Fort C. F. Smith

The historic battle at Fort C. F. Smith occurred on August 1, 1867, when Lieut. Sigismund Sternberg, with less than 20 enlisted men and a few civilians, guarding haymakers, about three miles from the fort, stood off more than a thousand Indians from about 9 a.m. to 5 p.m. The commander of the post, being aware of the fighting all that time, refused to allow a relief party to go out, although officers were eager to go, all day long; and finally, as the shades of evening approached, he consented to their very urgent appeals. In this battle Lieut. Sternberg and two men were killed, and no little loss was inflicted on the Indians. It was fully the equal of the "Wagon Box" fight in desperate defense, and the odds against the men in the corral of logs was about the same. There were fewer defenders than was the case at the Wagon Boxes, and the fight lasted twice as long. As was the case at the "Wagon Box" also, not many of the Indians were armed with anything better than bow and arrows, or the result in both instances might have been different. The site of this battle is known, but it has not been marked.

Fort Laramie Treaty

The Fort Laramie treaty of 1868 gave to the Sioux and Northern Cheyennes all the country between the North Platte and the Yellowstone, and from the Big Horn mountains to a line east of the Black Hills, for a perpetual hunting ground; or, in the language of the treaty, "as long as grass grows and water flows." However, the "license" with which the whites regarded this poetic agreement amounted to virtual rejection of it, almost from the start, and conflicts with these northern Indians kept up. The Indians, also, seeing that the treaty rights were not being respected by the whites, overran the boundary lines and committed depredations both south of the North Platte and north of the Yellowstone. While large Indian populations under Red Cloud and Spotted Tail had settled down on reservations there were bands of discontented Sioux, under Crazy Horse and Sitting Bull, and Cheyennes, under several leaders, who had no use for the reservations except for occasional trade, and they preferred to roam the wilderness unhindered, and to live on the buffalo in the way of their forefathers.

Surveys of Northern Pacific

The surveys of the Northern Pacific Railway, in 1872 and 1873, had to be conducted under strong escorts of soldiers, and attacks were frequent. These attacks occurred at points all the way across North Dakota and along the Yellowstone. What is known as "Baker's Battleground" where Major Eugene M. Baker, of the 2nd U.S. Cavalry, had a minor engagement, is a few miles east of the present town of Billings, and is marked in temporary fashion. General Stanley, whose command included nearly all of the 7th U.S. Cavalry, under General Custer, and infantry besides, had two engagements with the Sioux, in August, 1873, Custer being personally engaged in both of these. One of the fights occurred on the north side of the Yellowstone, a few miles west of where Fort Keogh is now, and the other, a week later (August 11), was on the same side of the river, on what later came to be known as Pease Bottom. Both of these sites have been identified and temporarily marked. Custer once made an effort to cross his men over in bull boats to fight the Sioux on the south side of the Yellowstone. The next day, however, the Sioux crossed by swimming their ponies over and attacked him on his own side, near the mouth of the Bighorn. In this fight Custer had a horse wounded and his orderly was killed. Lieut. Charles Braden was severely wounded.

Bozeman Campaign

The next year, 1874, a party of mining prospectors, organized at Bozeman, invaded the Indian country south of the Yellowstone and had several hard fights with the bands of Sitting Bull and Crazy Horse. From the standpoint of the invaders, this expedition, was successful. Although followed by large numbers of Sioux for more than a month, they went just where they pleased, with plenty of supplies hauled by horse and ox teams, and they treated the foe with contempt. In two of the battles the bodies of Indians, both alive and dead, fell into their hands and were treated in just the way Indians would have done had the situation been reversed. Invariably these men "dug in" every night, and the rifle pits in each of nine locations are still very well preserved, and some of these have been marked by wooden signboards. The manner in which they picked their ground for a fortified camp in each place would, I think, be a worthy study for the military historian. Their entire route up the Rosebud was traversed by General Custer two years later on the campaign from which he never returned.

General Custer Explores Black Hills

During this same year, 1874, General Custer made an exploration of the Black Hills, and his official reports, together with those of the geologists and newspaper correspondents who went with him, led the whole East to believe that the Hills were full of gold "from the grass roots down" as the current rumors expressed it. In spite of military forces on all the roads, to turn people back, and the destruction of outfits and wagon trains in some instances, no less than eleven thousand miners, according to creditable estimates, had gotten into the Black Hills by the fall of 1875. This violation of the treaty soon brought matters to a head with the Indians, for, by the spring of 1876, Sioux from all the Missouri River Agencies, and from the Red Cloud and Spotted Tail agencies in northern Nebraska had gone out and joined the hostiles under Sitting Bull and Crazy Horse.

Campaign of 1876

This brings us to the heavy fighting of the year 1876, the history of which has been much written, and I need not go into the details of the plans for the campaigns nor follow all the movements of the troops that were marched and countermarched over the plains and through the mountains that year. If there be some here who did not participate in those campaigns, however, let me say that the Sioux and Cheyennes who went out to fight that year carried firearms almost to a man; and not a few of them carried repeating rifles of the Winchester pattern, which were just then coming into favor with big-game hunters all over the country. No longer did Army officers idly boast that they would not hesitate to undertake to "ride through the whole Sioux nation" with few companies of veteran soldiers, as some of them had, in times past, been quoted as saying.

Powder River Fight

The first clash came on St. Patrick's day on the Powder, just a few miles north of the Montana line. Here Colonel Reynolds, who, according to his own statement, had never seen an Indian village before, with detachments of the 2d and 3d Cavalry, attacked and captured a camp of 104 lodges, but sans Indians, who ran off far enough to get their families out of harm's way and then returned and hung about the camp sharpshooting while the soldiers were trying to burn it. One Indian was killed and four soldiers — some dead and some alive but wounded — fell into the hands of the Indians. Before the destruction of the camp was complete, Reynolds ordered the thing abandoned and marched off. He drove off with him a large herd of captured Indian horses, but nearly all these were recovered by the Indians that night. The site of this fight has been well identified, but not marked, although government headstones for the four soldiers who perished there have, through the kind offices of General Mills and Major Lemly, been shipped out to Wyoming, at the nearest railroad point and will be placed on the battlefield next summer.

General Crook on Rosebud

Three months later, June 17th, General Crook, commanding in person, met the whole congregation of the Sioux and the Cheyennes at the head forks of the Rosebud, in an all-day fight. Crook's forces here amounted to 1,028 men, all told, and for an hour or two which way the conflict would turn seemed uncertain. He lost nine men killed on the field and more than 30 wounded (and had fired away so much ammunition that, thinking discretion the better part of valor), retired back to the foot of the Bighorn mountains, whence he had come. Could Crook have pressed on at this time there might never have been any Little Bighorn to record in history, for on the day of this fight, Custer was still on the Yellowstone; and the point where Custer did strike the Indians 8 days later, to his utter defeat and annihilation, is only forty miles from where Crook fought identically the same Indians on June 17th.

The battle of the Rosebud extended all the way from the bend of the creek, where Tom Penson's ranch now is, to the forks, a distance of about 2¾ miles. It has not been marked, but government headstones for the men killed there, nine in all, have been shipped to the nearest railroad point and will be set up on the battlefield. The remains of these men now lie scattered about the field, where some of them have been upturned by the plow, and along a side hill, where supposedly, they were dug up by Indians soon after the battle.

Battle of Little Big Horn

As for the battle of the Little Bighorn, you know that the site has been marked by a monument on which are inscribed the names of the men killed with both Custer and Reno, 263 in all, of whom 207 were killed with General Custer. This was a battle in three fights, the one in which Custer fell, and where the monument stands, being known as the engagement on Custer ridge. The sites of Reno's fight in the river bottom, where he lost 29 men killed, and on the bluffs where he lost 27 more killed and some 60 wounded, have no been marked but should be. Leaving Custer's part of this fight out of consideration entirely, these two fights under Major Reno were about the hottest affairs of the kind, where the troops got out of it still in shape to fight on, that the historian will find opportunity to study. There were "heaps" of Indians there and, as they say, they had "heaps of guns" — they were not handicapped for lack of firearms as they were in the fighting soon after the Civil War.

Generals Crook, Merritt, Carr and Terry

After the battle of the Little Bighorn, the Indians pulled straight for the Bighorn mountains. Soon after, General Crook's forces were reinforced by the addition of the 5th Cavalry, under Merritt and Carr, and the Indians led him a long chase. He followed their trail down the Rosebud to within a day's march of the Yellowstone, where he was joined by General Terry and some 1,100 men. The combined forces of about 2,500 men, struck across to the Tongue the trail led to the Powder, during the rainiest August even known in that country, and beast and man plodded on with great difficulty. Still, the trail led on toward the Little Missouri, and, at length, the buffalo being all chased out of the country, and the grass very poor or gone entirely, both commanders thought best to hunt for supplies.

Fort Abraham Lincoln

General Terry pulled straight for Fort Abraham Lincoln, on the Missouri, but Crook elected to make a bee line for the Black Hills, where he would, if he could reach them, be back in his own department and likely be able to find supplies in the mining camps. Crook had about 1,500 men, and his movement to the Black Hills has gone down in history as the "starvation march." Although his outfit was far more experienced in Indian fighting, yet he was in much the same fix as had been Colonel Cole with his 1,400 volunteer soldiers on the Powder 11 years before. More than 400 horses played out and had to be killed, the majority of the men were afoot, either without horses or leading them, the rations were exhausted and the men were living on horse flesh, wild plums and bull berries. Seeing that he would never get to destination with all his force unless unusual measures were taken he dispatched Captain Anson Mills ahead with the pick of the horses and 150 picked men to go to the Hills and return to meet him with supplies of food.

General Mills at Slim Buttes

But this march was not without glory, for Mills, plodding on through the rain and fog, ran into an Indian camp in broad daylight, sought cover, and the next morning fell upon them while they slept, or just missed doing so. He got the camp of 37 lodges, with the herd of fat horses, and held on. Without anticipating any such a result, a long-sought object was here attained, for, much by accident, they had "found Indians" — more than enough to put up a considerable fight against all of Crook's command. Mills had found the camp at the foot of Slim Buttes, on the east side; and just through a gap, but eight miles distant, was the whole outfit of Sioux and Cheyennes that Crook had been following all the way from the Bighorns.

When the Indians had heard from the refugees from the captured village what had happened, they got up onto their horses and rushed through the Buttes, but, very fortunately for Mills, Crook arrived simultaneously with his whole force and there was skirmishing and fighting all over a township of open country the rest of that day. Thus, Slim Buttes became a historic affair, and King and Bourke and Finerty have written classic accounts of it.

In this battle three men were killed, an officer lost a leg, and many were wounded. On the Indian side the loss in killed was more, and there were a few prisoners, whom Crook turned loose unharmed when he marched away the next morning. The site of this battle was lost for more than forty years, but it has been found, and a monument will be placed on the site of the village next summer. The remains of the men killed and buried there were taken up by the Indians, and they lie there on top of the ground until this day. Government headstones have been sent to be set where their remains will be reburied.

Battle of Red Fork of Powder River

With the exception of small parties of agency Indians who sneaked back to their reservations from time to time, the great mass of the Sioux and Cheyennes who were out fighting in 1876 remained out all the following winter. Crook planned to hit them in their winter quarters, and he found the Cheyennes under Dull Knife, on the Red fork of the Powder, up in the foot hills of the Bighorn mountains. There Colonel MacKenzie surprised them in the late days of November, 1876, and won the most decisive victory of troops over the Indians of that year, destroying their camp and driving the whole population out into bitter winter weather. In this battle Lieut. John A. McKinney was killed. The site is well identified, but not marked.

On the Yellowstone with Miles

Up north, on the Yellowstone, General Miles, with the 5th Infantry and some of the 2d Cavalry, operating from Fort Keogh cantonment, kept up the same tactics. After the middle of December, a portion of his command, under Captain Baldwin, with foot soldiers, wading through deep snow, attacked Sitting Bull's Indians twice, on the Missouri, and on Redwater Creek and on the latter occasion destroyed their village. The sites of these events have not been marked. Three weeks later, or in January, 1877, General Miles met the forces of Crazy Horse on Tongue River, about 90 miles from the cantonment, shelled them out with artillery and pursued them some distance up the stream. The site of this engagement is known but not marked. In the following May, General Miles surprised and captured the camp of Lame Deer, a Minneconjou Sioux chief, on what is now known as Lame Deer Creek, near Lame Deer agency of the Northern Cheyenne reservation. By mistake, Lame Deer, who was trying to give up peaceably, was menacingly driven to self-defense was killed and the camp was destroyed. The site is pointed out by Cheyennes who were present, but it is not marked.

Nez Perces War

Except for occasional raids that were made by Sitting Bull's band that had run over the line into Canada, there was now a lull in the fighting with the Sioux but, after outrageous treatment, the Nez Perces, hitherto a peaceable lot of Indians, took to war, or, rather, were driven into it, and they led General Howard far from his base. The heaviest of the fighting was with Captain David Perry of the 1st Cavalry, in White Bird Canyon, in June, 1877, on the Clearwater, in Idaho; at Big Hole, on the other side of the Bitter Root mountains; at Canyon Creek, north of the Yellowstone; and on Snake Creek, not far from the Canadian line, commonly known as the battle of Bear's Paw mountain. Here the remnant of the Nez Perces, under Joseph, after White Bird and his band had gotten away, surrendered. The site is well identified, but not marked. At Big Hole, where three officers were killed and several more wounded, including General Gibbon, the commanding officer, a granite monument marks the site of the battle. The sites of the battles in White Bird canyon and on the Clearwater have not been marked.

Bannock War

In 1878, the Bannock went to war, and there was some fighting in Idaho, but without large casualties on either side. The windup came when a number of Indians who had sought asylum east of the mountains were caught by General Miles with an escort on a pleasure trip, in their camp, on Clark's fork and routed, losing their lodges. In this fight a veteran officer, Captain Andrew S. Bennet, of the 5th Infantry, was killed. The site has not been marked, and the settlers, so I have learned by correspondence, do not agree as to the exact site.

Ghost Dance and Battle of Wounded Knee

As to the wars with the Apaches, I am not able to give you any information other than what I have gained from reading the books and magazines. I will conclude, therefore by jumping ahead twelve years to the culminating event of the Ghost Dance war, if it may be called a war, the battle of Wounded Knee. Anyhow, a good many troops were called into the fuss, and it fell to the lot of the organization that became so famous for Indian fighting, the 7th Cavalry, to fight the last of the hard battles of the Indian wars. I will not go into the details of the engagement any more than to say that neither side was expecting a fight, the Indians having surrendered the day before and had camped with the troops overnight. The blunder that started the firing was committed by one of the Sioux, so they admit themselves. The site of this battle is marked by a marble monument erected by Joseph Horn Cloud, a son of one of the Indians who was slain there, and the inscription is in the Sioux language. The names of the 47 heads of families who were killed there are included in this inscription, and the battle is designated the "Big Foot Massacre." The monument in memory of the soldiers who were killed there has been erected at the old home of the 7th Cavalry, Fort Riley, Kansas.

I will take occasion, in closing, to pay deserved tribute to the distinguished toastmaster of the evening, General Godfrey. I began with the battle of the Washita, in 1868, and he was there, and is now the only surviving officer who participated in that engagement. I told you about the Little Bighorn, and he was there, commanding a company. I have told you of Bear's Paw, and he was there, shot off his horse, desperately wounded. I finished with Wounded Knee, and, behold he was there. He participated in every one of the four historic battles that made this regiment so famous in Indian campaign, and these four stand out conspicuously among the illustrious events of the plains.

1921

At this meeting there were 36 Companions and 12 guests present. The usual order of business preceeded the annual dinner which was a normal order for all their annual meetings. (Hereafter, only data of special importance will be reported of each meeting.)

The only presentation printed in the *Proceedings* for that year was the one by General Charles King who spoke on the Sioux Campaign of 1876. Two other short — perhaps even informal — addresses were made but not printed. They were by General Nelson Miles who gave reminiscences of his Indian experiences, and by the Honorable Charles R. Davis, a Representative in Congress from the State of Minnesota, who gave his recollection of the Indian campaigns in Minnesota in 1862. Mr. Camp also made a very brief remark — also unrecorded — supplementary to his address in 1920.

One observation the *Proceedings* did feel of sufficient importance to print was the following:

"It is noteworthy that all the remarks made at this meeting had in them words of praise for the Indian — that he had many estimable and sterling qualities, so many, in fact, that he won the favor and in many cases the admiration of those whose duty sometimes called for hostile relations. Mr. Davis' remarks on his relations with the Sioux Indians, amongst whom he found playmates and friends in his early life and with whom he spoke in their own language breathed a spirit of warm sympathy and appreciation and admiration that struck a responsive chord in the hearts and minds of all present."

Address by General Charles King

Nearly a half a century has rolled by since the summer of the Sioux campaign, wherefore there must be far less time before than behind us, and I shall waste none of it in telling of the causes of that memorable clash. It was the climax of a long series of troubles beginning with the Grattan affair near old Fort Laramie in '58. It was the supreme effort of the strongest nation of the wild frontier, backed by the friends and allies, even better horsemen and warriors than Ogalalla, Uncpapa, Minneconjou or Brule — the famous Northern Cheyennes. It started with every hope and prospect of success, so far as such chieftains as Sitting Bull, Crazy Horse, Gall, and Rain-in-the-Face could see, yet Red Cloud, he who planned and plotted the Fort Phil Kearny massacre of 1866, and compelled the Great Father to abandon the Montana route by way of the Big Horn, and to withdraw his scant and scattered forces to the line of the Platte, was no longer in active service. They would have been better advised and better led had he been afield, rather than semi-paralyzed back at the agency.

Be this as it may, the young men of even the far Blackfeet and Sans Arc had swarmed to the camp of Sitting Bull in the heart of Indian story land. The Indian Bureau had at last given up all hopes of inducing them to come in and be good. The War Department had been besought to bring them to terms, and by early March there had ventured forth from Fort Fetterman across the ice-bound Platte a column of horses, headed by an undeniably gallant general of Civil War experience, but of savage warfare as undeniably expert, and again had the soldiers of the Great Father found the Sioux far too numerous and skillful even when amazed at the coming of cavalry through snow drifts and bitterest cold to look them up in their winter lair. Again had our guidons to come drifting back to the shelter of the forts, some of our leaders to face court-martials, our men the merciless chaffing of comrades of the infantry and civilians by the dozen in Cheyenne and Laramie. It was an unhappy springtide in the Department of the Platte. It was mid May before matters really got going again. Then three big expeditions — big as such things seemed to us in those days — launched forth to concentrate on the hostiles known to be in force somewhere south of the Yellowstone and north of the Big Horn range, and with George Crook and the infantry and cavalry of the Department of the Platte marching northward from Fort Fetterman, with Alfred H. Terry and his combined forces heading westward from Bismarck and Fort Abraham Lincoln, and John Gibbon, with most of the soldiery of the Upper Missouri at his back, striding for the junction of the Yellowstone and the Big Horn rivers, it began to look as though the Indian at last would have to fight with equal numbers instead of big odds in his favor. The question was whether our red brother would let us concentrate about him or come forth and fight us in detail, and the 17th of June gave answer.

Already on June 9th the Sioux had struck Crook's column and given it temporary pause. The Crow and Shoshone allies had been slow and cautious in coming to join him, and Crook believed he needed them. Pacific coast Indians he had fought successfully, even the hitherto intractable Apaches whom he whipped into subjection through skillful use of their own kind as scouts and trailers. He had won his star over the heads of the colonels in the Army as reward for his service. He knew the Indians and his nature well, no man in our day knew him better, but he never yet had fought the mounted warriors of the great plains.

He had been warned by Red Cloud's triumph over the Fort Phil Kearny garrison. He had been nettled and distressed at the failure of Reynolds' command to nab Crazy Horse ten years later, and he had underrated the prowess and valor of the Sioux and Cheyenne. He had taken the 5th Cavalry to Arizona and taught it mountain scouting and Apache fighting, and we loved and honored him for many a trait, notably that he personally led and shared in every peril and hardship, but, even in the 5th were officers and men who had fought the Indians of the Southern plains and certain strong bands of renegade Sioux, Cheyenne and Arapahoe before ever they went to Arizona, and some of our elders did not hesitate to say that Crook had a far different position ahead of him now, and they were not a whit surprised when, far to the southward, we got the tidings of that day's doings on the beautiful bluffs of the Rosebud — how Crook's picturesque allies, Snake and Crow, had come tearing back upon the column in wild excitement and disorder, shouting "Heap Sioux! Heap Sioux!" instead of the defiant battle cry. It was the only time in the whole campaign this expensive contingent actually got into the game; by the time we really met and fought the embattled warriors of Sitting Bull that summer, the last of our Crows and Shoshones had flitted back to their squaws, where most of them properly belonged.

Just as in December, '66, wily Red Cloud had enticed a strong detachment out from the walls of the hated fort on the Piney to the rescue of wood choppers, then in overwhelming numbers engulfed and annihilated to the last man, so on this memorable 17th of June it was doubtless the hope and plan of the red leaders to draw Crook's column on down the deep and tortuous Dead Canon of the Rosebud, then swarm upon it from every side. Anson Mills, whose battalion was the first to mount, to charge, to scatter such of the Sioux as were permitted to show on the northward bluffs, had indeed received orders to push for the village somewhere down stream, had already set forth on his perilous mission, with but a single battalion following in support, everybody else being busily engaged beating off the circling flocks of hostiles pecking away at the flanks and rear. It was God's mercy and Crook's second thought that sounded the recall not one moment too soon. It was a wise leader that accepted that lesson, and with another day had fallen back toward the wagons and temporary safety, while couriers went in post haste to Fetterman with the call for big reinforcements. The Sioux meantime, leaving thirteen dead upon the field — which meant at least temporary defeat — slipped away a less distance to the west, and there, eight days after they had practically turned back Crook — surrounded and overwhelmed Custer.

Never again until September was either Crook, Terry or Gibbon to encounter the big array at the beck of Sitting Bull. Then again it was Crook's command that stirred them up. Then again it was the squadron leader who opened the ball at the Rosebud who, far in advance of our bedraggled column, rode slap into their easternmost village, and in the first as in the last battle of the luckless "B. H. & Y."[1] the opening chorus was the charge of Anson Mills.

Meantime some rather remarkable things had happened. By easy marches Crook led his original force of barely eleven hundred back under the lee of the Big Horn to the south. By easy marches, after burying the dead of the gallant but ill-starred 7th Cavalry, Terry and Gibbon descended the Yellowstone. It was the summer of our discontent; it was the proudest summer the Sioux nation had ever known.

Under the strong escort Crook's wagons went back to Fetterman with the wounded —

---

1. The Big Horn and Yellowstone Expedition.

38

Guy Henry, the paladin of the 3rd Cavalry, among them. With what was supposed to be a sufficient force, Sibley and Frank Gruard were sent scouting out westward, and nothing but God's mercy brought them back, though Sibley's serene courage and Gruard's horse sense were the instruments of the Divine Will.

Riding by night and hiding by day, Schuyler of the 5th Cavalry had made the hazardous trip from Fetterman to find Crook, to join him as aide-de-camp and to tell him that his old Arizona friends had been gathered up from their winter stations in Kansas and were en route to Cheyenne, Fort Laramie, and thence to watch the reservations and head off reinforcements for Sitting Bull. There was nothing to do, therefore, but await developments, and nothing came until July 10th, in the person of scout Louis Richard, with the appalling news of the Custer disaster on that very Sunday in which, far to the southeast, the advance guard of the 5th Cavalry had discovered the broad Indian trail from Red Cloud toward Pumpkin Butte, and Anson Mills himself, ever restless and alert, had seen far over to the northwest the great white cloud rolling up from the lowlands of the Little Big Horn, and Richard bore despatches from Sheridan to Crook, acknowledging report of the battle of June 17th and bidding him, "Hit 'em again and hit 'em hard." They had been roommates at the Point, comrades in the closing campaign of Five Forks and Appomattox, and each knew the other well. "I wonder if Sheridan could surround three Sioux with one soldier," was all Crook had to say. He was up against an Indian proposition the like of which neither he nor Sheridan had ever known before.

And yet, could Crook only have men and pack mules, he was eager to set forth and meet it. Here it was midsummer and nothing accomplished. Two,—three weeks he waited, marveling at the non-appearance of the longed-for levies. He had looked for them by July 5th or 6th, and late in July learned to his annoyance that the 5th Cavalry had gone back to Laramie instead of coming on direct to him.

And thereby hangs a tale.

Obedient to Sheridan's orders, every captain with his troop and every troop mounting 55 men, the 5th Cavalry had spent the fall and winter of '75-'76 in garrison in Kansas, after their four years in and long march from Arizona. They had hailed with delight the rumor of field service, and the eight troops hurried by rail to Cheyenne were the envied of those left to guard the stables and quarters of their scattered stations. They were led by their Lieutenant Colonel Eugene A. Carr, who, with Bill Cody for guide, had so soundly thrashed Tall Bull's big band of desperadoes in '68, who had been regimental commander from the fall of '71, and fully expected to lead it through the big campaign he clearly foresaw. They were joined at Cheyenne by their old-time scout and comrade, Cody himself, fresh from the footlights and glorying in once more being in saddle. They had marched to Laramie, heard there much excited talk of the Rosebud affair, and thence had jogged swiftly northward. Great was the excitement at the Red Cloud and Spotted Tail Reservations east of Fort Robinson, and Major Jordan, there in command, was in eager telegraphic communication with Sheridan. By June 24th we were trotting swiftly down the valley of Old Woman's Fork of the South Cheyenne, and on the unclouded morning of Sunday, the 25th, afar to the north of it, our advance guard had found the very trail as to which Sheridan desired information, and, turning once more southeastward, had stirred up a few small war parties, too small and too swift to be overtaken, and on the 1st of July, just to the west of the Black Hills, had been joined by the late Inspector of Cavalry, Division of the Missouri, Wesley Merritt himself. Our old-time Colonel, Emory, had retired and the older-time brigade and division commander of Gettysburg, Five Forks and Appomattox, had come again to his own. He had joined the very day of his promotion. Moreover, he had the latest word from Sheridan.

The next morning came a long chase after swift-footed prowlers; the next, and the next, scouts up the valleys of Hat and Indian creeks, and not until the 6th did we reach the block house on the back track and the old Black Hills stage road that went by way of Rawhide Butte in to Laramie, and here on July 7th we got the news that Custer and five troops of the 7th Cavalry were wiped from the face of the earth.

Merritt sensed the situation on the instant. Nothing we could accomplish in chasing small bands from the reservation could now equal Crook's need of men. Expectant of immediate orders to join Crook, he called in his scouts, but there we waited four days longer before those orders came. "Back to Laramie and thence to Fetterman," they read, and when but one day's ride from the former post came urgent messages from Jordan at Fort Robinson. Wild excitement among the Southern Cheyennes! We might be needed there! Eastward, therefore, Merritt turned at once; marched until late afternoon away down on Rawhide Creek to the junction of the Red Cloud road from Laramie, and there, on the 15th, received Jordan's next despatch: "800 Southern Cheyennes start at daybreak to join Sitting Bull!"

They didn't get there. They had a broad, straight road to go, but in the opulence of pride, they were taking their families with them, disdainful of any opposition from Fort Robinson, or to be expected before they neared the camp of Crook. The cavalry, said their scouts, had hurried back to the Platte to get out of danger. They could go on their way rejoicing and they did. But, speeding day and night, back by the way he came, far to the west of their line of march, Merritt led the 5th; threw them across the path of the Cheyennes, 85 miles in 31 hours, and early on the morning of the 17th met, charged, and in an all-day chase drove them pell mell back to the agencies, amazed and discomfited; the young chief, Yellow Hand, dying in single combat in the initial clash with our outpost, Buffalo Bill's first *coup* of that campaign.

It was a big thing, but it had taken time. It took three days more to get in to Laramie, two more to fit out and start for Fetterman, and so not until August did we reach Crook. Then, with fourteen companies of seasoned infantry under Alexander Chambers, twenty-five troops of cavalry of the 2nd, 3rd and 5th regiments, a mule pack train with each battalion (or squadron) and a numerous and motley array of no-account Crows and not much more reliable Snakes, away we went, leaving wagons and impediments behind, with four days cooked rations and two weeks' provisions, on a search for Sitting Bull that was to last for six weeks. And when we finally found him we never suspected it, and could hardly have harmed him if we had.

By that time we were wearing what was left of the things we had on the glorious day we marched so blithely away to the fords of the Tongue River, and now our horses were worn out. For the first few days the scouts had kept saying the Sioux were only a few miles ahead; the valley of the Rosebud was thick with their tracks. Here and there and frequently we came upon the aerial sepulchres of the braves who had succumbed to wounds received on the 17th or 25th of June, but not a live hostile did we see or hear of.

Six days out, heralded by just such a wild commotion among our Indian allies, we encountered coming up the Rosebud the grand array of Terry, Gibbon and Miles, and beautiful was the deployment of the 7th Cavalry as they covered the front and came trotting out to meet us, and ludicrous was the scene when the two great commands finally came together. "Where on earth are the Indians?" was the question, and the answer was obvious. Leisurely and scientifically they had slipped away between us.

Leaving the Rosebud at the big bend, the very point at which the allied yet opposing forces met, the broad trail led away eastward. "They've crossed to the Tongue river," said the scouts. So to Tongue river we followed, all but Miles, with the 5th Infantry and the guns, who hurried back to the Yellowstone in hopes of heading the Indians on a possible northward retreat.

The weather had been gorgeous. Now it turned to gloom. Day after day, night after night it rained a deluge. Soaked and bedraggled, we reached the Yellowstone at the mouth of the Powder and went into bivouac. We had no tentage, we of the Crook expedition at least — and there he and Terry held frequent conference. There we wasted about a week waiting for tidings of the foe. The steamer "Far West" paddled up with supplies for five hundred men, and we had fully four thousand. Moreover, it now became obvious that so far from making for Canada, the great mass of the Indians might even be making for the Black Hills and the unguarded settlements. Terry, as senior, wished to campaign northward in his own department, and, being in command of the joint forces, might have so ordered Crook; possibly Crook believed it would follow, and that it was his duty to protect his own bailiwick. At all events, they parted company, and then eastward, past O'Fallon and Cabin creek and so on to the Beaver, and then down the Beaver to a point where we halted while George Randall and the scouts rode afar off to the Yellowstone. Not until long after did we know why. Crook, already short of supplies, had hoped that Terry would have them meet him at a designated point on the Yellowstone, and made the request at least, but Randall came back reporting not a sign of them. Eastward again we went and, by way of Andrews creek, down into the deep valley of the little Missouri, Indian signs everywhere, said the scouts. Then up the valley of Davis creek and so on out on the grand open plateau beyond, and another day brought us up standing near the headwaters of Heart river, Fort Abraham Lincoln five to six days' long march away to the east, the Black Hills ten to twelve days' march away to the south, and no three days' rations left in the pack trains.

Crook was up against it again. August had gone; September had come and not a hostile had he killed or captured since the fight on the Rosebud. Moreover, our horses were well-nigh starving, so scant was the grass; grain, of course, had long since disappeared. Our men were out even of tobacco, and no one unaccustomed to the use of the really fine old navy plug, then regularly issued, can begin to imagine what it meant to the soldier to be without it on such a campaign. Crook felt that the peril of the settlers called him imperatively southward. Though the Indian trails had scattered everywhere east of the Tongue, the general trend was toward the Little Missouri and thence, said Gruard, who had lived for years among them, they were probably making their way back toward the reservations or at least to the Black Hills. To march to Lincoln would try the wearied and dejected soldiery, and since they *had* to be tried, why not make the longer march to the Hills? It was almost a desperate call, a stern test of the discipline and loyalty of the Old Army, but I doubt if Crook hesitated a moment. To John Finerty, the gallant and gifted Irishman who represented the Chicago *Times* all through that summer's meanderings, he said, in answer to query as to how we could live, "We still have our horses!"

And horses it was! Two days later the order was issued: three horses to be shot each night in each battalion, and by that time most of them, like their riders, were scarecrows.

41

Earlier in the summer the long column of infantry, burdened only with their rifles and ammunition, would set forth on each day's march an hour ahead of the cavalry, to be overhauled and passed before noon. Once across the mud flats of the Little Missouri, all this was reversed. We of the mounted service would set forth as soon as the men had finished morning coffee and scraps of bacon, but in an hour most of the command would be afoot, dragging their dejected steeds, and long before noon, lean, gaunt and wiry, those blessed doughboys would be striding alongside and then ahead, casually asking could they give us a tow.

Eleven days and eleven nights it rained. We slept on the open prairie, — without removing so much as a boot, for many of us could not, — wet to the skin and sometimes chilled to the marrow. Some of us could not stomach horse flesh. Game was scarce and high. We bivouacked the night of September 7th on the banks of a little stream and saw Anson Mills, with 150 picked men and horses from the 3d Cavalry, push away southward. "Going ahead to the Hills," said one of the staff, "to buy up everything eatable at Deadwood and Crook City." We thought it might be a week before we saw them again. It wasn't 48 hours.

The morning of September 9th broke cold and cheerless, but for a wonder it wasn't raining. The clouds hung low in dripping mist over the broad expanse of prairie to the south. We had barely left our dismal bivouac, and were strung out in long columns of twos, some afoot, some astride, when afar up at the front there was symptom of excitement; then the signal to halt. Merritt and brigade headquarters were up there, close following Crook and his staff. Carr, Lieutenant Colonel commanding the 5th Cavalry, rode forward to see what was the matter. In five minutes he was back.

"Go back down the column," said he, "and throw out every horse that can't carry a rider three miles at a trot. Mills is surrounded by Sioux not twenty miles ahead!"

Before the foremost troop was weeded out, other officers had come spurring back and the news flashed ahead of me down the column. All had been something akin to dejection if not disgust; all as suddenly had become alert and eager. Few, indeed, in our ten "companies" seemed other than rejoiced that action had come at last. Many a man ordered to rein out showed reluctance, even resentment. Bob London, riding a wretched wreck of a steed was one of them. He was our lightest weight, physically, at least, but that horse couldn't have borne him five miles at a walk. He had already led him most of the way from Heart River. Over the next rider and horse I hesitated, and finally passed them, but said the rider: "I can't make this horse carry *me* any ten miles." London spoke up at the instant: "I can ride that horse; he'll carry my weight every inch of the way." "Take him," was the answer. "Fall out, Blank," and in this way perhaps a third of our number were left to come on with the infantry. The rest spurred onward over the muddy trail, and even the worn-out horses seemed to understand. "Anson Mills surrounded!" It sent a thrill throughout the entire command. By ten o'clock, off to the right front through the mists we sighted a long line of heights nearly parallel with our line of march, and just about eleven the head of column rode into a sort of amphitheatre among the buttes, caught sight of a herd of Indian ponies, placidly grazing, and off to the westward, facing the bluffs, a line of sprawling skirmishers, then a number of Indian tepees about a mound-like hill, around which the headquarters parties had ridden, and then, half way up the gentle slope, serene and smiling, Anson Mills himself, afoot, and almost unattended. He shook hands with Carr. "Look out for that ravine yonder," he said, pointing southward. "There's a wounded Indian or two in there, and they've picked off some of our fellows." Around to the south of the mound, on which Merritt's flag was already displayed, we dismounted, led our horses into the low, winding watercourse, now practically dry, sent a skirmish line forward to cover them, and still had not seen an Indian. It was three o'clock, — later, possibly, — before all Crook's force had reached the scene, and still not a hostile showed anywhere among those encircling heights or over the open ground to the east.

By way of diversion, however, somebody had started a move to get at those "one or two wounded Indians" in that ravine, not a hundred yards from the tepee Carr had picked out for regimental headquarters, and a hornet's nest was the result. There came a crashing volley from the dark depths that stretched one or two assailants and scattered the rest, and brought Philo Clark, of Crook's staff, with a score of others, officers and men, scurrying to the scene, and in ten minutes one of the liveliest side shows to an Indian battle was in full swing. Finerty in his "War Path and Bivouac" gives a graphic picture of it and of the death of poor Buffalo Chips, Cody's devoted follower, who ventured too close to the cave in which the fugitives were hiding and hoping for night or rescue.

Presently Crook himself appeared and bade Gruard get the ear of those Indians, promise them safety and coax them out. The firing ceased, though our men were hot over the death of White of the scouts, and Kennedy of "E" Troop, and four or five wounded. Then presently the cave men came forth, the Chief shot through the bowels, supported by a squaw and half a dozen strapping braves after him, with a little bunch of women and children — our first prisoners. They had slashed their way through the tepee walls when aroused by Schwatka's wild charge through the village and in the darkness and confusion had taken refuge in this little ravine while the rest of their people, a band of hunters from Crazy Horse's tribe, scurried off into the bluffs. One or two lay dead in the cavelike nook, two or three, men and women both, were wounded, but only one looked scared, — a poor old squaw, who clung to Crook's hand imploringly, and could hardly believe Gruard's assurance that they were to be fed and cared for, not tortured.

But when questioned as to where their red brothers were, they were dumb. 7th Cavalry guidons, Myles Keogh's gauntlets, scraps of cavalry uniform and equipment found among the lodges, unerringly told the tale of their participation in the great victory of the 25th of June, but not a word would they say as to the whereabouts of the big Indian village, which Gruard and others declared to be within striking distance.

And before five o'clock it struck.

The most spirited, thrilling, picturesque warfare I had seen that summer, was the dash of the Cheyennes down the slopes of the War Bonnett to the rescue of Yellow Hand and his followers who had stirred up our outpost, but this later afternoon affair in the dripping mists that hovered over the sodden prairie of Slim Buttes was on a grander scale, where numbers at least were concerned.

All on a sudden it opened and for nearly an hour it raged. From every coulee and ravine northward, west, and southwest, from behind every spur and ridge and divide, every mother's son of them well mounted and equally well armed. Sioux by the hundreds came dashing down upon our lines, their first and fiercest effort apparently aimed at the herds of the 3rd and 5th Cavalry. The crash of musketry, the shrill chorus of battle cries borne on the wind, was our first intimation at 5th Cavalry headquarters, and Carr's "Sound to Arms, Bradley!" our first summons to the fight.

We of the headquarters party of the 5th had unsaddled at the south side of the

43

amphitheatre. The attack broke on the west and northwest, then gradually encircled the big position. "B" Troop's herd, — all grays, — startled by the clamor, had broken away from the guards and gone galloping out to the south, but before even the Sioux could reach them Corporal Clanton and a few troopers, bare-backed, had spurred beyond and turned them eastward and then into the lines. In less than no time, silent, swift and disciplined, the men had sprung to ranks and were scrambling up the steep banks of the coulee. Then the lines opened out, skirmish fashion, and then, it was significant of their caution and discretion, the circling warriors veered away. Here were nearly double the number of white men who had faced and held them that day on the Rosebud. Here were no such numbers of Sioux as had swarmed upon Crook's 1,100, or Custer's puny force. Lots of lead they shot and lots of noise they made, but it was sweet to see how shy they were of those long lines of silent troopers sprawled or kneeling on the turf. And then from the center of the big, irregular circle, there came striding out a long column of infantry, heading for the heights southwest, and presently their Springfields joined in the clamor. It was getting dusk, and the flashes began to take on a ruddy tinge. It all wound up almost as suddenly as it began. I doubt if a thousand Sioux were present, either then or on the dripping, dismal morning that followed, when Crook, with the wounded on *travois,* the infantry and the 2d and 3d Cavalry, pushed on southward, a flock of fat ponies alongside, while Upham's battalion (five troops) of the 5th covered the withdrawal and had a right smart time of it getting out. Twice it looked as though they might be cut off, for the main body, in the long, absurd column of twos, then the rule in prairie marching, was strung out a mile or more southward. But, though the mounted braves made a spirited dash or two around the flanks of the long skirmish line retiring afoot, they quit presently and scampered back to save what they could from the burning village. A few of them followed at respectful distance to kill off stragglers or pick up abandoned horses, but Slim Buttes, to all intents and purposes, was the last fight of the summer so far as we were concerned.

The awful march of September 12th, through thirty miles of mud; the four days in which there wasn't a crumb of bread or a quid of tobacco to be had for love or money; the final fording of the Belle Fourche and the coming of the wagons from Deadwood, with bread, crackers, bacon, flour and coffee, and also something as a substitute for navy plug, were episodes not soon forgotten. Never before or since had I seen our regulars turned into ravening wolves. The sight or scent of food was too much for discipline. The first few wagons were mobbed in the twinkling of an eye and their boxes and barrels torn to shreds. Out of the mud I picked up three ginger snaps that hadn't been crunched under heel, and Mason and Woodson, my messmates, eagerly shared them with me.

A few days rest here and then came the leisurely saunter southward, nursing our horses. Glorious days and frosty, starlit nights, with roaring campfires, full stomachs, fun, feasting and song. Three weeks of loafing along, meeting our wagons, finally, brought round all the way from Fetterman and Laramie, and looking for the recruits by the hundred, and as many horses on their way to meet us — horses that had been fed, groomed and petted, while ours, poor brutes, had been starved and slaughtered.

On October 13th, Merritt led a long column of us scouting down the South Cheyenne, a week of luxurious ease, with tentage and warm clothing. Then back and southward again we went, to take part in the general roundup and disarming of the Ogallallas and Brules, deposing Red Cloud and exalting Spotted Tail, at the agencies. Here we gossiped a day or two, at old Fort Robinson, with Mackenzie and the 4th Cavalry, *en route,* as you will remember, in search for Dull Knife and his Cheyennes, whom they found in full force one sharp November night away up near the Big Horn range again, and spoiled a war dance and smashed up their village, but lost gallant Jack McKinney, riding in at the charge at the head of his little troop.

It was there at Fort Robinson, the fag end of October, Crook dissolved the "B. H. & Y." in a stirring order in Nickerson's best style, and again we jogged away southward, reaching our winter stations along the Union Pacific in abundant time and mood for Thanksgiving; but a strange sight to civilized eyes about Cheyenne, still in field garb, with hardly a trace of regulation uniform, bearded, gaunt and devil-may-care, but hard as nails, and, except in the case of a few elders semi-invalided at the outset, none the worse for the long months of hardship and privation. And then came payday, the first in half a year, and half the garrison of old Fort Russell went in to Cheyenne to see how soon they could spend it, and of all the sprees that blessed old frontier metropolis had aided and abetted, that was the gem of the lot.

And now for the summing up. What had we accomplished? We were out again, late the following summer, still further away to the northwest, even to Heart Mountain and the head of Clark's Fort, in the effort to enmesh Chief Joseph with his Nez Perces, who outfought Gibbon and the 7th Infantry at Big Hole, outfooted Howard and the men of the Columbia, outwitted Sturgis and the 7th Cavalry, and twisting, turning, dodging, with superb skill, was only tackled and thrown by Miles and the 5th Infantry within short march of the British line, adding Owen Hale, and Biddle to the long list of the gallants of Custer's old command that "bit the dust" under the leaden hail of the red riders of the north. We were out after the Cheyennes in '78, through the sand hills of Nebraska — a heroic, hard-used band that won the admiration of their captors of the 3d Cavalry, and broke loose still once again, only to be finally run down and almost begged to surrender, so unwilling were the soldiery to slaughter more of them. Did not Chase and Wessels, of the 3d, link arms and march up to their breastworks in vain effort to convince them they would risk death rather than shed the blood of such valiant foemen? Not until '79, after three years of ceaseless scout and fight, was Miles himself enabled to gather in the last remnant of Sitting Bull's exhausted followers.

And all, said our critics, because when we had them well nigh surrounded in '76 we "let them go scot free."

Let us look into this: The only time we can be said to have had them between our lines was during the early summer, when Crook, from the south, found them too strong on the Rosebud and wisely fell back to his wagons; when, eight days later, Custer swung hard at their center and died as the result; when Terry and Gibbon, two days later still, coming from the north, marched into a deserted village site on the left bank of the Little Horn, with a populous city of the dead on the other. Even then the wide west was open to the Sioux, in the event of disaster.

But they declined battle with Terry, Gibbon and what was left of the 7th Cavalry; moved off into the Big Horn Range until sure the adversary had retired to the Yellowstone, then returned to the Rosebud neighborhood until satisfied that, heavily reinforced, the columns again would essay to pen them; then leisurely moved their barbaric goods and chattels, families, ponies and dogs, eastward toward the Little Missouri. Mr. Camp has told us that Sitting Bull, with most of his warriors, went far to the southeast and camped close to Slim Buttes, sending in to Red Cloud eager entreaties to the Southern Cheyennes to come

45

out and join them, but the Southern Cheyennes had thought it all over since the 17th of July, and decided to hold aloof.

By the time our two thousand struck that outlying camp at Slim Buttes, men were weakening from hunger, and many horses were already gone. Thirty, at least, had been shot for food, a few had been abandoned, and a hundred were too weak to carry so much as a saddle. None, not one, was fit for a fight or chase. Sitting Bull and his warriors on their nimble ponies could have laughed at us. Such fighting as was done, except Schwatka's dash, was afoot. One thing it did accomplish: The Sioux became convinced the Great Father was at last in earnest and that no longer in driblets, but by battalions, his soldiery would be seeking them summer and winter from that time forth, as indeed under General Miles they did. Moreover, however clumsily from the Indian point of view, he realized that the white soldier could certainly fight. From that summer, therefore, the Red Man began to lose hope. The inevitable came when at last Sitting Bull's half starved followers gave ear to the truth and to General Miles, and the wily old chief saw fit to come in and be lionized. Except for the Ghost Dance excitement of the winter of 1890, the unhappy and unnecessary clash and killing at Wounded Knee, we saw the last of Indian warfare; — the word the chieftains pledged to Nelson Miles at Pine Ridge Agency that winter has been kept inviolate.

So it is all a memory now, but what a memory to cherish! A warfare in which the soldiers of the United States had no hope of honors if victorious, no hope of mercy if he fell; slow death by hideous torture if taken alive, sheer abuse from press and pulpit if, as was often inevitable, Indian woman or child was killed. A warfare that called us through the cliffs and canyons of the southwest, the lava beds and labyrinths of Modoc land, the wind-swept plains of Texas, the rigors of Montana winters, the blistering heart of midsummer suns, fighting ofttimes against a foe for whom we felt naught but sympathy, yet knew the response could only be a deathless hate. Who of our number would willingly at the outset have dealt a blow to the Christian Nez Perces? Who of our number would not gladly have spared the heroic band that broke from the prison pen at Robinson and died disdaining to surrender? Who of our number did not feel a thrill of soldier pity when that gallant fellow, Crazy Horse, was done to death resisting unlooked for arrest at old Camp Robinson?

A more thankless task, a more perilous service, a more exacting test of leadership, soldiership, morale and discipline no army in Christendom has ever been called upon to undertake than that which for eighty years was the lot of the little fighting force of regulars who cleared the way across the continent for the emigrant and settler, who summer and winter stood guard over the wide frontier, whose lives were spent in almost utter isolation, whose lonely death was marked and mourned only by sorrowing comrade, or mayhap grief-stricken widow and children left destitute and despairing. There never was a warfare on the face of the earth in which the soldier, officer of man, had so little to gain, so very much to lose. There never was a warfare which, like this, had absolutely nothing to hold the soldier stern and steadfast to the bitter end, but the solemn sense of Soldier Duty.

Yet, as it had just that one inspiration, so has it had at least one compensation that we may well hold and cherish. In no other warfare that I ever heard of were officers and men so closely drawn together. Wearing the same rough garb, sharing the same rations, or lack of them, — sometimes even the same blanket, facing the same peril and enduring the same hardship, there grew up between the rank and file and their platoon and troop leaders, at least, a sense of comradeship and sympathy that years of garrison service or long campaigning against civilized foemen could never have brought about. As to one's fellows, captain or subaltern or senior, the close touch, the constant intimacy, with all the veneer and polish of social life rubbed away until the man and the soldier stood alone revealed, enabled us to know each other as even in cadet days at West Point we did not know, and to find that in nine cases out of ten the sterling, stanch, manful attributes outweighed by far the little asperities, — the traits that somehow sometimes jarred just a bit in the monotone of garrison life; and men came back from such campaigns with ever growing regard for the comrades of the rude billet and bivouac, to the end that the friendships there cemented, the comradeships there tried and tested through peril, privation and hardship, have stood first and foremost through the long chain of years and found their best reward, their enduring form, in this fraternity of veterans of the old frontier, our honored Order of Indian Wars!

1922-1925

None of the addresses delivered at the meetings during these years reached publication in the *Proceedings*.

1926

There were 40 Companions and 6 guests present at this meeting and dinner. The presiding Commander that year, Brigadier General S. W. Fountain, had published a letter in the *Proceedings* the exact date of the next meeting, January 19, 1928, thereby eliminating a meeting in the calendar year, 1927. There was no official reason given for this change, but at this meeting Brigadier General James Parker submitted the following proposal:

> "Inasmuch as Washington, D.C., contains a larger number of members of the Order of Indian Wars during the Winter than at any other season, it is proposed that the annual dinner be held there in the Winter rather than the Fall."

This proposal was accepted and as a result the next meeting was not held twelve but fourteen months later.

At the 1926 dinner meeting the two speakers were General Godfrey, who gave an account of the Battle of the Washita (which was not printed in the *Proceedings*), and Dr. Frederick W. Hodge of the Museum of the American Indian, Heye Foundation, in New York, who spoke of the early life of the Zuni Indians and of their first discovery by white men. He also utilized motion pictures and slides to illustrate his talk. The presentation which did see print in that *Proceedings* was one by Colonel Peter E. Traub, "Sioux Campaign — Winter of 1890-91." The maps referred to in the manuscript were evidently used only during the lecture.

Sioux Campaign — Winter of 1890-'91

By Colonel Peter E. Traub

The causes that led to the serious disturbances of the peace during the winter of 1890 and '91, were so remarkable that an explanation of them is necessary in order to comprehend the seriousness of the situation. The Indians assuming the most threatening attitude of hostility were the Cheyenne and the Sioux. For several years following their subjugation in 1877, '8 and '9, the most dangerous element of the Cheyennes and the Sioux were under military control. Many of them were disarmed and dismounted; their war ponies were sold and the proceeds were returned to them in domestic stock, farming utensils, wagons, etc. Many of the Cheyennes under the charge of military officers were located on land in accordance with the laws of Congress, but after they were turned over to Civil Agents and the vast herds of buffalo and large game had been destroyed their supplies were insufficient and they were forced to kill cattle belonging to white people, to sustain life.

The fact that they had not received sufficient food is admitted by the agents and officers of the government who have had opportunities of knowing. The majority of the Sioux were under charge of the civil agents frequently changed and often inexperienced. Many of the tribes became re-armed and re-mounted.

They claimed that the government had not fulfilled its treaties and had failed to make large enough appropriations for their support; that they had suffered for want of food. The evidence of this is beyond question. The statements of officers, inspectors, both of the Military and of the Interior Departments, of agents, missionaries and civilians familiar with their condition leave no room for reasonable doubt that this was one of the principal causes.

The unfortunate failure of crops in the plains country during 1889 and '90 added to the distress and suffering of the Indians and it was possible for them to raise but little from the ground for their support. White settlers fared the same, but they could migrate and actually did to the Pacific Slope and East of the Mississippi. The Indians however were rooted to the spot, neither could they obtain employment upon or beyond the Indian reservations. They must remain in comparative idleness and accept the results of the drought — viz: an insufficient supply of food. This created a feeling of discontent even among the loyal and well-disposed and added to the feeling of hostility of the element opposed to every process of civilization.

The disturbed condition of the Indians, which made action necessary, was due in part to discontent felt for years by a considerable portion of them and intensified by the reduction in area of the Sioux Reservation and the division of that remaining into separate reservations.

Up to 1889, the Sioux Indian Reservation in Dakota comprised an area of about 34,000 square miles with boundaries as follows:

Starting at point where the 46th parallel of latitude crosses the Missouri River, thence down channel of said river to where it crosses the Nebraska State Line, thence west along this line to the 103 meridian, north along this meridian to where it crosses the South Fork of Cheyenne River, thence along the South Fork to its intersection with the North Fork or Belle Fouche — up the said Belle Fouche to the 103 meridian — thence north along said meridian to its intersection with South Fork of Cannon Ball River (known as Cedar Creek); down Cedar Creek to its junction with the North Fork of Cannon Ball River, thence down the Cannon Ball River to its intersection with the Missouri River, thence down said river (right bank) to point of departure.

In April 1889, Mr. Benjamin Harrison, then President of the United States appointed the Sioux Commission, consisting of General Crook and Messrs. Foster and Warner to negotiate with the Indians for the cession of land. The Indians that opposed the opening of the reservation were those that had always been opposed to every process of civilization; were those that eventually took part in the Ghost dances, defying the authority of agents and eventually taking the war path. But a sufficient number of signatures having been obtained, over 11,000,000 acres of land were thrown open for settlement in February, 1890, by proclamation. The Indians were distributed on separate reservations as follows:

1. *Cheyenne River Reservation* — Blackfeet, Minneconjou, Sans Arcs and Two Kettle Sioux.

2. *Crow Creek and Lower Brule Reservation* — Lower Brule and Yanktonai Sioux.

3. *Pine Ridge (Red Cloud) Reservation* — Northern Cheyenne and Ogalalla Sioux.

4. *Rose Bud (Spotted Tail) Reservation* — Minneconjou, Ogalalla, Upper Brule and Wahzahzah Sioux.

5. *Standing Rock Reservation* — Blackfeet, Unkapapa, Lower and Upper Yanktonai Sioux.

But the disturbed condition that made immediate action necessary was due more immediately to excitement caused by and belief by many of the Sioux belonging on the Standing Rock, Cheyenne River, Pine Ridge and Rosebud reservations, in the predictions of a pretended prophet and Messiah, which about a year previously had gained currency among these Indians and other tribes, particularly the Cheyennes and Arrapahoes, to the effect that a great change in the condition of all Indians would soon occur by which they would be freed from the domination of the white man; that game in abundance would again appear in their country and that all opposed to this transition would surely disappear. That the white man's period of oppression would cease and the noble red man take the ascendency intended for him. The special belief of a divine savior sent to rescue humanity from its oppressions repeats itself in ths history of many religions. Its latest manifestation is among the Indians of North America. Suddenly there arose a confident belief, widespread and pervading every class among these people, that a Messiah will soon appear among them to restore their lands, which have been acquired by the U.S. government, in many cases by arbitrary seizure or else by purchase in which the promised compensation was never paid.

A belief in a divine interposition in behalf of the aborigines had previously appeared among the Indians. It is said that Elskwatawa, the prophet brother of the great Tecumseh, preached a war of extermination against the whites, and told the story of a coming Messiah who would lead the Indians to assured victory. A similar belief prevailed among the Sacs and Foxs, and before the battle of the Bad Axe in Wisconsin, in August 1832, Black Hawk assured his followers that the Great Spirit would send a Messiah to them who would lead them to success in the struggle for the recovery of their lands. More recently, other prophets have told of a time in the near future when the wrongs of the red man would be righted by the interference of the Great Spirit.

During the summer of 1890 vague reports began to reach the East of an outbreak among the Sioux Indians that was soon to occur. At first these rumors were denied by the

52

authorities in Washington, until positive information of the Ghost Dances, or the so-called "Messianic Craze," and the concentration of the Indians was received. Early in December Gen. Nelson A. Miles said, "The danger of the situation in Dakota has not been exaggerated. The disaffection is more wide-spread than it has been at any time for years. The conspiracy extends to more different tribes that have heretofore been hostile with each other but that are now in full sympathy and are scattered over a larger area of country than in the whole history of Indian warfare. It is a more comprehensive plot than anything ever inspired by Tecumseh or even Pontiac." "Altogether there are in the Northwest about 30,000 who are affected by the Messiah craze; that means fully 6,000 fighting men. Of this number at least one-third would not go on the war path, so that leaves us with about 4,000 adversaries. There are 6,000 other Indians in the Indian Territory who will need to be watched if active operations take place."

The belief as taught by the Indians seems to have included the necessity of dancing, and it was said that during one of these dances the Messiah would appear. Accordingly this Ghost Dance or Christ Dance was inaugurated and continued during the night, without interruption, although in the daytime it was varied with the old time war dances. Little Wound wrote to the Reservation and said, "Our dance is a religious dance and we are going to dance until spring, if we find then that Christ does not appear we will stop dancing."

Of the dance itself the Protestant Episcopal Bishop of South Dakota, the Rev. William H. Hare, says, "The devotees of these ideas are dressed in their exercises in special garb (a shirt made of calico and worn like a blouse, being its chief feature), and amid harangues from their leaders and songs in which they cry, "the buffalo are coming," the people form a ring by joining hands, and whirl themselves round and round in wild dances, until they fall to the ground unconscious. They are then said to be dead. Their leaders promise that while in this state they will be transported to the spirit world, and will see their friends who have died, and the Son of God, and, accordingly, when they recover consciousness, they will tell of the strange visions they have enjoyed."

The supposed Messiah was a Pah Ute Indian named Quoitze Ow, commonly called Jack Wilson, belonging to the Walker Lake Reservation in Nevada. The pretensions of Jack Wilson were a continuation of those of a former Pah Ute prophet, and his association with the whites, and the religious instruction received by reservation Indians, accounts for his teaching that Indian Ancestors would reappear; that he would cause rain to come; the destruction of the wicked and opposers, by water, etc. The fame of this Indian spread from the Indians in the vicinity of Walker Lake, to the Indians of the Western Shoshone Reservation in Nevada, and thence to the Shoshones and Bannocks of the Fort Hall Reservation, Idaho; and from there to the Arapahoes and Cheyennes of Oklahoma Territory, and to the Cheyennes and Sioux in the Dakotas and Montana; and to other tribes. During the early part of 1890 delegations from all these reservations visited this Indian near Walker Lake, Nevada, and, on their return, gave versions of what they had seen and heard, varying in some respects, as might be expected, but agreeing in the promise of early freedom of all Indians from dependence on the white man, and of a state of plenty without labor. The teachings of these returning Indians found ready credence by a considerable part of the Indians on all the Sioux reservations, particularly Cheyenne River, Pine Ridge and Rosebud. Discontented leaders took advantage of the consequent excitement and restlessness, and of some causes of fair complaint by the Indians, and endeavored to regain lost influence with their people, and to set aside the authority of the agents. To what extent these leaders were influenced by belief in the prophesies of the so-called Messiah, and what their ultimate purposes were, are not clear from the information at hand; but the result of the excitement was, that by the latter part of October, 1890, a substantial part of the Indians belonging to the Cheyenne River, Pine Ridge, and Rosebud Reservations, were openly defiant of the authority of their agents, and a less proportion on the Standing Rock Reservation were so in spirit, although more circumspect in conduct.

Interposition by military force was necessary to support the legal authority of the Indian agents and check the disorder, thus preventing the outbreak, otherwise probable.

Short Bull, one of the Indians who had made the pilgrimage to Nevada, and who had become one of the acknowledged leaders of the hostile element, in a public harangue announced that he would shorten the time for a general uprising and called upon all the warriors to assemble in what is known as the Mauvaises Terres or Bad Lands, on the White River in Southwest Dakota, in November, 1890. Short Bull's speech, interpreted, was as follows:

"My friends and relatives: I will soon start this thing in running order. I have told you that this would come to pass in two seasons, but since the whites are interfering so much, I will advance the time from what my Father above told me to do so. The time will be shorter. Therefore you must not be afraid of anything. Some of my relations have no ears, so I will have them blown away. Now there will be a tree sprout up, and there all the members of our religion and tribe must gather together. That will be the place where we will see our relations. But, before this time, we must dance the balance of this moon, at the end of which time the earth will shiver very hard. Whenever this occurs I will start the wind to blow. We are the ones who will then see our fathers, mothers and everybody. We, the tribe of Indians are the ones who are living a sacred life. God, our Father himself, is the one who has told and commanded and shown to me to do these things. Our Father in Heaven has placed a mark at each point of the four winds; first, a clay pipe, which lies at the setting of the sun and represents the Cheyenne tribe; third, at the rising of the sun there lies hail, representing the Arrapahoe tribe; and fourth, there lies a pipe and nice feather at the south, which represent the Crow tribe. My Father has shown me these things, therefore we must continue the dance. If the soldiers surround you four deep, three of you on whom I have put holy shirts will sing a song, which I have taught you, around them, when some of them will drop dead, the rest will start to run, but their horses will sink into the earth; the riders will jump from their horses, but they will sink into the earth also; then you can do as you desire with them. Now you must know this, that all the soldiers and that race will be dead; there will only be five thousand of them left living on the earth. Now we must gather at Pass Creek, where the tree is sprouting. There we will go among our dead relations. You must not take any earthly things with you. The men must take off all their clothing and the women must do the same. No one shall be ashamed of exposing their persons. My Father above has told us to do this, and we must do as he says. You must not be afraid of anything. The guns are the only things we are afraid of — but they belong to our Father in Heaven. He will see that they do no harm. Whatever white men may tell you, do not listen to them. My relations, this is all. I will now raise up my hand to my Father and close what he has said to you through me."

This harangue was followed by the movement of some three thousand Indians from the Rosebud and Pine Ridge reservations, to that rough, broken country of high buttes, ravines and impassable gulches. The hostile element on the Cheyenne and Standing Rock agencies were prepared to join them. As the following of Short Bull and Kicking Bear moved to the Band Lands, they looted the homes of hundreds of Indians who had been trying for years to farm and, in part, support themselves, and carried with them many Indians who were peaceably disposed. This would have been the case on other reservations, had no protection been given to the loyally disposed, and decided measures been taken to suppress the hostile element.

The general condition at the end of November, 1890, was as follows: on the Standing Rock Reservation the Indians were at their homes; but the disaffected element under the leadership of Sitting Bull had been having the so-called Ghost Dances, had gained somewhat in numbers (principally by union of members of his tribe, the Uncapapas), and were in frequent communication with the disaffected belonging on the reservations to the south. The number of Indians on this reservation seriously affected by the prevailing craze, was about one-fourth of all, counting by families including some 300 males, from 16 years old and up.

On the Cheyenne River Reservation, under the leadership of Chief Hump, who had been Captain of the Indian Police at the Agency, were congregated in the region of Cherry Creek and vicinity, a considerable part of the Minneconjou Sioux, who were affected. The people of Big Foot's following, located in the vicinity of the junction of the Belle Fouche and Cheyenne Rivers, were also for the most part affected, and had been for some time inimical to the agent. The disaffected Indians of this reservation, counting by families, numbered about 1,000 persons and included about 300 men. They were in a state of open defiance of the authority of the agent, but had not committed depredations of consequence against, nor offered violence to, any white settlers in the region.

On the Rosebud Reservation, the greater part of the Brule Sioux were affected by the excitement, and many had moved to the Pine Ridge Reservation, where not so large a proportion of the Indians properly belonging were involved. The Brules were under the leadership of Two Strike, Crow Dog, Short Bull and Lance.

The general excitement however was highest, and disregard of authority of the agent was greatest, on the Pine Ridge Reservation, owing to the presence of a large number of turbulent Brule Sioux belonging to the Rosebud Reservation. The leader of the Ogalallas was Kicking Bear.

The state of affairs was not improving, orders were received directing the use of military force for the preservation of order and prevention of hostilities.

Not until the civil agents had lost control of the Indians and declared themselves powerless to preserve peace, and the Indians were in armed hostility and defiant of the civil authorities, was a single soldier moved from his garrison to suppress the general revolt. To prevent the threatened murder of the civil agents and employees at the Rosebud and Pine Ridge agencies, and the destruction of public property at those places, as well as to give protection to and encourage the loyal and peaceful Indians, troops were ordered to those points under command of General Brooke commanding the Department of the Platte, on Nov. 17, 1890.

To provide for contingencies troops were assembled at different times between Nov. 17 and Dec. 20, at the Rosebud and Pine Ridge agencies and other points in the Department of Dakota as follows: 7 companies of the Seventh Infantry, under Col. Merriam, were placed along the Cheyenne River to restrain the Indians of that reservation and intercept those from Standing Rock agency, which had a very salutary effect upon the Indians of both

55

reservations. In the meantime a strong force had been gathered at the Rosebud and Pine Ridge agencies.

Those at the Rosebud were under the command of Lieut. Col. Poland, composed of two troops of the Ninth Cavalry and battalions of the Eighth and Twenty-first Infantry; Col. Shafter with seven companies of the First Infantry controlled the country to the south and west of the Rosebud Agency, with station at Fort Niobrara. Those at Pine Ridge Agency under the immediate command of Gen. Brooke, were eight troops of the Seventh Cavalry, under Col. Forsyth, a battalion of the Ninth Cavalry, under Maj. Henry, a battery of the First Artillery under Capt. Capron, a company of the Eighth Infantry, and eight companies of the Second Infantry under Col. Wheaton. West from Pine Ridge Agency was stationed a garrison of two companies under Col. Tilford of the Ninth Cavalry; north of that with headquarters at Oelrichs was stationed Lieut. Col. Sanford of the Ninth Cavalry, with three troops, one each from the First, Second and Ninth Cavalry; north of that on the line of the railroad at Buffalo Gap, Capt. Wells, with two troops of the Eighth Cavalry and one troop of the Fifth Cavalry was stationed; north of that on the same railroad was Rapid City, Col. Carr of the Sixth Cavalry, with six troops was in command; along the south fork of the Cheyenne River Lieut. Col. Offley, and seven companies of the Seventeenth Infantry was stationed, and to the east of the latter command, Lieut. Col. Sumner, with three troops of the Eighth Cavalry, two companies of the Third Infantry, and Lieut. Robinson's company of scouts was stationed. Small garrisons were also stationed at Forts Meade, Bennet and Sully. Most of the force was placed in position between the large hostile camp in the Bad Lands, which had gathered under Short Bull and Kicking Bear, and the scattered settlers endangered by their presence. As the line under Col. Carr was considered the most liable to be brought in contact with the hostile force, the division commander established his temporary headquarters at Rapid City, S. Dakota, where this force was in close communication and from which their movements could be directed with the least delay.

The general disposition of the forces was such that by means of those placed at the Rosebud Agency, the Pine Ridge Agency and along the railroad running northerly from Chadron, Neb., near and west of the Pine Ridge Reservation. The Sioux Indians of this and the Rosebud reservations could be kept under observation and the regions to the south and the Cheyenne River Valley to the west be protected and movements of bands to the west or northwest be intercepted; by means of those assembled under command of Lieut. Col. Sumner, near the junction of the Belle Fouche and Cheyenne, and the garrisons with the additional troops collected at Forts Bennett and Sully, Fort Yates at the Standing Rock Agency, Fort Abraham Lincoln, the force at Dickinson, N. Dakota, that under Capt. Adams, First Cavalry, en route for the Little Missouri, and that assembled at Fort Keogh, the Indians of the Standing Rock and Cheyenne River Reservations were placed under restraint or observation and any excursions from these reservations could soon be met.

In the interim of peace the Indians had succeeded in getting together a large amount of ammunition and arms, particularly their favorite weapon, the Winchester rifle. They were consequently far better prepared for war than at any time previous in their history. The old theory that the destruction of vast herds of buffalo had ended Indian wars, is not well-founded. The same country is now covered with domestic cattle and horses and the Indians would have been able to loot the scattered homes of the settlers and live and travel upon the domestic stock.

A period of several years of peace and activity from serious field service had created a feeling of security on the part of the settlers and a degree of confidence on the part of the troops not warranted by the real condition of affairs. The efficiency of the troops had to some extent been impaired. This was noticeable in the want of proper equipment for field operations especially in transportation. There was a reasonable amount of transportation for the ordinary post or garrison service but it was entirely inadequate for field operations. The time to prepare them for active campaigning was so short that they were hardly equipped before their services were required in the field.

It was the design of the Division Commander, Maj. Gen. Nelson A. Miles, to anticipate the movements of the hostile Indians, and arrest or overpower them in detail before they had time to concentrate in one large body; and it was deemed advisable to secure, if possible, the principal leaders and organizers, namely, Sitting Bull, Hump, Big Foot, Short Bull, Kicking Bear and others, and remove them for a time from that country. To this end authority was given on Nov. 25, 1890, to William F. Cody, a reliable frontiersman, who had much experience as Chief of Scouts and who knew Sitting Bull very well and had perhaps as much influence over him as any living man, to proceed to Standing Rock Agency to induce Sitting Bull to come with him, making such terms as he (Cody) might deem necessary, and if unsuccessful in this to arrest him quietly and remove him quickly from his camp to the nearest military station. He was authorized to take a few trusty men with him for that purpose. "He proceeded to Fort Yates on the Standing Rock Reservation and received from Lieut. Col. Drum the necessary assistance but his mission was either suspected or made known to the fields of Sitting Bull who deceived him (Cody) as to Sitting Bull's whereabouts."

Buffalo Bill's Unsuccessful Attempt to Capture Sitting Bull

In Nov. 1890, General Ruger was ordered by the President to make a personal investigation of the actual condition of things among the Sioux. While at Standing Rock Agency, he was informed by Indian Agent James McLaughlin that it was practicable and advisable to have the actual arrest of Sitting Bull and other disaffected leaders on that reservation, made by the Indian police, both for the certainty of their capture and for the beneficial effects that would result in strengthening the authority of the agent and establishing the proper position of the Indian police. The Indian police might possibly make the capture without bloodshed or much excitement among the Indians. Sitting Bull's men were, moreover, constantly hanging about the Agency, ostensibly to have wagons repaired or for some other purpose, but really to keep him informed. This, in connection with the fact that Sitting Bull lived 40 miles from the post, and that an Indian on a fleet horse would reach him before a troop of cavalry could possibly get there, decided the authorities in favor of having the actual arrest made by the Indian police.

While Col. Drum, commanding Fort Yates at Standing Rock, and Agent McLaughlin were making plans for the capture of Sitting Bull and perfecting the details for carrying them into execution the moment the orders came, William F. Cody, commonly known as Buffalo Bill, appeared at Fort Yates with the authority of the Division Commander, to make the attempt to bring in Sitting Bull, either peaceably or by force; and for this purpose the commanding officer was directed to furnish transportation and a few trusty men.

This was on Nov. 27; it produced consternation on the part of Drum and McLaughlin. The probability was much against the success of this expedition. Failure meant the escape of Sitting Bull and his following, their flight to Pine Ridge, the presence of the leader of the

57

Sioux malcontents amongst the disaffected element in the Bad Lands along White River, the beginning of actual hostilities before the troops were in position around Pine Ridge, the probable destruction of property, looting of homes of settlers and, perhaps, all the attendant horrors of Indian warfare — murder, rapine and mutilation. But Drum and McLaughlin were the right men in the right place. The former at once telegraphed the gravity of the situation to Gen. Ruger, desiring, above all, to know whether the order was by proper authority. Gen. Ruger was very much surprised, as it was the first he had heard of the subject, the orders to Cody never having been transmitted to him. He at once telegraphed to Washington, through proper military channels, throwing the great weight of his experience and highly respected opinion against any such attempt at that time. McLaughlin telegraphed to the Secretary of the Interior in the most emphatic terms, and we will leave their telegrams speeding towards Washington, and return to Fort Yates.

By hook or by crook Buffalo Bill must not be permitted to leave on his errand. But how prevent it? Buffalo Bill liked whiskey; therefore, privately three officers were detailed to see that his appetite was more than satisfied. They did their duty nobly and Cody was retired for the night amid general rejoicing at the success of the scheme. It was now a question of electricity and alcohol — Would the telegraph bring authority to annul Cody's orders before the streak of dawn or would another detail be necessary to quiet Buffalo Bill? Great indeed was everybody's surprise to see the latter emerge from his temporary quarters sweet, smiling and happy, ready for the start to Sitting Bull's camp and asking for transportation and escort. In despair another detail attempted the subjugation of the wily scout, but he fairly thrived on rum and simply seemed to gain strength and energy for the fulfillment of his mission. Everybody delayed as much as possible but all excuses palpable and impalpable having been exhausted he left for Grand River, the home of Sitting Bull 40 miles away.

This aspect of the case had been conceived of by both Drum and McLaughlin, and, as a last resort, they had thought of a device that acted like a charm. Its development will be seen as the story progresses. Bill proceeded to Oak Creek, about 20 miles. Here, coming along the road toward the Agency, he met Louis Primeau, Indian Scout and interpreter at Standing Rock Agency, upon whom McLaughlin had counted in thwarting Buffalo Bill's attempt. Primeau and Bill were well acquainted, and the former was questioned as to Sitting Bull's camp and his whereabouts. Primeau replied that Bull had had a dance Friday night, and he said he intended going to Standing Rock that very next day to see his old friend, Agency McLaughlin; that Buffalo Bill must have missed him on account of Bull's having taken the north road to the Agency instead of the south one. To make doubly sure, he advised Bill to cut across country to the north road, and in case wagon tracks were seen going towards the agency, they were made by Bull, thither bound. This the party did, and by proper manipulation wagon tracks were seen leading to Standing Rock, and Buffalo Bill turned back from Grand River where Sitting Bull was probably at that moment haranguing his followers.

In the meantime, Col Drum had been in hot water awaiting the orders from superior authority. He kept Indian scouts at the adjutant's office, ready to leave at a moments notice to overtake Cody. The message came, and that there should be no mistake, Indian couriers were sent over both the north and south roads; but it so happened that while they were passing in the vicinity of Oak Creek, Buffalo Bill was cutting across country between the two roads so as to strike the north road. The Indian scouts, therefore, on both roads missed him and they went on toward Sitting Bull's camp with great care, and found everthing quiet,

Sitting Bull there, and no Cody on either road; and those scouts wondered.

Col. Drum was a little alarmed at not hearing from the scouts by evening and sent out two more on each road with copies of the President's dispatch; for it appears that the Secretary of the Interior and the Secretary of War went to Mr. Harrison in the middle of the night and, with his own hand, the Chief Executive wrote the dispatch, that Wm. F. Cody, known as Buffalo Bill, should not attempt the arrest of Sitting Bull or any other Indian whatsoever, and that he should leave the Indian reservation at once. The second courier on the north road found Cody in camp about five miles out from Fort Yates. The message was delivered, and Cody wrote in pencil the following: "The President's orders have been received and will be obeyed. I leave tonight, (signed) William F. Cody." The next morning (Nov. 30th) at 9 o'clock, he left for Mandan. Col Drum and Mr. McLaughlin had thus, by foresight, ingenuity and prudence, avoided the danger of the possibility of an unsuccessful attempt to capture the wily chieftain, Sitting Bull, who was so soon destined to pitch his lodge in the Happy Hunting Grounds.

Capture and Death of Sitting Bull

Sitting Bull was not a hereditary chief, yet he was the acknowledged leader of the hostile element when the Sioux was at war. Few Indians in the history of the United States have possessed the power of drawing to their standards so large a following, or of so thoroughly inbuing it with the spirit of animosity, hatred and revenge. His policy was ever against the whites and against civilization. He could instill into the savage heart and crystallize the savage brain, all those horrors whose results have been viewed with despair by the reading millions of our effete civilization.

It was universally admitted that he should be removed from the scene of trouble, and to that end orders were given on December 10th by General Miles, through General Ruger, to Col. William F. Drum, commanding at Fort Yates: "Make it your special duty to secure the person of Sitting Bull. Call on the agent to cooperate and render such assistance as will best promote the purpose in view."

For reasons before stated, it was decided to make the arrest by Indian police, these to be supported by troops, with orders to prevent a rescue, and, if necessary, protect the police. December 19th or 20th was agreed upon as the day to make the attempt, for then most of the Indians would be at the Agency for the issue of rations, and it was presumed that Sitting Bull would not come to the agency, as he had not been there on the preceeding ration day, but would remain at his home on Grand River. However, trustworthy information was received on the evening of Sunday, Dec. 14th, that Sitting Bull was preparing to leave the reservation to join the hostiles at Pine Ridge, and it became necessary that there should be no delay in making the arrest. The number of Indian police about Bull's camp had been materially increased, under pretence of getting out logs for a building on Oak Creek, but in reality to watch his movements, become acquainted with his camp, his house, and the surroundings; so that, even in the middle of the night, they could effect his capture and removal.

Everything being ready, as soon as it was dark, orders written in Sioux and English were sent by two reliable Indians, to be read to Bull Head, the lieutenant of police, by an agency school teacher in that neighborhood. The order specified that Sitting Bull was to be arrested before daylight on the morning of the 15th, and brought to the Agency, and that troops would be within reach in case a rescue was attempted. Later in the evening orders were issued for Troops F (Slocum) and G (Crowder), Eighth Cavalry, six officers and a hundred enlisted men, Capt. Fechet, Eighth Cavalry commanding, to march at twelve o'clock that night in the direction of Sitting Bull's settlement, for the purpose of preventing rescue, and, if necessary, to assist the police. It was the understanding that the police would send a courier to Oak Creek to inform the troops of the situation of affairs as soon as the arrest was made.

Although entrusted to Indians, all the details were perfectly executed. Up to 2 a.m. the 15th, a "ghost dance" and feast had been in progress at Sitting Bull's camp, and being tired out, the usual sentries around Sitting Bull's shack fell asleep; and not until the Indian Lieutenant of police, Bull Head, placed his hand on the sleeping chief's shoulder at 5:30 a.m., had the latter any idea of going to the agency. With the spirit of quick perception, he at once arose, and remonstrated with his own people, now clothed in uniform and armed with the authority of the U.S. government. There was a slight delay in giving him time to dress. Sitting Bull's wives were quartered in a separate lodge, but in his own shack there slept Crowfoot, a deaf and dumb son of the old chief; between these two there existed the greatest intimacy. When the boy saw what was happening, he strained to the utmost the flaccid muscles of his throat and larynx, causing that awful, unearthly sound, not loud but terrible. It was frequently repeated before the police gagged him, but unfortunately it had been heard by Catch the Bear, who emerged from his tepee just as Sitting Bull was being led captive between Lieutenant Bull Head and Sergeant Shave Head. Sitting Bull raised the cry of revolt and kept calling upon his followers to rescue him from the police; that if the two principal men were killed the rest would run away. Thereupon Catch the Bear fired, hitting and breaking Lieutenant Bull Head's thigh bone. As he was falling to the ground, Bull Head placed his pitol against Sitting Bull's side and fired, killing him. At least 75 warriors then attacked the 40 Indian police, who, however, got possession of the shack and stable adjoining. The fight was hot, and volunteers were called for to carry a report of the situation back to the approaching troops. Hawk Man offered to perform this perilous mission, and at the imminent risk of his life, he slipped through the encircling hostiles and carried the news to Fechet, who was met some three miles from Grand River.

In addition to his two troops of Cavalry, Fechet had a Hotchkiss and a Gatling gun, under charge of Lieut. E. C. Brooks, 8th Cavalry. Throwing out a light but extended line of skirmishers, he disposed his troops in column of fours, an interval of 300 yards between heads of columns, artillery between the heads, and advanced to the bluffs about 1500 yards from Sitting Bull's house. About 900 yards to his right front, on a knoll, was a party of about 50 Indians. Shots were being exchanged. Fechet then directed the Hotchkiss to be fired into this brush, and at the same time he displayed a white flag, the signal agreed upon between the Indian police and the troops. The effect was electrical, Indians began to scamper from the brush and retire across the river; a white flag was displayed by the beleaguered police from Sitting Bull's shack. The Hotchkiss was next trained upon the group on the knoll and they dispersed, fleeing up the river. F troop dismounted, advanced in skirmish line to and beyond the house, while Crowder in G troop, mounted, protected the right flank, and followed the retiring Indians up Grand River for two miles, when he was recalled. The skirmish line was about 600 yards beyond the house, clearing the brush, and then returned leaving pickets at the farthest points.

When the troops came up, the Indian police filed out of the shacks and formed company-front, and reported the absentees (four killed, two mortally wounded, one badly

60

wounded); but there was sufficient evidence of the noble defense they had made. Eight dead hostiles, including Sitting Bull, three wounded, and two relations of Sitting Bull prisoners.

Capt. Fechet's orders were explicit and did not include a pursuit of Sitting Bull's band, which would have resulted in unnecessarily frightening peaceful Indians; accordingly the command moved back to Oak Creek, and couriers and runners were sent in all directions reassuring the peaceably inclined and urging all others to remain on the reservation and come into the agency, as that was the only safe place for them.

Over 400 Sitting Bull Indians, men, women and children, fled south to the Cheyenne River Reservation. Of these, 160 surrendered to Agent McLaughlin at Standing Rock, in a few days, and 88 others who had reached the Morean River, returned and surrendered within two weeks. Of the remainder, 20 joined the hostiles at Pine Ridge, 38 joined Big Foot's band on Cheyenne River, and 166 surrendered to Capt. Hirst and Lieut. Hale, at the mouth of Cherry Creek. Thus ended the first act of the campaign, and peace was restored on Standing Rock Reservation.

Next came the move on the Cheyenne River Reservation against Hump and Big Foot.

Hump, it will be remembered, was the leader of the disaffected Minneconjou Sioux, numbering about one-fourth of all the Indians on the Cheyenne River Reservations. He had always been a power for good or for evil among the savages, and his good offices were to be obtained under almost any concessions. No man in the whole United States has as much influence over him as Capt. Ewers, Fifth U.S. Infantry, Ewers had been in charge of Hump and his Minneconjou followers, and had won their respect and love. At the request of Gen. Miles, Ewers was ordered from Texas, where he was then stationed, and directed to proceed to South Dakota and put himself in communication with this dangerous Indian and attempt to attach him to the U.S. government in the interests of peace. Ewers proceeded to Fort Bennett and, accompanied only by Lieut. Hale, made a trip to the hostile camp of Hump on Cheyenne River, 60 miles in the interior. It was fully believed by all the civilians and military near the Agency, that this dangerous Indian could not even be communicated with. But fortunately the characteristic of the American army officer is decision of character when the path of duty lies open before him. When Ewers and Hale reached Hump's camp, the Indian was some 20 miles away, up Cherry Creek. A runner was sent after him and as soon as Hump heard that Ewers was in the vicinity he at once came in to see him and was informed by the Captain that Gen. Miles desired him to take his people away from the hostiles and bring them into Fort Bennett at once. Hump complied with the request and brought all his people into the Agency with the exception of some 30 followers who broke away and joined Big Foot's band of discontents. Hump was at once enlisted as an Indian scout by Capt. Ewers and he afterwards performed valuable service in the interests of peace.

This removed a dangerous element and reflects the greatest credit upon those two brave officers, deliberately offering themselves up for sacrifice in the interest of peace. Battles and marches and campaigns gain the attention of the multitude, but that quiet spirit of devotion to duty, patience, courage, self-control, while not so conspicuous, gives rise to more lasting results, the clash and shock of combat, privation, torture, rapine and death are almost invariably the result of the non-exercise of the restraining and heroic virtues. Bearing this in mind, we shall be able to give proper credit to the mild, perservering qualities that enable men to accomplish great deeds without display and blare.

After this event Lieut. Hale rendered signal service in receiving the surrender of the 168 (afterwards increased to 227) Sitting Bull Indians at the mouth of Cherry Creek. These

Indians were crazy with excitement. Their leader, to their minds at least, had been unjustly killed and they themselves were fugitives deprived of their homes, eager and anxious to find congenial sympathizing spirits to make a proper stand against what they considered the injustice, nay the oppression of the U.S. government. Col. Sumner, from his camp, through couriers, had sent information to the Division and Department Commanders, that Sitting Bull Indians were expected that night, Dec. 18th, at the mouth of Cherry Creek. Capt. Hirst, Post Commander at Bennett, sent Hale to that vicinity, some 52 miles, to report condition of affairs and do his best in the interests of peace. Hale's action, as characterized by Gen. Ruger was gallant, conspicuous and praiseworthy. Every white man and half breed had fled from the vicinity. Word had been sent in that warriors had looted a ranch ten miles away and were expected at Cheyenne River in a short while, yet Hale stood to his post of duty.

Soon the Indians could be seen filing in battle array down the hillside into the little village at the junction of Cherry Creek and Cheyenne River. Hump rode into camp and together he and Hale went forth to meet the hostiles who fortunately listened to these two brave men. There was no interpreter present, but, by the sign language, Hale made them understand that he wished them to wait there until he could return to Bennett to bring out Hirst and an interpreter. They did so. Hale killed a beef for them and started on his 52-mile trip to Bennet, which place he reached in six hours. There was great danger of these Indians joining Big Foot and there was constant communication between the camps, but the Sitting Bull Indians were more scared than anything else and after a parley of some hours they surrendered to Hirst and on Christmas Eve they camped on the flat below the post. Soon after, they were removed to Fort Sully where they were guarded until the war was over.

And so by the foresight of Capt. Hirst in sending out Lieut. Hale and by the cool bravery and determination of both of them and by their skillful dealing with a band of Indians who were undecided as to whether or not they would go on the war path, 81 men and 146 women and children were prevented from joining Big Foot's band and participating in the desperate fight with Forsyth's command. With 81 effective men added to his strength, Big Foot would have emptied many more saddles of our hard-worked cavalrymen.

Let credit for a bloodless victory be given to Capt. Hirst and Lieut. Hale of the 12th Infantry.

Next came:

The Big Foot Affair

Big Foot's band had very early engaged in the Ghost Dance, and soon defied the authority of the Agent. In April, 1890, Capt. Hennessy, Eighth Cavalry, with two troops of cavalry and one company of infantry, belonging to the garrison of Fort Meade, was sent to camp near the junction of the Belle Fouche and Cheyenne Rivers, having for special duty the keeping under restraint of the Indians of Big Foot's following located in the vicinity, and, also, keeping other disaffected Sioux under restraint on the Cheyenne River Reservation. On Dec. 3rd, 1890, Lieut. Col. E. V. Sumner, Eighth Cavalry, with Troop D, Eighth Cavalry, from Fort Meade, arrived at the camp and took command. The force was increased, Dec. 12th, by Company C, Third Infantry, from Fort Meade. Sumner had, therefore, three troops of cavalry and two companies of infantry and, in addition, two Hotchkiss guns.

Sumner's orders were: "To keep the region to the east of the country between the

Cheyenne and White Rivers under observation. Keeping, at the same time, the village of Big Foot under control, and giving assurance of safety to the people in the region about it."

This region comprised the north fork of the Cheyenne River, known as the Belle Fouche. It swept round the north of the Black Hills, the richest section of country between the Mississippi River and the Pacific Slope. Along its banks were many settlers; and to prevent incursion on their homesteads and protect their lives, was an important duty to perform. This Black Hills region had been the bone of contention in the '76 campaign, and most of the hostile Sioux claimed that it belonged to them by right, and had been wrested from them by force; in which statement there was a great deal of logic.

For these purposes Sumner was authorized to move his camp nearer to Smithville, if thus they might be better accomplished. The telegraphic instructions from Department Headquarters further stated, that "it is probable the command of Capt. Wells (two troops of cavalry, stationed since April at Oelrichs, on railroad between Chadron and Rapid City) may be spared from its present post of duty; when it is intended to order it to join the command of Col. Sumner, and put a stop to the unauthorized going back and forth of parties between the upper and lower Sioux reservations."

In compliance with instructions, Sumner moved his camp up the Cheyenne nearer to Smithville, and opened a trail directly over the hill; he established an outpost at Davidson's ranch, twenty miles east at the head of Deep Creek, on the trail between Big Foot's village and Pine Ridge. This trail was not practicable for wagons, but could have been used by cavalry, and the outpost was established to give information of any Indians passing north or south.

A few days after Sumner's arrival in camp, most of the chiefs and headmen, including Big Foot, came to see him. They remained several days about his camp, and seemed not only anxious, but willing, to obey his orders and wished him to inform his superiors that they were all on the side of the Government, in the troubles then going on. Frequent and friendly communication was kept up with all these leaders until about Dec. 15th, when Big Foot came to camp to say good-bye, as he and all his men, women and children were going to Bennett for their annuities, again assuring Sumner, that none of the Cheyenne River Indians had any intention of joining the hostiles at Pine Ridge. Notwithstanding this assurance, it was apparent that Big Foot was making extraordinary efforts to keep his followers quiet, and seemed much relieved in having succeeded in getting them to go to Bennett. Sumner considered it his duty to give him all the support possible, and he never failed, in the presence of everybody, to show good feeling toward Big Foot, and the utmost confidence in his assertions.

About this time, Sumner received a telegram from Department Headquarters, dated Dec. 16th, saying: "It is desirable that Big Foot be arrested, and, had it been practicable to send you Wells with his two troops, orders would have been given that you try to get him. In case of arrest he will be sent to Fort Meade, to be securely kept prisoner."

But, under the circumstances and owing to the delicate situation of affairs at that moment, viz., his belief that Big Foot could alone control the young men, and was doing so under his advise and support, Sumner thought it best to allow Big Foot to go to Bennett a free man, and telegraphed to Division and Department Headquarters that Big Foot was on the way to Bennett, and could be arrested on his arrival there, and that if Big Foot returned he (Sumner) would try and get him. At this time Sumner had a troop of cavalry, Godwin's, at Big Foot's village, and a scouting party watching for Sitting Bull's Indians, near the mouth of Cherry Creek, under Lieut. Duff. On Dec. 19th, Duff sent back word to Sumner that the Cheyenne River Indians under Big Foot had stopped on their way to Bennett, and had assembled at Hump's camp to meet the Sitting Bull Indians then expected along at any moment, and those runners had overtaken Big Foot's band.

On receiving this information, Sumner at once marched down the river with two troops of cavalry one company of infantry and two Hotchkiss guns, and was soon in support of Godwin's troop, near Big Foot's village. On December 20th Sumner reached Narselles, and going into camp, received a letter from Big Foot, stating he was Sumner's friend and wished to talk. On December 21st, Sumner made an early start to join Godwin's troop, and, as he says, "either to fight or capture Big Foot, if any resistance was offered." While on the march and four miles east of Narselles, Big Foot came to him accompanied by two Standing Rock Indians. He expressed a desire to comply with any orders he had to give, and said all his men would do the same. He informed Sumner that he had 100 Indians of his own, and 38 Standing Rock Indians, and that he had harbored the latter, knowing them to be off their reservation and refugees; because they were brothers and relations; because they had come to him almost naked, and were hungry, footsore and weary; that he had taken them in, and fed them, and that no one with any heart could have done less. This satisfied Sumner, though he admits that, in the light of future events at Wounded Knee, he had undoubtedly been imposed upon with reference to the Standing Rock Indians, and that most of the warriors were kept out of sight, but close enough for an emergency. Sumner telegraphed to Miles that he expected to get the surrender of all the Indians the next day.

Capt. Hennessy, Eighth Cavalry, was directed to go to the Indian camp with Big Foot, get all the Indians, and return to Narselles' ranch, back to which point Sumner marched and camped the night of the 21st. At 3 p.m. Hennessy marched in with 333 Indians. This was a great surprise to Sumner who had stipulated that a feast would be given to the Indians. The latter made themselves very comfortable under the circumstances and the night passed quietly.

Sumner telegraphed the above facts to the Division Commander and, further, stated that he would take the whole crowd to his home camp, and, unless otherwise ordered, send them to Fort Meade; and further, on the 22nd, "I am holding on to, and feeding the crowd to prevent, if possible, the young men from going south. I will march in a few moments for my home camp with the whole outfit and expect to reach there this evening."

As the Indians were approaching their village on the march up the Cheyenne, it was apparent that Big Foot himself could not control the desire they had to get to their respective homes, and he came to Sumner and told him frankly, "I will go with you to your camp, but there will be trouble in trying to force these women and children, cold and hungry as they are, away from their homes. This is their home where the government has ordered them to stay, and none of my people have committed a single act requiring their removal by force." Sumner concluded one of two things must happen, either he must consent to their going into their village or bring on a fight. He chose the former, and, considering that Big Foot's presence and influence with them would be more powerful than anything he could do in restraining the young men from going south in a stealthy manner, he left Big Foot with his people, instead of arresting him and taking him to Meade. But Big Foot promised Sumner that he would see him next day, and would bring the 38 Standing Rock Indians with him. Sumner then went with his troop to his home camp, not even thinking it advisable to camp in the vicinity of the village, desirous only of accomplishing what he considered the wishes of the Department Commander; especially, believing that his plans were to settle matters if possible without bloodshed.

While in camp on the nights of the 22nd and 23rd, Sumner received a dispatch from Gen. Miles, stating that a report had been received that there were several hundred Indians near the little Missouri, and that there might be some truth in the report. Further, Miles stated, "I think you had better push on rapidly with your prisoners to Meade, and be careful that they do not escape; and look out for Indians. (Signed) Miles."

The only criticism I have to make upon Col. Sumner's action in the matter is simply surprise at his too-great confidence in Big Foot's promises, bearing in mind that he had for some time been inimical to the authority of the Agent, and that he was harboring Sitting Bull and Cherry Creek outlawed Indians.

It had, moreover, been made apparent by the Division and Department Commanders, that the person of Big Foot was desired away from the reservation, and it was with the intention of enforcing orders, that Col. Sumner had made his march down the Cheyenne River, and had received the surrender of these Indians. The work required of his command was very great, and it should surely have been reinforced, so as to have enabled him properly to accomplish his mission, and carry out his other orders. However, he should have kept more in touch with the enemy, so as to see that Big Foot faithfully carried out the numerous promises he had made. There was a failure to co-operate on the part of Sumner and Merriam that could easily have been avoided; and, had Merriam's command been crossed over the Missouri River (which might have easily have been done by planking the ice) and been pushed up the Cheyenne instead of being kept at Fort Sully and vicinity from Dec. 7th until Dec. 19th, waiting for the river to freeze over, the result would have undoubtedly been far different. He started from Bennett on the 21st and camped that night at Corn's on the Cheyenne. Here a courier from Bennett brought him the following telegram from Gen. Ruger: "Move with your regiment without delay to near the mouth of Cherry Creek and communicate with Col. Sumner's command. Should he need your assistance or co-operation at any time, you will render it." . . . "The presence there of your strong force will be beneficial and the command will be in better place for service in region generally. Make an expeditious march, send daily reports for dispatch from Bennett, communicate fully with Sumner's command." . . . (signed) Ruger. Upon which telegram Col. Merriam in his report remarks: "I was greatly surprised and puzzled by a portion of the above telegram. However willing I might be to assist Lieut. Col. Sumner, or any junior officer, the 122nd Article of War puts certain restrictions upon the method of procedure to that end, which would necessarily govern and reverse the situation." Whereupon Gen. Ruger makes the following notes: "I do not see anything that would surprise or puzzle one in the proposition that, in case of need, assistance should be given by a senior to a junior commander, or that commanders should co-operate in case of need for a common object. Whether at any particular time the senior commanders could or should assume command of both commands, would of course depend upon the facts and it would rest with the senior to decide the matter. The instruction to Col. Merriam was, as appears upon its face, given in the general sense, and should be received in a commonsense way. In the order of the President, of Oct. 31st, 1890, to the Secretary of War, relative to the Sioux trouble, the following is that closing sentence: 'In the meantime you will see that all necessary precautions are taken to have the troops in that vicinity to cooperate in the execution of any orders that may be given.' "

So that this command of Col. Merriam was frittering away valuable time, was complaining about transportation, about several companies being left behind to guard Indian prisoners and haggling over the spirit of Department orders, instead of doing its duty to the handle as good soldiers should.

But to return to Col. Sumner. Sumner stayed in his camp until noon of the 23rd, when, not hearing anything from Big Foot, who had promised to come in with the 38 Standing Rock Indians, nor from his own scouts whom he had sent to Big Foot's village, he ordered the march of his command, and was about moving out, when a Mr. Dunn, a citizen living on the Bell Fouche, came to camp to sell butter and eggs. Instead of moving on Big Foot, Sumner remained behind, and sent Dunn ahead with instructions to Big Foot, to go with his people to Bennet and, also, to tell him that Sumner intended to enforce the order. What Dr. Dunn told Big Foot is a question; he probably misrepresented Sumner's instructions into threatening Big Foot and his band with being shot down, if they did not comply. Sumner for quite a while thought that Dunn had played him false, and that the cause of Big Foot's flight was directly traceable to Dunn's statement to that Chief of Sumner's threat. But later the Colonel exonerated Dunn, on account of previous good reputation and apparent fidelity to the cause of peace, and decided that his statement had had no influence whatever on the flight of the band. At all events Dunn, while returning from Big Foot's camp, met Sumner on the march, and informed him that Big Foot had consented to go to Bennett.

Sumner went into camp about five miles from Big Foot. About seven that night, his scouts reported that Big Foot had gone south and had eluded and deluded him.

Sumner's opinion was, that the advance of Col. Merriam up the Cheyenne and the report of the disarming of the Standing Rock Indians at Bennett, caused a sudden change of plan in Big Foot's village, and that the young men, on account of the situation, were able to overcome all objections to going south. It must be said in justification of Col. Sumner, that positve orders for the arrest of Big Foot and the renegade hostiles did not reach him until the morning of Dec. 24th, the day after the flight.

Upon hearing the news, Miles telegraphed to Sumner: "Your orders were positive and you have missed your opportunity, but such does not often occur. Endeavor to be more successful next time. Hold your command in the vicinity but in close communication with Fort Meade."

Sumner did not pursue, his reasons being fear of Big Foot's return to commit depredations on the Belle Fouche and fear of the Indians reported to be in the northwest near Cave Hills, of S. Dakota. He sent couriers to Gen. Carr to send out a force to the east to intercept Big Foot and he himself went into camp near Big Foot's village.

In the meanwhile every effort was being made for peace. Gen. Brooke, in command at Pine Ridge and Rosebud, was using every means to create dissention in the hostile camp and to induce as many Indians as possible to return to their proper reservations. At the same time the troops to the west of the Bad Lands, formed a strong cordon which had the effect of gradually forcing the Indians back to the agency, the object being if possible to avoid conflict; although at any time from the 17th of Dec., 1890, to the 15th of January, 1891, the troops could have engaged the Indians and a serious engagement would have been fought. The fact that the Indians had lost confidence in the government was a serious embarrassment to the military. But the measures already taken were having a most desirable effect for it was reported in their camp that Sitting Bull and his immediate followers had been killed, that Big Foot had been arrested and that Hump had returned to his allegiance. This discouraged them, and the presence of a strong cordon of troops gradually forcing them back into the agency, without actually coming in contact with them, and the strong influence brought to bear through the aid of friendly Indians from Pine Ridge, caused them to break camp on Dec. 27th, 1890, and leave their stronghold (a series of natural fortifications, almost impregnable) and move towards the agency by slow marches. The troops under Col. Carr and Lieut. Cols. Offley and Sandford were slowly following in communicating and supporting distance. In fact, the fires of the Indians were still burning when the troops moved in to occupy the same ground. On Dec. 28th they camped still nearer the agency and on the evening of the 29th they were expected to camp at the agency itself. But an unforeseen event disturbed the plans of the Division Commander and prolonged the struggle and complicated it to such an extent that a bloody Indian war seemed the only solution of the problem. This event was the sad affair at Wounded Knee.

After Big Foot had eluded Sumner, he passed up Deep Creek, crossed the Band Land wall at Buffalo Pass and White River, near Red Earth Creek, and so on to Porcupine Creek, which he reached on Dec. 28th. As soon as the news of his escape reached Miles, Maj. Henry with his squadron of four troops of the Ninth Cavalry and Maj. Whitside with four troops of the Seventh Cavalry, and two Hotchkiss guns, under command of Lieut. Hawthorne, Second Artillery, were ordered out to effect his capture and disarmament.

Whitside, in accordance with orders from Gen. Brooke, left Pine Ridge at 1:20 p.m., Dec. 26th, and camped that night at Wounded Knee crossing. Next day his command scouted up and down the creek, looking for trails, and trying to communicate below with Maj. Henry.

At 12 a.m. on the 28th, Scout Little Bat, who had been sent toward the Porcupine to the east, reported Big Foot on the Porcupine coming toward Whitside. The latter at once caused his command to saddle-up, and took the trot. Within two miles of the Porcupine the Indians were seen on a hill, halted. The command was formed in double column of fours and dismounted, and line formed to the front, Hotchkiss guns in the center. Whitside then rode forward with Lieut. Nicholson, Seventh Cavalry, towards the Indians, who, to the number of about 120, well armed, two-thirds mounted — one-third dismounted, were advancing in line. Some of the Indian tried to get round Whitside's flanks, but were ordered back, and they obeyed. Big Foot was sick in a wagon, and at once surrendered to Whitside, who marched back to camp on Wounded Knee, the order of march being, two troops in advance, then the Indians, then the remaining two troops. Two troops, A and I, were detailed to guard the Indians during the night, which was done by placing a chain of sentinels around the camp and the two Hotchkiss guns on a hill overlooking the village.

Meanwhile, Whitside had sent in news of the surrender, and asked for re-enforcements to arrive before daylight the following morning, to assist in the disarming of the Indians, as he did not consider it safe to make the attempt with his small command.

At 8:30 p.m. Col. James W. Forsyth, Seventh Cavalry, with four troops (C.D.G.E.) of the Seventh Cavalry, and two Hotchkiss guns, arrived at Wounded Knee Creek and assumed command.

About 7:30 the next morning, after considerable trouble, the bucks of Big Foot's command, numbering 106, were collected 100 yards away from their camp, troops K and B being posted midway between. Having explained to them, that after having surrendered, they would be treated as prisoners of war, and that, as such, they would have to be disarmed, squads of 20 were cut off and told to bring their weapons to a designated place. The result of this was very unsatisfactory, only two broken carbines being brought. Keeping the bucks together, details of soldiers were made under officers to search the Indian camp, which resulted in securing 48 guns; the squaws making every effort to conceal the weapons by sitting on them, practicing deception, etc.

While this was going on, one of the Indians in "ghost dance" costume separated a little from the rest, and commenced to harangue the bucks. Forsyth paid no attention to him, as the interpreter told him that he was telling the Indians to be quiet and submit. Shortly after, however, he changed his address to one for the extermination of the whites, and he was silenced.

Just after this, the search through the Indian tepees having been completed, order was given to search the persons of the bucks. The weather was cold, and they had been permitted to wear their blankets; underneath, most of them had their weapons concealed.

Shortly after the move to disarm them, an Indian in "ghost dance" costume threw some dust into the air as a signal and the bucks made a break, opening fire on K and B troops, so that every shot that failed to hit a trooper or his horse, was sent through their own camp, where their squaws and children were located. They broke through and around the flanks of Wallace's (K) troop, and reached their camp, from which place they kept up a fire on the troops, drawing death toward their women and children.

The troops were completely taken by surprise, and fully 50 shots were fired by the Indians before a single soldier discharged his weapon; but recovering, they soon surrounded the Indians with a perfect sheet of flame, through which every once in a while a bounding buck would make his way. Bucks, squaws and children, mounted and dismounted, started for the hills, up the dry ravine. It was impossible to distinguish buck from squaw, in spite of the care exercised by both officers and men, whose action under the trying circumstances was most praiseworthy. The hot fight lasted about 20 minutes and skirmishing was kept up an hour afterwards.

Three troops were sent after those that went up the dry ravine, and they succeeding in killing six bucks and capturing five others (all badly wounded), and 19 squaws and children. But they were immediately attacked by 125 Brules, who had gotten wind of the fight and left the agency. In the fight that followed between the three troops and the 125 Brules the prisoners were dropped and the Indians driven off. The latter returned towards the Agency, which they attacked, drawing the fire of scouts and police, and spreading the report of the massacre of Big Foot to the peaceably inclined ones in the camps surrounding the Agency; which resulted in some 3,000 joining the hostile and assuming a threatening attitude.

The Indians from the Bad Lands, under Short Bull and Kicking Bear, would have camped that night near the Agency, but on hearing the news of the Big Foot disaster, they turned back, and assumed a hostile attitude at No Waters, eight miles from the mouth of White Clay Creek and about 17 miles from Pine Ridge Agency. The hostile camp now embraced 4,000 Indians, including over 1,000 warriors.

In this affair Capt. Wallace, six non-commissioned officers and 18 privates were killed; Lieuts. Garlington, Gresham and Hawthorne, 11 non-commissioned officers and 22 privates wounded. Capt. Whitney, Eighth Infantry, was ordered to make an investigation of Indians killed, etc., and he reported as follows: 62 bucks, one boy, killed, two bucks badly wounded; 40 squaws killed, one squaw wounded, one blind squaw unhurt; four small children and one papoose killed; 40 bucks and seven women killed in camp, 25 bucks, 10

68

women and two children in canyon, near and on side of camp; the rest found in hills; 58 horses and ponies and one burro found dead. Further he reported that there was evidence that a great number of bodies had been removed. Forty-eight guns and 150 horses were secured. After the fight the troops went back to the Agency.

As soon as the report of the affair reached Washington, Gen. Schofield telegraphed Gen. Miles the President's regrets that the affair had not been ended without bloodshed and further, "Give my thanks to the brave Seventh Cavalry for their splendid conduct." Miles at once telegraphed back: "It is stated that disposition of 400 soldiers and four pieces of artillery was fatally defective and a large number of soldiers were killed and wounded by fire from their own ranks and a very large number of women and children were killed in addition to Indian men. Do you wish your telegram of congratulation sent?" Schofield replied: "In view of this aspect of the case it will be better not to deliver my message to the Seventh Cavalry until I have seen your report after your investigating of the case."

1. That Forsyth had received repeated warnings as to the desperate and deceitful character of Big Foot's band and repeated orders as to the exercise of constant vigilance to guard against surprise and disaster under all circumstances.

2. That these warnings and orders were unheeded and disregarded by Forsyth who seemed to consider an outbreak of the Indians as beyond the pale of possibility, in the presence of the large force of the troops at hand.

3. An examination of the accompanying map shows conclusively that at the beginning of the attack not a single company of the troops was so disposed as to deliver its fire upon the warriors without endangering the lives of their own comrades. It is in fact, difficult to conceive how a worse disposition of troops could have been made. It would have been perfectly practicable for the entire command of upwards of 450 men to have been placed between the warriors and the women and children, with their backs to the latter and their faces to the warriors, where they might have used their weapons effectively if required. The testimony goes to show that most of the troops were forced to withhold their fire, leaving the brunt of the affair to fall on two companies until such warriors as had not been killed, broke through or overpowered the small force directly about them and reached the camp occupied by their women and children.

The battery of four Hotchkiss had until then been useless, the friction primers having been removed by order of the Captain commanding the battery, lest in their excitement the gunners might discharge their pieces and destroy their own comrades. These guns were opened upon the Indian camp, even then placing in peril troops C and D, Seventh Cavalry, which were obliged to retreat for some distance.

The fact that a large number of the 106 warriors were without weapons when the outbreak occurred is shown by the evidence that 48 guns were taken from the tepees and that a personal search of some 20 or more warriors resulted in finding them unarmed. This fact taken in connection with the extremely injudicious disposition of the troops and the large number of casualties were suffered at the hands of our men. Gen. Miles concluded by saying: "I can only partially account for the singular apathy and neglect of Col. Forsyth upon the theory of his indifference to and contempt for the repeated and urgent warnings and orders received by him from the Division Commander or by his incompetence and entire inexperience in the responsibility of exercising command where judgment and discretion are required."

Gen. Schofield in forwarding this document to the Secretary of War, Feb. 4th, said:

69

"The interests of the service do not demand any further proceedings in this case, nor any longer continuance of Col. Forsyth's suspension from the command of his regiment. The evidence in these papers shows that great care was taken by the officers and generally by the enlisted men, to avoid unnecessary killing of Indian women and children in the affair at Wounded Knee and shows that the conduct of the Seventh Cavalry, under very trying circumstances was characterized by excellent discipline and in many cases by great forbearance. In my judgment the conduct of the regiment was well worthy of the commendation bestowed upon it by me in my first telegram after the engagement."

By Endorsement, Feb. 12th, the Secretary of War, Mr. Redfield Proctor, completely exonerated Col. Forsyth and the Seventh Cavalry. After carefully reviewing the circumstances leading up to the time the Indians broke from the circle, he says: "The women and children were never away from the immediate company of the men after the latter broke from the circle. Many of them, men and women, got on their ponies and it is impossible to distinguish buck from squaw at a little distance when mounted. The men fired from among the women and children in their retreat. Cautions were repeatedly given, both by officers and non-commissioned officers not to shoot squaws or children, and men were cautioned individually that such Indians were squaws. The firing on the Indians by the troops was directed on the men in the circle and in a direction opposite from the tepees until the Indians after their break mingled with the women and children, thus exposing them to the fire of the troops and as a consequence some were unavoidably killed and wounded — a fact which was universally regretted by the officers and men of the Seventh Cavalry. This unfortunate phase of the affair grew out of circumstances for which the Indians themselves were entirely responsible. . . .

No doubt the position of the troops made it necessary for some of them to withhold their fire for a time in order that they might not endanger the lives of their comrades, but both Major Kent and Captain Baldwin concur in finding that the evidence "fails to establish that a single man of Col. Forsyth's command was killed or wounded by his fellows." This fact and indeed the conduct of the officers and men throughout the whole affair demonstrates an exceedingly satisfactory state of discipline in the Seventh Cavalry. Their behavior was characterized by skill, coolness, discretion and forbearance and reflects the highest possible credit upon the regiment, which sustained a loss of one officer and 24 enlisted men killed and two officers and 31 enlisted men wounded.

The situation at Wounded Knee Creek was a very unusual and a very difficult one; far more difficult than that involved in an ordinary battle, where the only question is that of gaining a victory without an effort to save the lives of the enemy. It is easy to make plans when we look backward, but in the light of actual conditions as they appeared to the commanding officer, there does not seem to be anything in the arrangement of the troops, requiring adverse criticism on the part of the Department. By command of the President Col. Forsyth will resume command of his regiment."

With one exception (the Cibicu massacre, of Col. Carr's command in 1883, by the White Mountain Apaches in Arizona) this is the first time in the history of the army, since the War of the Rebellion, that the military dispositions of officers engaged in war against Indians either in battle, pursuit or retreat, have been made the subject of official accusation and investigation by the commanding General of a Department or a Division, unless a charge of cowardice was connected therewith. As if by common consent a law of exemption has grown up under which strict military accountability has never been demanded and which like all practical rules, was founded in the necessities of the service, and is therefore the only fair rule to apply now. Under this rule the army has had cause to feel throughout all its grades, that no matter what enterprise was to be undertaken, no blasting of reputations honestly and previously established would follow a gallant and faithful discharge of duty, even though mistakes might be made. To pin the army down and make it feel that every operation against Indians not conducted in accordance with the prescriptions of book writers or the views of some one in authority would be followed by censure and investigation would result in its total demoralization. The enterprise, dash and daring which have been so conspicuous, would give way to fear of consequences and the time wasted in weighing probabilities and making dispositions by men fearful of their military repute would be profitably employed by the Indians in taking scalps or in the innocent amusement of torturing prisoners and ravishing women.

The next affair was the:

Fight at the Mission

On December 30th a small band of about 60 or 70 Indians came near the Catholic Mission, four miles from the military camp at Pine Ridge, and set fire to one of the small buildings. Col. Forsyth with eight troops of the Seventh Cavalry and a detachment of artillery was ordered by Gen. Brooke to go out and drive them away. He moved out, the Indians falling back before his command with some skirmishing, until they had proceeded six miles from the camp at Pine Ridge, there the command halted without occupying the commanding hills and was surrounded by the Indians. Skirmishing followed — Forsyth sent back three times for re-enforcements and fortunately Major Henry with four troops, Ninth Cavalry, and one Hotchkiss gun had just arrived in camp from his scout down White River after Big Foot, and moved at once to the scene rescuing the Seventh Cavalry from its perilous position.

Inspector General Heyl, who investigated this affair says: "It appears that skirmishers were not thrown out to take possession of the bluffs on the right and left of the valley until Major Henry arrived with his command and deployed it as shown on map enclosed. The position selection by Col. Forsyth on the slope by the shack beyond the bridge was not a judicious one, as the hills to the front and to the rear commanded his position. The Indians worked their way up the ravine in rear of the crest of the hill overlooking his troops and in that way soon gained possession of the ravines and hills in his rear. In fact that part of his command was actually surrounded and had it not been for the timely arrival of Major Henry with his battalion of the Ninth Cavalry the result would in all probability have been very serious. The number of hostiles with which Col. Forsyth's command was engaged Dec. 30th, '90, varies according to the best authority from 50 to 80.

In this connection it will be interesting to introduce two letters, one by Henry to Forsyth and the latter's acknowledgement of the same.

Camp on White River, Jan. 5th, 1891.

Gen. James W. Forsyth, Colonel Seventh Cavalry.

General: Will you please say to your officers that my officers and myself do not feel the services rendered to your regiment during the Mission engagement as entitled to the consideration which seems to be accorded us by the newspapers. No such catastrophe as indicated seemed imminent and we certainly are not desirous of gaining a little glory at the expense of your comrades. The "entente cordiale"

71

between the officers of the Seventh and ours is perfect and we hope the newspaper statements may not change the same.

Yours truly,
Guy V. Henry, *Maj. 9th Cav'y,*
Comd'g Battalion.

Pine Ridge Agency, S. D., Jan. 7th, 1891.

My dear Col. Henry:

Your letter of yesterday received. Please accept our thanks for the spirit of kindness and good feeling in which it was written and receive the assurance that that same feeling is reciprocated and has not, nor can it be changed by any newspaper article. There is no doubt, however, that your (9th Cavalry) timely arrival on the 30th, aided materially in the withdrawal of my troops, for at that moment it was hard to tell from which direction we were to expect the strongest force.

Very Sincerely,
James W. Forsyth, *Colonel 7th Cavalry.*

On Dec. 30th, the wagon train of the 9th Cavalry was attacked by Indians. One troop (D) had been left to guard it and the train had fallen about 1½ hours behind the battalion, returning to the Agency after the Big Foot search. They formed park within two miles of camp, defended themselves and sent in a courier to Henry, who at once came at a gallop in trepidation, to the rescue, driving off the Indians. The affair amounted to the exchange of a few shots and resulted in the death of one trooper shot in the first volley by an Indian dressed in the uniform of a cavalry soldier, with the yellow lining of his overcoat boldly displayed.

On January 3, 1891, an attack was made by about 100 Indians upon Capt. Kerr's troop of the Sixth Cavalry, which had not yet joined the regiment but which troop was hourly expected to come into position between Col. Carr and Lieut. Col. Offley.

Kerr, not knowing the close proximity of Col. Carr's command (then only four miles away on White River) formed his wagons into park and threw up some hasty entrenchments standing the Indians off — things were getting hot — he sent a courier who fortunately reached Carr's camp. Tupper's battalion was at once sent at a rapid gait to Kerr's assistance, making a gallant charge across the river filled with ice and cold as death. Tupper was supported by Carr himself and the Indians were driven back and Kerr brought safely in.

These various repulses had a tendency to check the westward movement by the Indians and to hold them in position along White Clay Creek until their intense animosity had subsided.

On January 7, 1891, occured the death of Lieut. Casey, 22nd Infantry, one of the purest, brightest, noblest officers in the service. The sadding thing of all is that his death was wholly unnecessary.

With the company of Cheyenne scouts that he had attempted to civilize and into whose heart he had succeeded in inculcating habits of discipline and domesticity, Casey reached the junction of White Clay Creek and White River on Dec. 20th, joining Lieut. Col. Sandford's command, consisting of the Leavenworth Cavalry battalion then encamped at that point. At this time the hostile camp of the Sioux was at "No Waters" on White Clay Creek about eight miles from its mouth and about 17 miles from Pine Ridge Agency. Casey employed his scouts until the day of his death in locating and watching this camp of the Sioux. On January 6th, by Lieut. Caseys' invitation, six or seven Sioux entered his camp and had a friendly talk.

On January 7th, about 9 a.m., Casey left camp with two scouts, telling Lieut. Getty that he was going out to get a view of the hostile camp. They proceeded up the right bank of White Clay Creek and a short distance from their own camp met a Sioux woman with whom Casey talked in English. He went on and within a short distance of the Sioux camp came upon a party of Sioux Indians (butchering cattle) with whom he shook hands. While White Moon, one of the scouts with Casey, was talking to these Indians, Casey left and had gone some distance toward the Sioux camp before White Moon noticed his departure. White Moon followed him, the other scout, Rock Road, having left and gone back. When he caught up to him Casey was talking to a halfbreed Sioux (Pete Richards).

On Pete Richards' right was another Sioux and to Lieut. Casey's left and rear, Plenty Horses, the murderer. While they were engaged in conversation, Plenty Horses shot Lieut. Casey through the head, the ball entering at the back and coming out under the right eye, killing him instantly.

White Moon rode toward him hoping to catch him before he fell but did not succeed. He caught his horse and took it back to camp, followed by Pete Richards, both of whom reported to General Brooke.

By permission of Gen. Brooke, who had established his headquarters with Sandford on Jan. 5th, Lieut. Getty took Casey's scouts and proceeding up White River, found Casey's body about one and a half miles from the Sioux camp; part of the clothing had been removed but the body had not been mutilated.

It was Getty's opinion that Casey started out with the intention of penetrating the hostile camp to have a talk with the principal chief and thought he could accomplish his object by boldness.

Casey's death was universally regretted as he was loved by all who had come in contact with the noble fellow. It cast a gloom over everyone and the shadow still hovers when our thoughts go back to that dark day, the 7th of January, 1891, when an Indian murderer's bullet cut short a true and faithful soldier's career.

Plenty Horses was delivered to the custody of the civil authorities and was tried on the charge of murder in the South Dakota Courts. The government's case was presented by Capt. John Green Ballance, 22nd Infantry, but Plenty Horses was acquitted, the learned judge holding that as actual hostilities existed Casey's death however inflicted must be considered as an act incident to war, he having voluntarily entered the hostile camp.

Plenty Horses was a graduate of the Indian school at Carlisle which fact of course should not militate against the process of civilizing the Indians, it simply goes to show that an Indian with a bad heart can no more be a made a good Indian that can the white man, under similar circumstances, be made a saint. Nature will out, nothing more is indicated by the dastardly deed. Churches and religious societies are surely but slowly quenching the fires of barbarism in these aborigines. The disappearance of blanket and breech clout, of long hair and highly painted faces, although mere external signs, marks the commencement of a change of heart and moral nature, that taken in the bud, in the young will lead to the love of Christ and his teachings.

At this stage Gen. Miles took station at Pine Ridge, where he could not only communicate directly with the Indian camp but also exercise a general supervision over all the commands.

Fortunately Congress appropriated funds necessary for complying with the obligations of the Sioux treaty and Gen. Miles was able to assure the Indians that the Government would respect their rights and necessities. Messengers were immediately sent, representing to them the injudicious policy of contending against the authorities and assuring them that the road to the Agency was the only safe one.

They were also advised of the distribution of the powerful commands inclosing their camp, barring all possibility of breaking through the line. The troops were thus once more steadily pressing the Indians back to the Agency. Fortunately again, their supplies of food had been increased and properly distributed and officers in whom they had confidence were placed in charge of the agencies; Capt. Hurst at Cheyenne River Agency, Capt. Lee at Rosebud and Capts. Pierce and Dougherty at Pine Ridge.

Under these circumstances on Jan. 15th the Indians moved up White Clay Creek and encamped within easy range of the guns of the large command under Col. Shafter at Pine Ridge, the troops under Gen. Brooke following immediately behind them, almost pushing them out of their camps. On the next day they moved farther in and encamped under the guns of the entire command and surrendered their entire force of nearly 4,000 people. The troops were moved into three strong camps of easy communication, occupying the three points of a triangle with the Indian camp in the center in close proximity to the troops.

While in this position they gave up some 200 guns, making in all some 600 or 700 guns surrendered by the Sioux Indians during the entire campaign. Short Bull and Kicking Bear and some 20 other leaders gave themselves up and were sent to Fort Sheridan under guard. Authority was given for ten Sioux chiefs, representing the different elements of the nation, to go to Washington to represent their affairs to the authorities and tell their own story.

The turbulent Brules from the Rosebud were taken back to their Agency in the dead of Winter, without escort, by Capt. Lee and reached their destination without casualty.

The Northern Cheyennes whose separation from their own people at the mouth of Tongue River in Montana, had caused them a good deal of discontent, were taken 300 miles across country covered with two feet of snow, the mercury in the thermometer almost out of sight, and safely reached their reservation.

Thus ended what at one time threatened to be a serious Indian war and the frontier was again assured of peace and quiet. Too much credit can not be given the troops who underwent the hardships and maintained the honor, character and integrity of the service, placing themselves between a most threatening body of savages and the unprotected settlements of the frontier in such a way as to avoid the loss of a single life of any of the settlers and establishing peace in that country with the least practicable delay. It was only 32 days from Sitting Bull's death to the surrender of the Indians at Pine Ridge, South Dakota.

And now once more the Indian has returned to his humdrum existence. During the past generation his mode of living received a wrench that caused him to look toward a Messiah as the only possible chance of a return to his previous habits of freedom, of tribe relationships, of happy hunting grounds all his own. The Sioux Campaign was the result of the last throe in "Poor Lo's" transition to the new order of things.

The camp fires that glowed in those bitter days are now cold. Around them, in jest and in earnest, we got to love and know each other's worth. But warm in our hearts are the memories of fallen comrades who sacrificed themselves on the altar of duty.

1927

No meeting held in the calendar year, 1927.

1928

There were 37 Companions and 11 guests who enjoyed the annual dinner and program this year. The addresses which were printed in the *Proceedings* were: "Items of Indian Service," by Brigadier General William H. Bisbee, read by Major George P. Ahern; "The Experience of Major Mauck in Disarming a Band Of Cheyennes On The North Fork Of The Canadian River In 1878," also read by Major Ahern; and "Lieutenant Fountain's Fight With The Apache Indians At Lillie's Ranch, Mogollon Mountains, December 9, 1885, and At Dry Creek, New Mexico, December 19, 1885."

Unpublished were General Parker's sketch of the Geronimo Campaign, a "humorous story of . . . first service in Indian Wars," by General Hutcheson, and Senator Tyson's "interesting account of his experiences in Indian Wars," in which he "paid tribute to the old Army who gained the West under many hardships."

75

L.F.BJORKLUND

Items of Indian Service

By Brig. Gen. William H. Bisbee, U.S. Army, Retired

Following the four years of Civil War two prominent duties appeared — political reconstruction of the South and opening our Western country to civilization.

By early Fall in 1865 our Volunteer Army was fast disappearing, the Grand Review had taken place in Washington and the usual disturbing aftermath of long war prevailed among thousands who must begin life anew. The unoccupied Western Territory was a safety valve for pioneers clamorous to occupy it with new homes. My best recollection is that the first regiment to protect this migration was the 18th U.S. Infantry in 1865, followed by the 13th U.S. Infantry, under Colonel I. V. D. Reeve, a year later, both with our Northwest Territory as the objective.

In November, 1865, my regiment, the 18th, then stationed temporarily at Louisville, Ky., proceeded by river steamer to Leavenworth, Kans., consuming two weeks' time filled with old-fashioned monotonous nostrums of slow progress, sandbars, soundings and landings for wood. Nobody knew where the channel of the "Great Muddy" was to be from one week to another. At Leavenworth we were joined by the 1st and 3d Battalions of 16 companies, (the full regiment comprising 24 companies, 8 companies to each battalion).

The 1st Battalion marched to stations on a southern line — Fort Ellsworth, Lara, Larned, Dodge, Aubrey and Lyon — on towards Denver, Colo.

The 3d Battalion, Maj. W. H. Lewis, (afterwards killed at White Woman Creek, Kans., by Northern Cheyenne Indians who had broken away from Darlington Agency, I. T., September, 1878), took stations on a middle line — Fort Sanders, Wyo., Fort Bridger, Utah, and Camp Douglas, near Salt Lake City.

Regimental Headquarters and the 2nd Battalion, after several days' preparations, marched to old Fort Kearny, Nebr., 190 miles west of Omaha, on the main Platte river, in a first leg toward an ultimate destination of old Fort Reno, on Powder River, Fort Philip Kearny, (to be built by the troops), and Fort C. F. Smith, in the Big Horn Valley, near Bozeman, Mont.

The two weeks' march was severe. Families had joined under special peace privileges, (mine, a wife and one son fourteen months old), in hopeful expectation of a restful life at some quiet frontier post, a dream from which we were soon to awaken. In the South our winters had been varied by mud and warm rains, now we were facing a winter march in the North and this year it began early and with plenty of snow. Fifteen degrees below zero was the average temperature, buffalo robes and heaviest woolen clothing were in demand, foodstuffs containing moisture, frozen from the beginning, potatoes, bread, etc., to be chopped out by hatchet as needed. Canvas laid on snow and icy ground, with blankets, was our bed. Such music as we had was supplied by crunching, creaking wagon wheels rolling over icy roads with accompanying howls of wolves and prairie winds.

New recruits deserted in unusual numbers in cowardly fear of Indian troubles, much increased by wild stories from straggling volunteers returning from the upper country. Some of these deserters, in seeking clear records and honorable pardons for pension purposes, later made claim of having been abandoned on the road, a false absurdity, for our transportation was ample to care for all disabled. The Civil War men, inured to hardships, remained steadfast and faithful.

Fort Kearny was an old, dilapidated garrison post of cottonwood logs and framework, where, upon arrival of our contingent, the eight companies were crowded into quarters for the winter. My assignment was one back room and a small space under a hall stairway. This was our parlor, dining room and sleeping apartment for six months. First Lieut. F. H. Brown, (B. Brown), a bachelor and Regimental Quartermaster, occupied the front room. His chief joy was to pack the room full of Pawnee Indians, fill them with "chow," in return for which they gave gruesome and noisy exhibitions of scalping war dances, buffalo hunts, etc., until Spring gave us relief in final orders for opening and protecting a wagon route from Fort Laramie to the Gallatin Valley, Mont.

The officers present were Col. H. B. Carrington to command the new Mountain District, Department of the Platte; Capt. Fred Phisterer, Adjutant, 18th Infantry and Assistant Adjutant General of the District; First Lieut. Fred H. Brown, Quartermaster; Capt. S. M. Horton, Chief Surgeon, Doctors Matthews, McCleary and Buelon, Assistant and contract surgeons; Brevet Maj. Henry Haymond, Capt. Commanding 2nd Battalion; Brevet Capt. W. H. Bisbee, First Lieut., Battalion Adjutant; Captains Nathaniel C. Kinney, Joshua Proctor and Thomas B. Burrowes; Lieutenants John J. Adair, Thaddeus Kirtland and Isaac d'Isay, company officers.

Jim Bridger was our guide. Let me digress here a moment to correct some of the faulty impressions given out about this good old scout. He was not the rough, lawless, gambler type, sometimes pictured to excite and misinform the comboy fans of today, and, although a more and less unimportant matter, a page may not be amiss in pen description of him by one of the few remaining men who knew him personally. History is best served in this way.

Bridger was a plain, farmer-like looking man, five feet ten or eleven in height, dressed in the customary "store clothes" garments, low crowned, soft felt hat, never affecting, in my recollection, long hair or showy fringed buckskin suits, though he may, on occasion, have donned them as a convenience. His habits accorded with his dress, plain and sensible. He appeared shrewd in estimation of Indian customs, cautious and observing in his line of work, apparently adopting the Indian ways of seeing without being seen. Never leaving camp unless ordered, he would come out of his tent, shade his eyes, cast them around the hills and say, "When you don't see 'em that's when they are full of devilment." His name of scout belied his calling in our expedition for we had no occasion to scout for Indians — they were nearby always.

Elaborate preparations were made for long and indefinite occupation of our new country, 700 miles from a railroad. Transcontinental railroads had not been started. Everything asked for was granted, from tent pins to sawmills. My personal allowance embraced two six-mule teams, an ambulance, three saddle horses, cow and chickens. The train consisted of more than 200 wagons. Someone gave it the name of "Carrington's Overland Circus."

From the mustered out 7th Iowa Cavalry, at Fort Kearny, we received a hundred or more horses for courier and other duties until cavalry could be supplied.

May 19, 1866, we started up the Platte Valley, via Plum Creek, Jack Morrow's ranch and Cottonwood Springs, for Fort Sedgwick, 200 miles distant. Here we found an uncertain stage of water at the crossing, with the usual treacherous channels and quicksands. Several days were wasted in constructing a raft — destined to failure — after which, upon the advice of Captain "Bill" (Charles E.) Norris, 2nd Cavalry, stationed there, the train, team by team, was pushed, "cussed" and driven across the stream, nearly a mile wide, the leaders, swing and wheelers swimming and gaining foothold alternately, quicksands requiring rapid work or immediate sinking beyond recovery.

June 6, en route again for the last civilized place, Fort Laramie, 100 miles northwest. It was getting warm, buffalo gnats growing wicked, wood and water less plentiful. Buffalo chips served as fuel. Ambulances carried the heat-exhausted and lame recruits.

Each day was much like another, the march at earliest dawn, the same adventures with rattlesnakes, the inopportune thunder storms, routine of evening guard-mount and sound slumber.

At Fort Laramie a big "pow-wow" with the Sioux Indians was in session. A Peace Commission to consider and determine the right of way to Virginia City from the East found strong opposition from the Indians who claimed knowledge of an old treaty forbidding it. Red Cloud, Head Chief of the Ogallalah Sioux, with a following of 2,000 or 3,000, was disgruntled, saying he would not leave us a hoof and left the conference. Large quantities of presents had been given to satisfy them and, though accepted, did not satisfy. Waiting citizens were insistent and daring in their desire to go through and settle in the Northwest. Indian rights, if they existed, were set aside, bad feeling resulted, with the soldiers, as usual in those days, placed on the frontier line to maintain order or do what they could. A few days were spent at the post to replenish various requirements as we cut loose from civilization. Ward and Bullock were sutlers at the large frontier store. Indians filled every available space, dressed, half dressed and undressed. Squaws dressed to the same degree of completeness, papooses nude or almost nude, all mingling with soldiers, teamsters, emigrants, speculators, half-breeds, squaws men, and interpreters.

The scene was characteristic of existing life in the Wild West. Under the eaves of buildings, by doorsteps and porches were groups of Indians in assorted sizes, sexes and conditions, with the element of cleanliness just as critically wanting as usual among the aborigines.

"Man-afraid-of-his-horses" joined Red Cloud in opposition to our advance into the Powder River country without treaty agreement and declined to treat or give up their hunting lands on any consideration.

Our part was to go forward, which we did on June 17th, with our 600 or 800 men who, in comparison with the skilled marksmen of today, with improved, breech-loading, repeating firearms, made our recruits, with muzzle loaders and ignorance of handling them, a poor second in the task before us, resulting in the sacrifice of more than 200 lives in course of the next year.

At Bridger's Ferry we learned that the stock of Mr. Mills, a squaw man, had been run off by Indians the night previous. The day we reached Fort Reno, Smith and Leighton's (sutlers) herd of mules and horses were run off by Indians. Major Haymond, with a party of men in pursuit, were rewarded by nothing but a pony abandoned by the Indians, loaded with presents from the Peace Commission at Laramie.

First count for the Red Man. Indians in small parties occasionally appeared on our march, saying they were going to fight the Snakes (Shoshones) over the mountains, though in truth they were "sizing us up."

Friday the 13th came our next admonition — two trains had been attacked. At Clear Fork a swarm of Indians had come into camp for the usual "pow-wow" and "size up." We were peacefully inclined, having nothing as yet to fight for, but suspicion grew strong that they were treacherous.

July 15th, the permanent site for the post of Phil Kearny was marked out and ready for the work of building. On the 17th our herd of mules was stampeded by Indians who jumped over one of the recruit pickets, grabbed the bell mare and, of course, the herd followed. Major Haymond and I, with a few men, pursued them in a running fight for fifteen miles but the odds were against us and we lost the mules as Red Cloud had promised.

Nearby we found "French Pete" and his party of five men killed and scalped just over the hill on the Bozeman road, signs indicating that this unlawful load of whiskey had led to his destruction, despite his squaw wife who was spared.

July 22nd, at Buffalo Springs, one man was killed. Indians near the post at Reno drove off six mules and killed two citizens.

July 23d, Louis Cheney's train was attacked, one man killed, horses and cattle stolen.

July 24th, midnight, brought word from Captain Burrowes, who had gone to Reno for supplies, that a train had been attacked, endangering a party of newly appointed officers joining. Private Callery, foolishly ahead of the company, had been killed and on reaching the scene, Lieut. Daniels was found dead, scalped and mutilated, with over a hundred arrows in his body, a custom of Indians being to count a "coo" for every stroke given a victim while alive.

29th, citizen train, attacked at Brown Springs, had eight men killed. Mr. Grover, an alleged Frank Leslie artist, employed in the sawmill, was inclined to stroll carelessly on Sundays, unarmed. One Monday morning I found him dead, scalped and badly mutilated, lying face downward across the roadway, a sign that he had not been brave.

Thus it went on day by day and month by month, the soldiers heavily engaged in the timber four miles away, cutting saw logs for stockade and with little power to do more than defend themselves, animals and property.

August 12th, 14th and 17th, Indians drove off horses and cattle, killing citizens, Postlewaite and Williams.

September 8th, twenty mules driven away from a citizen herd within a mile of the post.

13th, Crary and Carter's hay camp was attacked, one man killed and 209 head of cattle run off with a band of buffalo the Indians were chasing. Private Donovan came in with an arrow in his hip, going out again after extraction.

14th, Privates Gilchrist and Johnson, a few yards in advance of a hay guard, were cut off and killed. Nothing was found but a small piece of clothing. Wolves had even carried the bones away.

27th, Private Patrick Smith, scalped at the log camp, crawled half a mile to the block houses and lived 24 hours with an arrow in his breast. Drawing it out by the surgeon caused his death. Days were filled with incidents of this nature, with an average of one or two scalpings a week. Mail communication with the East was kept up by relays, via Fort Laramie, oftentimes at monthly intervals, with a sacrifice of life.

During that Winter we did not hear from Fort C. F. Smith for three months and, fearing disaster to their two companies, Sergeant Grant and a companion volunteered to make an attempt to go through the hostile country — ninety miles. Success attended them. The garrison was found safe by reason of its location near the "Crow" Indian country, a friendly tribe. There had been no serious Indian troubles at the lower stations. Phil Kearny and Reno had them all. One day, the usual wood train attack being announced, the Colonel assumed the privilege of commanding a relieving party. During this special work a stray Indian was seen not far distant from the troops. Lieutenants Grummond and Bingham, mounted, ran for him in hopes of capture. The lone Indian meantime shouting and dodging their bullets and sabres. Soon more Indians appeared among the hills and ravines, making retreat the only course, whereupon a break was made for a hill where three soldiers were seen. No sooner had this point been reached than scores of redskins developed. No course remained but a dash for the main body, in doing which Bingham was killed immediately. Sergeant Bowers, of my company, fell nearby, the two others wounded, Lieut. Grummond only escaping unharmed. That night, in relating his adventure to me, he stated that upon rejoining the command he very hotly asked the Colonel if he was a fool or a coward to allow his men to be cut to pieces without offering help.

The constraint of constant confinement to stockade limits became unbearable, relief by risky strolls was sought at times, never free from danger, one occasion including three ladies who had but a few moments before returned from a short walk, developed the dash of 30 or 40 Indians across the path they had left, heading directly for Picket Hill, upon which two sentinels were always kept daily posted. Instant action was required and taken by men running to the rescue. In superintending the progress of work, Captains Fetterman and Ten Eyck, Lieut. Link and myself and two orderlies, riding ahead of the wood train, stopped at the edge of the timber to water our animals. Suddenly, from behind a huge log fifty yards away came yells and shots from ambushed red skins. Taking immediate shelter, for better observation and to await reinforcements from the train guard in rear, we plainly discovered larger parties awaiting our further approach. One lone Indian only came into the open — plainly a decoy leading us to a trap. It was not accepted beyond driving the young brave to cover.

The culmination came in December. On the morning of the 21st our pickets on Picket Hill gave signals of many Indians on the wood road. It was evident that the usual attack was being made on the train and relief was speedily on its way from the Fort — eight odd soldiers in number, under command of Brevet Lieut. Col. Wm. J. Fetterman, accompanied by Captain Fred H. Brown, Lieut. Grummond and two citizens, experienced frontiersmen. The matter of driving the Indians from the attack was speedily accomplished. Col. Fetterman, actuated by a spirit of humiliation over so much previous defeat at their hands, obviously attempted to chastise them, as was our custom, but small bands appeared to oppose it. Red Cloud was, however, playing his game. The Indians in sight were but a decoy and, after leading our troops over the next ridge into Reno Valley, to ground of their own choosing, 3,000 Sioux quickly surrounded and, within the hour, massacred them all. Not a man escaped. Relief was started from the post but so few in number that the Indians only jeered and challenged them to come down from the ridge on which they had halted to obtain a view of the field. Nothing could be seen of Fetterman or his party. Later in the day, having completed their butchery, the Indians withdrew and 46 bodies were brought back to the Fort, the remainder of the 83 the next day. All but six had been killed by arrows and all were horribly mutilated, a work generally left to the squaws.

Following this diaster, published statements appeared in book form, in effect that Col. Fetterman disobeyed orders, leading to the destruction of his command, the first statement coming in a book under the alleged authorship of Mrs. Carrington, though bearing much evidence of the Colonel's style in diction and larger knowledge of the subject matter than a woman could ordinarily possess.

The statements set forth that Col. Fetterman was ordered to relieve the wood train and under no circumstances pursue the Indians across the ridge. Very specific orders, these. I have never believed that such an order was given so positively in this particular instance, basing my disbelief on many plausible grounds from my official standpoint of Company Commander, Battalion Adjutant, Regimental Adjutant and Assistant Adjutant General of the District.

It was not the custom to give orders forbidding pursuit and punishing of marauding Indians, nor do I recall any ever being given. On the contrary, many cases occurred when they were not given. Once, when Major Haymond and myself, with a few men, pursued for fifteen miles a band that had jumped over recruit pickets on herd guard and stampeded the mules. Again, when Col. Fetterman, Capt. Ten Eyck, Lieut. Link and I were with the wood train, as previous related. Once when Lieutenants Grummond and Bingham pursued the lone Indian when the Colonel (C) was present in command. At another time, when Lieut. Brown and I, with such men as we could hastily pick up, drove off Indians who were attempting one night to drive away our beef cattle, in rear of the post. Signal fires denoted Indians, two or three officers had gathered in the office of the Colonel, who, turning to us, said "Lieut. Brown, you are the senior present and have the right to drive these Indians off." I will not record the remarks of Brown, as we left the room disgusted, and proceeded, with a few men, to round up the cattle. Again, when Mr. Brown and I pursued a small party that had been seen nearby, towards Lake d'Smedt. Why, then, this special order not to pursue and attempt to punish as usual? Was it premonition of an ambush or an aftermath? Somebody was responsible, either the higher military authority for not supplying more troops to oppose these 3,000 Sioux, the Post Commander, for mismanagement, or not making better efforts, or Colonel Fetterman, who, with all his command, was now dead — unable to answer.

At all times Col. Fetterman was an ideal soldier, thoroughly disciplined in the importance of obedience, making it unthinkable that he would flagrantly disobey. That he was led to an ambush is undeniable, as was his feeling of unrest and humiliation over the prevailing trend of affairs in service under an officer who had not served in the field or been acquainted with hostile rebel shots during our four years Civil War.

This he, Fetterman, made plain to me ten days before his death, in our last interview, and is here recorded in defense and memory of a brave friend.

The Powder River territory was abandoned and given over to the Indians from the following year until the campaigns of General Crook, ten years later, became necessary in subduing and placing them on reservations.

In concluding this partial narrative of events in the '60s on our then American Frontier, taken in conjunction with American history before and after, it may well be said, in retrospection, that, in rescuing from savages and transforming the wilderness into teeming gardens and fields, the Army of our people has been a most important factor.

Since writing the foregoing I received from Mr. A. B. Ostrander, under date of February 2, 1927, information bearing directly upon the subject matter of the Fetterman affair as follows:

"When I was composing my book, *An Army Boy of the Sixties*, I had before me a copy of the report of the Board of Inquiry on the Fetterman massacre and there for the first time I read Carrington's testimony that he had given such a specific order and so, on page 167 of my book, I incorporated his statement after having read the same in other documents, but I got a calling down. At one of our G.A.R. Encampments I met an old comrade whom I had known at Phil Kearny by the name of F. M. Fassendan. He was of our battalion. He died in the Soldiers Home in Tennessee last year. I sent him a copy of my book and he wrote back to me as follows in effect: 'You are all wrong in your story about Carrington giving orders to Colonel Fetterman not to cross Lodge Trail Ridge. At guard mount that morning I was detailed as headquarters orderly and reported directly to the Adjutant's office. I was there when Major Powell and Colonel Fetterman came in and heard Fetterman ask for command of the relief party and when that was settled Colonel Carrington turned towards Colonel Fetterman and said, "Colonel, go out and bring in that wood train," and not a word was said about how, or route, or where not to go.'

Lieutenant Fountain's Fight With Apache Indians at Lillie's Ranch, Mogollon Mountains, December 9, 1885, and At Dry Creek, N.M., December 19, 1885

My fight with a part of Geronimo's band at Lille's Ranch Snow Creek, Mogollon Mountains, New Mexico, on evening of December 9th, 1885, was the culmination of a "stern chase" on a large circle, marching from November 27th till December 9th.

I was in camp near Alamo, New Mexico, under the command of Major Samuel S. Sumner 8th Cavalry, who commanded also troop M 8th Cavalry, stationed at Malone. The stations were 90 miles apart and Major Sumner had located at Silver City where he could receive telegraph and mail information more readily than at either of the camps. He was convinced that a band of ten or more hostiles were in the Mogollon Mountains and ordered the two troops to meet him at Duck Creek, Cactus Flat near the L. C. Ranch. The troops reported to him on Thanksgiving Day, November 26th. I furnished the Major with later news that convinced him the hostiles had left the Mogollons and were headed for the Indian reservation at Turkey Creek, five miles from Fort Apache, Arizona. The next morning he ordered me back to my camp and Troop M to Malone. But he directed me to send 2nd Lieutenant Cabell with a detachment via Mule Springs into the San Francisco range to scout the country till he found the hostile trail and then follow it into the reservation. Lieutenant Cabell took the trail and I the Alamo road. That night I camped at Higgins' ranch. During the night a courier from Major Sumner delivered the letter, telling me the hostiles had been on the reservation, had had a fight, had broken away and were probably largely reinforced and might overwhelm Cabell; that I should take measures to save him. I aroused the command, marched to my camp at the Alamo, twenty miles to replenish supplies and then marched to the "Little Blue" about eighteen miles. The next day I reached the crossing of the "Big Blue." Here I expected to find Cabell's trail but scouted the country in that vicinity without seeing any evidence of it. I, therefore, went into camp feeling sure that he would come later and he joined me that night.

The next day we marched to the crossing of Eagle Creek, which is only five miles from the Turkey Creek Indian reservation. Here I struck a fresh trail of a Cavalry command coming from the reservation and followed it. It proved to be Lieutenant Reed with a detachment of the 10th Cavalry. His information confirmed the report of the hostiles. The following day we scouted the country for trails but found none and moved down Eagle Creek till we struck the trail to Clifton, Arizona. I took that trail and Lieutenant Reed continued his march to Fort Grant. At Clifton there were rumors of the hostiles being in the vicinity, that "Al Seebers" with the Apache scouts was in pursuit and that the hostiles were making for the Mogollon mountains.

The next day I started for the Mule Spring Ranch via Char-Coal camp, where a day later we picked up the hostile trail about 10 a.m. and followed as rapidly as possible till near sundown when we arrived at Mule Springs. The hostiles had been there and looted the place. The trail I had followed from Char-Coal camp was the ordinary traveled route and was distinctly marked. One very large footed horse and another with a right front foot bare were specially noticed. I camped near the ranch house and then while it was still light enough to see, scouted the country carefully and located a scattered outfit that was quite as large as the band I had followed. This I concluded must be Al Seebers and his scouts — a very encouraging sign, for it looked as though he must be very close to the hostiles. Later that night Captain Sproule 8th Cavalry arrived with his troop, having marched from some place on the Gila, hoping to head off the hostiles before they reached Mule Springs. He decided to remain the next day and directed me to return to my camp at the Alamo, supply my detachment and scout into the Mogollon mountains, via Clairmont trail while he would enter the mountains via Mogollon trail. We would then have the hostiles between us. That night two men came from the L. C. Ranch on Cactus Flat to see what had happened at Mule Springs. They reported that on the previous day about 4 p.m. they were at Mules Springs and had just corralled some horses and mules when they saw the hostiles and they mounted their horses and rode away.

The cowboys warned me not to take grain or fodder from the fields as Mr. Lyda, the manager of the L. C. Ranch, who also controlled the Mule Spring Ranch had told them not to allow the United States troops to take any supplies from the place. However, I fed grain and fodder to my horses and left a receipt for it.

The next morning I marched as rapidly as possible to reach Cactus Flat before the mail carrier passed, so that I might send dispatches to Silver City and Fort Bayard. When I reached the road I found Lieut. and Assistant Surgeon Maddox, who was my camp Surgeon at Alamo, with a few men and ten Navajo scouts. Reports had come to him that the hostiles had killed some travellers on the road and he had marched to attack the hostiles and protect the country. I selected ten men and horses and the Navajo scouts that I thought would last as long as I could, taking such supplies as were available and sent the rest of the men under Lieutenant Cabell to Camp Alamo about thirty miles north. With the ten men, two civilian guides and the ten Navajoes I took the hostile trail. I also sent a courier to Captain Sproule telling him what had occurred.

The Navajo scouts soon loitered on the trail and when urged they said: "You are not strong enough — too many hostiles." I tried to make them understand that we were following Al Seebers and his scouts as well as the hostiles and that made the trail look large. They may have understood me but they did not believe it. Finally, I told McKinney, my civilian guide, that I would not be delayed by meandering the trail and ordered him to lead directly to the Mogollon gap, where I would take the chances of finding the trail. We reached the water hole at the gap just before dark. The hostile trail was there and led on into the mountains south of the Mogollon trail. I camped there for the night, having no feed for my horses and not much for my men. There were range cattle about and my sergeant — Van Meter — came to me and wanted permission to kill a beef. I told him that I would kill one before we left the cattle range unless we picked up some beef that the Indians might abandon. During the night it snowed and made the trail hard to follow. McKinney pointed out a "high-gap" through which he thought the hostiles must pass. We marched as direct as possible for the gap and reached it about 10 a.m. The hostiles had evidently camped there as fires were burning and the trail out was on top of the snow.

(Before reaching the gap we heard a cow bellow and could see buzzards fly into the air. We finally could see the cow. She would leave her dead calf and graze, then the buzzards would drop down on the calf and the cow would rush at them and stand over the calf and bellow. Her udder was greatly distended and she showed great distress. No one suggested that we should use the calf for food.)

There were signals indicating that the hostiles would move north, though the trail was leading east. The signals annoyed me — for whom could they be signalling? Certainly not to Al Seebers and his scouts. The trail indicated thirty or forty animals and the big foot and bare foot were still there. About noon McKinney told me the country East was very rough and really led nowhere and the hostiles would turn north soon so as to cross Diamond Creek Canyon at the only crossing that he knew. Whereupon, I concluded to cut north. When I reached the Mogollon trail I found water and good grass. I halted, unsaddled and grazed for an hour and a half. About one hour's march brought us to an abandoned ranch — a few of the hostiles had been there. Later we reached the edge of the Diamond Creek Canyon. Detachments of the hostiles had come in and gone down the trail, the big foot horse still with them. Signals indicated north which was their line of travel. The trail was quite fresh and I used such case as I could to avoid ambush. We crossed the Creek at the Butcher Brothers' ranch. They had both been killed there by the Indians the previous June and the place was abandoned. On the north side of the Canyon we found an exhausted horse. This indicated to me that the hostiles contemplated returning and suggested to me the plan to wait there for them, but that would have left Lillie's ranch on Snow Creek and Papanoe's on the Gilita at the mercy of the hostiles, and I pushed on. Lillie's first ranch had been looted but evidently no one was there at the time and little damage was done. His home ranch was five miles away and to reach it before or with the hostiles was my desire. The trail struck Snow Creek, which ran through an open valley two hundred or more yards wide, at right angles, Lillie's ranch being on the far side. The sun was just down, the ranch house was on fire and the hostiles were leading their horses from the corral where they had placed them while they looted the house. I counted nineteen Indians but I saw only those about the burning house and corral gate — others had already mounted and taken the trail. I could have opened fire on them but could not charge mounted because my horses were so nearly exhausted. I dismounted, formed my men in line, leaving Sergeant Moore and Private Beatty to look after the horses and moved forward, warning the men not to fire till I ordered, for I wanted to get upon the hostiles and cause a thorough stampede. So I moved at a run leading the men through the creek and beyond the open fire. The hostiles were surely stampeded, only one getting away mounted and he was shot from his horse and the horse wounded. I ran to the door of the burning house and called, hoping if any one was inside and alive we could save him. Old man Prior was there but he was dead.

We followed the Indians as far as was advisable, keeping up a running fire. I returned with the men to the corral, which was under a bluff. In the meantime, the hostiles had opened fire on my horses. I left Sergeant Van Marter in charge at the corral with instructions to move the captured stock and supplies to our side of the creek later. I then moved down the creek under the protection of the bluff till opposite Sergeant Moore's position and called to him to keep up the fire while I crossed the valley to join him. The Indians had one loud sounding gun which I had noticed. When I was about half way across the valley the ground in front of me was torn up and that gun boomed, causing me to make such a jump that I tumbled, my men thinking I had been shot. However, I was soon in motion and joined Sergeant Moore. When I was on the ground, in a flash of memory I recalled the story of a soldier who, while retiring from the first battle of Bull Run, said he heard a bullet passing twice. When asked how he could have heard it twice, he replied, "The first time it passed me, the second I passed it." It was an old story and a real comfort to think of at that time. We moved the animals to safety, the hostiles keeping up a rattling fire upon us without inflicting any serious damage. The big gun was not heard again. They probably used their last cartridge on me.

In commenting upon my report to the effect that I had counted 19 hostiles, the Division Commander said that the ten hostiles when leaving the reservation had taken 9 squaws with them. I am awfully glad that I did not count a greater number else the reservation might have lost all of its squaws.

Sergeant Van Marter brought his men, captured animals and supplies to our side where we remained for the night. At daylight I was able to note our spoil. Among the animals were two mules and ten horses of the "L. C." brand which I returned to the owners at the White House Ranch. The big foot horse was there. He was a large brown horse and a good one. I gave him to the guide, McKinney. He was killed under him in the fight with the hostiles ten days later. There were coffee, sugar, flour and bacon in abundance, for which I was most thankful.

The man, Lillie had recently returned from Socorro with winter supplies. He was an eccentric man of good family and considerable means of Newark, N.J. and chose to lead a hermit's life in these mountains. His body was lying in the field some distance from the house. Old man Prior who was a visitor at the time was burned in the cabin. I got his "Marlyn carbine" from the hostiles and gave it to Papanoe the next day.

The Indians had disappeared during the night. The signals found now indicated south. That was a relief to me, for Papanoe's ranch was eight miles north. I found him in a state of blissful safety. As a means of defense he had a broken shotgun and no ammunition. He told me of Lillie having just returned with a load of supplies and recognized the carbine as belonging to old man Prior. I gave it to him and all of the ammunition belonging to it. I suggested that as a matter of safety he should go to Alamo with me but he said that he felt safe where he was, that the hostiles would leave the mountains on account of the snow and would go south via Mogollon Pass. That was my opinion also and I was anxious to return to my camp and send a detachment to the White House ranch to meet and escort a train of supplies due at this time from Fort Bayard.

Upon arrival at my camp near Alma, after receiving a hearty welcome from Lieutenant Cabell, Surgeon Maddox and the men of the troop, I gave orders for Lieutenant Cabell and his platoon to proceed at daylight to the L. C. ranch on Duck Creek and escort a train of supplies that should be there. I felt sure the hostile bands in the mountains would unite and raid the valley.

When Lieutenant Cabell returned he reported to me that a few miles from Alma, he met Mr. Lyda, the manager of the L. C. ranch and a deputy sheriff. He told them that he had two mules and ten horses of the L. C. brand that Lieutenant Fountain had captured from the hostiles in a fight he had with them at Lillie's ranch in the mountain. Mr. Lyda was delighted with the news, turned and rode back to the ranch, where Lieutenant Cabell later learned that he and the sheriff had inteded to arrest me for taking the corn and fodder at Mules Springs the night I camped there. I was very glad that the corn episode was settled in that way.

On December 18th, I left my camp with Lieutenant Cabell, surgeon Maddox, 28 men, 10 Navajo scouts and 10 days' rations, intending to scout the country as far as the Mogollon pass. Just a few miles before I reached Dry Creek, where I planned to camp that night, I met a courier from Silver City with a telegram from the District Commander at Sante Fe, N.M., directing me to proceed to Clifton, Arizona, to protect mines in that vicinity while they finished the necessary work before the end of the year to establish their claims. To obey that order would have left my section of the country without protection. That night at my camp I learned from cattle men at Higgins' ranch, that they had seen evidence of Indians on their rides, which confirmed me in my opinion that the hostiles had left the Mogollons and were in the valley or had gone back to the reservation. I answered the District Commander's order to that effect and informed him that I would locate the hostiles before going to Clifton. The courier left early the next morning and delivered my telegram at the office in Silver City.

Later that morning, December 19th, I left Sergeant Van Marter and two men in charge of the camp at Higgins' ranch, and directed Lieutenant Cabell to mount the troop. Sergeant Moore in charge of the Navajo scouts was slow in getting them out. I made some remarks and by my presence expedited their mounting. We trotted out to join Lieutenant Cabell. The command was not in marching order, no advance guard or flankers. I was not alarmed but I was anxious and moved rapidly, joined the command, came down to a walk, because the road was in a side cutting and too narrow for me to pass easily, when a single shot was fired. I looked along the column, thinking some person had fired at game — which was positively forbidden. I saw no evidence of such a shot. A volley followed quickly. There was some confusion but no panic among the men. Lieutenant Cabell and most of the men dismounted at once. I dismounted and fastened my horse to a bush on the lower side of the road and the men in my vicinity did the same. We returned the fire of the hostiles who were visible on the ridge beyond the upper side of the road. Their fire was not scattering and I moved forward with Lieutenant Cabell and many of the men. Privates Gibson and Wishard were killed just as we crossed the road — Wishard had enlisted under the name of McMillan. — Corporal McFarland's horse was killed and he was wounded in the first volley.

I did not see the Navajo scouts and asked Sergeant Moore where they were. He was provoked and replied "God only knows." As a matter of fact they had quickly disappeared, but when under cover dismounted and moved up a ravine and joined me as I gained the ridge. Doubtless their presence was noted by the hostiles and had effect in moving them from their chosen position. About the same time, Sergeant Van Marter, one private and old man Elliott rushed in on the right. They had heard the firing, saddled and mounted their horses. Mr. Elliott knew the ground and suggested the line of approach and led them in the most gallant manner. The sight of the old man, bare-headed with white hair flying, was picturesque and inspiring. The firing was continued at close range, so close that I am sure I recognized one of the hostiles and spoke to him at San Antonio, Texas, when Geronimo and his band were turned over to me by Capt. Lawton. I said: "You and I exchanged shots in the fight at Dry Creek and missed each other." He replied quickly: "No it was not I — I never missed my man." Natchez, who was with me, took in the reply and smiled in a knowing manner. — The ridge was their chosen position and when driven from it they disappeared in the timber and rough land to the west.

88

The first shot had killed guide McKinney's horse; the volley that followed wounded Surgeon Maddox, killed Corporal McFarland's horse and wounded the Corporal. Later, while hospital steward Babcock and private Beatty were assisting Surgeon Maddox, he was shot through the head and killed, Lieutenant Cabell slightly wounded and Blacksmith Collins mortally wounded and two horses severely injured. As soon as I could I went to Collins. He asked me to pray for him. I had my little prayer book with me and read to him the prayers for the dying. He realized his condition, was calm and followed the prayers with appreciation. He died soon after. I wrote the story of his death to his father, for I knew it would be a comfort to him.

My men stood the shock of attack without panic and doubtless had in mind instructions given to us by Major Sumner in the early days of the campaign: — "If you are attacked by the hostiles you must hold your ground — some are sure to be killed or wounded and if you vacate the ground, the hostiles will mutilate them.

I recall Lord Robert's remarks to the effect that an officer who allowed his command to be ambushed, should be shot. But I also had in mind General Crook's saying that troops in pursuit of the Apaches, should be strong enough to receive a shock and move on, otherwise the Apache would not be engaged. By reason of their ability to move, mounted or on foot in their rugged country, they would elude ordinary pursuit and could not be surprised or overtaken. I did not plan to be ambushed, but I did expect to come in contact with the hostiles and always depended upon my men to stand the shock and move on. They proved their training, drove the hostiles from their chosen position and from the Mogollon country to which they never returned.

The Experience of Major Mauck in Disarming a Band of Cheyennes on the North Fork of the Canadian River in 1878

It happened in the winter of 1878; I was a lieutenant then, in the Fourth cavalry. My captain was Mauck. He's dead now. Short, sturdy, erect in his carriage, a very brave man he was. Mauck had the job of taking a band of Northern Cheyennes from their homes in the north to the Indian Territory. There were some sixty bucks, with their women and children, about 250 in all. They were prisoners in a way, for though they had been peaceable for years and had distinguished themselves in two campaigns as scouts in the government service, they were leaving their old camping grounds, and what is dear to an Indian heart, the graves of their fathers. They had fought for Uncle Sam against the Sioux and the Nez Perces, but that availed nothing. When it came time to move them and seize their land, it was "Forward, march!" just the same. But their protests were very bitter, and their reluctance extreme, and nothing but the logic of a batallion of mounted soldiers got them under way.

From Fort Sydney, Nebraska, where our battalion took charge of them, across the prairies of Western Kansas, was a weary march. Wood and water were sometimes thirty miles apart, which meant a two days' march from stream to stream for overloaded ponies worn down with previous marching and a halt at night without water or fuel, and this, mind you, in December with snow on the ground. Six weeks our journey lasted, and as we got to know the individual Indians of the band, every day our sympathy and interest increased. A scout that we had, who was our interpreter, knew the Indian character well. His name was Amos Chapman. The Indians seemed to like him, and talked to him freely, so that with what we saw and with what we learned from him and through him, we were constantly getting new insight into Indian character, and developing new interest in this particular band. It was a favorable band to study, too, for the Cheyennes are the very flower of the Plains Indians, and their men are brave and their women clean and chaste.

We would have liked to part with those Indians upon terms of mutual esteem, but it was not fated to happen that way. One snowy evening as we lay in camp on the north fork of the Canadian river between Fort Supply and Fort Reno, a courier overtook us with a dispatch. We were then about two days' march from the agency that we were bound for. The dispatch directed our commanding officer to stop whenever the order reached him and disarm the Indians, and take away their war ponies. It seems that the agent of the Cheyennes in Indian Territory had protested against this band being sent down armed from the North, and as a result, the order to disarm them had probably been issued by the War Department, at the request of the Department of the Interior. It was doubtless a matter of clerks and copying, and endorsements, and a functionary's nod, and a signature hastily scrawled in Washington, and that was all. But to us it was a different business, with a mighty serious difference. To disarm any Indian is like handcuffing him, for it leaves him helpless to defend himself, and deprives him of the only means of support that is natural to him, which is hunting. What made this case harder — ten times harder for us if not for them — was that we knew that both the guns and the ponies that belonged to these Cheyennes had been earned by them in the government service, and distinctly given to them on different occasions as the reward of courage and fidelity. So when Major Mauck got the message he understood that a serious thing had happened to him. Amos Chapman, the interpreter, had got leave to go over to Fort Supply to spend the night and join us again in the morning. Mauck sent for him to come back immediately.

Now Chapman was a remarkable man. He had served under Sheridan, McKenzie, Custer and other Indian fighters, and had lost a leg in a battle with Indians. Through years of border warfare he had been distinguished for his courage, but when he got Mauck's message he refused to come. If those Cheyennes were going to be disarmed, he said for his part he wasn't in it. It would simply be a useless slaughter, and the man who acted as go between in such a business would be the first man killed. Fifty dollars a month and a ration, he said, afforded him a very inadequate inducement to mix himself up in any such piece of business. His mind was pellucid on that point, and it seemed fixed, and no interpreter came to camp that night.

But Chapman's reputation for courage was well founded. Courage was in him which had entered into his conduct too long to let him shirk any hazardous job that seemed legitimately his. It was true that his life was worth more to him than $50 and a ration a month, but there was that inside of him, that would not allow him to stay in a post when he knew there was fight in prospect fifteen miles off.

Mauck and I slept together that night, and we took to bed with us the secret that no one else knew, that there would probably be a bloody fight next day. As we lay there and talked about it all, we felt as I suppose a man feels who has a duel arranged for the next morning. We were glad enough when the night was over and Amos Chapman with his wooden leg, gave the lie to his own message by riding into camp in the gray of the morning on his mule.

The Indians were encamped a few rods off. Mauck sent word to them to stay in camp, and that he was coming over to talk with them. Presently he and Chapman went over to the largest teepee, where a dozen of the older bucks had assembled. They sat about in council.

90

The proposition was laid before them; was received with true Indian inperturbability, and rejected with dignity and decision. Chapman argued and protested with them a few minutes, until seeing the wrath of the bucks getting hotter, he said to Mauck that if they were going to get away alive they must be about it. So Mauck got up and slowly and quietly moved toward the entrance, with Chapman after him. Not a moment too soon. He had scarcely risen from his place, when a knife slit down the canvass of the teepe from the outside, and a furious young buck sprang through the opening, crying: "Let me kill _____ thief! Let me kill him!" And he would have killed him if Mauck had not moved when he did. But that instant peril passed, the other chiefs restrained the hot head and Mauck and Chapman got back to camp and the protection of the troops.

Then came the execution of that injurious order. We moved up our four troops of dismounted cavalry and ranged them on two sides of a trapezoid, so that they should not fire into one another. The Indians came out of their camp and faced us. Grim looking warriors they were, with their carbines and Winchesters at full cock and the squaws and children behind them with knives and hatchets in their hands. The confronting lines were not thirty yards apart, and as we stood there looking into their eyes, flashing with resentment, not the less deep because it was reasonable, our officers at least felt that their time had come, for every lieutenant of us was as well known to every Indian as daily intercourse for six weeks could make him, and we all knew that if a shot was fired an officer would be the first victim.

But though the Cheyennes were grim, they were not so grim as little Mauck. Straight he stood at the front of his line, the natural target of every Indian there. For Indians, you know, like all savages, are concrete in their feelings, and when they have been injured, or are threatened with an injury, they do not generalize about their misfortunates but form definite opinions as to who has done them harm. These Cheyennes were satisfied that Mauck intended to rob them of their arms and their ponies for his personal profit and use, and their feelings toward him were such as such a conviction would warrant. But it was all the same to Mauck. He had not made the situation, and he could not dodge it.

A Cheyenne warrior named Iron Shirt was the most violent. He made a speech to the soldiers, in which he reminded them that the ponies it was proposed to take away from the Indians had formerly belonged to the Nez Perce, against whom the Cheyennes had fought as government scouts, and had received the captured ponies from the commanding general as a reward for their services. In the same way he said the Cheyenne's arms had been given to them by Gen. Custer for similar services in another Indian war, and they had had the assurance of General Sheridan that they would keep them. These features of the situation being adequately dwelt upon, the Indians pulled out from the little packages they wore around their necks their discharges as government scouts, showing how some had been discharged as corporals and sergeants, and all with good "character." These they tore to pieces, saying that they were "lying papers," and that all white men were liars; and declaring that although they were outnumbered four to one, that that was a good day to die, and that they would die right there. Some of the Indian boys got frightened and slipped away back to camp and scrambled up on their ponies with intent to make off, but the women howled to them and they jumped off, and came back with their knives in their hands, to take their stand with the rest.

For three hours the Indians raged at bay, and Mauck and his command stood almost in silence and waited for whatever might come. At last a half-breed named George Bent,

91

whose father was a white man, and in whom the Indian feelings took a modified force, came boldly forward, his cheeks pale, expecting every moment to be shot in the back, and so agitated by the prospect that the perspiration, that cold day, rolled down his face. He laid his rifle in silence on the ground at Mauck's feet. His family followed him. That turned the scale. The old chief came forward next, and made a heartbroken protest against what he called the treachery and dishonesty of the whites. He was entrapped, he said, and could not help himself, so he laid down his gun. And so, one after another, they gave up their arms. Only three or four of their ponies were taken from them. The rest they absolutely needed and were allowed to keep. That was all there was of it. How long it took no one noticed at the time, but I was astonished when it was all over to find that it was 3 o'clock in the afternoon. The Indians never doubted for a moment that Mauck had robbed them for his individual gain. Full of hatred and distrust of white men and their promises, they were driven on to the reservation, where, of course they turned their energies to raising horses, selling skins, and earning money however they could, with which to buy more guns.

And so there was no fight; no report of the matter was ever made to the War Department, and of course, Mauck never got credit for winning a hard battle without striking a blow. I doubt if half a dozen officers of the army, outside of the eight that were there, even so much as heard the story of those hours of suspense, far more trying than any fight."

"Well, captain," asked the report, "if the fight that you looked for had come off, would the squaws and children have been killed?"

I don't see what could have prevented it. Certainly those who were not disabled would have made themselves very active. If I had been shot through the legs I suppose some old squaw would have run in and ripped me up with a knife. In a fight in '67 a trumpeter was disabled and the squaws caught him and skinned him alive. Still soldiers dislike to kill squaws. I have known them to take care of Indian babies, whose mothers were killed, for days together, and keep them alive on sugar until they got into camp.

1929

General Parker's short sketch of the Geronimo Campaign given at the 1928 meeting was expanded into a full paper delivered at the session at the Army Navy Club in 1929. There were 44 Companions and 16 guests present.

The *Proceedings* for that year printed the following addresses: "The Geronimo Campaign," by Brigadier General James Parker; "The Surrender of Geronimo," by Lieutenant Charles B. Gatewood, compiled by Major C. B. Gatewood, son of Lieutenant Gatewood, and with editing and biographical sketch of Lieutenant Gatewood by General Godfrey, the whole read by Major Ahern; "Some Unwritten Incidents Of The Geronimo Campaign," by Lieutenant Thomas J. Clay; and "A Plea For Cooperation," by Colonel Samuel C. Vestal, in which he pleaded the cause for contributions to the archives of the Historical Section, Army War College.

Those papers and remarks heard at this dinner meeting which were not printed include the "humorous anecdotes by [Mr. Will C. Barnes] of his boyhood experiences in Indian Wars," General Charles King decrying "the efforts of some historians to represent William F. Cody (Buffalo Bill), merely as a 'showman' [citing] several incidents which portrayed his true character as a scout and soldier and the distinguished service he rendered to the Army in its campaign against the Indians," and a few remarks by General Godfrey on the Black Hills march citing "the incident which probably caused the separation of the two Commands." It is unfortunate all these choice remarks and reminiscences were not captured in print in the *Proceedings* for historians of today to ponder and interpret.

The Geronimo Campaign

By Brig. Gen. James Parker

At the time of the Geronimo outbreak I was stationed at Fort Apache, Ariz., commanding Troop K, 4th Cavalry, and performing the duties of Post Quartermaster and Commissary. On May 17, 1885, Geronimo's band, camped near the Post, went on the war path and we started in pursuit, Troops A and K, 4th Cavalry, Captain Allen Smith in command. On May 22, following the trail of the hostiles, we arrived at Devil's Creek, a deep canyon, and camped. An hour afterwards, Captain Smith being absent bathing, we were attacked by the hostiles. I took command and we ascended the heights, drove off the Indians and captured their camp.

On or about June 3rd, I relinquished command of my troop, having been ordered back to Fort Apache to perform my duties as Quartermaster. In January, 1886, I reported to Fort Huachuca as Adjutant of the 4th Cavalry.

Early in June, 1886, General Miles arrived at Fort Huachuca. To get an idea of the country he and I climbed to the summit of El Moro mountain near the post. I have never been slow at suggestions and I took this opportunity to ask General Miles if I could make one. "I have recently come from Fort Apache where the Chiricahuas not with Geronimo are located," I said. "Whenever there is news of a raid, the Chiricahuas, in order not to become involved in the fighting, go into the post and are quartered in the quartermaster corral. I would suggest a false report of a raid be spread and when the Indians are in the corral, they be surrounded by the troops, disarmed, taken to the railroad and shipped east as prisoners of war. Geronimo's band in the field will then be isolated, will no longer receive aid and comfort, as heretofore, and will surrender." "Why that would be treachery," said the General. "I could never do that." "Treachery or not," I replied, "it will end the war and save hundreds of lives of innocent citizens."

The General appeared to regard the proposition with disfavor. But nevertheless it was only a few weeks later when the Chiricahuas at Fort Apache, being assembled to receive rations, were surrounded by troops, disarmed and sent by railroad to Florida. This was in August. In September, Miles, in his negotiations with Geronimo, used this fact to bring about the surrender.

Descending from El Moro we climbed another mountain, and at the end of that day we had ascended five peaks. This gives an idea of Miles' physical energy.

In June, 1886, I resigned the adjutancy of the 4th Cavalry and asked to be sent to a troop. Accordingly, I was assigned to H troop, 4th Cavalry, at Cloverdale, Ariz., which I reached 4 days later after a march of over 100 miles. I had two men with me. At Cloverdale, an abandoned ranch, I found Lieut. Abiel L. Smith whom I relieved of the command of H troop. Also at the camp was a company of the 8th Infantry, Capt. John F. Stretch, 1st Lieut. James Pettit and 2nd Lieut. R. L. Bullard.

Thirty-six hours after I got there, there arrived at the camp two Americans, Anderson and Jones, fine looking frontiersmen. It appeared that their profession was smuggling, carrying tobacco and other wares into Mexico. They informed us that they had picked up a trail of hostiles in Guadalupe Canyon.

95

I hastened to mount my troop and start in pursuit. Anderson and Jones led me to a point in Guadalupe Canyon where the Indians had killed a cow and had camped for several days. It was apparent that they had been there when I passed two days before. Hidden among some rocks they had not seen me, or it would have fared hard with my party.

The trail led north, passing over the crests of the mountains. Being obliged, on account of the roughness of the trail to often dismount and lead our horses, we made that day only 20 miles.

The next day we made 30 miles. At night my horses having had no water we were obliged to leave the trail and descend from the mountain to the plain, where we camped at Gray's Ranch. It was very hot and my horses had suffered greatly.

The next morning Jones and Anderson, who I found could follow a trail like the most expert Indians, proposed that instead of going back to where we had left the trail, we should try to cut it further north, at Skeleton Canyon. Adopting their advice, after a march of 16 miles, and having reached the top of the divide, we struck the Indian trail fresh, the horses' droppings still smoking. Following it rapidly, the trail turned and went south. Pursuing it some distance it entered a region strewn with large boulders and rocks where our horses could not be led except with great difficulty and delay.

As the Indians were hampered by their animals I felt sure that on foot I could overtake them. Dismounting my troop we left the horses and dashed up through the rocks. But our efforts were fruitless. After a march of 7 miles on foot we had not overtaken the Indians. The heat was intense though and the men exhausted by their efforts were in great want of water. Some of the soldiers cut the pulp out of the cactus and chewed it, but this gave little relief. I was obliged to conduct them back to their horses. Thus the Indians had got several hours' start. We made this day 32 miles, 14 miles on foot. The command was very tired.

As the Indians had evidently seen us coming up Skeleton Canyon, had taken the alarm and were fleeing back to Mexico, it seemed unlikely we would be able to overtake them. In the next 3 days we made through appallingly rough country, seventy-seven miles. Near Cajon Bonito, a remarkable and beautiful canyon descending into Mexico, the trail was finally obliterated by a heavy downpour of rain.

July 2nd we returned to Cloverdale when I forwarded my report of the scout to the District Commander, Colonel Beaumont, at Fort Bowie. The substance of this report having been telegraphed to General Miles at Albuquerque, he at once ordered that I proceed into Mexico with a command "on the trail of the hostiles."

The treaty with Mexico providing for crossing the boundary says: "It is agreed that the Regular Federal Troops of the two Republics may reciprocally cross the boundary line when they are in close pursuit of a band of savage Indians." "The pursuing force shall return to its own country as soon as it has fought the Indians or lost the trail." While the conditions in my case were not exactly those mentioned in the treaty it was evident to me that General Miles, a man of resources, thought he could stretch them to justify my expedition. Only a First Lieutenant, I felt flattered at being selected for the command.

After some delay due to the late arrival of pack mules and of scouts, I started for Mexico July 24th, 1886. The expedition consisted of thirty cavalrymen, twelve infantrymen, eleven packers, forty pack mules, two wagons with teamsters, interpreter Montoya, and the scouts; Hank Frost and fifteen Yaqui Indians. The officers with me, a more congenial, efficient lot I never saw, were First Lieutenant W. B. Banister, Surgeon; Second Lieutenant W. T. Richardson, 8th Infantry, in charge of the cavalry; and Second Lieutenant R. L. Bullard, 10th

Infantry, quartermaster and commissary.

My orders were to "take up the trail of six hostiles you were pursuing, follow it into old Mexico, and try to intercept or overtake, destroy or capture them." Of course, it was understood that in attempting this I might have to fight the main body of the hostiles. I carried forty days' rations. I was further ordered to communicate, if practicable, with Captain Lawton, whose expedition was still in Mexico in which case, the order stated, we might "be of mutual assistance."

At Carretas a courier from Cloverdale reached me with orders for me to halt my column and await the arrival of Lieutenant C. B. Gatewood, 6th Cavalry, with a party consisting of interpreter Wratten and two Indians. On July 21st Gatewood arrived. He showed me his papers. One was a letter from General Miles to Colonel Beaumont, District Commander. In it Miles said "Lieutenant Gatewood with two Indians will pass through your post. The Indians have instructions to go to the hostile camp to carry a communication to the hostiles. * * * It is desirable that they be put on the trail of the six Parker was following, as there are indications that they desired to surrender! You may hold that command of Parker's near the line for further service or until the disposition of the hostiles can be ascertained."

The orders from Beaumont stated: "the District Commander directed that you furnish Lieutenant Gatewood with a sufficient escort to enable him to perform the duties he is intrusted with. The escort need only be large enough for the protection of Lieutenant Gatewood and his Indians against Mexicans and hostiles. The District Commander further directs that you keep your command in readiness for further orders, either at Carretas or at Cloverdale as you may judge best."

"But," said I to Gatewood, "this trail is all a myth — I haven't seen any trail of hostile Indians since July 1st, three weeks ago, when it was washed out by the rains."

Gatewood seemed startled by the statement. "Well," he said, after some reflection, "if that is so I will go back and report there is no trail."

"Not at all," said I, "if General Miles desires that you be put on a trail I will find one and put you on it. In any case I can take you with me and hunt up Lawton and he surely will be able to find a hostile trail — he is probably on one now."

Gatewood dissented. He pleaded he was sick and was not in fit condition to travel. "Very well," said I, "we will wait here until you are better." Gatewood, with some unwillingness, assented. He said that in any case he would require an escort of at least twenty-five or thirty mounted men.

After reflection I determined to escort Gatewood with my entire command. I accordingly wrote the District Commander as follows: "* * * To furnish an escort of this size, twenty-five or thirty men, will take half of my command * * * The small remnant of this column remaining after Lieutenant Gatewood's escort is deducted would possess no efficiency and be of no use. I have therefore determined to take along the entire outfit. While this determination conflicts with the orders I have received I believe it is the only course open to me consistent with the interests of the service and the ends desired by the Department Commander."

I have taken pains to go into this matter at length for as a result of this decision of mine the way was opened for the negotiations with and final surrender of Geronimo.

After Gatewood's arrival we remained in Carretas for six days, at the end of which time he announced that he was sufficiently recovered to proceed.

The trail over the divide led down into the valley of the Bavispe River, a branch of the

Yaqui River.

Bavispe Valley, which contained the little towns of Bavispe, Baceras, and Huachiners, is entirely separated from the rest of the world by high mountains. Not a wheeled vehicle had ever been seen there.

Marching for three days through the Valley of Bavispe, on July 30th we left the river and travelled southwest over a high rolling plateau camping at some water holes.

Sixty miles from Bavispe we arrived July 3rd at Bacadehuachi, a curious looking town situated on a rock at the bay of some remarkable mountains, where we heard for the first time of Lawton's whereabouts. They told us he was south of Nacori on the Yaqui or Haros River. That he had been there some days, and was vainly searching for an Indian trail. That the Indians were in hiding and had committed no depredations for some weeks. I met there a party of peons gathering acorns in the mountains — it was one of their principal foods.

Marching south thirty miles down the Nacori River we arrived August 3rd at Lawton's camp on the Haros or Yaqui River. This river which falls into the Gulf of California near Guaymas, is here a broad, swift stream, unfordable when we reached it.

Before arriving at Lawton's camp we came upon a party of Lawton's scouts under Assistant Surgeon Leonard Wood, working on a raft which they were building with a view to crossing the river in order to scout southward towards Sahuaripa. Wood, who seemed in excellent spirits, was in the river tying together some palm tree trunks which barely floated. The crossing looked to me like a somewhat hazardous proposition.

At the camp I found Captain Lawton, Lieutenants R. A. Brown, Walsh and A. L. Smith, (all of these officers have since distinguished themselves — Walsh and Brown as Brigadier Generals in the World War, and Smith as Assistant Quartermaster General.) I found Lawton in a pessimistic mood. He had been then in the field since May 5th, three months, searching vainly to overtake Geronimo in the immense area of Northern Mexico, wild and rugged in the extreme, difficult to traverse. As a result of his exertions his command was pretty nearly used up — all the officers except Wood were suffering from minor ailments (Wood himself had been sick). The weather was very hot with rains every day or night. Many of the men were sick. For several weeks he had lost touch with the hostiles, who had disappeared — he was sending Wood and the scouts south of the Haros River towards Sahuaripa to ascertain if they could be located in that direction.

When told about Gatewood, Lawton objected strongly to taking him with his command. "I get my orders from President Cleveland direct," he said. "I am ordered to hunt Geronimo down and kill him. I cannot treat with him." I said, "Lawton, you know as well as I do, that now General Miles has made up his mind to open negotiations for Geronimo's surrender, that that is the way he will be brought in. As for finding him and killing him, it is as difficult to find him in this immense mass of mountains as to find a needle in a hay stack." I said further, "if I keep Gatewood with me, I may in the end effect the surrender of Geronimo. But my scouts are worthless, while yours are good; and furthermore you are liberally supplied with transportation, money, guides and spies — your command is larger and your facilities are much superior — I, myself, am nearly out of rations. And again if there is any honor to be gained from this surrender you, after all you have done, deserve it."

I stayed three days with Lawton. Before I left him he agreed to take with him Gatewood and his Indians. "But," he said, "if I find Geronimo I will attack him — I refuse to have anything to do with this plan to treat with him — if Gatewood wants to treat with him he can do it on his own hook." "Oh, nonsense, Lawton," I said.

I must admit that my action in turning over Gatewood to Lawton was not approved by my officers Banister, Bullard and Richardson. They did not share my great admiration for him and they thought I was doing myself an injustice by depriving myself of this opportunity. I think, however, that in doing as I did I was acting in the best interests of the service. My action quickly bore fruit.

At Lawton's suggestion I determined to scout eastward from Nacori across the Sierra Madre towards Casas Grandes where it was thought by him the hostiles might have taken refuge. Accordingly, leaving Gatewood with Lawton, August 6th, we arrived August 7th, at a point east of Nacori looking down on the enormous canyons and broken country which we were to traverse.

But we were not destined to cross the mysterious country of tremendous ravines that we looked down upon from the end of this valley. News came that evening by courier from Lawton that the hostiles had appeared in the West near Ures. So sending word to Lawton that I would march to cooperate with him, we set out the next morning for Bacadehuachi and Huepare which we reached August 11th.

The next day there arrived in Camp Lieutenant Spencer of the Engineer Corps and we were gladdened by receiving letters from home, the first we had gotten for a month. Lieutenant Spencer also gave us the interesting news that we had at Carretas barely escaped attack or capture by a large force of Mexican militia from the State of Chihuahua which had arrived at our camp there the day after we had abandoned it and after we had crossed over the pass into the State of Sonora, whither, being state troops they could not follow us.

The next day I sent Lieutenant Richardson with ten men and twenty pack mules to Carretas to meet the wagons with rations at that point and transport the rations to my command.

August 16th, Lawton's command arrived at our camp at Huepare. Lawton confirmed the news received by courier that the hostiles had been located to the west, and asked me to move north through the valley of the Bavispe keeping on the east of the Terras mountains while he moved on their west side. He still expressed great reluctance at taking along Gatewood and his Indians. The next day he left for Douto, to pursue the hostiles.

On August 18th when near Nacosari, Lawton wrote me saying the hostiles had passed Nacosari going north, killing and plundering, and that some of them came down a hill near Fronteras calling for Jose Maria, a guide of Lawton's, and saying they wanted to surrender. Lawton asked me to move towards Fronteras keeping southeast. This letter did not reach me until too late to comply with it, as I had passed the border when I received it.

Making short marches we moved north through the difficult country between Bavispe and San Bernardino Ranch, on the American border.

August 25th, I proceeded to my old camp at Cloverdale. September 1st, in accordance with instructions from Colonel Beaumont, I moved my troop eight miles to a camp at Cottonwood Springs on the west side of the mountains. From several sources we had heard that Geronimo had surrendered and was with Lawton's command, north of San Bernardino. So taking Bannister, Bullard and an orderly with me I started out to find him.

Riding down Cottonwood Canyon toward the plain we saw at a distance a herd of horses, which we believed without doubt to be Lawton's. Presently we neared a place where the stream entered a ravine on the edge of the plain. Here to my great surprise, Geronimo with whom I was well acquainted, passed, riding a white mule and, apparently ignoring our presence. Going a little further we entered the ravine or more properly speaking, canyon. It had been selected by the Indians as their camp and it was with feelings of astonishment and some trepidation that we saw the bucks, seated up on the walls of the canyon, with their rifles in their hands, eyeing us grimly.

Nevertheless affecting to not notice them we passed through the canyon to the further end. Looking out over the plain we saw no signs of Lawton's camp, so we retraced our steps through the canyon again. It was only when we emerged that we breathed freely.

Several miles to the northward we found Lawton with his men, and I had a long conversation with him in which he described the situation. What it was can best be judged by a recent typewritten statement sent me two weeks ago by Brig. Gen. Abiel Smith, who at that time was with Lawton's column. The correctness of Smith's account is vouched for by General R. D. Walsh, who also was with Lawton. It also agrees generally with Lawton's and Gatewood's official reports which I have in my possession.

"The first intimation that Lawton had a desire on the part of the hostile Indians to surrender, came from Wilder, who interviewed two squaws from Geronimo's band that came into the town where Wilder was encamped.

"When Lawton received this information he directed Gatewood, with his two friendly Indians that Miles had sent down from the reservation in Arizona, along with R. A. Brown and his U.S. Indian Scouts and a few regular soldiers, to push ahead on the trail, so that the two Indian Messengers from Miles could join the hostiles. This was done and after traveling about thirty-five miles Gatewood and Brown went into camp on the Bavispe River. The two Miles Indians had by this time joined the hostiles.

"The next morning one of the Indian Messengers returned to where Gatewood and Brown were encamped and asked Gatewood to go out a short distance and meet representatives of Geronimo's band for a talk. This Gatewood did with an interpreter and one or two others of his party. During the talk Geronimo, himself, appeared. He told Gatewood that they would not come in as Miles' Indians had requested. Gatewood, after informing Geronimo that he could not add anything to what the Miles messenger had brought them, returned to his camp where Brown and the rest of his party were.

"By this time Lawton with one officer, A. L. Smith, and a couple of civilian guides, arrived at the camp. Gatewood reported the result of his visit and interview with the hostiles and announced his mission was ended and he would report back to Miles.

"Lawton decided that the party should remain where they were on the Bavispe River with the hope that the hostiles would again seek an interview.

"The main part of Lawton's command with the supplies were back on the trail thirty-five or forty miles at this time. Lawton directed one of the officers, A. L. Smith, with him to go back and hurry forward a few mules loaded with food.

"The next morning a request from Geronimo came into the camp for Lawton, himself, to come out and meet him. Lawton went out and was greeted most affectionately and effusively by Geronimo. This time the principal topic of conversation seemed to concern the question of food. Lawton told Geronimo that they had little or nothing with them in the advance camp, but that one of his officers had gone back to hurry forward rations. Geronimo then said when the food came in he would come back and have a talk with Lawton.

"The following day early in the morning, six pack mules with supplies arrived, and almost at the same time Geronimo and Natchez, and a couple of his warriors joined Lawton in camp.

"After eating a hearty meal they all sat around, A. L. Smith was present, and listened to the terms on which Geronimo was willing to surrender. Lawton told Geronimo that he could not grant him any terms, but would take down his demands and forward to General Miles, and if not accepted by Miles, would give Geronimo twenty-four hours' notice to get away.

"It was further agreed that Geronimo's band should be supplied with rations and the two commands should travel back to the U.S. border together.

"After arriving on the border, Lawton communicated by heliograph with Miles. At first, Miles declined to come down and listen to any terms. Lawton was informed that he should not bring the Indians back to the United States unless he had hostages; and to take possession of the bodies of Natchez and Geronimo by any means whatever, and to hold them beyond any possibility of escape.

"Later, on the same date, Miles decided to come down to Skeleton Canyon where the Indians were and to listen to what Geronimo had to say.

"He came on September 3rd, and after a conference in the ambulance with only Geronimo, Natchez and an interpreter and himself present, Miles announced that Natchez and Geronimo should return with him in the ambulance that day to Fort Bowie, and that the other hostiles would follow the next day into the Post with the troops.

"Immediately after the conference Natchez came directly to my tent from the ambulance and informed me, as he stated, that the war was over and that he and Geronimo would go with Miles."

As Smith says, on the afternoon of September 3rd, General Miles arrived at Lawton's Camp — the hostiles receiving the terms of surrender from his lips, were reassured, laid down their arms and surrendered. What these terms were, no one knew. The Indians taken to Bowie station, were placed aboard a train and sent to Florida, there to rejoin the rest of their tribe which had previously been deported. Later the tribe was taken to Alabama, and still later to Fort Sill, Indian Territory.

It must be conceded that Geronimo, who had engendered this causeless outbreak, which had cost the country millions of dollars and unnumbered lives of peaceful settlers foully murdered, received but little punishment for his crimes. Geronimo differed from a common murderer, only by the fact that he was an Indian and an assassin on a large scale.

It is not improbable that the authorities at Washington were in favor of punishing Geronimo and his men for their crimes. There was a story widely circulated at the time that after the Indians had been put on the train at Fort Bowie, and as the train was about to start, a telegram from Washington was handed to Captain Wm. A. Thompson, 4th Cavalry, then acting as Miles' Adjutant General, and that Thompson after reading the telegram was then in his pocket. The train departed, and the telegram was then given to General Miles. Did the Government in this telegram disapprove of General Miles' disposition of the Indians? And did they later reverse their decision?

In my opinion one of the principal reasons that they surrendered was that they knew by this time that the rest of the tribe had been removed to Florida. Geronimo's small band, then, was isolated, they no longer had any friends or relatives in that country to give them aid and comfort. The hope of gaining recruits was gone. They could not expect again, as often before, to be restored to their reservation.

September 30th, I returned with my troop to Fort Huachuca, having marched, since June 18th, over eleven hundred miles. I felt chagrined that in reports and orders my services had received so little recognition. But I was proud to feel I had been nevertheless a factor in the success of the campaign. On May 22, 1885, at Devil's Creek, I had commanded and beaten the enemy in the only serious fight during the campaign. In May, 1886, I had suggested to the Department Commander the removal of the Chiricahua tribe to the Eastern States, which suggestion, afterwards acted upon, proved the key to the situation. On June 28, 1886, I had intercepted and driven back into Mexico a party of hostiles. On July 27, 1886, being in command of an important expedition, I had taken the responsibility of disregarding my orders, marching two hundred miles away from my post in order to make the mission of General Miles to the hostiles a success. On September 2, 1886, I again failed to obey an order which would, if carried out, have made the negotiations with Geronimo for his surrender fruitless.

In conclusion, what Lawton and Gatewood accomplished was a remarkable achievement, and both of these officers should be awarded, if possible, posthumously, a medal for distinguished service.

Curiously enough the only actor in this drama who received substantial reward was Leonard Wood. He received a Congressional Medal of Honor for "distinguished gallantry" in this campaign. The award of this medal has been the subject of considerable discussion.

A photograph of Geronimo and Natchez, now in the pictorial division of the historical section of the General Staff, bears an inscription written by Britton Davis, substantially as follows: "Gatewood deserves all the credit for capturing Geronimo — Lawton never saw Geronimo until after the surrender." This is a sample of some of the fables told about this campaign. How Britton Davis picked up this astonishing information, I do not know — at the time of the surrender he was out of the service, employed at the Corralitos Cattle ranch in Mexico, over 100 miles distance.

It is not necessary for me to say more than that this statement is confuted by the story of the pursuit and capture as Smith and I have given it, and as related in the printed reports not only of Lawton but also of Gatewood. A. L. Smith, commenting on this statement of Britton Davis, told me Lawton had, in fact, when on the march, many interviews with Geronimo.

The real credit for the success of this campaign was due to General Miles. He supported Lawton in every way. He deported to Florida the remainder of Geronimo's tribe, and thus deprived Geronimo of a base of operations, and a home. He discovered that to run down and capture Geronimo's band within a reasonable time was not practicable, that it would be better and save more lives of citizens to treat with him. He sent into Mexico, Gatewood, for that purpose. To obtain Geronimo's surrender he promised to protect him from the civil authorities of Arizona and New Mexico who were keen to arrest and hang him. To carry out this program, in spite of orders from Washington, he shipped Geronimo and his band out of the dangerous territory before the civil authorities had become aware of what was going on. For this he received the censure of the President. But he delivered the southwest and northern Mexico from a century-old thralldom of murder and ravage.

Lieutenant Charles B. Gatewood
6th U.S. Cavalry
And the Surrender of Geronimo

(Compiled by Major C. B. Gatewood, U.S.A., Retired, son of Lieutenant Gatewood)

COPYRIGHTED, 1929, BY MAJOR CHARLES B. GATEWOOD
EDITED BY BRIG. GEN. EDWARD S. GODFREY

EDITOR'S NOTE

"The surrender of Geronimo" is a modest, concise and convincing statement of the last, long, soul-trying pursuit of, and negotiations with, the most vicious and treacherous Indians in our North American Tribes. It denotes the courage, the sense of duty, the loyalty of Lieutenant Gatewood in particular and, in the general sense, reflects the honor and glory of our Army.

Lieutenant Charles B. Gatewood

Charles Baehr Gatewood was born April 6, 1853, of a family whose successive generations have nearly all been represented by one or more members in our Army or Navy ever since the beginning of the Revolutionary War. Appointed to the United States Military Academy from Virginia, he was graduated and commissioned a Second Lieutenant in the Sixth Cavalry in 1877.

From then until the fall of 1886, he was on active duty in Arizona and New Mexico, in command of Indian Scouts and in the field almost constantly throughout most of the Apache campaigns and disturbances of any importance during that period. For some years he was also the acting Indian agent with full powers in charge of the White Mountain Apaches and others with agency headquarters at Fort Apache.

He was with Colonel A. P. Morrow in the critical fighting with Victorio around the Lakes Guzman, Mexico, in the fall of 1879, and was specially commended by that officer. During the remainder of that year and in 1880, he and his Scouts took an active part in several of the major engagements, and many of the lesser ones, with Victorio's forces, including the bitter fight under Captain C. B. McLellan in rescuing Captain Carroll and his troops of the Ninth Cavalry from the clutches of Victorio. He was a member of General Crook's historic expedition of 1883 into the unknown recesses of the Sierra Madre mountains of Mexico; and he initiated the surprise attack on the camps of the Chiricahua chiefs, Bonito and Chatto, defeating the Indians, rescuing a number of captives, and paving the way to the final submission of all the renegade Chiricahuas. For this he was mentioned in War Department orders. He took part in many other campaigns and scouts up to and including the Geronimo campaign; again being mentioned "for bravery in boldly and alone riding into Geronimo's camp of hostile Apache Indians and demanding their surrender."

It was published in General Orders of 1885, Department of Arizona, that "Lieutenant

Gatewood has probably seen more active duty in the field with Indian Scouts than any other officer of his length of service in the Army." His knowledge of the Apache character was deep and practical; his acquaintance with individuals of the different tribes was extensive; and his reputation among them became widespread from the Mescaleros of New Mexico to the Yumas of the Colorado River.

In May, 1885, a minor portion of the Chiricahua tribe, under Natchez, Nana, Geronimo, Mangus and Chihuahua, broke from their reservation near Fort Apache, and started what is usually referred to as the "Geronimo Campaign." With a detachment of his Scouts, Gatewood accompanied Captain Allen Smith's command of two troops of the Fourth Cavalry from Fort Apache, in the first pursuit of the renegades to be organized. At Devil's Park Canyon, New Mexico, the Indians' rear guard suddenly drove back the pursuing Scouts and sharply attacked the troops in bivouac. They were repulsed, but meanwhile the main body of Apaches, who had that day traveled from ninety to one hundred and twenty miles, escaped. During the next twenty-three days, the renegades successfully eluded the many commands sent after them — except for a few minor engagements — then crossed unseen into Mexico and disappeared among the inaccessible canyons of the Sierra Madres.

There was still persistent rumors of hostile Indians in the Black Range and the Mogollons of New Mexico; and General Crook hesitated to follow the main body of renegades south until assured that none was left to commit outrages in his rear. He sent Gatewood with one hundred Scouts to search those mountain ranges thoroughly and expel any hostiles found therein. None was found. Crook then started his operations into Mexico, under Captains Crawford, Wirt Davis and others, which finally resulted in the surrender of Chihuahua and the major portion of the renegades to General Crook and their deportation by him to Florida. Geronimo and Natchez, with twenty-two fighting men, continued the war against General Miles, who meanwhile had relieved Crook.

General Miles had hoped to run down and capture or kill Geronimo and his band, but four months of the most strenuous campaigning with a fourth of the whole Regular Army failed to do this. In July, 1886, General Miles decided to send Gatewood, then at Fort Stanton, New Mexico, with two Chiricahua Scouts to the hostiles with a demand for their surrender.

Gatewood traveled several hundred miles into Mexico, found and entered the hostile camp alone, argued with the Indians for a day and a half, and finally received the promise from Natchez and Geronimo that the entire band would go and meet General Miles in the United States and surrender to him: provided that their lives be spared; that they be sent out of Arizona until the sentiment against them had abated; and that they be reunited with their families. Also, they would keep their arms until the formal surrender; Gatewood would accompany them on their march to the United States; and the command of Captain H. W. Lawton, which was nearby, should protect their flank and rear, at a distance of several miles, however, during the journey. These terms were agreed to between Lawton, Gatewood, Natchez and Geronimo. The program of march, the meeting with General Miles and the surrender to him were carried out as had been agreed, though not without difficulty; and the band was sent to Florida. The subsequent history of these as well as the other Chiricahuas is recorded in Senate Executive Documents No. 117 of 1887, and No. 35 of 1889, and in other publications, all of which will well repay their reading.

After the surrender, Gatewood, presuming upon his ten years of unbroken Indian service and the impairment of his health due thereto, applied for a staff corps appointment, but this was denied, and he was detailed instead as an aide to General Miles. Upon release from four years of this duty, he rejoined his troop at Fort Wingate, New Mexico, and was almost immediately ordered with his regiment to the Dakotas to take part in the Sioux War of 1890-'91. But his health, already undermined, broke down after a few weeks of the severe winter campaign and he was practically an invalid for a year. Recovering sufficiently to report for duty at Fort McKinney, Wyoming, he saw a bit more field service when the military quelled the so-called Cattle War in the Big Horn and Jackson's Hole country. Shortly afterward, he was seriously injured in leading the fight against a fire which destroyed nearly half the post. With health gone and body crippled, he was ordered home for retirement, and died in May, 1896.

His reward, for services that have often been described as unusual, was like that of many another soldier who has given his all that his country might grow and prosper: for himself a free plot of ground in Arlington Cemetery, and to his widow a tardy seventeen dollars a month.

For several years there was an unfortunate controversy as to the bestowal of credit generally in the Geronimo campaign, but in this Gatewood took no part. But finally, he was prevailed upon by the editor of a leading magazine to write his story of the surrender of Geronimo. He died before final arrangements for publication could be made; but his story was written; and his manuscript, just as he wrote it, has been preserved all these years. Proofs of every essential statement contained therein have been painstakingly collected and assembled, and they are now complete. General Lawton, himself, gave to Gatewood the credit for having effected the surrender of Geronimo.

Lieutenant Gatewood's narrative follows:

The Surrender of Geronimo*

By Lieutenant Charles B. Gatewood, *6th U.S. Cavalry*

I

In July, 1886, General Miles, after an interview with some of the friendly Chiricahuas at Fort Apache, Arizona, determined to send two of them, Kayitah and Martine, with myself to the hostiles under Natchez and Geronimo, with a message demanding their surrender and promising removal to Florida with their families, where they would await final disposition by the President. General Miles gave me written authority to call upon any officer commanding United States troops, except those of a few small columns operating in Mexico, for whatever help was needed. And, to prevent my possible capture as a hostage, he particularly warned me not to go near the hostiles with less than twenty-five soldiers as an escort. He ordered the soldiers to be furnished me by the commanding officer of Fort Bowie.

Our party was organized at Fort Bowie, Arizona: the two Indians; George Wratten, interpreter; Frank Houston, packer, and myself. Later, "Old Tex" Whaley, a rancher, was hired as courier. We were furnished with the necessary riding and pack mules; but upon mention of our twenty-five soldiers, the commanding officer showed so little desire to part with so large a portion of his command that we forbore to insist. Whereupon he seemed much relieved and promised cordially that my escort should be supplied from the command of Captain Stretch, south of us at Cloverdale near the Mexican line.

We set out, and in three days arrived at Cloverdale. There we found that a company of infantry at very reduced strength, ten broken-down horses and a six-mule team comprised the whole outfit. Captain Stretch having been my instructor at West Point, it did not seem right that I should rob him of his whole command. Instead, we merely accepted his invitation to dinner, and then journeyed on into Mexico.

Soon after crossing the line, we fell in with a troop of the Fourth Cavalry under Lieutenant James Parker, with Infantry detachments under Lieutenants Richardson and Bullard, a total of some thirty to forty men — again too few to furnish my escort without disrupting the command. We went on together to Carretas, Mexico, and, as Parker had no news of the hostiles, I waited there five days with him, for news and to recuperate from old injuries revived by the ride from Bowie.

I decided to get in touch with the command of Captain Lawton, who had excellent facilities for gathering information, in the hope that he knew where the hostiles were. We started out, accompanied by Parker's command, and on August 3rd arrived in Lawton's camp on the Arros River, high up in the Sierra Madre mountains, some two hundred and fifty miles by trail below the border. Lawton had no information of the hostiles' whereabouts, nor any news of them within two weeks. Having no escort — which I should of course have taken from Bowie — I put myself under Lawton's orders, with the distinct understanding, however, that when circumstances permitted I should be allowed to execute my mission. Parker with his command returned north.

---

* Copy slightly condensed from the original manuscripts and notes.

While on the Arros River, news came that the hostiles were far to the northwest. We moved in that direction, and about the middle of August learned that Geronimo's party was near Fronteras, Mexico, making some overtures to the Mexicans on the subject of surrender. My little party, with an escort of six men that Lawton gave me, left the command about two o'clock that morning and at night camped near Fronteras, having marched about eighty miles.

The next morning at Fronteras, we learned that two squaws from the hostile camp had been there with offers of peace to the Mexicans, and had departed, going east, with three extra ponies well laden with food and mescal, the strong drink of Mexico. Lieutenant Wilder, of our Army, had talked with them in regard to their surrendering.

II

In the meantime, the Prefect of the district had secretly brought about two hundred Mexican soldiers into Fronteras and was planning to entice the Apaches there, get them drunk, and then kill all the men and enslave all the women and children. Geronimo told me later that never for a moment had he intended surrendering to the Mexicans, but wished merely to deceive them for a while so that his band could rest, buy supplies and have a good drunk. The Prefect did not suspect that; and he was much annoyed at the presence of the American troops and tried to get them to leave; but, since the treaty between the two republics gave them the right to be there, his requests availed him nothing. But he demanded that the Americans should not follow the squaws, with implied threats if we did.

Taking an escort of six or eight men that Wilder gave me from his troop, and Tom Horn and Jose Maria as additional interpreters, I started as though for Lawton's camp, twenty miles or more to the south; but after going about six miles we quickly darted up a convenient arroyo and circled around toward the north, so as to strike the trail of the squaws. We picked it up about six miles east of Fronteras. Then, from time to time, members of the escort were sent back to tell Lawton where the trail was leading.

Slowly and cautiously, with a piece of flour sacking on a stick to the fore as a white flag, we followed the squaws for the next three days, over rough country full of likely places for ambush. By the third day the trail was very fresh; and we found where it joined that of the main body. It entered the head of a narrow canyon, leading down to the Bavispe River about four miles away — a canyon so forbidding that our two Indians, who were ahead, stopped to consider the situation. Hung up in a bush just before us was a pair of faded canvas trousers, which *might* be a signal for us to go forward without fear, and again might *not*. Everybody gave a different opinion of what should be done, and we finally went on all together — an unwise formation — but that canyon proved to be harmless, and then I was sorry I had not been brave and gone ahead.

A few miles farther, we reached and crossed the Bavispe River, near its most northerly sweep where, after flowing north, it makes a wide bend and flows south. Here we made our camp for the night in a cane-brake just under a small, round hill that commanded the surrounding country for half a mile. With a sentinel on the hill, with the two Indians scouting the trail several miles beyond and with the hiding places the cane-brake afforded, we felt fairly safe; though this peace commission business did not at all appeal to us. The white flag was high upon the stalk of a nearby century plant, but we all felt that it took more than any flag to make us bullet proof. As it turned out, Geronimo saw us all the time but never noticed

107

the flag, though he had good field glasses; and he wondered greatly what fool small party it was dogging his footsteps.

About sundown that day Martine returned and reported that the hostiles occupied an exceedingly rocky position high up in the Torres Mountains in the bend of the Bavispe, some four miles from our camp. Both Indians had been there and had delivered General Miles' message; and Geronimo, keeping Kayitah with him, had sent back Martine to say that he would talk with *me* only, and that he was rather offended because I had not come straight into his camp myself. Knowing Geronimo, I had my opinion of that; but Natchez, the real chief if there was any, sent word that we would be safe as long as we started no trouble, and he invited me to come up right away. His influence among the band being greater than any other, I felt much easier; especially since Lawton's Scouts, thirty in number, under Lieutenant R. A. Brown, had arrived in camp, and Lawton, with the rest of his command, was supposed to be near. It was too late to visit the hostiles' camp that night, so we remained in the cane brake.

III

The next morning August 24, 1886, we moved out on the trail with Brown and his detachment. Within a mile of the hostile camp, we met an unarmed Chiricahua with the same message for me that had been delivered the night before. Then, shortly, three armed warriors appeared, with the suggestion from Natchez that his party and mine should meet for a talk in the bend of the river, that Brown and his Scouts should return to our camp, and that any troops that might join him should remain there too. These conditions were complied with. Our little party moved down to the river bottom, after exchanging shots and smoke signals with the hostiles to indicate that all was well.

By squads the hostiles came in, unsaddled and turned out their ponies to graze. Among the last was Geronimo. He laid his rifle down twenty feet away and came and shook hands, said he was glad to see me again, and remarked my apparent bad health, asking what was the matter. Having received my reply, and the tobacco having been passed around — of which I had brought fifteen pounds on my saddle — he took a seat alongside as close as he could get, the revolve bulge under his coat touching my right thigh; then, the others seated in a semi-circle, he announced that the whole party was there to listen to General Miles' message.

It took but a minute to say, "Surrender, and you will be sent with your families to Florida, there to await the decision of the President as to your final disposition. Accept these terms or fight it out to the bitter end."

A silence of weeks seemed to fall on the party. They sat there with never a movement, regarding me intently. I felt the strain. Finally, Geronimo passed a hand across his eyes, then held both hands before him making them tremble and asked me for a drink.

"We have been on a three days' drunk with the liquor the Mexicans sent us from Fronteras," he said. "But our spree passed off without a single fight, as you can see by looking at the men in this circle, all of whom you know. There is much wine and mescal in Fronteras and the Mexicans and Americans are having a good time. We thought perhaps you had brought some with you."

I explained that we had left too hurriedly to bring any liquor, and he seemed satisfied. Then he proceeded to talk business. They would leave the war-path only on condition that they be allowed to returned to their Reservation, re-occupy their farms, be furnished with the

108

usual rations, clothing and farming implements, and be guaranteed exemption from punishment. If I were empowered to grant these modest demands the war could end right there!

I replied that the big chief, General Miles, had told me to say just so much and no more, and it would make matters worse if I exceeded my authority; this would probably be their last chance to surrender, and if the war continued they would eventually all be killed, or if they surrendered later the terms would not be so favorable. This started an argument, and for an hour or two Geronimo narrated at length their many troubles — the frauds and thievery perpetrated by the Indian agents and the many injustices done them generally by the Whites. Then they withdrew to a cane-brake nearby and held a private conference for an hour or more.

When their caucus had adjourned it was noon, so we all had a bite to eat. After lunch we reassembled. Geronimo announced that they were willing to cede all of the Southwest except their Reservation, but that to expect them to give up *everything,* and to a nation of *intruders,* was *too* much; they would move back on the little land they needed, or they would fight until the last one of them was dead. "Take us to the Reservation — or *FIGHT!*" was his ultimatum as he looked me in the eye.

I couldn't take him to the Reservation; I couldn't fight; neither could I run, nor yet feel comfortable.

IV

But Natchez, who had done little talking, here intervened to say that, whether they continued the war or not, my party would be safe as long as we started no trouble. We had come as friends, he said, and would be allowed to depart in peace.

His words greatly reassured me, as well as gave me the opportunity to tell them that the rest of their people on the Reservation, between three and four hundred, the mother and daughter of Natchez among them, were being removed to Florida; and therefore if they went back to the Reservation it would mean living among their enemies, the other Apaches. This piece of news was an unexpected blow. Geronimo asked me sternly if it were true or if it were only a ruse to get them into the clutches of the White Man. I convinced him that it was true. This put an entirely new face on the matter; they went back to the cane-brake for another confidential session.

For an hour they talked together, then reassembled. Geronimo announced that, although they would continue the war, they wished to discuss the matter further, and if they could find a beef for a barbecue they would talk all night. But a search of the neighborhood revealed no beef, and, as they did not see how they could hold a night conference without the barbecue, I was greatly relieved that I did not have to talk all night as well as all day.

After much smoking and general conversation, Geronimo harked back to the main subject. They knew General Crook, he said, and might surrender to him, but they did not know General Miles. "What is his age, his size, the color of hair and eyes; is his voice harsh or agreeable; does he talk much or little, say less or more than he means? Does he look you in the eyes or not? Has he many friends? Do people believe what he says? Do officers and soldiers like him? Has he had experience with other Indians?" These, and many other keen and searching questions did he ask; and finally, "Is he cruel or kind-hearted?"

His questions required a full description of the General in every respect. They all listened

109

intently to my answers. After a pause, Geronimo said, "He must be a good man, since the Great Father sent him from Washington, and he has sent you to us."

Towards sunset I suggested that I return to my camp, where Lawton had arrived that day and had remained at my request. But Geronimo asked me to wait to listen to a request they wanted to make. After some preliminaries, he said, "we want your advice. Consider yourself not a White Man but one of us; remember all that has been said today and tell us what we should do."

As earnestly and emphatically as possible I replied, "Trust General Miles and surrender to him."

They stood around looking very solemn. Then Geronimo said they would hold a council that night, and he would let me know the result the first thing in the morning. But again before I got away, they reopened the subject of getting better terms; and they wanted me to go alone, or with one of them, across country to the nearest American post, to get in touch with General Miles and ask him to modify his terms. They promised that a number of their warriors would guard me from harm on the journey, though I might never see them, and they would all wait nearby to hear what decision I brought them from the General. But I replied that it would be a useless journey; that General Miles had already made up his mind and nothing I could say would make him change it.

Then, after shaking hands all around, my little party started for camp. On the way, Chappo, Geronimo's son, overtook us and, after riding for awhile, in answer to my question said that he had his father's permission to stay close by me that night. But our Scouts and Chappo's people had never been friendly. There was a great chance of his getting a knife in him during the night; and as that would never do I explained the matter to him and bade him return, telling his father why he was sent back. I found later that my action had a favorable effect on the band.

Arrived at our camp. I narrated to Lawton all that had happened that day.

V

The next morning, the pickets passed a call for "Bay-chen-day-sen," my pet name among the Apaches, meaning "Long Nose." With the interpreters, I met Natchez, Geronimo and several of the band some hundreds of yards from camp. Geronimo wanted me to repeat at length my description of General Miles. When I had done so he stated that their whole party, twenty-four men, fourteen women and children, would go and meet the General and surrender to him. They asked that Lawton's command act as a protection to them from other troops during the journey. Other conditions were that they should retain their arms until the formal surrender, that individuals of either party should have the freedom of the other's camp, and that I should march with them and sleep in their camp. These terms were agreed to between us; and then we all entered the camp where, upon explanation of the whole matter to Lawton, he approved the agreement.

The rest of the hostiles moved down near us, General Miles was informed of the situation and a place of meeting designated; and we started for the United States that same day, August 25th.

The next afternoon, we halted to camp, the disappointed Mexican commander from Fronteras suddenly appeared very close, with about two hundred infantry, and created a stampede among our new friends. While Lawton's command remained to parley with the

Mexicans, I fled with the Indians northward for eight or ten miles; then halted to observe developments behind us. Soon a courier arrived saying that Lawton had arranged a meeting between Geronimo and the Mexican commander, so that the latter could assure himself that the Indians really intended to surrender to the Americans.

It was only with great difficulty that we persuaded the Indians to a meeting; they wanted nothing to do with the Mexicans; but finally arrangements were agreed upon. A new camp was established near where we were, and soon the Prefect, with an escort of seven armed men, arrived. Then, Geronimo, with his party, came through the bushes, all heavily armed, very alert and suspicious.

As I introduced Geronimo to the Prefect, the latter shoved his revolver around to the front. Instantly, Geronimo half-drew his, and a most fiendish expression came over his face — the whites of his eyes at the same time turning red. But the Mexican put his hands behind him; Geronimo let his revolver slide back into its holster, and the danger of serious trouble was past.

The Prefect asked Geronimo why he had not surrendered at Fronteras. "Because I did not want to be murdered," retorted the latter.

"Are you going to surrender to the Americans?"

"I am; for I can trust them not to murder me and my people."

"Then I shall go along and see that you *do* surrender."

"No," shouted Geronimo: "*you* are going *south* and *I* am going *north.*"

And so it was; except that a Mexican soldier came with us, and returned eventually to his superior with official notice from General Miles that the much dreaded Chiricahuans had been sent to Florida.

VI

A day or two later — our party had been marching several miles ahead of Lawton's command — we halted early for camp and waited for the pack-train to catch up with our supper rations. But hour after hour went by and no pack-train — nor command. Lawton, who was with us that day, became anxious and went back to hunt them up, leaving Lieutenant T. J. Clay, Surgeon L. Wood and a soldier with us.

Dinner time came and all we had for us four was one small can of condensed milk. Wandering about camp, I saw the squaw of Periquo, brother-in-law of Geronimo, preparing a tasty meal of venison, tortillas and coffee. I entered into conversation with Periquo and presented his squaw with the can of milk; and I must have looked hungrily at the food, for, with much dignity and grace, Periquo invited me to partake. Then, motioning to Clay, Wood and the soldier, he invited them also. We needed no second invitation. The dinner was well cooked and everything was clean; our host gave up his own table-ware for our use and waited on us himself, and his squaw was pleased to see us eat so heartily.

Next morning there was still no pack-train, and we learned it had wandered off many miles on a wrong trail. But our Indian charges again saw to it that we did not go hungry.

We reached Guadalupe Canyon on the boundary line. Some months previously the hostiles had killed three or four troopers of a detachment stationed here. Both parties started to go into camp near the springs which are the only water within several miles when, suddenly, our Indians, who had manifested uneasiness since their arrival, began to mount their ponies and leave camp, women and children going first. Then I learned that some of the command had become inflamed with angry desires for vengeance for the killing of their comrades and were proposing to attack the Indians. Lawton was temporarily absent.

Seeing Geronimo going up the trail, I immediately rode after him; but out of the canyon they all took up a lively trot, and I had to gallop my mule to overtake the old man. The troops having followed slowly without any hostile move, we came down to a walk. After some conversation, Geronimo asked me what I would do if the troops fired upon his people. I replied that I would try to stop it, but, failing that, would run away with him. Natchez, who had joined us, said, "Better stay right with us lest some of our men believe you treacherous and kill you."

I cautioned them to keep the best possible look-out for any of the numerous bodies of troops in that region. We went a few miles farther, and, Lawton, having returned, camped, but spent an uneasy night.

Through all this, as well as previously on several occasions, the Indians had been urging me to run away with them into the mountains near Fort Bowie, to get into communication with General Miles direct. But I knew the General was not at Bowie, and I feared that if I left them to locate him they might easily be attacked by one of our many columns or by the Mexicans and run out of the country; so I argued strongly against their plan.

Our troubles were not over, for the next day there was again some hot headed talk of killing Geronimo. Present conditions were difficult for me, if not impossible; so I told Lawton I wished to join another command, that I had been ordered simply to deliver a message, and had done that and more was not required. He stressed the necessity of my remaining, spoke of the "trouble" we would both be in if the Indians left, and wound up by saying that he would if necessary use force to keep me. I stayed.

VII

About the last of August, we arrived at Skeleton Canyon, Arizona, and General Miles came September 3rd. Geronimo lost no time in being presented; and the General confirmed the terms of surrender. Geronimo turned to me, smiled, and said in Apache, "Good, you told the truth!"

Then he shook hands with General Miles and said that no matter what the others did *he* was going with him.

But in the meantime, Natchez with most of the band was several miles out in the mountains, mourning for his brother who had gone back to Mexico a few days before for a favorite horse and who, he feared, had been killed. Since Natchez was the real chief, and Geronimo only his Secretary of State, his presence was necessary to complete the surrender. At Geronimo's suggestion, I took the interpreters and the two Scouts and accompanied him to Natchez' camp. There I explained to Natchez that the big chief, General Miles, had arrived and that, among the Whites, a family affair like a brother's absence was never allowed to interfere with official matters. He said that, although it was hard for him to come before he knew his brother's fate,he wished to avoid any seeming disrespect to the big chief and therefore would come at once. He gathered his people together, came in and was as much pleased with General Miles as was Geronimo.

General Miles wanted to take the two leaders on ahead with him to Bowie, thus separating them from their band. But they were still very suspicious, or had been up to that time, and it required no little diplomacy to get them to consent, which they finally did. They

112

made the trip in one day — the rest of us taking three. The surrender of Geronimo and his band was complete!

From Bowie the Indians were sent to Florida, after a delay in Texas; and finally were removed to Alabama — for them a grimly suggestive name, for it means, "Here We Rest."

Postscript

Lieutenant Gatewood's narrative, written before 1896, ends here.

All of the Chiricahua tribe, the loyal and peaceful as well as the recalcitrant, were sent to Florida. For a long time, the men were confined separately from their families. Their meager wealth brought from Arizona was soon dissipated, without provision for them to acquire more or to do honest labor. Used to long sustained marches across vast stretches of territory, they were cooped closely in restricted quarters without sufficient natural exercise. Their light and scanty clothing received but few additions, and they suffered from cold and attendant sickness in the damp chill of the Gulf coast winters. In that moist climate, so different from that of Arizona, they readily contracted pulmonary diseases from which in about three years a fourth of them were dead. Misfortune and tragedy fell heaviest upon the little children. If this was just retribution to some, it was injustice for many who had long been peaceful and had helped ably to bring the war to an end. It should be said that those charged with their immediate care did all for their miseries that the means provided would allow.

At length, their condition prompted one or more Congressional investigations which finally secured for them more humane living conditions, and later a removal to Oklahoma. In 1914, some were allowed to return toward their old homes as far as the Mescalero Reservation in New Mexico.

The two faithful Scouts, Martine and Kayitah, without whose services the surrender might not have been accomplished, were sent to Florida with the men they had hunted. In 1927, after waiting forty-one years for any sort of reward or recognition for those services, they were finally granted the small pensions to which their military enlistments had long entitled them.

George Wratten died several years ago, after many years service as interpreter for the exiled Apaches. Frank Huston, at last accounts, was still living, as were several of the old troopers who were temporary members of Gatewood's expedition.

It has required time and labor to obtain separate and independent proofs of all the principal happenings told of in this narrative of Gatewood's — a narrative at variance with many accounts of this same incident that have been published — but finally all such proofs have been assembled complete.

Our Apaches of today are submissive, law-abiding and industrious where once they ruled practically supreme by terrorism and robbery. For three hundred years and more, they defied the advance of civilization and maintained against all comers their arrogant dominance over an immense country. The surrender of that last little band under Chief Natchez (erroneously spoken of as Geronimo's band) extinguished the last flicker of effort on the part of the Apache nation to regain that proud position. Therefore, the so-called "Surrender of Geronimo" was a significant event in the history of our West.

Some Unwritten Incidents Of The Geronimo Campaign

By **Thomas J. Clay,** *Lieutenant, U.S. Army, Retired*

In 1885, I was in command of my company of the 10th Infantry, at the Supply Camp at Langs Ranch, New Mexico; while there I was taken seriously ill with dysentery, and General Crook had me ordered back to my station, Fort Union, New Mexico, for treatment. As soon as I was able to travel, I was given a sick leave, and went home to Kentucky where I remained for several months before I reported back to duty.

I had not fully regained my health, but volunteered for duty with Lawton's command, then somewhere in Mexico. I was ordered to report to General Miles at Willcox, Arizona, and went with him to Nogales, Arizona, where he had a conference with Governor Torres, then governor of Sonora, Mexico. The governor gave me letters to the Prefecto's of several districts through which we might have to pass.

General Miles ordered me to proceed to Fort Huachuca, and there take command of a detachment of infantry, under command of Lieut. Smiley, and several wagons with supplies for Lawton's command, which was supposed to be in the Yaqui River Country in southern Sonora. If the command was in that section, I was ordered to enlist twenty Teremari Indians as scouts, and scout through the Yaqui River Canyon and try to locate the hostiles. After passing the town of Baucuachi I met a courier with dispatches from Lawton, who told me that the Indians had turned north with Lawton in close pursuit; so I cut across country to intercept him.

I carried one thousand dollars in gold for Lawton's command. I joined Lawton in camp south of Cachuta Ranch and was appointed Battalion Adjutant. I told Lawton of the letters I had received from Governor Torres, and he, Dr. Wood and I, with a detachment of cavalry, rode into Fronteras and had a conference with Prefecto of Arispe. After the conference we went to a small Mexican restaurant, where we had dinner consisting of Tortillas, Frijoles and Mexican wine.

I rode back to camp alone, over a trail I had only been over once before. The distance was about twenty miles, and the hostiles were supposed to be very near the town, but in what direction was not known. The night was one of the darkest I ever saw. I reached camp about one o'clock a.m.

Hearing that Lieut. C. B. Gatewood, 6th Cavalry, was holding the Indians, over a range of the Sierra Madre Mountains to the east of Fronteras, we crossed the range and went into camp on a small river several hundred yards from where the hostiles were camped. During the day Gatewood prevailed upon Geronimo, Natchez and several others of the band to come to our camp and have a talk about going up to the line, and there have a talk with General Miles about surrendering. They consented to do so.

Next morning the hostiles broke camp and started for Skeleton Canyon. After giving orders to Lieut. Smith to follow on our trail with the command, Lawton, Gatewood, Dr. Wood, George Wratten, the Interpreter, and I followed the Indians.

Late that afternoon they made camp, and after waiting for some time in vain for Smith to

114

put in an appearance, and Lawton, thinking that he must have taken a trail to the West, with George Wratten left us and cut across country to intercept him and bring him back on the right trail.

Gatewood, Dr. Wood and I stayed with the hostiles that night and remained with them till the next night, when Lawton and the command got in.

The order of march of the Indians the day we were with them was as follows: Natchez with the main band started out first, with his men deployed in a skirmish line about a mile in length. After he had been gone about half an hour, Geronimo, with the old men, women, children and pack horses, followed in the rear of the center of the line. This order of march was kept up all day.

Natchez, a son of the great Apache Chief Cochise, was really in command of the fighting men while Geronimo was only the adviser. During the march from where we first came in contact with the hostiles till we reached Skeleton Canyon, Lawton was very nervous and apprehensive that the Indians might make a break and get away, and I and all the other officers at that time gave Gatewood the credit for holding them together.

When General Miles met us at Skeleton Canyon, all the principal Indians came to talk with him with the exception of Natchez, who was missing. Gatewood went back to look for him and found him on a ridge some distance from camp, looking toward Mexico. He asked him why he was not with the other Indians, and he replied: "I am looking for one of my relatives who I sent back to Mexico after some cached horses which we left there, and as he has not returned, I fear something wrong has happened to him." Gatewood said to him: "Natchez, you promised me that when we got to the line you would talk to General Miles about surrendering." Natchez thought a moment and said; "That's so," and he immediately joined the others.

After the Indians surrendered unconditionally, Geronimo and his head men were placed in an ambulance, and I was ordered to ride behind it, with instructions to kill any one who attempted to escape. It was a hard old ride of seventy miles in eleven hours on a rough-gaited mule. Before we got to Fort Bowie, Arizona, Lieut. Wilder rode ahead of the command and came back with a bottle of whiskey. General Miles asked him where he was going. He replied; "Clay must be very tired of riding behind the ambulance, and I thought I would get him a drink." General Miles said; "No, wait till Clay gets the Indians in the guard house and he can take all he wants to drink." I got them safely in the guard house and had my drink afterwards.

Afterwards, I, with Lawton, Wood and others of the command, took the prisoners to San Antonio, Texas, where we turned them over to the commanding officer there to hold them preparatory to their being sent to Florida.

Lieut. C. B. Gatewood at one time was in charge of the Reservation where Geronimo and his men were located, and by the interest he had taken in them and their affairs, he had inspired them with great respect for him and confidence in his judgment.

When the hostiles started north from south of Montezuma, Sonora, where Lawton had followed them, Gatewood, with two Apache Scouts, was ordered to go down into Mexico and try to get in communication with Geronimo and get him, if possible, to have a talk with Lawton about surrendering. Gatewood found them and went into their camp at a time no other white man living could have gone in and come out alive. He persuaded them to have a talk with Lawton. If it had not been for their confidence in Gatewood, and the advice he gave them, I do not believe they would have surrendered when they did.

115

A Plea For Cooperation

By Colonel Samuel C. Vestal, *Chief of Historical Section, Army War College*

"I have come here to-night to ask that you do what you can to contribute to our archives in the Historical Section all such matter as will go to make up the story of those long, dreary days and risky fights against the savages."

In the field of military history the United States had and will have a most difficult task to hold its own. Many foreign countries have already produced histories not only of their own wars; but the Germans and the British have written official accounts of the wars of other nations. The United States has produced a short epitome of the Russo-Japanese War; but it has taken many years for us to come to the point of producing for the public and for military men and statesmen a complete and faithful account of any of our own wars.

The fault has been in ourselves, not in others. Unfortunately it has taken a long time to build up the feeling in our army that military men can write interesting history, that they should write our military history, and that this history should be an official staff publication of the government.

The Historical Section of the Army War College is launched upon the project of producing, first in pamphlet form and then in volumes, the military history of our participation in the World War. It will be the first official history of any of our wars. Twenty-four officers are now researching, along many lines, in the various repositories of Washington. Army officers in London, Paris, Berlin, Vienna, and Rome, representatives of the Historical Section, have supplied us with a vast amount of material from the war offices of foreign countries, both friend and foe in the last war. They have also sent us a great number of maps and photographs.

Happily a great part of our own records is available and easily accessible. These records are in a fair state of preservation. But now is the best time to use them. If we delayed many years, we would undoubtedly find, on account of the inferior paper upon which orders, messages and reports are written in time of action, that much of the evidence would become illegible or effaced.

From the psychological point of view we are in an excellent position to write World War History. Ten years after the war we can write with less prejudice and less personal leaning and hence with a nearer approach to truth than we could have written immediately after the close of hostilities; and the records are still fresh.

As time goes on, many memoirs, diaries, and other documents are published by those who participated in the war. These writings often supply important facts and they are invaluable sources for color and setting.

There is one very serious drawback to the writing of the history of the World War and of every other war in which America has participated. It is a curious phenomenon that seems to accompany our free ideas and free institutions. Few who have not been engaged in historical research know of its existence; but it is a thing that strikes at the faithfulness and fullness of our annals. It is the right that so many public men and others in the services of the Government feel they have to take with them and stow in their own vaults and crypts public documents which appeal to them as being more private than public, more personal than official. In most cases the reverse is true.

Such papers are the basic sources of history. Often they contain the only key to the understanding of a vital situation. Cabinet members, congressmen, soldiers and sailors, acting under the mistaken notion that they have a proprietary right to public documents of their own production, have carried off valuable records when they relinquished office. The purpose has often been to write memoirs at some future time, or to record for posterity, happenings upon which the documents throw light. In a countless number of instances, these fragments, so necessary to the construction of any true and complete picture of a war, have been forgotten in the attic and never used at all. The repositories in Washington contain but a small part of the documents that should be stored in the public archives.

Every scrap of paper recording the public action of a public servant is the property of the nation. Even contemporary personal diaries and personal correspondence assume this character to a large extent as time goes on.

It is scarcely necessary to say that the collection of the bits of evidence scattered in the private homes and vaults throughout the United States is a most difficult task. Unless some distinct preventive has been applied beforehand or the separate survivors of a war may be personally solicited, much of our history must necessarily lie fallow.

I could recount for you for hours instances of our attempts to beg back for the Government valuable papers which have been carried over the country in the manner I have outlined. One instance will serve to show the volume of such material which is abroad in the land and inaccessible to us. When the representatives of the First Division came to our office to arrange the orders and other documents of that division for a little more than a year of actual war, they found here and there great vacancies in their material and many minor gaps. They determined to supplement the official documents in our archives with what they could gain from private custody. They went over the rosters of the members of the division who they thought might have in their possession documents not filed in Washington. They sent a representative, a very able army officer, on a trip through the country, in order to interview men who might have copies of missing documents and to request them to give their material to the First Division, or, in effect, back to the Government. Almost fifty per cent of the matter that the First Division now has on hand was obtained by such scouting over the country and most of the papers obtained in this way were extremely vital to the story of the First Division; for, it must be confessed that those who preserve and cherish documents are not poor judges of the value of historical documents.

If this condition of affairs prevails in the year 1929, how much more noticeable must it have been in earlier times when the methods of conducting the public business were much more lax than they are today? I dare say that the absence of continuous, complete series of documents has been the great handicap that has operated to prevent the writing of the history of our wars.

This and other causes account for the sterile condition of the war history of our country. America is first in so many lines of endeavor! Is there any reason why she should not be first in the recording of military annals?

It may be stated beyond peradventure that there is only one story of any of our wars that deserves to be called a full and authentic account of an American conflict. Many accounts of the American Revolution have been written. It is possible that the best of these are the work of British writers; but no one has done for this epoch-making conflict what Thucydides did for the Peloponnesians, Livy and Polybius for the Punic, and Oman for the Peninsular War, and what Guizot did for the British Revolution of 1648. I do not wish to be misunderstood as saying that no one has written a meritorious history of the American Revolution. There have been several excellent accounts of this war; but none do full justice to the story. For the War of 1812, there is no history worthy of the name. Although the Civil War has had many recorders of its sweep and tenacity, no one has done for it as a whole, what the great historians of the past have done for the great wars of earlier times. The Count of Paris and Ropes have shot close to the mark; but one of these accounts is unbalanced and the other is unfinished. Likewise the writers on the Spanish-American War show hurry and temporary enthusiasm, but they do not record the bigness of that enterprise, its deep significance, and its far-reaching effects.

Of the Mexican War we have a history that challenges comparisons with the best histories that time has produced. It is the "War with Mexico," by Justin H. Smith. By his Darwinian-like efforts and years of labor covering all the main libraries and repositories in this country, by interviewing an assemblage of private witnesses, by a journey over the battle-fields of Mexico, a study of the archives of the City of Mexico, and research among the records of Madrid, he produced two volumes which are unchallenged by any of the accounts of our other wars.

One history out of the sum total of all our wars is our total stock in trade as a nation. And that one history was produced by a private person through his dogged preserverence. The voluminous records of the War of the Rebellion have done much for historians; but a work commensurate with such a vast collection has not yet been produced.

We come now to a phase which is of more immediate interest to those who are present. Our earlier Indian Wars have been graphically told by Colonel Roosevelt in the "Winning of the West"; but the Seminole War, the Black Hawk War, and the wars of the fifties and sixties have not yet been told even as fully as the pictures in the "Winning of the West." The great Indian wars that went on simultaneously with the Civil War and the later wars of the seventies and eighties when the number of hostile Indians had greatly increased and the slaughter had become more serious, have been recorded only in fragmentary records, some good, some bad, some spurious. What single book can you find that will give you a general and comprehensive knowledge of our Indian Wars? It is extremely doubtful whether we can ever have any such history unless we can supplement what the Government already has with what is in the possession of private individuals.

Within my hearing are men who undoubtedly have in their possession very authentic and most interesting and important documents which will give fascinating sidelights upon the campaign against the Indians upon our western plains. You treasure these things as private keepsakes. These documents when pieced together will make a continuous history of the effort of the white man against the red man in the trans-Mississippi region and give the public the first comprehensive and truthful account of what has so often been misunderstood.

Not long ago there came into the Historical Section by personal appeal, the diary of a surgeon who was with Gibbon's column when it marched toward Custer. The little volume, apparently seldom read since 1876, has in it here and there pieces of atmosphere and facts which will add greatly to any story of Custer's fight. The diary has lain, since the time when it was written, unemployed and inaccessible to historians. It is now in our possession through accident.

There are many of you here who have, or who know others that have, reports, photographs, correspondence, copies of orders, and other writings that will shed great light upon this, the most fascinating part of the history of the United States. When you pass away, these valuable relics will be more or less unappreciated by posterity and they will doubtless be lost. I have come here tonight to ask that you do what you can to contribute to our archives in the Historical Section all such matter as will go to make up the story of those long, dreary days and risky fights against the savages.

Already we have a fine collection of photographs. General Miles has been the most generous contributor to the section of photographs and other documents. We ask you to contribute any pictures taken upon the ground. If you so desire we will return the originals, each with a copy, probably larger than the original. Likewise we will return documents after we shall have made copies. It is our idea that an official history of our Indian Wars may be undertaken at the earliest possible date to commemorate appropriately for our people the hardy achievements which you did so much to bring about.

The great cities and prosperous rural communities of a mighty nation now fill the land where you fought the Indian. Two foreign wars have been fought since that day. People are prone to forget earlier history in the light of more recent events. The band of participants in our Indian Wars grows less and less each year. The Historical Section knows the importance of these wars and wishes to see them occupy their proper place in our history. To do this adequately requires your cooperation. Grant it to us and you will do your country service and yourselves and your children and grandchildren justice.

To this gallant band, this hardy remnant of a brave and glorious past, to these fine facts that I see before me, I would say: May your deeds and those of your associates who have passed on be rightly recorded and hold the place in the nation's thought that they deserve.

L.F. BJORKLUND

1930

At this year's meeting there were 44 Companions and 6 guests to sit for dinner. For the first time the *Proceedings* published the menu:

MENU
Supreme of Fruit
Celery   Olives   Radishes
Mock Turtle Soup
Filet of Sole, Tartare Sauce   Breast of Chicken, Virginia Style
Candied Sweet Potatoes   Broccoli au Beurre
Hearts of Lettuce, Roquefort Dressing
Meringue New Orleans   Cakes
Demi-Tasse
Cigars   Cigarettes

Printed in the *Proceedings* for this year were a series of letters concerning General Parker's address relating the surrender of Geronimo and Britton Davis' objection to an observation contained within. Also included in print were "The Armistead-Kauffman Unit," some remarks by General Fountain on his service years in New Mexico in the early 1870's, and remarks by General William A. Brown on "Citation Stars For Indian War Brevets." The *Proceedings* listed Generals Charles King and Edward Godfrey as being the main speakers with their subject being "Recounting The Story Of The Sioux Campaign of 1876," which was not printed.

In order to correct an inadvertent injustice, the following correspondence is published for the information and guidance of the members.

4145 Marlborough Ave.,
San Diego, Calif.,
April 9, 1929.

The Commander, Order of Indian Wars,
2020 Munitions Building,
Washington, D.C.

My Dear Commander:

The published account of the annual proceedings and dinner held January 26th past has just reached me. With no little astonishment I find published the following attack on my veracity by General James Parker.

"A photograph of Geronimo and Natchez, now in the pictorial division of the historical section of the General Staff, bears an inscription written by Britton Davis, substantially as follows: "Gatewood deserves all the credit for capturing Geronimo — Lawton never saw Geronimo until after the surrender.' This is a sample of some of the fables told about this campaign. How Britton Davis picked up this astonishing information I do not know — at the time of the surrender he was out of the service, employed at the Corralitos Cattle ranch in Mexico, over 100 miles distant."

The explanation of my endorsement on the photo is very simple. I have always maintained, and feel prepared to prove to the satisfaction of any unprejudiced person, that Geronimo actually surrendered the morning of August 25th, 1886, at his second conference with Gatewood; that Lawton left the matter of negotiating the surrender entirely in Gatewood's hands, and during the campaign had no meeting with Geronimo earlier than the morning of the 25th, after the actual surrender.

In my forthcoming book, "The Truth About Geronimo," now in the hands of publishers, I hope to make these facts plain to fair-minded people. In contentions with prejudice and self-glorification I am not interested. But I am interested when accused of mendacity — of fabricating one of "the fables told about this campaign." As I was given no opportunity for a hearing before the Order published and circulated this stigma, my only recourse now is to assert as my right that the Order give equal publicity to this, my letter. That done, my resignation from the Order will be submitted for acceptance.

Very respectfully,

(Signed) BRITTON DAVIS

R.F.D.1,
Newport, R. I.,
June 15, 1929.

Gen. S. W. Fountain,
Commander Order of Indian Wars.

My Dear General:

In reference to the letter of Lieut. Britton Davis, copy herewith, I wish to make the following explanation.

I am very sorry, however unintentionally, to have offended Britton Davis, for whom I have always had the highest regard. I was a witness in 1884-5 to a part of his faithful and devoted service as the officer in charge of the Chiricahua Indians. This work, attended as it was by extreme peril, has never received the recognition it merited.

As to the expression in my paper to which Britton Davis objects, I suppose when he claimed that Lawton never saw Geronimo until after the surrender, that he, Britton Davis, meant to imply that Lawton never saw Geronimo until after the surrender at Skeleton Canyon September 4, 1886, when Geronimo and his band laid down their arms. As it is the only surrender I know of, I inferred that Davis was misled by some of the popular legends current at the time. In no respect did I attack his veracity.

As to the date of Geronimo's surrender, I refer to Gatewood's own official report, printed and published in the Department of Arizona, 1886.

Yours truly,

(Signed) JAMES PARKER

4145 Marlborough Ave.,
San Diego, Calif.,
July 18, 1929.

Gen. S. W. Fountain, U.S.A., Retired,
Commander Order of Indian Wars,
2020 Munitions Building,
Washington, D.C.

My Dear General:

I am just in receipt of your favor of the third instant enclosing copy of letter from General Parker.

I sincerely appreciate your kindly efforts to have this unfortunate and, to me, mortifying incident set right. But for the fact that these charges appeared in the official publication of the Order I would never have paid any attention to them. But to have remained silent would have given my sanction to them.

The question as to *when* Geronimo surrendered is purely an academic one. The Miles-Lawton partisans claim that it was when he met Miles at Skeleton Canyon. I claim that he actually surrendered the morning of his second talk with Gatewood, when he *accepted the terms* of surrender. That he and his band kept their arms until they reached Skelton Canyon was due solely to fear of attack by Mexicans. Had there been no fear of this they would have surrendered their arms then and there as readily as they did later. General Parker confirms my view in his statement that *previous to September 1st* "from several sources we had heard that Geronimo had surrendered and was with Lawton's command, north of San Bernadino."

Howbeit, this question of "when" is in my opinion of little moment. The paramount question is "Who is most entitled to credit for Geronimo's final surrender?" It has been claimed for several. My interest lies in doing justice to the memory of a friend and fellow officer to whom justice was denied in his lifetime. This I hope to do in "The Truth About Geronimo."

Yours very sincerely,

(Signed) BRITTON DAVIS

123

THE ARMISTEAD-KAUFFMAN UNIT

Donated by Mr. R. King Kauffman

Captain Armistead's Company of the 6th Infantry accompanied Albert Sidney Johnston's Utah Expedition to California, and was sent from San Francisco to take station at Fort Mojave on the Colorado River. Supplies were carried for a stated period with the command. The steamer with supplies for a later date was wrecked, and before that information was received at San Francisco and another supply ship sent, the command at Mojave was living on reduced rations. The Indians were hostile and numerous, so much so, that the soldiers could not hunt and fish and in that manner add to their food supply. The command had been living on one pint of flour per man per day. It soon became evident to Captain Armistead that the men could not keep up their strength on such a limited diet. He therefore determined to attack the Indian village. The command, which was warned of the coming fight on the afternoon of August 4, 1859 and during the night marched to the vicinity of the Indian village, consisted of Captain Armistead, Lieutenant Marshall, First Sergeant A. B. Kauffman and fifty other enlisted men.

At daylight the village was attacked, the Indians were between two and three hundred strong. They were completey surprised but were rallied by their leaders and fought fiercely, charging the troops repeatedly with their war clubs which were repulsed by the troops with bayonet. Twenty-three of the hostiles were found dead on the field.

Dried meat and fish were found in abundance in the village. Chief Sin-ka-hunt came in to Mojave and made peace with Armistead and furnished supplies to the troops.

Sergeant Kauffman was commissioned in the army and commanded Troop E, 8th Cavalry and was stationed for a short time in 1868 at Fort Mojave. Chief Sin-ka-hunt was still alive. He and Kauffman had many talks recalling the days of 1859. The Mojaves had kept the peace which they had made with Armistead.

Armistead subsequently became a General officer in the Confederate army and led Pickett's grand charge at Gettysburg, falling mortally wounded inside the Union lines at the high tide of the rebellion. History of the Battle of Gettysburg cites that Gen. Alexander S. Webb and other officers, "by their heroic and reckless conduct rallied the troops at this point."

In June, 1900, I, (General Fountain) met General Webb at West Point and asked him of the death of General Armistead. We were walking from the graduating exercises. He stopped and holding up his walking stick said: "This stick was part of the staff of Armistead's flag and I carry it, not as a trophy of war but in remembrance of a man whom I dearly loved." That stick is now in the Museum at the United States Military Academy, West Point.

REMARKS OF BRIG. GEN. S. W. FOUNTAIN

In October, 1872, the District Commander at Santa Fe, N.M., ordered the Commanding Officer at Fort Wingate, N.M., to send me with a suitable detachment, mounted, to explore and survey a practicable wagon road from Fort Wingate to Fort Tulerosa — directly South — and authorized me to employ a guide at the rate of three dollars per day. Upon inquiry no guide could be found. Three Navajo Indians offered their services, saying that they did not know any route but they would take me through for one dollar each a day. The Commanding Officer authorized their employment and I made the exploration and survey. The District Commander had wisely added a post script to his order, saying perhaps Lieutenant Fountain may not know what a practicable wagon road is, so order him to take a six-mule team with him. I afterwards learned that the Commanding Officer at Tulerosa was ordered to send a Lieutenant and ten Infantrymen to make the exploration and survey going north. They had failed to get beyond what became known as San Augustine Plain and turned back and were ordered to Fort Wingate via Fort Craig and Albuquerque, about 440 miles. My route was 152 miles and became a well traveled road. I enjoyed my exploration and had no trouble in putting into use a practicable wagon road. I had the three Indians under my observation for over two weeks. I saw that two of them did the work that was required and the third remained a silent observer. I spoke to Benow the leader and was able to make him understand that I considered number 3 a loafer and wondered why they had him as an associate. Benow made it plain to me that number 3 was a Medicine Man and the others would not have come without him. My service with the Navajoes continued until 1875 during which time I learned their habits and claim to have been a benefit to them, for I taught them the honor of labor and the value of thrift.

Ten years later I became associated with a band of them during the Geronimo Campaign and Benow was with them.

I was in command of my troops and camp near Alma, N.M., at the mouth of Clairmont Gap, Mogollon Mountains, and was informed that Captain Rogers, 13th Infantry, with a band of Navajo Indians would locate in my vicinity. A few days later he arrived. I met him and located his camp and later the pack train came in. The men said Lieutenant O'Brien had passed them just as they entered the "Tin can trail" leading from the Mesa-land to the Clairmont Gap. It was plain to me that O'Brien after descending the trail had turned to the left and entered the mountains instead of turning to the right towards my camp. Captain Rogers and I arranged for a detail under Lieutenant Cabell to proceed at daylight and pick up O'Brien's trail. In the meantime the Indians had started a fire and their Medicine men went into conference. In a short time they told us Lieutenant O'Brien had gone into the mountains and seemed to be "loco." Lieutenant Cabell and party left at daylight. The Indians made medicine during the morning and said that Lieutenant O'Brien's horse had gone lame and he was leading it. During the day Medicine men reported that O'Brien had found some white men and left his horse with them and got some food from them and would come into our camp in a few days via the Silver City road. I ordered Lieutenant Farber, with a small detachment, to proceed via the Silver City road, to the Mogollon Pass, which was 45 miles from Clairmont Gap. My thought being that O'Brien would come out of the mountains there. The Indians in the meantime took everything as a matter of course, the lieutenant will come to camp by the Silver City road. Lieutenant Farber reached the Mogollon Gap about the same time as Lieutenant Cabell's party. Lieutenant Cabell reported that O'Brien had left the travelled trail and was now separted from water and would soon perish unless found. He ordered Farber to cross Cactus Flat for necessary supplies. In the meantime his detachment would cut the country hoping to pick up O'Brien's trail.

Farber secured supplies and started back to the Mogollons when he saw a wagon train coming from the direction of Silver City and rode to meet it. To his surprise Lieutenant O'Brien was sitting on the leading wagon. O'Brien said he found himself overlooking a vast plain and concluded he would find a road leading somewhere. Farber gave him supplies and left him to travel with the train which two days later arrived at my camp, our efforts having had no influence over O'Brien rescue. Upon his arrival the Indians expressed no surprise. They only said, "We told you so." Lieutenant Cabell's report verified the Indian story of O'Brien's wandering, his horse having been recovered from Jone's Cabin where he left it.

REMARKS OF BRIG. GEN. WM. C. BROWN

Citation Stars for Indian War Brevets

There are still on the Army Register the names of 21 officers who have been brevetted for gallantry in action in Indian Wars, three of whom — Generals Gordon, Sumner and Kress — have also brevets for Civil War service.

The citation in every one of the Indian Wars brevets states that the award was given "for gallantry in action."

Had these awards been announced in War Department Generals Orders, as they should have been, and as was done in cases of brevets awarded for Civil War Service, the officer concerned would automatically have been entitled to wear a silver star in the lapel button provided by the War Department for wear with civilian dress.

These Indian War brevets were all granted under the Act of February 27, 1890, and the nominations (a total of about 150), were made in 1894 and 1895.

Shortly after the Civil War many brevets were granted for services *not* in action and therefore the recipients would not under the law of July 9, 1918 be entitled to wear the silver star. The Indian War brevets are of a different class, for the citations of *every one* were for gallantry in action. It was clearly an oversight on the part of the War Department not to publish these awards in General Orders, and for this reason it is claimed that an executive order on the part of the Secretary of War is all that is necessary to give the 21 survivors the right to wear the silver star.

It is to be presumed that the fact that the act of gallantry in each individual case of Indian War veterans was considered and acted upon favorably at the time their brevet nominations were sent to the Senate, and that *that* question has already been definitely decided.

Suggestion is made that the Order of Indian Wars take this matter up with the War Department with a view to ascertaining whether this very slight and belated recognition cannot now be given.

Indian War Papers of the Late Walter M. Camp

Shortly after Mr. Camp's death, some four years ago, I corresponded with his widow at 7740 South Union Avenue, Chicago, to get Camp's papers on Indian War history, and notes taken on the sites of some 41 Indian engagements, turned over to the Historical Section, Army War College, where they would be accessible to the public. I have stopped several times in Chicago for this purpose, on two occasions being assisted by Gen. Charles King.

Finding that the government has no money for the purchase of such material, the matter was taken up with the Librarian of Newberry Library, Chicago, with a view to their purchase by that library in case examination should indicate considerable value, and purchase could be made on satisfactory terms. About ten days ago General King and I consulted Mr. George B. Utley, Librarian, Newberry Library, and I later saw Mrs. Camp's lawyer and got him interested.

Mr. Camp, as many of you know, was an editor and had spent twenty summers in visiting old battle grounds, interviewed a large number of witnesses, both white and red, learned something of the Sioux dialect, and was preparing to write a history of our relations with the Red Man.

If these papers, believed to contain a large amount of valuable data, impossible now of replacement, are not secured their loss would be irreparable.

1931

There were 37 Companions and 11 guests who enjoyed a dinner of breast of guinea Virginia style and all the trimmings this year.

Brigadier General James T. Kerr was the main speaker for the evening; his chosen subject was "The Story of the Modoc War of 1873." Two addresses which were not printed in the *Proceedings* were "A Description of the Lava Beds and Present-Day Appearance of the Territory in Which the Modoc War of 1873 Took Place," given by Dr. Thomas N. Vincent, and the one by the Reverend J. Buell Shomaker, National Chaplain of the Society of Veterans of Indian Wars, who gave a short account of the work his organization had been doing in the way of securing adequate pensions for Indian War veterans.

Address of Brig. Gen. James T. Kerr
The Modoc War of 1872-73

The Modoc Indians, along with other tribes, occupied a section of country in southeastern Oregon and northeastern California. The tribe was a small one in number, in 1874, according to the Office of Indian Affairs, 247, so it is reasonable to assume about 300 as their number in 1873. The outbreak of 1872-73 was not participated in by the tribe as a whole, the chief of the tribe, Old Schonchin, with about 100 of his followers, remaining peacefully on the reservation. The leader of the hostile band, Capt. Jack, was a subchief of the tribe, and although the greater part of his band were Modocs, several renegades from other tribes joined him when he defied the authorities. The number of warriors in his band has been variously estimated from 40 up to 120, but probably 75 to 80 is a fair estimate.

The field of this War was mostly in the Lava Beds which cover an area of about 75 square miles in northeastern California, immediately south of Tule Lake, which covers about the same area; or at least it did in 1873. It has since been drained, and its former bed, except for a small pond, is now a prosperous farming country. Bordering the lake and lava beds on the west is a precipitous bluff a few hundred feet high.

Maj. Chas. B. Hardin, Ret., has written an account of this war for the Historical Section, Army War College, he having served through the campaign as an enlisted man in Bernard's troop, 1st Cav. He describes the lava beds, quoting from another writer, as follows: "Conceive a smooth, hard surface of 80 square miles of hardened lava 500 feet thick, underlaid at frequent intervals throughout its entire extent with mines of dynamite sufficient to rent it to pieces, and then conceive these mines to be exploded simultaneously, breaking the surface into millions of fragments of all sizes and shapes, and piling them into confused heaps over the surface, leaving caves here and there, and deep fissures and chasms at intervals in the debris, and you have some idea of the roughness of this region."

He further states that the stronghold or fort in which the Modocs took refuge, lies on the edge of the lake and about 3 miles east of the high bluff on the west side of the lava beds. This was a strong fort naturally, but the Modocs greatly strengthened it by constructing covered ways and breastworks of loose stones. This stronghold is elevated slightly above the surrounding country, and has several of the largest fissures, caves, and underground passages to be found in the lava beds. The largest cave in the stronghold, a circular crater with overhanging sides, and with several underground passages radiating from it, was called "Jack's Cave" and would hold about 50 persons. There were several similar caves, not so large, and one large fissure from 6 to 10 feet in width and 10 to 15 feet in depth, which bisected the stronghold, running north and south, and which by reason of overhanging sides in many places, afforded great protection.

Col. John O. Skinner, Ret., who also served in this War, states that the Indians had ingeniously placed irregular lines of stakes in places, so that in falling back from one position to another, by following the line of stakes they could not be seen by the outlooks of the advancing skirmish lines.

The Modocs are described by Col. Wm. Thompson in his book entitled, "Reminiscences of a Pioneer," as being far below the tribes of the northern country in general appearance, not possessing the steady courage of the Nez Perces nor the wild dash of the Sioux, but in cunning and savage ferocity they are not excelled even by the Apaches, and in war they rely mainly on cunning and treachery. He was an old settler in that part of the country and knew the history of the Modocs. He was on the staff of the Governor of Oregon during the war and was present at some of the fights.

In the years following the California gold rush of '49, the section of country occupied by the Modocs and other tribes near them, was gradually invaded by white settlers, with the usual result of clashes between them, so the government, in accordance with its policy of establishing Indians on reservations, entered into a treaty with the Klamaths, Modocs, and the Yashookin band of Snakes, by the terms of which these Indians ceded to the U.S. all claims to the lands occupied by them for a monetary consideration to be paid in installments, and agreed to live on a reservation set apart for them adjacent to Great Klamath Lake, Ore., to the northwest of the country then occupied by them. This treaty was signed by the chiefs and sub-chiefs of the Modocs, Oct. 18, 1964, ratified by the Senate with certain verbal amendments July 2, 1966, the amendments consented to by the Indians in Dec., 1869, and promulgated by the President Feb. 18, 1870. During 1869 while the treaty was still pending, Old Schonchin, the head chief, with about 100 of his band, went to the Klamath Reservation where they settled down and remained. Capt. Jack, with the remainder of the tribe, refused to go at that time. Jack raising strenuous objections to the amendments, but he was finally induced by the other chiefs to agree to them, and he signed the amended treaty, and in Dec., 1869, he and his followers went to the Klamath Reservation. No sooner had they settled there than friction developed between his band and the Klamaths. It appears the latter were the aggressors; for instance it is alleged that when Jack's band were cutting rails for their own use the Klamaths came with their teams and carried off the rails. Protests by Jack to the Agent brought no relief, even after Jack's band was moved with his consent to another part of the reservation a few miles away from the Klamaths, as the latter followed them up and continued their harassing tactics. Finally Jack called his band together and left the reservation, going back to his old country on Lost River after a stay of only about 3 months on the reservation. On the surface it appears that Jack made an honest effort to settle down, and that the Agent failed to give him proper protection, but on the other hand, Old Schonchin and his followers managed to get along amicably with the Klamaths, so it is probable the tame life of a reservation Indian did not appeal to Jack's wild nature. He had gone reluctantly to the reservation and the annoyances of the Klamaths gave him a pretext for leaving.

During the following year and a half, the Superintendent of Indian Affairs for Oregon was constantly making efforts to induce Jack to return, but to no avail. On account of the admitted unfriendliness of the Klamaths, he recommended to the Commissioner of Indian Affairs that another reservation be set aside for Jack and his band. No action was taken by the Commissioner on this recommendation, and meantime the settlers were constantly complaining to the Indian agent, the Governor of Oregon and the military authorities of thefts and other depredations by the Indians. While no armed clashes occurred, the settlers were very apprehensive and the situation was becoming critical. Jack consistently avowed that he wanted to get along amicably with the whites, that there was room enough for all, and that as long as the whites let him and his people alone, they need have no fear. There appears to be no evidence that Jack personally was guilty of depredations, but his band contained some lawless individuals whom he could not or would not control, and the settlers doubtless had just cause for complaint.

In the summer of 1871 the Superintendent, in order to avert armed clashes which seemed imminent, sent two commissioners to the Indians, and as a result of consultations it was understood the Indians should be allowed to remain where they were pending action by the Commissioner of Indian Affairs on the question of another reservation for them, provided always that they refrained from thefts and other disturbances. No action was forthcoming, however, in regard to another reservation, the Commissioner of Indian Affairs intimating in a subsequent statement that as the Indians had left the reservation while in defiance of the authority of the U.S., other bands might be encouraged to similar action.

Under date of Jan. 25, 1872, the Superintendent of Indian Affairs requested the Comdg. Gen. Dept. of Columbia (Canby) to remove Jack and his band to Yainax Station on the Klamath Reservation, basing his request on a petition signed by 44 settlers asking for their removal, which was accompanied by affidavits setting forth depredations committed by them. Gen. Canby forwarded this request to the Comdg. Gen. Division of the Pacific (Shofield) stating among other things that he understood the agreement entered into by the two commissioners (heretofore referred to) was to be a settlement of the question until some permanent arrangement could be made for the Indians, and that unless they had violated some subsequent agreement, he did not think the immediate application of force as requested would be either expedient or just. He was not surprised at the unwillingness of the Modocs to return to the Reservation where they would be exposed to the hostilities and annoyances of the Klamaths. He stated that in other respects the Modocs were not entitled to much consideration. He would sent troops to such places as to protect the settlers.

With regard to the agreement referred to, the Supt. of Indian Affairs stated that when the agreement with the two commissioners was entered into in the summer of '71, the Modocs were located at Clear Lake, some miles distant from where they now were and they had not remained there as they agreed to do.

These papers having in due course reached the Commissioner of Indian Affairs, through the War Dept., that official in a letter dated April 12, 1872, called attention to the fact that the Indians had not refrained from thefts and other depredations as they had agreed to do, and had thus forfeited any claims to further forbearance under that agreement, and directed that Supt. of Indian Affairs to remove Jack and his band to the Klamath Reservation if practicable, and if removed to see that they were protected from the Klamaths. If they could not be removed, report was to be made as to the practicability of locating them at some other point. The Supt. sent J. D. Applegate to Jack to try to induce him to come in but without success. Applegate was of opinion that the headmen should be arrested and that this could probably be done without serious resistance by a display of military force, although admitting the possibility of resistance and consequent bloodshed. Under date of June 17, 1872, the Supt. reported to the Commissioner of Indian Affairs the failure of Applegate to induce Jack and his band to return, although Applegate has known these Indians intimately for many years, speaks their language fluently and possesses their confidence to an extent greater than any one else. He stated that the leaders were desperadoes, brave, daring and reckless, and had for so long been permitted to do as they pleased, they imagined they were too powerful to be controlled by the government and that they could with impunity defy its authority. He therefore recommended that the headmen be arrested and held at some place remote from the tribe till they should agree to behave themselves, this action not be to taken before the last of Sept. as it would be difficult to carry it out before the beginning of winter. Upon receipt of this report the Commissioner, under date of July 6, 1872, directed the Supt. to remove Jack and his band to the Klamath Reservation, peaceably if he could but forcibly if necessary, at the time suggested, Sept. He would use his discretion about making arrest of the leaders, avoiding any unnecessary violence or resort to extreme measures.

The Supt. still did not despair of finding some means of inducing the Indians to return before winter set in, and delayed calling for military force until Jack refused to have any further talks and defiantly refused to return to the Reservation. The Supt. then, under date of Nov. 27, 1872, requested the Commanding Officer, Fort Klamath, Maj. Green, 1st Cav., to furnish at once a sufficient force to compel the Indians to return to the Reservation. He stated it was the desire of the Dept. that it be done peaceably if possible, but if it became necessary to use force, then it was requested that Capt. Jack, Black Jim, and Scarface Charley be arrested and held subject to the Superintendent's orders. It was further stated that these leaders with only about half their warriors were then encamped near the mouth of Lost River, and if a force were immediately sent to that place, it was thought they might be induced to surrender without further trouble.

This request was received by Maj. Green at 5 a.m., Nov. 28, 1872, and he issued orders for Capt. Jas. Jackson, 1st Cav., to proceed at once with all available men of his troop to Capt. Jack's camp, endeavoring to arrive there before tomorrow morning, and if any opposition is offered on the part of the Modoc Indians to the requirements of the Superintendent, he will arrest if possible Capt. Jack, Black Jim and Scarface Charley. He will endeavor to accomplish all this without bloodshed if possible, but if the Indians persist in refusing to obey the orders of the government, he will use such force as may be necessary to compel them to do so. Second Lieut. F. A. Boutelle and Asst. Surgeon Henry McEldery were ordered to accompany the command.

Capt. Jackson left Ft. Klamath about 11 a.m., Nov. 28, his troop numbering 36 men, besides 4 with the pack train. What occurred is set forth in his hasty report of Nov. 30, and a more detailed report of Dec. 2, here summarized. He jumped Capt. Jack's band soon after daylight Nov. 29, completely surprising them. He repeatedly demanded their surrender and disarming and had his interpreter repeat these demands, and asked for a parley with Capt. Jack. Capt. Jack, Scarface Charley, Black Jim and some others would neither lay down their arms nor surrender, and some of them began making hostile demonstrations against him and finally opened fire. He poured volley after volley into the hostiles, took their camp, killing 8 or 9 warriors and drove the rest into the hills. His own loss was one man killed and 7 severely wounded. He states the camp he attacked was on the south side of the river, and that another small band on the north side was attacked by a party of 10 or 12 citizens and their surrender demanded, but when firing began in Capt. Jack's camp, these Indians opened fire on the citizens and drove them to the refuge of Crawley's Ranch. One citizen was killed and 2 others coming up the road unconscious of any trouble, were shot, one of them mortally and the other severely wounded. He stated his force was too small to pursue and capture the Indians, as he had to care for his wounded and protect the citizens at Crawley's Ranch. He destroyed Capt. Jack's camp, made arrangements to ferry his wounded across the river in canoes, then took his troop about 8 miles up the river to a ford where he crossed and then down again to Crawley's Ranch from where he submitted his reports and would await re-inforcement and further instructions. He stated from the best information he could get that he had killed or mortally wounded not less than 16 hostiles including Capt. Jack, Scarface Charley and Black Jim. (He was mistaken, however, as to the 3 named, as subsequent events showed). By Dec. 2, when he made his more detailed report, he had learned that the Indians who had bested the citizens on the north side of the river, had then gone along the lake valley killing settlers, but not molesting women or children. He did not know how many had been killed (but as it was later learned, the victims numbered about 12, who were ruthlessly shot down as they were at work unarmed, about their ranches). He believed the band had taken refuge in the rocks and caves of Tule Lake, but would send out a company of Klamath scouts just arrived that morning to take up the trail and keep them from raiding till more troops arrived.

The results of this initial encounter indicated only too plainly that too small a force had been sent to accomplish its object if the Indians were really bent on resistance. Lieut. Boutelle, in an account of the campaign written for Dr. Cyrus Townsend Brady's Book, "Northwestern Fights and Fighters," published in 1907, and presumably written shortly before that date, states that before Jackson's command left Fort Klamath, he (Boutelle) spoke to the Commanding Officer, inviting his attention to the Department Commander's instructions, and suggesting that a stronger force be sent; that there was no reason to think the Indians would not fight, and that this small force would be inadequate, just enough in fact to provoke a fight. (The instructions of the Dept. Commander were that "if the intervention of troops became necessary, the force employed should be so large as to secure the result at once and beyond peradventure.") Maj. Green had to decide what force would be sufficient under the existing circumstances. The Supt. had located a band of about half Jack's force and would furnish a guide to conduct the troops to their camp. If this force could be induced to surrender, or captured or destroyed it would probably end the trouble. To ask for additional troops would entail delay and probably defeat the attempt to surprise the Indians. He therefore decided on immediate action as the Supt. had requested, and sent the only troops of Cavalry which was at hand.

Of course after this first encounter and the ensuing murder of the settlers, all available troops were assembled, including two companies of Oregon Volunteers called out by the Governor. Lieut. Col. Frank Wheaton, Comdg. the District of the Lakes, was assigned to command the troops, which consisted of Capt. Jas. Jackson's Troop B, 1st Cav. (at Crawley's Ranch), Capt. David Perry's Troop F, 1st Cav. (at Van Brener's Ranch, 12 miles west of lava beds), Capt. R. F. Bernard's Troop G, 1st Cav. (at site of Land's Ranch, 13 miles east of lava beds), Maj. E. C. Mason's battalion, 21st Inf., consisting of Co. C, Capt. G. H. Burton, Co. B, 2nd Lieut. H. D. Moore, and a detachment of 20 men of Co. F under 1st Sgt. John McNamara, a section of mountain howitzers, Lieut. W. H. Miller, 1st Cav. Comdg., 2 companies, Oregon Volunteers, A and B under Capt. Hugh Kelley and A. C. Applegate, commanded by Gen. John J. Ross, Oregon Militia, a detachment of 24 men of California Volunteers who had volunteered for the occasion, and a company of Klamath Indian Scouts under Capt. Dave Kelly, in all about 400 men. Maj. John Green, 1st Cav., was second in command. On Jan. 12, Col. Wheaton issued orders for the disposition of his troops for the attack on the Modoc stronghold in the Lava Beds where they had been located, the attack to begin at daylight Jan. 17. The command was divided into two parts, Bernard's and Jackson's Troops and the Klamath Scouts being east of the Lava Beds, and the remainder of the troops under Maj. Green on the west side. The general plan provided for the troops on both sides to be deployed so the northern flanks should rest on or near Tule Lake, and advance simultaneously. When sufficiently near the Modoc stronghold, the western line was to execute a half wheel to the left and connect up with the left flank of the eastern line, with a view to preventing the escape of the Indians to the south and force them north towards the lake. Communication between the lines was to be kept up by signal flag, but unfortunately a dense fog covered the field during practically the entire day, so each side was unaware except as could be guessed by the sound of firing, as to how the other was advancing. The attack was made as arranged but the difficulties of advancing were much greater than expected, both on account of the fog and the nature of the ground. The advantages were all in favor of the Indians who were under cover, and as the advancing troops emerged from the fog they were shot down at close range, generally without seeing where the shots came from. One soldier who fought gallantly all day, being wounded four times, said he did not see an Indian all day. The troops advanced notwithstanding heavy losses, until the left wheel movement was attempted, when the right of the west line, about 2 p.m., came to a deep precipitous fissure which it was found impossible to cross without excessive losses. The junction of the southern flanks was then abandoned, and an effort made to connect the northern flanks along the lake shore. This movement was only partially successful, for although contact was effected, a gap was caused in the western line, and the intended enveloping operation failed. By this time it was nearly dark, and Col. Wheaton decided upon withdrawal, being convinced he could not capture or dislodge the Indians with the force he had. The troops were withdrawn to their camps and Col. Wheaton requested 300 more men and four mortars, feeling confident that with this addition to his force he could take the stronghold. His casualties were 16 enlisted men killed, and 5 officers and 44 enlisted men wounded. In a subsequent report of Gen. Canby to Hdqrs. of the Army he stated that 8 Modocs were killed and many injured.

Before any further military operations could be gotten under way, the President decided to suspend all offensive action, and on Jan. 23 instructions were sent to Gen. Canby to use his troops to protect the inhabitants but if possible to avoid war. Additional troops had been, in the meantime, ordered to the scene and Col. A. C. Gillem, 1st Cav., had superseded Col. Wheaton in command. Gen. Canby acknowledged receipt of the instructions and stated that orders in conformity therewith would be given at once, and at the same time sent a separate telegram to Gen. Sherman, which is interesting as showing Gen. Canby's attitude at that time, and is here quoted in full:

"Portland, Ore., Jan. 23, 1873, to Gen. W. T. Sherman, Comdg. The Army, Washington, D.C. I am satisfied that hostilities with the Modocs would have resulted under any circumstances from enforcement of the Commissioner's order to place them on the reservation, new facts showing clearly that they were determined to resist and had made preparations to do so. If the arrangements for their removal had been carried out, the lives of the settlers who were murdered by them might have been saved, but hostilities still would have resulted, and these blows would have fallen elsewhere and later. On the approach of a force too large to resist, they would have betaken themselves to the mountains or to their caves, and kept up the war from these points. Since the commencement they have twice attacked trains, evidently for the purpose of securing ammunition for carrying on the war. I have been very solicitous that these Indians should be fairly trated, and have repeatedly used military force lest they might be wronged, until their claims or pretensions were decided by proper authority. That having been done, I think they should now be treated as any other criminals, and that there will be no peace in that part of the frontier until they are subdued and punished. Col. Gillem acknowledges receipt of instructions of this morning, and asks if Capt. Jack shall be notified that he will not be molested if he remains quiet. If not inconsistent with the President's desire, I propose to instruct him to hold communication with Capt. Jack, to prevent his getting supplies of any kind, and to treat as enemies any of his party that may be found in the settlements without proper authority, but to make no aggressive movement until

136

further notice." Gen. Sherman replied that the telegram would be laid before the President, and added "Let all defensive measures proceed, but order no attack on the Indians till the former orders are modified or changed by the President, who seems disposed to let the peace men try their hands on Capt. Jack."

The Peace Commission, which was to consist of three members, would take some time to arrive on the ground, and meantime Gen. Canby went in person to the field of operations. He made efforts to get in communication with Capt. Jack and offered to send wagons to bring in his sick and wounded. The offer was accepted but when the wagons went to the appointed place at the time agreed upon, no Indians appeared. Gen. Canby was of opinion Jack was merely playing for time awaiting warmer weather, and made such disposition of his troops as to guard as far as practicable all means of egress of the Indians from the Lava Beds, and at the same time give protection to the settlers. These movements of troops were, of course, observed by the Indians, and doubtless increased their apprehensions as to the intent of the authorities. Gen. Canby and Col. Gillem met Capt. Jack and one other chief on March 23 by agreement, but Gen. Canby reported the results were unsatisfactory. The substance of all that could be elicited from Capt. Jack was that he didn't want to fight and wanted to go to his home on Lost River. He wanted all the soldiers moved out of the country, and if anybody wanted to talk to him they must come to his camp, and if anything was to be done for him it must be done there.

The essential instructions to the Peace Commission were as follows: It will be required to proceed to the Modoc country as rapidly as possible, and before entering on the active discharge of its duties, will confer with Gen. Canby of the U.S. Army, and in all subsequent proceedings of the commission it should confer freely with that officer and act under his advice as far as it may be possible to do so, and always with his cooperation. The objects to be attained by the Commission are these, first, to ascertain the causes which led to the difficulties and hostilities between the troops and the Modocs, and secondly to devise the most effective and judicious measures for preventing the continuance of the hostilities and for the restoration of peace. It is the opinion of the Dept. (Interior) from the best information in its possession that it is advisable to remove the Modoc Indians with their consent to some new reservation, and it is believed that the Coast Reservation in Oregon, lying between Cape Lookout on the north and Cape Perpetua on the south and between the Coast range of mountains and the Pacific Ocean, will be found to furnish the best location for these Indians. The Commission will, therefore, be directed to make an amicable arrangement for locating the Indians on some part of this Reservation provided it is possible for it to do so, and provided the Commission after full investigation does not consider some other place better adapted to accomplishing the purpose of the Department, and in any case before concluding final arrangements with the Indians, to communicate with the Commissioner of Indian Affairs and receive further advice. The Commission will in no way attempt to direct the military authorities in reference to their movements. It will be at liberty, however, to inform the Commanding Officer of the wish of the Dept. that no more force or violence be used than in his opinion shall be absolutely necessary and proper, it being the desire of the Dept. in this as well as in all other cases of like character, to conduct its communications with the Indians in such manner as to secure peace and obtain their confidence if possible, and their voluntary consent to a compliance with such regulations as may be deemed necessary for their present and future welfare.

Mr. A. B. Meacham was appointed Chairman of the Commission and remained in that capacity to the end. He had formerly been Supt. of Indian Affairs for Oregon and was familiar with Modoc affairs. The other two positions were not so easily filled, some appointees declining to serve and others resigning after a short service, the two final members being the Rev. Dr. Eleazer Thomas, a Methodist clergyman of Petaluma, Calif., who had some experience as a missionary among Indian tribes, and Mr. L. S. Dyar, the Indian Agent at Klamath reservation.

The Commission organized Feb. 18, 1873, at Fairchild's Ranch, and opened communications with the Indians. It found difficulty in arranging terms with them for a conference, as Meacham under date of Feb. 27 wired the Secretary of the Interior, "Modocs positively reject every proposition as to terms and place of meeting of Council. Offers such as we cannot accept." On March 2 he wired again: "We have proposed surrender as prisoners of war, to be removed by Gen. Canby to Angel Island, protected, fed and clothed, and a permanent home found in Arizona. They are favorably considering, we think will accept, will know definitely in a few days." On March 4 he wired, "Modocs emphatically reject all offers and propositions. They propose to meet in full force, Meacham and Applegate with 6 men unarmed in Lava Beds. This undoubtedly means treachery. We are still willing to meet them in conference but not on their terms. They have an accession of 24 warriors, not Modocs without doubt. We will send message of protection to all who come out. The mission is a failure. Instruct immediately; time is of most importance. Courier awaits."

To this the Secretary of the Interior replied: "I do not believe the Modocs mean treachery. The mission should not be a failure. Think I understand now their unwillingness to confide in you. Continue negotiations. Will consult President and have War Dept. confer with Gen. Canby tomorrow."

On March 7 Meacham wired: "The Modocs have reconsidered and by their message have accepted terms offered by Commission on the 3d inst. * * * Capt. Jack's sister came as messenger from him yesterday and returned today. We will have a permanent peace if no treachery intervenes. If all right shall Commission confirm the terms above?" On the 8th he wired: "Modocs have named Monday to meet our wagons near the Lava Beds * * *" But on the 11th he wired: "No Modocs appeared at the appointed time and place. They first favorably considered terms offered by Commission as telegraphed you, then positively rejected next day; reconsidered and accepted, named Monday to come; failed to come in. Every honorable means to secure peace have been exhausted. Modocs break every promise. Have talked to our messengers, 'stop fighting, withdraw soldiers and let us alone on Lost River * * *' "

Two days later, March 13, Gen. Canby wired to Gen. Sherman, "The Modocs failed yesterday at time and place appointed by themselves. * * * I do not regard this last action of the Modocs as decisive, and spare no effort to bring about desired results."

About this time the Secretary of the Interior was evidently not satisfied with the personnel of the Commission, as on March 24 Gen. Sherman wired Gen. Canby: "Sec. Delano (Int. Dept.) is in possession of all your dispatches up to March 16, and he advises the Sec. of War that he is so much impressed with your wisdom and desire to fulfill the peaceful policy of the government that he authorizes you to remove from the present commission any members you think unfit and appoint others in their places, reporting through me to him such changes." Gen. Canby made no changes, however, wiring to Gen. Sherman: "The Commission as at present organized will, I think, work well. Yesterday the Modocs again invited conference, and Col. Gillem, who was with the party examining the Lava Beds, had a short interview with two of the most intelligent, both, however, of the peace party. He is of opinion they are more subdued in tone and more amenable to reasoning than at the last previous interview. I think that when the avenues of escape are closed, and their supplies cut off or abridged, they will come in."

It may be here remarked that during the truce, members of Jack's band frequently visited the camp of the troops, where they were fed and kindly treated. These visitors presumably belonged to the so-called peace party of Jack's band, and their attitude may account in some measure for Gen. Canby's optimism.

On Apr. 7 Meacham wired to the Secretary of the Interior from the camp at Lava Beds, to which the Commission had meantime moved from Fairchild's ranch. "First meeting since our arrival here, Modocs insisted on amnesty for all, home on Lost River. Second meeting they abandoned Lost River and demanded Lava Beds for home. We do not believe lasting peace would follow settlement of Modocs in this country. We meet them tomorrow to discuss only amnesty and a new home. They are wavering and indicate willingness to talk over these terms."

These meetings were held at what was called the Peace Tent, pitched between the lines at the edge of the Lava Beds, about three-fourths mile from Gillem's camp.

About this time occurred an incident which revealed the treacherous intent of the Indians, if taken at its face value, which Meacham and Dyar and most of the officers and practically all of the enlisted men did. The interpreter for the Commission was a white man named Riddle, whose wife was a Modoc squaw called Toby. She was friendly to the troops and was also trusted by the Modocs and frequently visited their camp. She usually assisted her husband as interpreter. When she was on a visit to the Modoc Camp early in April, one of the Indians followed her as she left the camp and told her not to come to the camp any more and to tell the Commissioners not to meet the Indians in council any more, as the Indians intended to kill them. She told Riddle of this and he told the Commissioners, and Meacham states he told Gen. Canby. The latter, however, and Col. Gillem as well, did not appear to attach the importance to it that subsequent events showed it deserved.

The conference which was to have been held on April 8 as referred to in Meacham's telegram of the 6th, did not take place that day, as Jack insisted on meeting at a place near his camp which was entirely hidden from sight of the troops' camp by a bluff. The Commissioners wisely refused to meet there. After several futile attempts to agree on the conditions of this meeting, the Commissioners finally, on April 10, sent Riddle and Toby with a written message to Jack, requesting a conference at the Peace Tent the next day, to have a permanent settlement of the difficulties. They wanted to make peace with them and move them off to some warm climate where they could live like white people. This was the substance of the message as interpreted by Riddle, who then handed the message to Jack telling him he should bring it to the Peace Tent with him next day. Jack threw the message on the ground saying he could not read it and had no use for it and that he would meet the Commissioners close to his camp and nowhere else. He said he would meet them, 5 in all, without any arms, and he would do the same, that he would not take any arms with him.

The understanding then was that Gen. Canby and Col. Gillem were to accompany the 3 Commissioners, making 5 in all, but Col. Gillem was sick on the 11th and unable to go along. Riddle and Toby returned to the Commissioners with Jack's message and Riddle told them the Indians were all forted up around there and had been killing beef, and he thought it was useless to try to make peace any longer, and if Capt. Jack would not meet them at the Peace

139

Tent, if he were in their places he would not meet them any more. The commissioners conferred, and Meacham and Dyar protested against any further meeting with the Indians. Dr. Thomas insisted on meeting them and said he would go alone if no one else went. Gen. Canby was consulted and it was finally decided, Meacham and Dyar reluctantly consenting, to send a message to Jack that they would meet him at the Peace Tent. This message was taken the morning of Apr. 11 by Bogus Charley, a member of Jack's band, who had been used previously as a messenger. He pretended to be friendly and had stayed at the troops' camp the night of the 10th. He returned in about an hour, accompanied by Boston Charley and said Capt. Jack had agreed and was already at the Peace Tent with 5 men all unarmed. When this message was received, Riddle made one more effort to dissuade the commissioners from going. He asked them and Gen Canby to go with him and Toby to Col. Gillem's tent, which they did. Gen. Canby, however, remained outside the tent while the others went in. Riddle, addressing Col. Gillem, said, "These men are going to hold a conference with them Indians today and I don't believe it is safe. If anything happens to them today, I don't want no blame laid on me hereafter, because I don't think it is safe for them to go, and after it is over I don't want no blame laid on me. (Riddle states that Col. Gillem gave a big laugh and said if the Indians done anything he would take care of them). Toby went up to Meacham and said, "Meacham, don't you go for they might kill you today. They might kill all of you today," and she held on to him and cried. Dr. Thomas, addressing Riddle, said he ought to put his trust in God, that God Almighty would not let any such body of men be hurt that was on as good a mission as that. Riddle replied that he (Dr. Thomas) might trust in God "but I don't trust any of them Indians." Meacham asked Toby if she thought the Indians would kill him, and she replied, "I have told you all I *can* tell you. They may kill you today and they may not." The party then left the tent and Meacham told Gen. Canby what had taken place inside. Gen. Canby replied substantially as follows: "I think there is no danger, although I have no more confidence in these Indians than you have. I think them capable of it but they dare not do it; it is not to their interest." He said Col. Mason was only a short distance from their stronghold and before they could get back to it Col. Mason could be upon them. He had had the road watched with a glass from the signal station since daylight, and there were but 5 Indians at the Peace Tent and they were apparently unarmed. He had no fears under the circumstances.

Meacham tried to persuade Dyar not to go, saying that as chairman of the Commission he (Meacham) had to go, but he could see no necessity for Dyar to go. Dyar replied that if the others went he would go, too.

Meacham made one more appeal to Gen. Canby, suggesting that if things did not look right when they got to the Peace Tent, they should agree to anything the Indians wanted in order to make their escape. Gen. Canby and Dr. Thomas both emphatically disagreed to this, Gen. Canby stating he had never deceived any Indians, and he would enter into no agreements he did not intend to fulfill.

So the little procession started for the Peace Tent, Gen. Canby in full dress uniform without saber, and Dr. Thomas, walking ahead, Meacham and Dyar following, mounted. Riddle and Toby went along as did also the two Indian messengers, Boston and Bogus Charley. Mr. Dyar, unbeknown apparently to the others, had put a small pistol in his pocket, and both he and Meacham took what money they had in their pockets and left it with a friend before starting.

When the party arrived at the Peace Tent they found a small fire had been kindled a few feet from the tent, about which six Indians, including Capt. Jack, were gathered. The agreement was there should be five in all. This was noted at once by Meacham, especially as Bogue Charley and Boston, who were members of Jack's band, were also present, and although they professed friendliness, he knew that if treachery were intended they would join Jack. More significant still, he was soon convinced the Indians were armed in violation of their agreement. They carried no arms openly, but he was sure he could see the outlines of revolvers in the pockets of their coats and shirts. (These Indians were not "blanket" Indians, but wore the usual frontier clothing of the white man. Most of them understood and spoke English, more or less.) The Indians ranged themselves in a general way on the side of the fire towards their camp, and the Commissioners seated themselves on convenient rocks on the other side. Gen. Canby had taken along a box of cigars, which were passed around. After desultory conversation for several minutes while all smoked except Dr. Thomas, Gen. Canby arose for a brief formal talk to open the conference. He said in substance that when he was a young officer he was detailed to remove two different tribes of Indians, one from Florida and one from some other point in the southwest, to west of the Mississippi River, and that at first they did not like him, but when they got acquainted they liked him so well they elected him Chief among them. That years afterwards he visited these Indians in their new home and found them prosperous and happy, and they came a long way to meet him and shake hands with him. That the greater part of his life had been spent in the U.S. Army, in the Indian service, that he had never deceived them and had always dealt fairly with them. That he came here at the request of the President of the U.S. and that the President had ordered the troops here and they could only be removed at the President's order. That they were here only for the purpose of seeing that this commission did its duty and performed what it agreed to do. That these people (addressing them) should do what they agreed to do, and that the citizens should not interfere. That unless the President ordered it he (Gen. Canby) could not take the soldiers away.

Dr. Thomas then spoke, and from a kneeling position he said, "Toby, tell these people that I think the Great Spirit put it into the heart of the President to send us here. I have known Gen. Canby for 14 years, I have known Mr. Dyar for a few years and Mr. Meacham for 18 years, and I know their hearts, and I know they are all your friends. I know my own heart and I believe that God sees us, what we do, that he wishes us all to be at peace, that no more blood should be shed.

Capt. Jack then spoke and the main thing in his talk was that he wanted the soldiers taken away. Meacham or Canby replied that the President had sent the soldiers there and they could not be taken away without his orders. Schonchin then said he wanted Fairchild's Ranch on Hot Creek for a home, that he had been told he could have that place. He was asked who told him, whether Fairchild or Dorris, and he replied, No, but from others he had learned he could have that place. Then Schonchin said, "Unless the soldiers are taken away and you give us Hot Creek or Fairchild's Ranch, we don't want to talk any more." While Schonchin was talking Jack got up and walked out several yards to one side and then returned just as the interpreter had about finished. As Jack returned Meacham observed two Indians rise from concealment behind the rocks about 100 yards distant and come running toward the tent each carrying 2 or 3 rifles. Meacham said to Jack, "What does this mean?" rising to his feet at the same time. Jack called out "Atuck" (meaning "all ready"), at the same instant drawing a pistol from his inside breast pocket, aimed at Gen. Canby at a distance of about 5 feet and pulled the trigger. The weapon misfired, and he re-cocked it and fired, and Gen. Canby fell severely wounded. At the same time Schonchin drew a pistol and fired at

Meacham, and other Indians, including Boston, who, with Bogus Charley, had gone to the meeting with the Commissioners' party, fired on others of the Commission. Gen. Canby and Dr. Thomas were killed. Their bodies were found a few yards away from the fire, so they probably staggered away a few steps after the first shot took effect. The Surgeon testified that Gen. Canby's body showed 3 wounds and Dr. Thomas' several. Schonchin's first shot missed Meacham, and as he tried to get away Schonchin continued to fire and he was wounded 4 times before he fell unconscious 30 or 40 yards away. Dyar escaped uninjured. He seemed to take in the situation quicker and got a start. One or two Indians ran after him firing as they ran, but he returned the fire with his pocket pistol and slowed up his pursuers, making his escape. Riddle also escaped without injury although he was pursued and fired at. Toby was not fired upon but one of the Indians who brought up the rifles struck her on the back with a rifle and knocked her down, not injuring her materially. Jack ordered him to let her alone, and she was not further molested. The Indians stripped the clothing from the bodies of Gen. Canby and Dr. Thomas, and one started to scalp Meacham supposing him to be dead, and had made a cut 5 inches long on one side of his head when he was apparently frightened off, probably by the sound of approaching troops. When the troops arrived he was found to be still alive and he regained consciousness in a few minutes. He was at first thought to be mortally wounded, but none of his wounds proved to be dangerous, and he was able to be about in a few days.

The Peace Tent was not in sight from Gillem's Camp owing to the conformation of the ground, but could be seen from the signal station part way up the bluff, where a sharp watch was kept, and when the firing began the troops were notified and they advanced as rapidly as possible, but when they reached the scene the Indians had already fled to their stronghold in the Lava Beds. Col. Gillem considered it too late in the day, about 3 p.m., for concerted action for an attack on the Indians that day, so the troops returned to camp.

The foregoing account of the incidents and conversations pertaining to the tragedy of Apr. 11, is summarized from the testimony of Meacham, Dyar, Riddle and Toby at the subsequent trial of the principals in the murders.

Meantime another scene in the tragedy was being enacted in Maj. Mason's camp east of the Indians stronghold. This is realistically described by Maj. Hardin as follows:

"We now come to the day's happenings at Mason's camp. The writer was a member of the camp guard that day, and was posted as 1st relief on the outpost nearest the stronghold. Lieut. Wm. L. Sherwood, 21st Infantry, was Officer of the Day, and visited this post soon after the writer was posted. He seemed unusually cheerful. 'Well,' he said, 'this is the last day of the war and now we can all go home and rest.' Like all the other enlisted men I believed in Toby's warnings of treachery, so I replied, 'This may be the last day of the war, but I don't believe it. I think we shall have one more good battle before the war ends.'

" 'Oh, nonsense,' he laughed, 'you must not be such a croacker. We shall have peace today.'

"He made other remarks of this nature, I still showing that I was skeptical. Then he directed me to keep a sharp lookout for a flag of truce, as perhaps some of the Modocs might wish to visit our camp. Should any Indians appear in view of my post, I was to make friendly signs and try to call them in. If they would not come in I was to call the Sgt. of the Guard, that he (Sherwood) might be notified. He then left me and had been gone but a few minutes, when two Indians appeared at a distance of about 400 yards, waving a white flag. At first I could only see the flag and then their heads appeared. I stood up on the wall that was built about my post, leaving my carbine out of their sight, and waved my hand calling for them to come on in. They stood upright, but would not come nearer. I could hear their voices calling to me, but could understand or distinguish no words. I was seen and heard in camp, and soon Lieut. Sherwood came out alone. This was about 10 a.m. He asked me what the Modocs had said, and I replied I had understood nothing but they seemed to be calling for some one. He said, 'Well, I am going out to see what they want.' 'Don't go, Lieut.' I said, 'they will surely kill you.'

"He laughed and said something about my lack of confidence, and asked if I did not know that the Chiefs were to meet the Commissioners that day. To this I replied 'Yes, and it will be the end of the Commissioners, too.'

"Seeing me pull a stone out of the wall in my front, he asked, 'What are you doing that for?' I replied that I was an excellent shot and thought I could hit one of those Indians, and meant to keep him covered during their talk. He remonstrated a bit, but being assured by me that the Modocs could not see what I was doing, that I was not nervous and would not fire unless they made a bad break, he left me to meet the Modocs, while I, sitting down out of sight of the Indians, adjusted my gun sight to what I thought to be the proper elevation, and with my good old Sharp's carbine, cal. 50, at a dead rest, covered the taller of the two Modocs and kept him covered during their brief interview with the Lieut. This talk ended all right, the Indians going back among the rocks, and Lieut. Sherwood returning to my post to give me additional orders about as follows: These Indians will come out again at about 1 o'clock. They wish to talk to the "Big Tyees," Maj. Mason, Col. Bernard and Maj. Jackson. Turn over orders to your relief to have me notified when they appear.

" 'I thought so.' I said. 'What do you mean?' he asked. I answered, 'I mean they let you go so they might catch bigger game.' He laughed and returned to camp, where it appears he failed to convince Bernard, Mason or Jackson that they had any business to talk peace while unaccompanied by their troops. I am only guessing at the stand taken by these officers. All that I know positively is that none of them went out for the afternoon talk.

"Shortly after noon the Indians again appeared and Lieut. Sherwood and Lieut. Boyle, 21st Inf., went out to meet them. All over camp the men were sitting in groups with carbines or rifles in hands. The Cavalry horses had been turned out to graze and these were, without orders, rounded up at the end of camp, each trooper sitting near his saddle, ready to use it quickly. We of the guard not on post, had a slightly elevated position, from which we could see the level piece of ground on which the meeting took place. A line of hog-back conformations of lava rock concealed the spot where the meeting took place, from those who were on lower ground. The two Indians advanced unarmed, as in the morning, meeting the officers on open ground. But something happened quickly to disturb that meeting. I never knew what it was, but I do know that almost immediately after they met, the parties separated, the officers turning back toward our camp, at first walking rapidly and then breaking into a run, and the Modocs hurrying back to where they had left their rifles at the top of a little mesa. Picking up their rifles the Modocs opened fire upon the officers. As the officers came back they were concealed from our view by a hog-back formation of lava, but up to the time when they were so concealed, though the Indians had fired several shots, the officers appeared to be unhurt. When I could no longer see the officers I hurried down to where the guard had formed. With the Sergeant in command the guard rushed out toward the hog-back behind which the officers had disappeared, but we were intercepted by an officer belonging to Gillem's camp and a visitor in our camp. This officer, bareheaded and greatly

143

excited, assumed command and ordered the sergeant to move over toward our left. The sergeant tried to tell him where we should find our officers, but the self-appointed commander would listen to nothing.

"* * * The sergeant was compelled to obey, but at the same time he was determined to protect the attacked officers. Turning to me he said, 'You know where they are. I cannot get away from this lunatic. You drop back and when clear run up this draw and hurry to that hog-back. The officers are down behind that.'

"By this time the Modocs had ceased firing. I did as directed and was soon speeding toward the hog-back. As I drew near I saw Lieut. Boyle running alone toward camp. Running up the near side of the hog-back and peeping over, I saw Sherwood lying on the ground. I called to him asking if he was badly hurt and he answered saying he was. I remember noticing that his voice was strong and firm, and I concluded that he was not so badly hurt. By this time the main body of the guard under its wild commander who was still shouting orders, was nearly 200 yards to my left. I stood up and shouted, 'Here he is.' Right then the new commander lost control. The guard broke away from him and rushed down to where I was. By this time several men were arriving from camp. The guard advanced to the point where the Modocs had fired, deployed as skirmishers and laid down, covering the party preparing to move the Lieutenant to Camp. From where we took position we could see, across an arm of the lake, the tent of the Peace Commission, and almost immediately after we had taken position, we heard the shots that were killing the Commissioners. Just before this the signal flag of our camp was waving a message to the signal station at Gillem's camp, but the message could not be acted upon in time to save the Commissioners, though it did start up wild yells from Gillem's men, who were immediately rushing out of camp, and perhaps so served to hasten the return of the Modocs to their stronghold. The troops of Mason's camp hastily formed and rushed out, and it was with difficulty that the officers stopped their rush to the stronghold. Had our commanding officer not kept his head, the war would have been ended on that day, but at a fearful loss to the troops engaged."

It may be here added that Boyle escaped unhurt, but that Sherwood's wounds were mortal — he died 3 days later. Maj. Hardin says of him. "The officer, through his habit of finding occasion for speaking pleasantly and cheerfully to enlisted men, had made himself very popular. His death was a great shock to all of us, for we had entertained hopes of his recovery."

Following Gen. Canby's death, Col. Jefferson C. Davis, 23d Inf., was assigned to the command of the Department of the Columbia and ordered to join at once. He was at Indianapolis, Ind., and it would be several days before he could join. Col. Gillem made plans for an attack to begin at daylight April 15. Additional troops had arrived and the command on the east under Maj. Mason consisted of 3 cos. 21st Inf., 2 troops 1st Cav., a section of mountain howitzers under Lieut. Chapin, 4th Arty., and a company of Indian Scouts. Those on the west under Maj. Green comprised 2 troops 1st Cav., 3 Batys., 4th Arty., serving as Inf., 2 Cos. 12th Inf. and 1 Bty. 4th Arty., with Coehorn Mortars, 12 pounders. The general plan of attack was the same as for that of January 17. Both sides were to advance and a junction of the southern flanks effected enveloping the Indians on 3 sides and forcing them toward the lake on the north. But again it was found impracticable to effect a junction. Both lines met stubborn resistance but made considerable advance until darkness stopped operations, except that the mortar battery kept up a fire during the night. The attack was resumed on the morning of the 16th, and on this day a junction of the northern flanks was effected, thus cutting off the Indians from their water supply in the lake. By nightfall our troops were close to the caves where the Indians were making their main stand. During the night the Indians made unsuccessful efforts to pierce our lines to obtain water. On the morning of the 17th the advance was cautiously resumed, and it soon became apparent that the main body of the Indians had left the caves, leaving only a rear guard which was soon driven off to the south, leaving the stronghold in the possession of the troops. Col. Gillem feared the Indians had escaped from the Lava Beds to the South, and on the morning of the 18th he sent Cav. and Ind. Scouts to the south of the beds but no trail could be found. On the 20th it was found they were still in the lava beds about 4 miles south of their old stronghold. Col. Gillem did not think his force was large enough to surround them, so devoted a few days to recuperation and care of his wounded. His casualties were 6 enlisted men killed and 1 officer (Lieut. C. P. Egan, 12th Inf.) and 13 enlisted men wounded.

And now occured another tragedy of this campaign. On April 26, Maj. Green sent Capt. Evan Thomas, 4th Art., with Btrys. A & K (as Infy.), Co. E, 12th Inf., and a detachment of Indian Scouts, comprising 5 officers, a contract surgeon, about 70 enlisted men and 14 Indian Scouts, to proceed to a point which was visible from the camp and about 4 or 5 miles to the southeast, to see if he could locate the Indians but not to bring on an engagement unless obliged to, and also to ascertain whether it were practicable to take the pack train and mortar battery to that point. Leaving camp about 7 a.m. the force moved cautiously and reached the designated point about noon without seeing any signs of Indians, and halted for lunch before starting the return journey. The commanding officer seems to have assumed that as no Indians had been seen, there were none in the vicinity, and had permitted the advance guard and flankers to be drawn in. Whether he authorized this or it was done without his knowledge, is not known, but nearly the entire force was grouped about in an open space having lunch when suddenly it was fired on by Indians concealed in the rocks. A portion of the command became panic stricken and fled, eventually straggling back to the camp they had left in the morning. The officers were able to rally several men and with these fought desperately, but the Indians had the advantage of position, and killed or wounded all the detachment. The attack soon became known as the troop camp and a force was sent to the rescue, but darkness came on as the rescuers had nearly reached the field, and meeting fire from the Indians, they bivouacked till morning when the extent of the disaster was discovered. Capt. Evan Thomas, Lieut. A. B. Howe, Lieut. Arthur Cranton, all of the 4th Art., and Lieut. Thos. F. Wright, 12th Inf., were killed, and Lieut. Geo. M. M. Harris, 4th Art., and Contract Surgeon B. Semig were wounded, Harris mortally, dying about 2 weeks later. Thirteen enlisted men were killed and 16 wounded. The rescuing party returned to the main camp with the wounded and bodies of the dead, except that of Lieut. Cranston whose body could not be found after a long search. It was found, however, about 10 days later.

On the evening of May 2, Col. Jefferson C. Davis arrived at the camp and assumed command. Additional troops had meantime arrived bringing the strength up to about 600. On May 4 he made a report to Div. Hdqrs. stating it had been his intention upon arriving to make another attempt to dislodge the Indians, but he found that the disaster to Thomas' command on the 26th of April, coupled with the fact that heavy losses had occurred in all the recent fighting and but little success attained, had left a perceptible feeling of despondency in the command. He would therefore make no forward move at present. He stated with regard to the disaster of April 26, that an error had been made by the officer in command in not pushing his skirmish line further to the front and flanks before halting, but that this mistake could have been easily and quickly remedied, had the men, as a few did, stood by the officers and obeyed orders. This they did not do. The result was conspicuous cowardice on the part of the men who ran away and conspicuous bravery and death on the part of the officers and men who stood.

On May 8, Col. Davis wired Div. Hdqrs. that on the previous night he had sent out the Indian Scouts who reported the Modocs had gone in a southeasterly direction and he would send out troops after them. The report of the commander of these troops is not available, but the following is from the account of Maj. Hardin who took part in the affair:

"On the 9th of May a mounted command composed of Light Baty. B, 4th Art., serving as Cav., Troops B and G, 1st Cav. and the Warm Spring Indians, all under the command of Capt. Henry Hasbrouch, 4th Arty., started out to find the Modocs. That evening they camped at Lake Soras (sometimes called Dry Lake) a very small, dry pond covered with gravel. The battery went on further, making camp at the edge of the 'Pinery' about 2 or 3 miles further south. Capt Hasbrouck remained in command at Lake Soras. It appears that as we were out to find the Modocs no special precautions were taken to prevent their finding us. All the horses were turned loose under a small guard, for the night, and no other sentinels were posted. At daybreak on May 10th, all of the horses were rounded up on level ground, between the bivouac of the troops and a semi-circular ridge of rocks on our north and west and about 100 yards distant from our bivouac. Just about 1st call for reveille, a Warm Spring Indian ventured into the rocks at the edge of the rocky formation to catch his pony, and was shot through the head by a hidden Modoc. The men in camp, thinking this was an accidental shot fired by some member of the guard, were making comments thereon. I was sitting up facing the rocks pulling on a boot, when I saw a line of Modocs pop up their heads and fire a volley. This at first caused some confusion. Men rolled over behind saddle and bundles of blankets, no covering however small being ignored, fastening on belts and pulling on boots, under a hail of bullet. The officers at some distance in our rear, having to put on boots and coats, could not immediately join us and assume command. There was a possibility of a panic; but this was happily averted by Sgt. Thos. Kelly of our Troop, who sprang up and shouted, "Gosh dash it, let's charge!" Bernard was not there but his pupil was. The men responded beautifully, and by the time we had gotten fairly started our officers were with us, with Capt. Hasbrouck sprinting for the lead. It was a beautiful charge with Troops B and G all mixed together, and as fine a man as ever lived, of the 4th Arty., leading. Our loss was 5 killed and 12 wounded of a force of 50 men. We carried the position and went on beyond it, until the scattered Modocs had entirely ceased firing and disappeared. We captured a considerable quantity of ammunition, etc. * * * To be sure our losses were heavy but the morale had not suffered. The prompt charge had done the work, and the same would have done the work on April 26th. Afterwards the Modocs told us they had lost 5 killed. We only came into possession of two of these. One of these was Ellen's Man, one of the murderers of the Peace Commission. After Skirmishing through the rocks until no shots were being fired at us, and recall had been sounded, we returned to camp and breakfast.

"One of the outstanding figures of the affair was our contract surgeon, John O. Skinner (now Lieut. Col., Ret.), who promptly established a dressing station behind a small ridge of lava, less than waist high, which afforded shelter for a man lying down but not much for the operator. Here I found him working alone when I led a wounded man back. I was about to leave him, as I did not particularly like the position, and too many bullets were howling about there; Skinner held me back by declaring that he must have help, and while working upon one man, he calmly directed my efforts to stopping the flow of blood from another man who had been shot through the arm, the shot severing the main artery. Under his cool direction I succeeded in this my first undertaking of the kind, and perhaps a life was saved. This was not the first time that J. O. Skinner had distinguished himself during the campaign. After his name in the Army Register appear the initial "M.H.," an honor fairly won. After describing the collecting of the stampeded horses he continues: "then, with but a short rest, we made an all night march back to our camp on the lake."

Col. Davis in his annual report of Nov. 1, 1873, gives a brief description of this fight, concluding the following: "The troops have had, all things considered, a very square fight and whipped the Modocs for the first time. But the whole band was again in the rocky stronghold."

They were found to be near the site of Thomas' fight of April 26th. Official reports of subsequent military operations are rather meager, as it will apear the command was soon to operate in small detachments, and reports of these subordinate commanders, if submitted, are not available. To summarize from Col. Davis' annual report: Hasbrouck's command was directed to follow the Modocs on foot and never to lose sight of them. Maj. Mason with his Infantry and Mendenhall's foot Artillery, was moved down through the lava beds as near the enemy as possible and opposite Hasbrouck's command. The Indians, he says, were now threatened with attacks from two sides, sandwiched but not surrounded. He says his troops being by this time much recuperated and inspirited, he decided to carry out the plan he had formed when he first arrived, viz, to move all the troops into the lava beds and form a series of bivouacs from which they could fight when opportunity offered, or could rest and take things easy like the Indians did. Several days of comparative inaction followed, and then it was discovered the Indians had quietly under cover of darkness deserted their position in the lava beds. It was not then known but it was later discovered that the Indians by this time were running short of supplies and had become so much exhausted by the necessity of being on the alert day and night, that the dissensions which had always existed to a greater or less extent in the band, had become more pronounced and led to quarrels and the division of the band into two parties, bitter enemies. The trail of the Indians was found to lead in a westerly direction, and Hasbrouck's command was mounted and sent in pursuit, and after a hard march of 50 miles overtook a band and had a sharp running fight of 7 or 8 miles, taking some captives. The Indians scattered and as night was coming on, Hasbrouck withdrew to Fairchild's Ranch for the night. From some of the captives it was learned that this band would like to surrender, and through the medium of friendly Indians they finally came in and laid down their arms, the band numbering about 75, including old men, women and children. But Jack was not in this band. Rumors indicated that he had gone to the south or east, and the captives confirmed this. In either case the settlers might be in danger. All the Cavalry including Indian Scouts was ordered to rendezvous at once at Boyle's camp, east of Tule Lake, and it was to be divided into 3 detachments under Captains Hasbrouck, Perry and Jackson respectively, Maj. Green in general command. This concentration would require about 3 days, and meantime one of the Modoc prisoners, who before the division of the band was known to be in the confidence of Jack, offered to find him. Col. Davis says he knew the Indian was an unmitigated cutthroat, and for this reason was loath to make any use of him that would compromise his well-earned claims to the halter. He does not state who this Indian was, but from subsequent statements it is believed he referred to Hooker Jim. He wanted 8 other Indians to go with him, fearing Jack's camp on Willow Creek east of Wright's lake, about 15 miles from Applegate's Ranch, to which place Col. Davis had gone to await their return. On receipt of this information, Hasbrouck's and Jackson's commands were ordered to come at once to Applegate's Ranch, where they arrived at 9 a.m. May 29, with Maj. Green. After resting the horses for a short time, the command set out at 1 p.m. and jumped Jack and his band on Willow Creek, a stream forming the headwaters of Lost River. The Indians fled in the direction of Langell's Valley. In the meantime Capt. Perry's command had arrived at Applegate's Ranch on May 22, and was at once sent out to follow the trails. Lieut. Col. Frank Wheaton arrived here the same date, he having been again placed in command of the troops in the field, vice Gillen, relieved. The Indians had scattered and Col. Davis says the final operations partook more of the nature of a chase after wild beasts than war, each detachment vieing with the others as to which should be first in at the finish. The final captures, including Capt. Jack, were effected by June 3, except there were 2 or 3 hostiles, supposed to be still alive, of whom no trace could be found, and further search for them was abandoned. By June 5, the troops and prisoners were assembled at the Tule Lake camp, and Col. Davis was making arrangements to execute some 8 or 10 of the ringleaders. He states he had the material for the scaffold already cut out and was investigating as to which ones he should hang, when instructions came from the War Department to hold all the prisoners under guard till further instructions as to their disposition. The entire command with the prisoners was then marched to Ft. Klamath, where a Military Commission was convened to try the ring-leaders. There was some correspondence as to which individuals should be brought to trial, and it was finally decided to try only those directly implicated in the murders at the Peace Tent, Capt. Jack, Schonchin John, Boston Charley, Black Jim, Barncho and Sloluk, 6 in all. The two last named were the men who came running to the tent with rifles when the attack began. There were 4 others directly concerned. Ellen's Man, who was killed in the Soras Lake fight, Hooker Jim, Bogus Charley and Shacknasty Jim. Col. Davis said that he considered Hooker Jim as probably the worst criminal in the band, but he seemed to be the only one in Jack's confidence who knew his plans, hiding places, etc., and he had accepted his offer to find Jack, when he surrendered at Fairchild's Ranch, although being careful not to promise his immunity. Moreover, consider that Hooker Jim had had a quarrel with Capt. Jack and deserted him, it was at considerable risk that he and his three companions went to Jack's camp and brought back word as to his whereabouts, leading to his capture. It was presumably because of the implied immunity in accepting his service that the 3 last mentioned above were not brought to trial. The Judge Advocate of the Commission stated that there were 3 Indians concerned in the attack on Lieuts. Sherwood and Boyle, but of these one was dead, one was still at large and the third could not be identified, so no action could be taken against those concerned in this attack.

The trial began July 2 and lasted till the 9th. The 6 prisoners were found guilty of murder in violation of the laws of war and of assault with intent to kill in violation of the laws of war, and sentenced to be hanged. The sentences were approved by the President August 22, 1873, and ordered carried into execution on October 3rd. Before that date arrived, the sentences of Barncho and Sloluk were commuted by the President to life imprisonment, and they were sent to Alcatraz where they served till death. The other 4 were duly executed October 3rd at Ft. Klamath.

The commutation of the sentences of Barncho and Sloluk was probably due to a letter of the Judge Advocate of the Commission, in which he stated they were of a very low order of intelligence and in nowise leaders of the band. During the trial they sat or lay on the floor taking no interest in the proceedings, much of the time apparently asleep, and palpably unable to comprehend what it was all about.

The remainder of the prisoners with their families were sent to a reservation in the Indian Territory. 1909 Congress authorized their restoration to the Rolls of the Klamath Reservation but few of them seem to have returned there. In 1927, the latest figures available, there were still 209 living on the Klamath Reservation.

The casualties of the troops during the war were reported as follows:

TOTAL

Wounded, 3 officers, 61 enlisted men, 1 citizen, 2 Indian Scouts, ... 67

Killed, 8 officers, 39 enlisted men, 16 citizens, 2 Indian Scouts 65

Aggregate killed and wounded 132

No statement is given as to the casualties of the Modocs. Dr. Brady in his book above referred to, estimates their deaths to have been about one-third of ours, and his guess is perhaps as good as any.

At the trial of the prisoners by the Military Commission, when the defense evidence was all in, the Judge Advocate stated he had intended to submit the case without remark, but that Capt. Jack in his own defense had made the charge that Maj. Jackson had started the whole trouble by firing first on the Indians in the fight of November 29th. He therefore introduced in evidence Maj. Jackson's official account of the fight, which indicated the Indians had fired first.

It may be stated that other writers have accepted the Indian's version in placing the blame on the military authorities. Maj. Jackson was evidently under the impression that the Indians fired first, as shown by the wording of his report, previously quoted. Maj. Boutelle, however, in his account of the fight written for Dr. Brady's book, written some years after the occurrence to be sure, but as he was the principal actor in the beginning of the fight, it may be taken as accurate, says, "As soon as we formed in the Modoc camp, Maj. Jackson, through Applegate, who knew the Indians individually, attempted to summon Capt. Jack, but could neither get a talk with nor a sight of the chief. While these attempts at a parley were going on, the Indians, under the influence of Scarface Charley and others, were undoubtedly preparing for combat. Applegate saw there was trouble brewing as fast as possible. Scarface Charley had withdrawn to one end of the camp and was talking in a very excited manner with a number of other Indians. He had a rifle in his hands which he waved defiantly and 3 or 4 lay on the ground beside him. Maj. Jackson finally rode over to me and said, 'Mr. Boutelle, what do you think of the situation?' 'There is going to be a fight,' I replied, 'and the sooner you open it the better, before there are any more complete preparation.' He then ordered me to take some men and arrest Scarface Charley and his followers. I had taken the situation in pretty thoroughly in my mind, and knew that an attempt to arrest meant the killing of more men than could be spared if any of the survivors were to escape. I was standing in front of the Troop. I called out to the men, 'Shoot over these Indians,' and raised my pistol and fired at Scarface Charley. Great minds appear to have thought alike. At the same instant Charley raised his rifle and fired at me. We both missed, his shot passing through my clothing over my elbow. * * * He goes on to say that he and Scarface talked the affair over afterwards, and they could not determine in their own minds as to which actually fired first. He continues, 'The fight at once became general, * * *' It therefore appears that the first two shots were those of Lieut. Boutelle and Scarface Charley, and they were practically simultaneous. But no matter who actually fired first, Maj. Jackson's action needs no defense, although he probably would have needed defense if he had withheld his fire any longer. His orders required him to bring the Indians back to the reservation, peaceably if he could, but if it became necessary to use force, then to arrest the three leaders. He exercised much patience in trying to induce them to submit without force. The Superintendent of Indian Affairs, and probably others, thought that a display of military force would be all that was necessary. But there had been a display of military force all about the Indians for months, and they only became more insolent in their determination not to submit. Maj. Jackson by a well executed and well timed march, surprised them, thus placing a military force face to face with them in the most effective way to test the efficacy of a display of force. When they refused to surrender and showed a hostile attitude, the time for action had arrived. He was faced by a force partially concealed in camp which he had every reason to believe was as large or larger than his own, while his men were in the open. Any further delay might mean the destruction of half of his command at the first volley. He showed a very nice discrimination as to the instant to resort to force, after giving the Indians a fair chance to comply peacefully with his orders.

The outstanding feature of the War was, of course, the treacherous murder of Gen. Canby and Dr. Thomas, and the simultaneous attack on the east side, resulting in Lieut. Sherwood's death. Gen. Canby's death can only be attributed, as expressed in the order announcing it, to "his entire self-abnegation and fidelity to the expressed wishes of his government." His own deliberately formed judgment as to the proper procedure, is set forth in his telegram of January 30 to Gen. Sherman, above quoted. His reply to the protest of Meacham against this final conference showed that he realized there was great danger of treachery. But the Peace Commission had already had one or two conferences with the Indians and nothing had happened, presumably after the threat of treachery had been revealed to them (although this is not certain as the exact time of the warning is not given). If this conference were given up, then the Peace Commission must be acknowledged a failure, and his loyalty to the administration which so heartily and repeatedly expressed its desire for a peaceful settlement would not permit him to give up without one more effort, with himself present at the council. He could not bring himself to believe that the Indians, with such a superior force of troops all about them, would take such a suicidal step as to treacherously attack the commission. So he went fearlessly forth, as it proved, to his death.

The high esteem in which he was held is beautifully expressed in the following General Order:

HEADQUARTERS OF THE ARMY

Washington, Apr. 14/73.

G.O. No. 3

It again becomes the sad duty of the General, to announce to the Army the death of one of our most illustrious and most honored comrades—

Brig. Gen. Edward R. S. Canby, Comdg. the Dept. of the Columbia, was, on Friday last, April 11, shot dead by the Chief, "Jack," while he was endeavoring to mediate for the removal of the Modocs from their present rocky fastness on the northern border of California to a reservation where the tribe could be maintained and protected by the proper civil agents of the government.

That such a life should have been sacrificed in such a cause, will ever be a source of regret to his relatives and friends, yet the General trusts that all good soldiers will be consoled in knowing that Gen. Canby lost his life "on duty" and in the execution of his office, for he had been specially chosen and appointed for this delicate and dangerous task by reason of his well-know patience and forebearance, his entire self-abnegation and fidelity to the expressed wishes of his government, and his large experience in dealing with the savage Indians of America.

He had already completed the necessary military preparations to enforce obedience to the conclusions of the Peace Commission, after which he seems to have accompanied them to a last conference with the savage Chiefs in supposed friendly council, and there met his death by treachery, outside of his military lines, but within view of the signal station. At the same time one of the Peace Commissioners was killed outright, another mortally wounded, and the third escaped unhurt.

Thus perished one of the kindest and best gentlemen of this or any other country, whose social equaled his military virtues. To even sketch his army history, would pass the limits of a General Order, and it must here suffice to state that Gen. Canby began his military career as a cadet at West Point in the summer of 1835, graduating in 1839, since which time he has continuously served 38 years, passing through all the grades of Major General of Volunteers and Brigadier General of the Regular Army. He served his early life with marked distinction in the Florida and Mexican Wars, and the outbreak of the Civil War found him on duty in New Mexico, where after the defection of his seniors he remained in command and defended the country successfully against a formidable inroad from the direction of Texas. Afterward transferred east to a more active and important sphere, he exercised various high commands, and at the close of the Civil War was in chief command of the Military Division of the West Mississippi, in which he had received a painful wound, but had the honor to capture Mobile and compel the surrender of the rebel forces of the southwest.

Since the close of the Civil War he has repeatedly been chosen for special command by reason of his superior knowledge of law and civil government, his known fidelity to the wishes of the executive, and his chivalrous devotion to his profession, in all which his success has been perfect.

When fatigued by a long and laborious career, in 1869, he voluntarily consented to take command of the Dept. of the Columbia, where he expected to enjoy the repose he so much coveted. The Modoc difficulty arising last winter, and it being extremely desirous to end it by peaceful means, it seems almost providential that it should have occurred in the sphere of Gen. Canby's command.

He responded to the call of his government with alacrity, and has labored with a patience that deserved better success, but alas, the end is different from that which he and his best friends had hoped for, and he now lies a corpse in the wild mountains of California, while the lightning flashes his requiem to the furthermost corners of the civilized world. Though dead, the record of his fame resplendent with noble deeds well done, and no name on our Army stands fairer or higher for the personal qualities that command the universal respect, honor, affection and love of his countrymen.

151

Gen. Canby leaves to his country a heart broken widow but no children. Every honor consistent with law and usage shall be paid to his remains, full notice of which will be given as soon as his family can be consulted and arrangements concluded.

By command of Gen. Sherman.
Wm. D. Whipple,
Asst. Adjutant General.

1932

The paper read before the assembled Companions (38) and guests (8) was a departure from the normally expected subject. This year, "in keeping with the spirit of the national bicentennial celebration commemorating the birth of George Washington, the lengthy address delivered by Brigadier General George W. McIver had as its subject "The Services of George Washington In The French And Indian War." This was followed by remarks of Lieutenant Colonel Charles E. T. Lull who directed his remarks to the value of collecting historical material relating to Indian Wars of the United States.

At the regular business meeting which transpired before the dinner the Official Board and Council were presented with a very interesting proposal. As reported in the *Proceedings,* it is as follows:

A blank petition and letter from Honorary Companion E. A. Brininstool, petitioning the Governor of Montana to take some action towards having the grave of Lieut. Crittenden removed from the National Cemetery and restored to its original location — where he fell — was read. After discussion, it was ordered that the papers in the case be referred to the Investigating Committee for investigation and report at the annual meeting.

REPORT OF INVESTIGATING COMMITTEE

Re: Recommendation of Mr. E. A. Brininstool, of Los Angeles, Cal., that the Order join in a general petition to the Governor of Montana, that the body of Lieutenant Crittenden (killed in the Custer Fight), be transferred from the National Cemetery, Custer Battle Field, to its original location, where the officer "fell in battle."

The Committee carefully examined all the papers in the case, and where complete evidence appeared to be lacking, wrote letters to the Governor of Montana, Mr. Brininstool, Commander of Post of American Legion, Hardin, Montana, and the Superintendent, National Cemetery, Custer Battlefield. Attention is also invited to report of an interview with the Chief, Memorial Division, Office Quartermaster General. This report, which appears to throw an entirely new light on loose statements that the body was disinterred by the State of Montana because of being on the right of way of a highway connecting the Custer and Reno Battlefields, alleges positively (1) that the reinterment of the body was approved by the Secretary of War long before the said highway was constructed; (2) that the original grave was not within the survey of the highway; (3) that removal of the body was ordered by the War Department, for its perpetual care and protection — vandals having well-nigh destroyed the original headstone; (4) that in its original location, it was totally impracticable for the War Department to prevent vandalism, or to keep the grave in proper condition; (5) that the reinterment was executed with due and fitting ceremony, and honors paid by the local post of the American Legion; and (6) that the present location of the body in the National Cemetery, insures protection and perpetual care, amid surroundings which are greatly in contrast to the former location of the grave on a sandy waste. It should also be noted that up to the time of reinterment, no surviving relative could be located by the War Department, to pass upon the removal of the body, although every effort was made.

In view of all the circumstances and facts before the Committee, the latter recommends that no change be made in the present location of Lieutenant Crittenden's remains; and that Mr. Brininstool be informed by the Recorder of the recommendation of the Committee, and of the reasons therefore, as stated in paragraph above.

For the Committee of Investigation:

(Signed) CHARLES D. RHODES,
Chairman.

Memorandum of an interview, February 16, 1932, had by General Rhodes with Lieut. Col. James H. Laubach, Q.M.C., Chief Memorial Division, Office Q.M. General, re: disinterment of the remains of Lieut. Crittenden from the Custer Battlefield:

The matter came up over a year ago. Information reached the Quartermaster General that Crittenden's grave was sadly neglected, and that the original monument or headstone had been seriously defaced by tourists chipping off pieces as souvenirs. On an inspection trip to the Pacific Coast, Lieut. Col. Laubach personally visited the Custer Battlefield and submitted to the Quartermaster General a special report and recommendation regarding the grave. The latter, about 250-300 yards from the little National Cemetery where all the other victims of the Custer Fight are buried, was found not at all close to the road joining the Custer and Reno battlegrounds. The grave was on the government reservation and not on state land. It was found impracticable — so Col. Laubach reported to the Quartermaster General, for the Superintendent of the Cemetery to either give the grave care, through the piping of water for turf and flowers; neither could he, although he lives within the Cemetery boundaries, give the grave protection from vandals. Accordingly, Col. Laubach recommended that the remains be removed to the Cemetery, with military honors, provided no relatives of Lieut. Crittenden could be found to determine for the Crittenden family, what should be done with the neglected grave.

For several months, every effort was made to find a surviving relative. The Commanding General, 9th Corps Area, was especially active in trying to discover some survivor of the immediate family, but to no purpose. The case was then given, again, very careful and serious consideration by the present Quartermaster General, and not content with making his own decision, something he had every right to do, General De Witt went to the Secretary of War and explained all the complexities of the case. The Secretary thereupon ordered that the recommendation of the Quartermaster General be carried out, and the remains were carefully disinterred by the Quartermaster Corps, and reinterred with military honors by the local military and American Legion of Hardin, Montana, in the National Cemetery of the Custer Battlefield.

The Quartermaster General, about that time, also secured funds by which the Cemetery, hitherto, a rather desolate and barren spot, was furnished with piped water for irrigation, and also initiated the planting of trees and shrubs, with a view to beautifying the spot. In time, the Cemetery will be quite attractive, it is stated.

Since the disinterment of Lieut. Crittenden's body, a rather distant relative has turned up, a native of Kentucky; and he it is who in part, has through his Congressman and others, entered his objection to removal of the remains from the original location — the latter not being at all a certainty as "where he fell in battle."

To sum up: the removal of the remains was done by the Quartermaster General from government land to other government land, and not by the State of Montana; it was done to protect the grave from vandalism and neglect; and in the opinion of the Quartermaster General, it should remain in the Cemetery, where it can, for all time, receive perpetual care and protection. It is also pointed out that the reinterment was made long before a State or other improved highway was contemplated, and that evidently, the latter did not enter into the question at all.

(Signed) C. D. RHODES.

Upon completion of the reading of the report of the Investigating Committee and, after considerable discussion in which some of the members verified certain facts developed by the Committee, it was moved, seconded and ordered that the following resolution be adopted.

WHEREAS the remains of Lieutenant John J. Crittenden are now interred in the Custer Battlefield National Cemetery, and

WHEREAS the grave containing said remains is under the jurisdiction of the Superintendent of that Cemetery and will receive perpetual care and attention while under his jurisdiction, and

WHEREAS to remove said grave from his jurisdiction would expose it to vandalism and neglect, therefore,

BE IT RESOLVED by The Order of Indian Wars of the United States, in annual meeting assembled, that the restoration of the grave of Lieutenant Crittenden to its original location would not be to the best interests of all

155

concerned, and

BE IT RESOLVED FURTHER that The Order of Indian Wars of the United States be and is hereby placed on record as opposed to any act or petition for the removal of and to the removal of the remains of Lieutenant Crittenden from their present location in the Custer Battlefield National Cemetery.

BE IT RESOLVED FURTHER that a copy of this resolution be furnished The Quartermaster General of the Army, Mr. E. A. Brininstool and Mr. A. B. Ostrander.

L.F.Bjorklund

Washington in the French and Indian War

By Brig. Gen. George W. McIver

Foreword

With the approach of the Bicentennial Year of Washington the Council of the Order of Indian Wars of the United States deemed it appropriate to have read at the annual meeting and dinner of the Order, February 20, 1932, an account of the services of Washington in the Indian Wars of his period. Investigation showed that he took no part in any Indian War waged solely between the Whites and the Indians, but that he participated in the French and Indian War, known in Europe as the Seven Years War.

This war was begun officially in 1756, but there were preludes and hostile acts long before any formal declaration of war. In addition to relating these preliminary events in which Washington bore a distinguished part, the writer has sought to bring out Washington's associations and contacts with the Indians, both as allies and as enemies, before and during the war.

The Causes of the War

In 1748, Washington was living at Mt. Vernon with his half brother, Lawrence Washington, who was his guardian. In that year he went to William and Mary College to take a course in surveying and in July, 1749, he was appointed a public surveyor in Virginia. The two or three years spent at this occupation in the western part of Virginia provided a schooling and an experience very valuable to him in his later career. At the age of nineteen he was given the appointment of Adjutant General in Virginia with the rank of Major, a position which brought him to the notice of the acting Royal Governor of Virginia, Robert Dinwiddie. In 1748, although a treaty of peace had just been concluded, political conditions and events in America were making another war inevitable. Primarily the conflict was to come from disputes over frontiers and boundaries between the rival Canadian and English colonies, their respective claims being backed up by the mother countries in Europe. These colonies had been at war before, but past wars had been on account of European disputes. The war that was at hand, entirely different in its origin and motives, was to be started by a young provincial officer in the backwoods of Pennsylvania; but the flame kindled in America was also to set Europe on fire. By virtue of the explorations of La Salle, France laid claim to all the territory lying between the Mississippi River and the Allegheny Mountains. Virginia claimed a strip of territory in extension of its north and south boundaries clear out to the Pacific Ocean and in addition claimed the territory in western Pennsylvania around the headwaters of the Ohio River.

The Ohio Company was a trading and development company organized in 1749 by prominent Virginians and London merchants. It had been granted half a million acres of land in the Ohio River valley under certain conditions and it was the threat of French encroachment on these lands that led to protests made by Governor Dinwiddie, of Virginia. The French were engaged in linking up Canada with the colony of Louisiana through the means of a series of forts, Missions and trading posts and the occupation of the Ohio valley was part of the plan.

In 1748, Count Gallissoniere, then Governor of Canada, proposed to bring over ten thousand French peasants from France and plant them in the valley of the Ohio and on the borders of the Lakes. This plan was not carried out, but military occupation of the Ohio River country was undertaken in 1753. In the spring of that year reports were brought to Virginia by traders that French soldiers had crossed Lake Erie, fortified themselves at Presqu-Isle (now Erie, Penna.) and pushed forward to the northern branches of the Ohio. Robert Dinwiddie, a Scotchman, Lieutenant Governor of Virginia at this time and in fact the actual Governor in place of the absentee Governor, Lord Albemarle, was a strenuous opponent of French aggression and as soon as he heard of the arrival of the French force at Presqu-Isle he warned the home government of the danger and urged the immediate construction of forts on the Ohio. There came a letter in reply, signed by the King, authorizing him to build the forts at the expense of the Colony, and to repel force by force in case he was molested or obstructed. Under this authority the Governor decided to send a note to the French Commander, challenging his right of occupation and summoning him to withdraw. In casting about for an agent to convey the message his choice fell upon the young provincial officer, Major George Washington, twenty-one years of age, whom he had met for the first time in January of the previous year. The dispatch of this message was the first in a series of events of the utmost importance to America and to mankind. In making the choice of an envoy the Governor was giving to Washington an opportunity to perform his first important public service. It was the first step in a career which was to lead him to become the central figure in a group of great men who laid the foundations of American liberties and American institutions.

By this time the Ohio Company had built a trading post at the mouth of Wills Creek on the Potomac River on the site of the present town of Cumberland, Md.

In the letter of instructions given to Washington by Governor Dinwiddie he was directed to proceed to Logstown on the Ohio and hold a communication with Tanacharisson and the other chiefs of the friendly mixed tribes in that vicinity; inform them of the purport of his mission and request an escort to the headquarters of the French commander. He was also told to acquaint himself with the numbers and the dispositions of the French on the Ohio and vicinity. Logstown was an important Indian village situated on the Ohio River about seventeen miles below the site of the present city of Pittsburgh. It was the home of Tanacharisson, also called Half King, a Seneca Chief, who was also the head chief ot the mixed tribes who had migrated to the Ohio River and its branches. He was called Half King for the reason that he and his people were subordinate to the Iroquois Confederacy.

The Mission to the Ohio

Washington set out from Williamsburg October 31, 1753, and proceeding to Fredericksburg he employed there a Dutch soldier of fortune, Captain Jacob Van Braam, to accompany him as French interpreter. Going next to Alexandria he went from there to Winchester, Va., then a frontier town, where he procured horses and camp equipment. He then pushed on over a newly constructed road to the trading post at Wills Creek, where he arrived November 14th. Here he met Christopher Gist, an employee of the Ohio Company, whom he engaged to accompany and pilot him. He secured the services also of John Davidson, an Indian interpreter and of fourteen frontiersmen as servants and helpers.

The party, now increased to a total of eight persons, set forth the morning of November 15th through a wild and difficult country made almost impassable by recent snow and rains. The party arrived in the vicinity of the junction of the Allegheny and Monongahela Rivers November 22nd, and while here, Washington, after making an examination of the ground, decided upon its suitability as the site for a fort. In his report of his expedition he said in part: "I spent some time in viewing the rivers and the land at the fork which I think extremely well situated for a fort as it has the absolute command of both rivers." French engineers subsequently confirmed his judgment by constructing Fort Duquesne at this point. In this vicinity lived Shingis, the head chief of the Delawares, and Washington visited him and invited him to the council at Logstown. He accepted the invitation since he was at this time friendly, but later he changed his allegiance and took up the hatchet against the English. Washington and his party arrived at Logstown late in the day on November 24th. The Half King was absent at the time, but he returned the next day and Washington had a private interview with him, learning much about the designs of the French. The next day Washington met the chiefs at the council house; made them a friendly speech; told them of his mission to the French commander and asked for their advice and assistance. He concluded his speech by presenting the Indian token of friendship, a belt of wampum. A reply was made by Half King, who assured him of their friendly feeling for the English and declared their intention of renouncing all friendly relations with the French. He also promised an escort for Washington's party in proceeding to the French commander's headquarters.

On November 30th, Washington continued his journey, his party having been augmented by the chief Half King and three other Indians. After several days' travel in the rain and snow, they arrived December 4th at the old Indian town of Venango (site of the present town of Franklin, Pa.), situated at the point where French Creek enters the Allegheny. Here had been an English trading establishment, but the French had seized it in the previous August and turned it into a military outpost. Captain Joncaire was in command of this post with two subalterns. Joncaire was the son of a French officer and an Indian mother and had grown up with the Indians. He was highly thought of by the French authorities for his ability to conciliate the Indians and win their favor. He received Washington and his party with great civility, inviting them to supper, where they were regaled with an abundance of wine. Washington said of this incident: "The wine soon banished the restraint which at first appeared on their conversation and gave a license to their tongues to reveal their sentiments more freely."

The revelations made at this time indicated plainly to Washington that the French had every intention of remaining permanently in the Ohio valley. When Washington advised Joncaire of the purpose of his mission, he was told he should apply for an answer to the General Officer who was at Fort Le Boeuf (on the present site of the town of Waterford, Erie Co., Pa.) on French Creek about sixty miles away. Several French guides were furnished to conduct the party to Fort Le Boeuf, but before leaving Venango on December 7th, Washington was obliged to do his utmost to keep his Indian companions from deserting him. Joncaire had from the first been active in trying to induce them to leave Washington's party. After four days of difficult travel, Fort Le Boeuf was reached, December 11th.

Washington was very politely received by the French commander, whose name was Legardeur de Saint-Pierre (Lagardeur de Saint-Pierre was killed in action at the battle of Lake George, New York, September 8, 1755), a veteran officer of long service. Washington

161

described him as "an elderly gentleman with much the air of a soldier." At this time he had just returned from a three years' absence in Manitoba, where he had been sent by his government on a mission of exploration and discovery, the main purpose of which was to find an overland route to the Pacific Ocean. His station and base of operations while there had been Fort LaReine, a French trading post on the Assiniboine River three hundred miles west of the present city of Winnipeg, Manitoba. The letter sent him by Governor Dinwiddie expressed surprise that his troops should build forts upon land "notoriously known to be the property of the Crown of Great Britain." "I must desire you," continued the letter, "to acquaint me by whose authority and instructions you have lately marched from Canada with an armed force and invaded the King of Great Britain's territories." * * * * "It becomes my duty to require your peaceable departure, * * *" Saint-Pierre took three days to draw up the answer. In it he said he should send Dinwiddie's letter to the Governor of Canada, the Marquis Duquesne, and await his orders; that in the meanwhile he should remain at his post, in accordance with the orders he had received from his superiors. Washington was well treated throughout his stay at Fort Le Boeuf and no form of courtesy was lacking. At the same time every kind of persuasion and artifice was used on the part of the French to induce Half King and the other Indians to desert his party. Neither gifts nor brandy were spared and it was only by the utmost pains and effort that Washington could prevent his red allies from remaining at the fort. While waiting, Washington occupied himself in observing and taking notes of the plan, dimensions and strength of the fort, the personnel of the garrison and the number of canoes available, all of which was in due time reported to Governor Dinwiddie. After having sent the pack horses ahead, Washington returned to Venango by canoe, arriving there December 22nd. Here he was obliged most unwillingly to part with his Indian companions. One of them, named White Thunder, had become disabled through an accident and as he was unable to walk, the others decided to remain with him. On the 25th of December, Washington and his party set out by land from Venango on the way home. Having travelled three days with the horses now weakened from lack of forage, he became impatient at the slow progress and determined to make better time by leaving his party behind and going ahead. Taking Gist with him, he set off on foot, leaving Captain Van Braam in charge of the other men and the pack horses to follow by easy marches. A day or two later, while passing an old Indian settlement called "Murdering Town," they were fired upon by an Indian at close range, but the Indian missed his aim and no damage was done. He was quickly captured while trying to reload his gun and Gist wished to kill him at once, but Washington interposed and he was set free. To escape from such an unfriendly neighborhood they walked all night and all the next day. This brought them to the banks of the Allegheny, which they found filled with floating ice. While trying to cross on an improvised raft, Washington was pitched into the cold stream and saved himself with difficulty. The next stopping place was at Frazier's place on the Monongahela at the mouth of Turtle Creek, near the scene of Braddock's defeat a year and a half later. He paused here two or three days and being concerned about the importance of cultivating the friendship of the Indians he took the opportunity of paying a visit of ceremony to an Indian Princess of the Delaware tribe called by the English, Queen Aliquippa. As tokens of friendship and good will Washington presented her with what he called a "match coat" and a bottle of rum, the latter being especially appreciated. Leaving Frazier's place on the 1st of January, they arrived in two days at Gist's house. Here they separated and Washington, having purchased a horse, continued on his way alone, reaching Williamsburg January 16th. He immediately delivered to the Governor the letter of the French

162

commander and made a report of the events of his mission. In making the entire journey he had covered about one thousand miles. He had been beset with problems and difficulties at every turn, but owing to his talents and his character, he had been equal to every occasion. His success pointed him out to the Governor and to the public as one eminently fitted, notwithstanding his youth, for important trusts involving civil as well as military duties. From this time forth he was a marked man. The information given by Washington of what he had observed on the frontier convinced Governor Dinwiddie that the French were preparing to take military possession of the Ohio River valley. He was also impressed with Washington's recommendation that a fort be constructed at the forks of the Ohio. To give effect to this, a Captain Trent was sent to the frontier with authority to raise a company of one hundred backwoodsmen, who were to be employed in the construction of a fort at the appointed place. The construction was actually begun, but the work was interrupted by the French before much progress had been made. After much controversy between the Governor and the House of Burgesses of Virginia, ways and means were found for raising a regiment of six companies in Virginia to meet the emergency. Joshua Fry, an English gentleman, was made Colonel of the regiment and Washington was appointed Lieutenant Colonel. Receiving his commission March 31st, he was at the same time directed to take the troops, then quartered in Alexandria, and march with them towards the Ohio, there to aid Captain Trent in building forts and in defending the possessions of His Majesty against the attempts and hostilities of the French.

His First Campaign

Washington left Alexandria April 2nd, his command of two companies numbering about ten officers and one hundred and fifty enlisted men. Proceeding by way of Winchester he arrived at the trading post of Wills Creek April 20th. Upon his arrival or very soon thereafter, he learned that the French had taken the unfinished fort on the Ohio on April 17th. Thirty-two men under Ensign Ward were engaged in the work of construction when the French under Contrecoeur, coming down from Venango, appeared and demanded an immediate surrender. Contrecoeur had an imposing force including artillery, so that prudence suggested submission to the demand of the French commander. Under the terms of the surrender, Ward was allowed to depart with his men and working tools. The Indian Chief, Half King, was with Ward at the time and accompanied him during the negotiations. When Ward arrived at Wills Creek with his party on April 25th, he was accompanied by two warriors bearing speeches from Half King, one addressed to Washington himself, the other with a belt of wampum being addressed to Governor Dinwiddie. In these speeches he plighted his adherence to the English cause and claimed assistance from his brothers of Virginia and Pennsylvania. One of the warriors was sent on to Governor Dinwiddie with the speech and belt of wampum. The other was sent back to Half King bearing a speech from Washington addressed to "The Sachems, Warriors, of the Six United Nations, Shannoahs and Delawares, our friends and brethren." In this communication he stated that he was on the advance with a part of the army to clear the road for a greater force coming with guns, ammunition, and provisions and he invited Half King to meet him on the road as soon as possible to hold a council. A full copy of this speech of Washington's is to be found in "The Diaries of George Washington," by John C. Fitzpatrick, and it is of special interest from the fact that the signature is shown to include Washington's Indian name "Conotocarius." According to the author just mentioned, the English equivalent of this name is "Devourer of Villages." This was the name given by the Indians to Washington's great grand-father, John Washington, who had been a Colonel of Militia in Virginia; and George Washington had fallen heir to the title when he first became known to the Indians. It is not known whether the tradition concerning his name is one which had been preserved in the Washington family or whether it had been handed down by the Indians.

The action of the French in taking possession of the fort on the Ohio through a show of superior force was an overt act of war or something very close to it, and Washington had good reason for feeling anxious and disturbed about the situation in which he now found himself. He was in an advanced position at a remote post in the wilderness with a handful of raw men confronting an enemy close at hand greatly his superior in numbers, discipline and equipment. Reporting at once the conditions of affairs to Governor Dinwiddie he asked for reinforcements and equipment including mortars and heavy cannon. He also suggested to the Governor that he invite the southern Indians, the Cherokees, Catawbas, and the Chickasaws, to come to his assistance. Prudence might have suggested to him that he remain in his position at Wills' Creek and await reinforcements, but a policy of inaction at this juncture might have been construed as a weakness and have led to an alienation of the friendly Indian tribes. He wished to keep faith with Half King and his other Indian friends and insure their adherence to the English. With this object in view, he decided to advance as far as Red Stone Creek on the Monongahela, where store houses had been built by the Ohio Company. This point was a little more than half the distance between Wills' Creek and the fort on the Ohio which the French had just occupied. Before setting out from Wills' Creek, April 29th, at the head of one hundred and sixty men, he had already detached a party of sixty men to make a practicable road along the route he proposed to follow. He soon overtook the working party and then all hands were set to work at road making; but with all their labor they could not make more than four miles a day. On the 9th of May he was not further than twenty miles from Wills' Creek. Every day he was receiving accounts of conditions on the Ohio, these coming chiefly from traders falling back before the invasion of the French. He learned from them that the French were busy constructing a fort at the forks of the Ohio on the site he had himself chosen. From them he also learned that Half King at the head of fifty warriors was on his way to join him. On reaching the Youghiogheny, a branch of the Monongahela, where it was necessary to build a bridge, Washington spent several days exploring the stream in the hope it might prove navigable, but in this he was disappointed. On the 23d of May he received a message from Half King saying, "It is reported that the French army is coming to meet Major Washington. Be on your guard against them, my brethren, for they intend to strike the first English they shall see. They have been on the march two days." On the same day it was reported to him that a French force was at the ford of the Youghiogheny, eighteen miles away. He now hastened to take a position at a place called Great Meadows, where he began the construction of a fort, later to be called Fort Necessity. This position was about fifty-two miles from Wills' Creek. On the 27th, Christopher Gist came in from his settlement on the north side of Laurel Hill with the information that fifty Frenchmen had been at his home at noon the day before. The same evening a messenger came from Half King with the information that he had found the tracks of two men who were probably members of the French party. Undeterred by a dark and rainy night, Washington at the head of a detachment of forty men, set out at ten o'clock for Half King's camp. Arriving at about daybreak, a council was held with Half King and he and his warriors agreed to join in attacking the French. With two Indians leading the way the tracks seen the day before were soon found. Marching in a single file through the forest, the party came to the hollow in the woods where the French lay concealed. They snatched their arms the moment they saw Washington and his party; Washington gave the word to fire and a short fight ensued, in which Coulon de Jumonville, an ensign in command, was killed with nine others of his party and twenty-two captured, including two subaltern officers. One Canadian escaped to bear the news to the French commander, Contrecoeur. In Washington's party one man was killed and two or three wounded.

After it was over the prisoners told Washington that the party had been sent to bring him a summons from Contrecoeur. Jumonville had in fact been provided with a written summons to be delivered to any English he might find. It required them to withdraw from the domain of the King of France and threatened compulsion by force of arms in case of refusal. Much effort was made on the part of the French authorities to discredit Washington by claiming that the slaying of Jumonville was, under the circumstances, an act of murder. Washington himself was unaware of the summons and to the best of his knowledge and information Jumonville was not an envoy on a peaceful errand, but the commander of a strong reconnoitering party whose manner of approach to his camp was to be interpreted in connection with the recent seizure by the French of the English fort on the Ohio. There was much of provocation in the summons, and efforts to give it effect were bound to bring resistance and bloodshed sooner or later. The obscure skirmish fought on May 28th, 1754, was the real beginning of the Seven Years' War, although war was not declared officially until nearly two years later.

Washington returned to his camp and, expecting soon to be attacked, he sent to Colonel Fry, then at Wills' Creek, for reinforcements. At the same time men were set to work on Fort Necessity to give it greater strength. The prisoners were forwarded to Winchester under guard; and on June 6th, Washington learned of the death of Colonel Fry at Wills' Creek. Through this casualty, Washington became the Colonel of the Virginia regiment. Reinforcements arrived from Wills' Creek, bringing the strength of his own command up to three hundred men; and at about the same time he was joined by Half King with about thirty Indian families including several of the friendly Delawares.

On June 10th, Captain Mackay's independent company from South Carolina, numbering about one hundred men, arrived, but this was an accession from which Colonel Washington was to derive little comfort or advantage. These men, although recruited in the colonies, were soldiers of the King, and Captain Mackay, holding a royal commission, could not bring himself to acknowledge a provincial officer as his superior. In every way he sought to be separate and independent and finally Washington wrote of him to Governor Dinwiddie: "I can very confidently say that his absence would tend to the public advantage."

On June 16th, Washington resumed his slow advance towards his objective, Red Stone Creek, leaving Captain Mackay with his company at Fort Necessity as a guard. On June 18th, eight Indians of the Mingo tribe, purporting to come from Logstown on the Ohio, arrived at Colonel Washington's camp and asked that a council be held; that they had brought a speech with them which they must deliver with speed. Their protestations of friendship for the English were so loud as to give an appearance of insincerity. Suspecting evil intentions, he declined to given them an audience until Half King could be present. The next day a council was held in the camp at which the Half King, several of the Six Nations, Delawares, Loups, and Shawanoes, to the number of forty, were present.

The first spokesman, representing the Six Nations, addressed a speech to the Governor of

Virginia. This speech was in part complaint, concerning threats which they alleged the English had made against them and in part interrogation as to Colonel Washington's plans against the French. Washington replied with a speech which was very conciliatory in its tone. He denied the alleged threats, saying that they had come from false reports started by the French. He reminded them of their old treaties of friendship with the English, assured them that their best interests lay in adhering to the English cause and urged them to join him in the war against the French. The council was resumed on June 20th, when a spokesman of the Delaware tribe addressed a speech to his Brethren, the Governors of Virginia and Pennsylvania. When this was concluded the same speaker addressed the Six Nations. These speeches were in the nature of reminders of old friendships, and they pledged a continuance of this relationship. When the council was resumed June 21st, Washington made a reply to the speeches of the Delawares, and, after this, the council came to an end. By this time he was certain that the Mingoes, who had come from Logstown, were French spies. He, accordingly, allowed them to acquire much incorrect information. In his own words: "They returned though not without some stories prepared to amuse the French, which may be of service to make our own designs succeed." After much laborious work in road building over the range called Laurel Hill, Washington and his command reached Gist's place, thirteen miles from Fort Necessity. From this point he busied himself in getting information concerning the French. Numerous scouting parties and runners were used, and some of these went as far as Fort Duquesne. Through the use of white men who knew the country and Indians borrowed from Half King, his service of information appears to have been very good. Very soon he received definite intelligence that strong reinforcements had reached Fort Duquesne and that a large force would soon be detached against him. He at once abandoned the plan of proceeding further on his way to Red Stone Creek. First inclined to defind himself at Gist's he began to dig entrenchments and sent word to Captain Mackay to join him at once. Captain Mackay arrived June 28th. After a consultation with his officers, it was decided not to await the enemy at Gist's, but to retire to Fort Necessity. He was now short of food supplies and transportation and the morale of his soldiers was impaired. Influenced by these considerations and hoping that supplies and reinforcements from Wills' Creek might reach him in time, he decided to defend himself there in preference to continuing the retreat. At this time he was deserted by all his Indian allies, including Half King, hitherto his faithful friend.

The French now had a preponderating force on the ground, and there was every indication that they would soon have the upper hand in the territory under dispute. Aware of this prospect and not wishing to be identified with a losing cause, the Indians withdrew either to assume a neutral attitude or to join the French. It was with them more a matter of self-interest than of sentiment.

Washington reached Fort Necessity July 1st and began at once to improve its defensive arrangements. It was built in an open meadow in the form of a square, each side measuring about thirty-five yards in length. There were palisades and the entrances were guarded by three bastions. The meadow was bordered by wooded hills and the foot of the nearest hill came within less than a hundred yards of the fort. Captain de Villiers, a brother-in-law of Jumonville, coming from Fort Duquesne at the head of about five hundred French and Canadian soldiers and several hundred Indians, was on his way to attack Colonel Washington's command at Fort Necessity. His advance arrived in the near vicinity of the Fort in the early morning of July 3rd. Probably a direct assault on the fort over the open level ground of the meadow would have been repulsed, but the enemy refrained from this course and kept under the cover of the nearby woods. From this shelter, the height of which gave them a partial command of the interior of the fort, they kept up a harassing fire all day, making the situation still more difficult for the garrison. At eight o'clock p.m. the French commander requested a parley which was finally agreed to. The terms of capitulation offered by De Villiers and accepted by Washington after some negotiation permitted him to leave the fort with his arms and baggage and to march to Wills' Creek without molestation. His artillery, consisting of nine swivels, was not to be surrendered, but was to be destroyed. The terms, which were written in French, were finally signed about midnight of July 3rd. Captain Van Braam, Washington's companion on his mission of the year before and now a captain in the Virginia regiment, had been used as an agent during the negotiations on account of his supposed knowledge of French. Whether from imperfect knowledge of the language or through design, Captain Van Braam made a mistranslation to Washington, whereby French words meaning "the assassination of Jumonville" were made to read in English "the death of Jumonville." The French commander, De Villiers, afterwards availed himself on this part of the articles of capitulation to cast a slur on the conduct of Washington. Agreement was made that the prisoners who had been taken in the skirmish with Jumonville should be restored and as a guarantee to hostages, Captain Van Braam and Captain Stobo, were delivered up to the French, to be retained till the prisoners should return. It was moreover agreed that the party capitulating should not attempt to build any more establishments at the place or beyond the mountains for a year.

In the action of July 3rd, Colonel Washington lost thirty men killed and seventy wounded out of his entire force of about four hundred, Captain Mackay's company included. All the horses and such cattle as he had with him had been killed. Early in the morning of July 4th, he marched away from the fort with drums beating and colors flying. Lacking transportation, much of the baggage was left behind, and the wounded men who were unable to walk were carried on the backs of their comrades. Wills' Creek, fifty-two miles away, was reached without incident and from that point Colonel Washington and Captain Mackay proceeded to Williamsburg and reported to the Governor the events of the campaign. Notwithstanding the unfortunate outcome, the conduct of the commander and the troops was highly approved by the Governor and applauded by the public. As soon as the House of Burgesses assembled, they passed a vote of thanks to Colonel Washington and his officers for their bravery and gallant defense of their country. A grant of three hundred pistoles (a pistole was worth about $4.00), about eleven hundred dollars, was voted for the benefit of the enlisted men who had served in the campaign. Shortly afterwards, Governor Dinwiddie undertook a reorganization of the Virginia forces. The number of companies was to be increased to ten; but they were to be independent companies with no officer holding a higher rank than that of captain. Feeling affronted at the proposed reduction in his rank, Washington resigned his commission and returned to his home.

The Braddock Campaign

After several months of quiet life at Mount Vernon, Washington was again called to the field through a series of events growing out of his own activities in the summer of 1754. The affair at the Great Meadow and the other acts of French hostility on the Ohio had roused the British ministry and in consequence the Government began preparations for active military operations in America, although war was not yet declared and was not declared in fact until May 18, 1756.

In November, 1754, a plan of campaign was devised for 1755 calling for operations against four different objectives, viz: Beau Sejour in Nova Scotia; Crown Point on Lake Champlain, New York; Fort Niagara, New York, between Lake Ontario and Lake Erie; and Fort Duquesne deemed to be the key point of the Ohio River valley from which the Virginia forces had been ejected. The Duke of Cumberland, the Captain General of the British Army, was charged with the organization of the campaign and though his selection Major General Edward Braddock was appointed to take charge of all these operations, but he was to lead in person the expedition against Fort Duquesne which was deemed to be the most important objective. General Braddock was a veteran of more than forty years' service, much of it spent in active campaigning in Europe. Commissioned early in life in the Coldstream Guards of the British Army, nearly all of his service as a regimental officer was spent in that organization. As a Lieutenant he had served under the Great Duke of Marlborough in Flanders and as a field officer he was at Dettingen, Fontenoy and Culloden. It was natural that he should be wedded to the ideas and methods of the rigid school in which he had been brought up. He had seen vindicated many times on hard fought fields. Faithful to the traditions of his type he was something of a martinet, arrogant, opinionated and irritable. With all his faults he was personally brave; he was very considerate of his officers and he was appreciative of real merit when he saw it, as in the case of Washington. On the human side he was not devoid of sympathy, as Washington came to know, and in his last hours he expressed his gratitude to those who had served him.

Two regular regiments, the 44th and 48th Infantry of the Line, at that time serving in Ireland, were designated to go with General Braddock to America and to these troops were added a company of artillery and a detachment of engineers. The Infantry regiments at the time of sailing were each five hundred strong, two hundred short of the complement. It was intended to supply the shortage of four hundred men through the enlistment of recruits in the colonies and the Governor of Pennsylvania was asked to furnish them; but this plan was not realized and eventually the recruits needed came for the most part from Virginia, a small number coming from Maryland. The expedition sailed from the harbor of Cork, January 14, 1755, in thirteen transports and three ordnance store ships under the convoy of two men of war. The ordnance store ships carried large cargoes of arms, ammunition and other stores for the use of the provincial troops. General Braddock and his personal staff left England for America December 21st, on the man of war *Norwich*, one of three warships composing Commodore Keppel's squadron. These ships dropped anchor in Hampton Roads, February 20, 1755. Colonel Sir John St. Clair who was to be the Quartermaster General of the expedition, had preceded General Braddock to America, having arrived in Virginia about the 10th of January, 1755. He at once began to acquaint himself with the nature and scene of his duties and to study the problems of transportation and supply. The transports bringing the troops parted company during the course of a long and stormy voyage, and arrived separately at Hampton, the first of them on March 2nd and the last on March 15th. Almost as soon as General Braddock arrived he proceeded to Williamsburg for a conference with Governor Dinwiddie. When all the transports had arrived orders were given for all the ships to proceed up the Potomac River to Alexandria where the troops were to be disembarked and put into camp. General Braddock himself reached Alexandria March 20th, but before he arrived all the troops had been landed. The base of supplies of the expedition against Fort Duquesne was to be Wills' Creek, which had been made a fortified place and was now called Fort Cumberland. The distance from this point to the objective, Fort Duquesne, was about one hundred and forty miles by way of a somewhat winding course through a wild and difficult country. For a good part of the way roads had to be built by the troops as they went along. Owing to this condition, the estimate of the transportation required at Fort Cumberland amounted to two hundred wagons with draft animals and fifteen hundred saddle and pack horses, a requisition finally filled by the farmers of Pennsylvania through the intervention of Benjamin Franklin. Other transportation was needed to attend the troops in their march from Alexandria to Fort Cumberland, and this was obtained with difficulty. The plan of campaign included the use of Indian allies and immediately upon his arrival General Braddock began to make inquiries as to the number who might be expected to join him. Through negotiations on the part of Governor Dinwiddie with the southern Indians, the Cherokees and Catawbas, a contingent of four hundred warriors from those tribes was promised, but this reinforcement never materialized. Through the efforts of George Crogan, Indian Commissioner in Pennsylvania, about fifty warriors belonging to tribes in the Ohio Valley were induced to join General Braddock at Fort Cumberland. These Indians were under Scarooyadi and other chiefs who had been Washington's allies the year before, Scarooyadi being the successor to Half King who had died in October, 1754. These Indians were not strong in their allegiance to General Braddock since they drifted away gradually until only eight of them were left at the time of the battle on the Monongahela, one of the latter being the chief Scarooyadi. It has been said that General Braddock alienated them by his forbidding manner and through not taking them into his confidence, but there were probably other reasons not connected with General Braddock's treatment of them.

The sight of the great flotilla of transports on the Potomac and of the soldiery in Alexandria, now like a garrisoned town, renewed Washington's interest in the military service, and he conceived the wish to join the army as a volunteer. This desire became known to General Braddock, who at the same time learned of his personal merits, his experience in frontier service and his special knowledge of the country into which the army was about to go. The result was a letter from Captain Robert Orme, one of Braddock's aids, inviting Washington to become a member of the staff. The appointment which carried with it the rank of captain was accepted at once, but a delay was authorized, and he did not report to his chief until May 10th. There can be no doubt that Washington's service with this well ordered, well disciplined little army, in the official family of a general experienced in the forms and routine of command, was of great use to him in his later military career. Braddock's army followed two different routes in proceeding to Fort Cumberland. Colonel Peter Halkett with six companies of his regiment, the 44th, left Alexandria for Winchester April 9th. Lieutenant Col. Gage followed him in a few days over the same route with the other four companies as escort for the artillery. The 48th regiment, under Colonel Thomas Dunbar, set out by way of Frederick, Maryland, crossing the Potomac from Alexandria April 12th and landing at a place on the Maryland side of the river called Rock Creek (probably at or near the mouth of Rock Creek) eight miles from Alexandria and five miles from the lower falls of the Potomac.

This regiment was accompanied by a detachment of seamen, three officers and thirty enlisted men detailed from Commodore Keppel's fleet, who were to go along with the army to be used at the water crossings. General Braddock and his staff following Colonel Dunbar's route arrived at Frederick April 21st. Washington joined him at that point on May 10th and was announced in orders as Aide-de-camp. As the road to Fort Cumberland on the Maryland side of the river was not yet completed, it was necessary for General Braddock and Colonel Dunbar and his troops to recross the Potomac and proceed to Fort Cumberland by the

Winchester route. According to the best indications available, this crossing was made at or near the present town of Williamsport, Md., the line of march thereto taking them over or near the Battlefield of Antietam. By the 19th of May all the forces were assembled at Fort Cumberland. In addition to the regulars and the seamen, there were two independent companies from New York, one of them commanded by Captain Horatio Gates; one independent company from South Carolina and one from Maryland. Of Virginia levies, there were five separate companies called rangers, numbering less than fifty men each; two carpenter or pioneer companies and one troop of light horse about thirty strong. In addition to these there was a company of rangers from North Carolina numbering eighty men. Owing to delay in the arrival of needed transportation, the command remained in camp at Fort Cumberland, nearly three weeks. During the interval at Fort Cumberland, Washington was sent back to Williamsburg to obtain public funds for the paymaster and in making the round trip his average rate of travel was forty miles a day. During the halt at Fort Cumberland, he had the opportunity of observing military routine in its strictest forms. Particular attention was given to the new recruits and the ranger companies with the idea of improving their drill and discipline, and all the organizations had field days in which each man was given twelve rounds of powder. A reference to the orders and instructions issued at this camp gives an idea of some of the customs and disciplinary measures prevalent at the time.

The Sutler was not allowed to sell to enlisted men more than one gill of rum a day, this being issued daily at eleven o'clock under the supervision of a commissioned officer. The rum had to be mixed with three gills of water before being drunk. Any non-commissioned officer or soldier found gambling was given a penalty immediately of three hundred lashes. Spectators of the games were deemed principals and punished accordingly. Any soldier found drunk in camp was sent to the quarter guard and given two hundred lashes the following morning. Any soldier or camp follower detected in stealing any of the provisions was given a death penalty.

Colonel Halkett with the 44th regiment set out on June 7th; Lieut. Col. Burton with the independent companies and the rangers marched on the 8th, and Colonel Dunbar with the 48th followed on the 10th. General Braddock left with Colonel Dunbar's command. The strength of the army as it left Fort Cumberland aggregated two thousand one hundred and fifty officers and men, not counting civilian teamsters, servants and other camp followers. At this time, twenty-eight women, the wives of regular soldiers, were sent to Philadelphia. Orders concerning the security of the command on the march were strictly enforced; and up to the time of the battle there was no apparent negligence or lack of vigilance. The march discipline appears to have been good; but owing to the narrow and difficult road the marching column often had a length of four miles. In seven days the command reached Little Meadows, twenty miles from Fort Cumberland. With the view of making better progress, it was decided at this point to divide the command into two parts, one of which, lightly equipped, was to push ahead under General Braddock, while the other, with the heavy baggage, under Colonel Dunbar was to follow. This step appears to have been due in part to Washington's recommendation. Apparently he did not hesitate to express his views frankly to his chief although they did not always meet with a kindly reception. The leading division of the army was composed for the most part of the 44th and 48th regiments, with ten pieces of artillery and the sailors from the fleet. One company of each of these regiments was left with the rear division along with the men of these regiments who were less fit for service and several provincial units. The remainder of the advance division was made up of independent

170

companies and rangers, the whole amounting to a little more than thirteen hundred officers and men; but one hundred men joined before the battle on the Monongahela took place. With the advance under General Braddock, there were twenty gun carriages, thirteen caissons, seventeen wagons and more than two hundred saddle and pack horses. About this time Washington became ill with a fever, and it was two weeks before he was able to return to his duty. It was during his illness that he was the object of a solicitude on the part of General Braddock which showed how much he was esteemed by that officer. On June 30th, General Braddock arrived at the ford of the Yougiogheny called Stuart's crossing, about forty miles from Fort Duquesne.

On July 8th, the advanced body reached the Monongahela at a point not far below its junction with the Yougiogheny. The halting place on this date was about fifteen miles from Fort Duquesne, and it was here that Washington rejoined his command following his illness.

The narrow and rocky road resembling a defile along the river on the eastern side seemed to the General too difficult to attempt so he resolved to cross the river in search of a better route and recross it a few miles further down in order to gain access to the fort. The river at these fords was shallow and the banks were not steep. By this time Contrecoeur, the commander at Fort Duquesne, was aware of the near approach of the formidable army that was on its way to attack him. He had with him a few companies of regular troops, a considerable number of Canadian militia and about eight hundred Indians, the latter being of doubtful value in a pitched battle. He debated at first whether to retire or to remain and surrender the fort after making a show of resistance. Under him were three other captains, Beaujeau, Dumas and Ligneris, and the first named one of these induced him to undertake to meet the enemy on the march and ambuscade them if possible at the crossing of the Monongahela or some other favorable spot. Beaujeau was given command of the sallying party; but the Indians were at first reluctant to join in the enterprise. They were finally persuaded, and Beaujeu left Fort Duquesne at about nine o'clock the morning of July 9th. His detachment consisted of two other captains; four lieutenants; six ensigns and twenty cadets of the regular army; seventy-two French regulars; one hundred and forty-six Canadians and six hundred and thirty-seven Indians. Among the latter nearly a dozen different tribes were represented. Some of these were baptized Indians, settled in Canada like the Abenakis and Hurons; but the rest were wild Indians like the Pottawattamies and Ojibwas from the upper lakes; the Shawanoes and Mingoes from the Ohio Valley and the Ottawas from Detroit commanded on this occasion by one of the greatest of all Indians, Pontiac, subsequently the leading spirit in the great Indian conspiracy to which his name has been given. According to General Braddock's plan for July 9th, Lieutenant Colonel Gage, with the advance guard, crossed the river before daybreak, marched to the second ford, and recrossing there took a position to secure the passage of the main body. The advance under Lieut. Col. Gage was composed of two companies of Grenadiers; one hundred and sixty-five infantry; the independent company under Captain Horatio Gates and two six pounder guns. An hour later Colonel St. Clair moved out with a working party of two hundred and fifty men to construct roads and make the fords passable for the wagons and artillery. The main body took up the march at six o'clock, and, after passing the first ford, reached the second crossing between eleven and twelve o'clock. By this time Lieut. Col. Gage had passed the second ford and was established on the other side. On the north side of the Monongahela at this point, there was a clearing where the Frazier house stood, and a glade covered with trees without undergrowth. Beyond this the road curved to the left and followed a course parallel to the river along the

171

base of a line of hills that here bordered the valley. These hills and all the country were covered with a dense growth of timber and underbrush, and the road which ran through this forest was only twelve feet wide. Bordering the road on both sides was a considerable amount of fallen timber left there by the workmen when the road was first cut through. The main body and the train which now included one hundred head of cattle, had entirely cleared the second ford by one o'clock; and before two o'clock the march was resumed, the troops keeping their original order in the column. The most advanced element was a small party consisting of the guides, engineers and six light horse. In a general way it was a normal march formation in an enemy's country, somewhat more compact than usual, with the 48th regiment in front, followed by the 44th. This unit was followed by the wagon train and the cattle, and these were followed by the provincial troops as a rear guard. There were numerous flank guards one hundred yards or more from the marching column. The fatal omission was in the failure to send out numerous patrols far out to the front in the direction of Fort Duquesne as might have been done by Colonel Gage after he crossed the second ford. Beaujeu had intended to lay an ambuscade or make a surprise attack at or near the second ford, but he was late. Some of his Indians were intractable, and it had taken him something like four hours to cover a distance of nine miles. There was no ambuscade, the action that ensued being the result of a meeting engagement, the French being much less surprised at the meeting than the English were. Colonel Gage's leading element had passed well beyond the low ground near the river and was ascending the rising ground covered with the forest growth when an engineer officer named Gordon, who was with the advance, suddenly saw a group of the enemy running forward along the road. In front of them was a French officer wearing a fringed hunting shirt with a silver gorget on his breast. This officer turned out to be Beaujeu. When he saw the English he stopped, turned and waved his hat. His followers quickly deployed across the road and opened fire. This was soon returned by the leading grenadiers and by the six pounders with such effect that Beaujeu fell dead, and, for a little while, there was confusion in the French ranks. Order was soon restored by Captain Dumas, the next in rank, and throughout the remainder of the action this officer showed excellent leadership. Almost immediately after the first burst of fire at the head of the column, the Indians began to creep along through the woods on both flanks of the English, and the latter soon found themselves exposed to a fire from an invisible enemy coming from both sides of the road in which they stood. At almost the first volley, the flanking parties ran back to join the main column in the road.

The part of the advance guard which first engaged the French, was soon subjected to a fire at close range coming from both flanks as well as from the front. Under this disadvantage the party could not long make a stand. The survivors, falling back in disorder, left the two six pounders to be seized by the French and, meeting the troops of the next echelon coming up to their support, tried to pass them in the narrow road. This was the beginning of the confusion. The extension of the French and Indians along both flanks of the English continued unopposed until finally the train and rear guard were brought under fire.

The situation and the terrain were peculiarly well suited to the flexible open order system of tactics which the French and Indians knew how to use. They were correspondingly disadvantageous to the British soldier drilled to precise marching, shoulder to shoulder, and to a mechanical delivery of his fire at word of command. Probably there were no commands laid down in the book by which these men could have been deployed in single rank in the woods. For the most part the efforts of General Braddock and his officers were devoted to

172

keeping the men in regular line formation in the road and in trying to make them deliver an orderly fire. Not only was the enemy well concealed in the woods, but there was good cover. There were several gullies running along parallel to the road and about fifty or sixty yards away from it. These made natural firing trenches from which the bright uniforms of the British soldiers in the road could be plainly seen. There was also a wooded hill on the right from which a heavy fire came, and General Braddock made an effort to have this hill carried; but the attempt was a feeble one, and it failed. Except for the efforts of the Provincials, this was the only move made to break away from the confines of the road. These troops coming forward from the rear attempted to make some headway by going into the woods and using Indian tactics, but their movement brought them between two fires, and they suffered severely without achieving anything. With men falling on all sides from a fire delivered by an unseen enemy, the British soldiers began to feel that they were caught in a trap and helpless. Added to this was the terror caused by the wild yells of the Indians. Under these demoralizing influences, discipline could not survive, and it was not long before all semblance of order disappeared. In place of the regular formations, the men huddled in large groups as though seeking protection in this way and fired their muskets into the air without taking aim. General Braddock showed great courage throughout the action, riding up and down the length of his line storming like a madman. He thought that all would be well if the men could be made to stand firm; but beyond this he had no plan.

Finally, at the end of about three hours, when the ammunition was exhausted he gave the order to retreat and just at that moment he received a mortal wound in the lungs. Prior to this he had had five horses killed under him. Washington loyally seconded all the efforts of his chief, riding with him or carrying his orders as required. Once the retreat was begun, he did everything possible to keep it from degenerating into a panic, but in this he failed. Captain Orme wrote of him to Governor Dinwiddie: "Mr. Washington had two horses shot under him, and his clothes shot through in several places; behaving the whole time with the greatest courage and resolution." There can be no doubt that beneath Washington's calm exterior there lay a fiery courage never displayed except in the face of great and imminent danger. Although he expressed a wish to be left on the field, General Braddock was carried to the rear by Captain Stewart, a Virginia officer, on a tumbril to a point about half a mile from the ford where about a hundred men had been rallied. Here he was attended by Dr. Craik. Captains Orme and Morris, the other aids, having been wounded, Washington was directed by General Braddock to go to Colonel Dunbar's camp, then forty miles away, with orders for him to hurry forward provisions, hospital stores and wagons for the wounded. He rode all night and reached Dunbar's camp the following afternoon. News of the defeat had preceded him, and he found the camp in a state of panic. The infection reached Colonel Dunbar himself, and the subsequent conduct of that officer was highly discreditable to him and to the service he represented. The escort with General Braddock continued the retreat with him until they reached Great Meadows, where he died July 13th and was buried in the road. Washington and Captain Stewart were faithful in their attendance to the last.

The victory of the French had been complete; but no attempt at pursuit was made beyond the ford. The total present in Braddock's army on July 9th was fourteen hundred and sixty officers and men. Of eighty-six officers present, twenty-six had been killed and thirty-six wounded. Of the total present, four hundred and fifty-six had been killed and four hundred and twenty-one wounded. The disproportionate number of killed may be accounted for by the fact that the wounded left on the field were killed by the Indians after the action. Twelve men were taken prisoners, and all of them were burned at the stake the night of the battle. All the artillery was lost, as was also nearly everything in the way of transportation, pack horses, cattle, baggage and stores. The loss of the French and Indians did not exceed seventy men all told.

Washington's commission as Captain was vacated on the death of General Braddock. There is evidence to show that in the course of their association he confided to General Braddock that he aspired to a career in the British Army and that the General looked favorably upon this desire.

Later on Washington wrote Lord Loudoun as follows: "With regard to myself I cannot forbear adding that had General Braddock survived his unfortunate defeat I should have met with preferment agreeable to my wishes. I had his promise to that effect, and I believe that gentleman was too sincere and generous to make unmeaning offers where no favors were asked."

Three Years of Frontier Service

The calamities resulting from Braddock's defeat did not end with the loss of several hundred soldiers in battle, for it brought on the provinces the miseries of an Indian War. Those among the tribes who had thus far stood neutral, wavering between the French and the English, hesitated no longer. The defeat and the retirement was the signal for the western savages to take up the hatchet against the English. Braddock's trail became a thoroughfare for Indian war parties, and their ravages turned the frontier of Pennsylvania and Virginia into a scene of terror and desolation. Many of the raids were instigated by the French commander at Fort Duquesne and as a rule the Indian raiding parties were accompanied by French detachments including one or more junior officers. This condition brought Washington back into the service of Virginia once more. Notwithstanding the total failure of the late campaign in which he had borne a part and the reproaches heaped upon the memory of the unfortunate commander, yet the prestige and character of Washington were greatly enhanced. Contrary to his will, he gained advantage from the defeat and ruin of others. He had returned to his home on July 26th and on August 14th he received his commission as Colonel of the Virginia regiment to be raised for the defense of the western frontier. In addition to being appointed Colonel, he was designated as the Commander-in-Chief of all the Virginia forces to be raised for the war. He was then twenty-three years and six months old. On September 14th he repaired to Winchester, which was fixed as the place for his Headquarters and where he was to remain with two intermissions for something like three arduous years. In February, 1756, he rode on a trip to Boston, Massachusetts and return for the purpose of getting an official decision concerning points of rank and authority which had arisen between himself and Captain Dagworthy, a Maryland officer holding a King's commission, — an issue decided in his favor by General Shirley, then Commander-in-Chief of the colonies. In the latter part of 1757, probably worn out by his labors, he was stricken by a serious illness and was obliged to return to his home for four months. His chief responsibility at Winchester was the defense of the frontier. To provide shelter and rallying points for the inhabitants in times of danger, the House of Burgesses made provision for a chain of twenty-one forts extending along the frontier from Fort Cumberland on the north of the North Carolina line. Some of these forts were already in existence. Others were constructed as a result of Washington's survey of the line of defense made soon after his arrival at Winchester. Recruiting and equipping troops demanded his best efforts and he took pains besides to renew advances to the friendly

Indians. Throughout the summer of 1756, Washington exerted himself in carrying out measures determined upon for frontier security. The fort at Winchester was begun and pushed forward as as expeditiously as a poorly organized service would permit. It was named Fort Loudoun after Lord Loudoun who was coming out from England to be Commander-in-Chief in the colonies in place of General Shirley. Recruiting went along very slowly and by April of 1756 only six hundred men had been enlisted out of total of twelve hundred authorized. Many of the officers were incompetent, and there was practically no organized staff service. He reported to the Governor that his command stood in need of almost every necessary thing. There were many desertions, and public opinion was such that these offenders were often sheltered by the people. In the absence of a code imposing proper penalties for desertion and other military offenses, discipline in any proper sense seemed an unattainable thing. Washington wrote to Governor Dinwiddie saying: "The militia are under such bad order and discipline that they will go and come when and where they please without regarding time, their officers or the safety of the inhabitants, but consulting solely their own inclinations."

In another letter to the Governor he said: "I would again hint the necessity of putting the militia under a better regulation * * * I must once more beg leave to declare that unless the Assembly will enact a law to enforce the military law in all its parts, that I must with great regret decline the honor that has been intended me. I see the growing insolence of the soldiers, the insolence and inactivity of the officers who are sensible how confined their punishments are in regard to what they ought to be." Through his persistence an act was passed by the Assembly putting into operation a military code which provided for the punishment with adequate severity of insubordination, desertion and mutiny; reinforced the authority of commanders to enable them to maintain order and discipline among the officers and soldiers and authorized commanders in times of emergency to avail themselves of the means and services of individuals. Through the operation of this wholesome law as administered by Washington, the militia service was greatly improved. Not long after the enactment of the new code, Washington reported to the Governor that two men had been executed for desertion. The usual punishment for drunkenness was one hundred lashes. No one felt more strongly than Washington the importance at this juncture of securing the assistance of the Indians. "It is in their power," he said, "to be of infinite use to us, and without Indians we shall never be able to cope with these cruel foes of our country." He wrote from Winchester, October 10, 1755, to Andrew Montour, a man of note on the frontier, having great influence with the Indians of the Ohio Valley, in part as follows: "I hope you will use your interest in bringing our brothers once more to our service; assure them as you truly may that nothing which I can do shall be wanting to make them happy; assure them also that as I have the chief command I am invested with power to treat them as brethren and allies, which I am sorry to say they have not been of late. Recommend me kindly to our good friend Monocatoochee (another name for the Chief Scarooyadi) and others; tell them how happy it would make Conotocarious to have an opportunity of taking them by the hand at Fort Cumberland and how glad he would be to treat them as brothers of our great King beyond the waters." To Governor Dinwiddie he wrote in the same month: "The French policy in treating with the Indians is so prevalent that I should not be in the least surprised were they to engage the Cherokees and Catawbas unless timely and vigorous measures are taken to prevent it." To Speaker Robinson, of the Assembly, he wrote: "Our detachments, by what I can learn, have sought them diligently, but the cunning and vigilance of the Indians in the woods are no more to be conceived than they are to be equalled by our people. Indians are the only match for Indians, and without these we shall ever fight upon unequal terms."

To Governor Dinwiddie he wrote, April 24, 1756: "Your Honor spoke of sending some Indians to our assistance, in which no time should be lost nor means omitted to engage all the Catawbas and Cherokees that can possibly be gathered together and immediately dispatched here."

Again on September 8, 1756, he wrote to Governor Dinwiddie: "I am glad the Cherokees have determined to come to our assistance and to hear the firm attachment of them and the Catawbas to our interest. They will be of particular service, more than twice their number of white men."

The Capture of Fort Duquesne

Early in 1758 plans were revived for the capture of Fort Duquesne, a step long advocated by Washington as the best solution of the problem of frontier defense. The expedition was to be commanded by Brigadier General Forbes, of the British Army, and it was to advance through Pennsylvania approaching Fort Dusquesne from the east instead of by the Braddock route from the south. Washington, with such of his Virginia troops as could be spared, as to form part of General Forbes' command. By this time there were two regiments of Virginia troops, the other regiment besides Washington's being commanded by Colonel Byrd. Early in July, the advance of General Forbes' army under Colonel Bouquet had reached Raystown, Penna. (now Bedford, Pa.) on July 2nd, Washington, with a part of his regiment, arrived at Fort Cumberland from Winchester and began the construction of a road to Raystown, thirty-four miles east of north of Fort Cumberland. Once the road was constructed, the question arose whether the army should proceed in a direct course to Fort Duquesne from Raystown, hewing a new road through the forest, or march thirty-four miles to Fort Cumberland and thence follow the road made by Braddock. Washington was very earnest in advocating the latter course, but he was overruled, and the other route decided upon. About the middle of September, Washington, being still at Fort Cumberland, was directed to march to Raystown with his troops and join General Forbes at that point. This accession of Virginia troops including his own and Colonel Byrd's regiments amounted to about sixteen hundred officers and men, and it brought General Forbes' army to a strength of more than six thousand.

In setting out on the march to Fort Duquesne Washington was given command of the advance of the army composed in part of his own regiment, which was to clear the road, throw out scouting parties and repel Indian attacks. It was November 5th before Loyalhannon was reached, forty miles from Raystown and fifty miles from Fort Duquesne. It was from Loyal-hannon that Major Grant set out on the foray against Fort Duquesne which resulted in his defeat. In this affair which failed owing to the bad management of Major Grant, a part of Washington's regiment was involved, losing six officers and sixty-two men. When French prisoners brought word of the weakened state of the garrison due to the desertion of many Indians, it was determined to expedite the movement by leaving behind the heavy baggage and pushing forward a strong detachment lightly equipped. Upon the appearance of the English before the fort, the French Commander withdrew his garrison of five hundred men, blew up the magazine and set fire to the fort. On November 25th, Washington, at the head of the advance guard, marched in and hoisted the British flag over the ruins. The fort was reconstructed in part, renamed Fort Pitt and garrisoned by two hundred men of Washington's regiment.

Thus came to an end French domination in the Ohio River valley. A treaty of peace was soon concluded with all the Indian tribes between the Ohio and the Lakes. With this campaign, Washington's service in the French and Indian War came to an end. Very soon thereafter he resigned his commission and returned to his home.

This period of his life is of special interest in view of the numerous references to Indians made in this correspondence and from these references some conclusions may be drawn as to his opinion about Indians, and his attitude towards them. Apparently he thought well of the Indian as a warrior, his estimate being that in forest warfare one Indian was the equal of two white men. Recognizing the military value of the Indian, and being a practical man, he preferred to have him as a friend and ally rather than as an enemy. In accordance with this preference his attitude towards Indians in all his associations with them was one of conciliation and friendliness. In all the records that we have of him there is nothing to show that he was ever guided in his actions towards them by any feelings of prejudice or enmity. His rule of conduct with them was one of justice and fair dealing, but it was unfortunately true that his own views and policy on this question were not shared by the majority of his countrymen, whose attitude towards the Indians was one of dislike and contempt. This sentiment of the majority was reflected to a large extent in the English colonial governments, who, all along neglected to cultivate a proper understanding with the Indians.

It should be remembered that Washington's point of view was that of a military man whose experience with the Indians had been gained in border warfare. He also had some peace time experience with them as a negotiator; but his early life had been spent in an environment from which the Indians had long been excluded and probably he gave little thought to them as social beings. It was a natural thing that the frontier settlers, who were in a position to see the worst side of the Indian character, should be less tolerant than Washington.

Unlike some other periods of his life, Washington's frontier service, which has been briefly surveyed, was devoid of anything spectacular. With a long frontier to be guarded, the warfare, which was one of small skirmishes, furnished no opportunity for personal distinction in action, but the demands made upon his resources and address as a commander were numerous and pressing. Aside from his arduous duties, he was obliged to meet a certain amount of criticism; to hear murmurs of discontent and cries of distress. To add to his vexations, Governor Dinwiddie, jealous of his own authority, was inclined to interfere unduly with the military management on the frontier and he did not always support Washington in his measures. Washington finally came to realize that the Governor's former attitude of friendliness had changed to one of dislike and distrust; but the difficulties arising from their altered relations were borne with patience and good temper. These were trying years and apparently he was working in a barren field; but his zeal in the public service and his talents brought him recognition and at the end of the war he was enjoying the confidence of his fellow citizens in a great measure than ever before.

References

Washington Irving's *Life of Washington.*
John Marshall's *Life of Washington.*
Montcalm and Wolfe, by Francis Parkman.
A Half Century of Conflict, by Francis Parkman.

The Diaries of Washington, by J. C. Fitzpatrick.

General Washington, by Gen. B. T. Johnson.

Life and Times of Washington, by Schroeder-Lossing.

Braddock's Expedition, by Winthrop Sargent.

Journal of the Braddock Expedition, by Captain Robert Orme, Aid-de-Camp to General Braddock.

Journal of the Braddock Expedition by a Naval Officer.

AUTHOR'S NOTE: Several of the passages appearing in this article have been paraphrased from the works of Washington Irving and Francis Parkman.

Remarks by Lieut. Col. Charles E. T. Lull

Collection of Historical Material Relating to Indian Wars of the United States

Sir National Commander and Companions of the Order. One of the most interesting events in history is that of the 100 Years War between France and England. We all recall this spectacular period from our youthful studies; but, how many of us stop to realize that the United States has had its own 100 years' war which, by every criterion, is of far greater significance than its counterpart of the Middle Ages. I refer, of course, to the American conquest of its own continental empire — the winning of the West.

The history of the American 100 years' war has never been written as a whole. Many of its more spectacular events have been recorded; but so far no Napier has arisen to give us a coordinated narrative of this, our greatest struggle. Unfortunately, the facts on which this narrative must rest are passing into oblivion and unless something is done, they will be more and more difficult to determine. It is a responsibility particularly appropriate to the traditions of this Order to safeguard the records of these events before they have passed beyond recall.

As time goes on, and we get farther and farther from the drama in which they took part, the actual participants become fewer and fewer and their personal recollections, more and more uncertain. There remain, however, a great number of contemporary documents which present the facts as known and experienced at or shortly after the time of their occurrence. Where these documents took the form of official reports or of papers of purely military nature, most of them found their way into the custody of The Adjutant General and we need not worry about them. But military records are not sufficient for historical work. Even for military history, they must be supplemented by other kinds of material. This material is to be found in such records as personal diaries, contempoary narratives, and, above all, in personal correspondence of the individuals concerned. In a period in which small groups of cultured persons lived in isolation on the frontier, the casual letter of an officer, a lady, or even a child, may reveal conditions of utmost importance to historical research. We all know of such material. It is to be found in the possession of participants still living, or the descendants and relatives of those who have passed on. It is generally stored in some attic, or maintained as an heirloom or curiosity. As long as the family stays in one place, it probably rests undisturbed, but in case of a move, it is very liable to be destroyed.

Our present problem is to find this material, and to get it into suitable depositories where it can be safeguarded and made available for historical research. The ideal would be to bring it all together in some central depository where it could be of the greatest value to historians. Opportunity for such an assembly is offered by the Library of Congress where manuscripts are received, safeguarded, classified, and indexed so that they can be consulted with the least time and effort by the investigator. The Library has an exceedingly gracious way of acknowledging material turned over to its custody and will hold it under any reasonable conditions that the original possessor may request. When material of value is treasured as a possession with which its own owner does not wish to part, the Library is prepared to make copies and return the original.

To deposit in the Library of Congress is desirable, but, for manifest reasons, not always practicable. Owners may prefer to donate documents to other institutions such as libraries, schools, and local historical societies in which they may have a particular interest. Such a course is entirely in line with what we are trying to accomplish. The essential purpose being, of course, to save the documents themselves from oblivion and have them where they will be cared for and can be used.

The task of finding the material and persuading its holders to part with it or allow it to be reproduced is the one which presents the greatest difficulty and the one in which the individual members of the Order can, and it is hoped will, be of greatest assistance. Publicity through the newspapers, service and historical journals, and magazines, supplemented by radio, should be of great value in uncovering sources otherwise difficult to find. It has been suggested, however, that in many cases the most effective method would be to discover the possessors of this material by inquiry and through the general "grapevine" chain of acquaintance, and obtain it by personal solicitation and direct correspondence with the parties concerned. To start the ball rolling in this connection, it would be greatly appreciated if any Companion, himself the possessor of such material, or knowing the names and addresses of persons liable to have any, would communicate the fact to the Recorder of the Order. A final obstacle with which we are liable to be confronted is that of unwillingness on the part of the owners of valuable historical documents either to part with them or to allow them to be copied. This unwillingness sometimes arises from considering the documents as heirlooms too precious to be allowed into profane hands and, most unfortunately, to a desire to use them as a source of revenue, a desire which is usually accompanied by a most exaggerated conception of their intrinsic value. I think you all will realize, of course, that a document may be very precious as an heirloom and of great interest to scientific research and yet have little or no money value. There is also, unfortunately, little or no money available for the purchase of these historical documents and no prospect, that we can see, of obtaining funds for this purpose. It is essential, therefore, that all ideas of commercial consideration be eliminated and that the possessors of material be made to appreciate the desirability of contributing it for patriotic reasons and for the purpose of erecting a lasting monument to their own people whose record of service to their country might otherwise be lost to history.

In closing, I desire to acknowledge the untiring efforts and suggestions of General W. C. Brown, original Companion of the Order, in bringing this matter to a head. I would like, also, to thank Colonel Ahern and the members of the Council for their kind assistance, courtesy, and encouragement.

1933

The annual meeting held this year was somewhat different from those of previous years; for the first time the assemblage — 37 Companions and an unspecified number of guests — met for a luncheon and not a dinner. They met at the Army Navy Club — as was usual — at one o'clock — which was not usual.

Immediately following the Luncheon Captain Carter, acting as toastmaster, introduced Brigadier General William C. Brown, who spoke briefly regarding steps which had been taken looking to the purchase of W. M. Camp records. Following this he gave a brief summary of the results of various engagements with Indians in 1876 in Eastern Montana, including Miles' conference and fight with Sitting Bull, October 22, 1876, at Cedar Creek. Neither were printed in the *Proceedings.*

Stress was given to information secured from the diary of Lieutenant Frank D. Baldwin, 5th Infantry, which indicates that instead of Sitting Bull having been driven across the Missouri River, December 7, 1876, as indicated by Heitman and the official reports, it is probable that Sitting Bull, learning of Baldwin's approach to Fort Peck from the West, withdrew of his own volition from Porcupine Creek south across the Missouri to Bark Creek, where his strong position of some 500 warriors made an attack at that time by Baldwin with his force of 110 men inadvisable. Baldwin's two consecutive night marches, December 6-7 and December 7-8, the latter in a temperature of 40 below zero in this maneuver, are believed to be unique in Indian War annals. Baldwin's opportunity came later when Sitting Bull, having moved East to the head of Redwater Creek, was attacked and his camp captured by Baldwin December 18, 1876.

In June, 1932, through donations by the citizens of Terry, Montana, and vicinity, the site of the latter engagement was marked by a seven foot monument.

The *Proceedings* did, however, carry an obituary on one of the most famous of Western Military figures, Brigadier General Edward S. Godfrey, who had served his country faithfully during the most explosively exciting years of expansion. His obituary was as follows:

The following obituary of Brigadier General Edward Settle Godfrey, written by his brother, Calvin P. Godfrey, was read during the Necrology ceremony:

A grand cavalryman of the old school has passed on. Seldom, indeed, has the career of a typically military personality been so intimately identified with so many notable events as that of General Godfrey. His service spanned that period of our country's relatively most rapid and really phenomenal agrarian development, by and during which the wonderful West emerged from lawlessness. That greatest of all American evolutions was truly an ideally staged empire drama of adventure, of privation, of encounter, of conquest, and of settlement.

He therefore was necessarily an actor in the popularly outstanding chapters of American history that treat of the early land lure and of the later gold and silver lures; of exploits of noted scouts; of achievements of the pony express; of thrills of the buffalo chase; of the give and take of outlawry and ruthless reprisal; of adventures and sacrifices of the overland coaches; of transcontinental railway victories over savage and beast and stubborn vasts of virgin domain. These chapters were of a period that brought forth whatever of the real man all its characters had. And, midst dangers both many and great, General Godfrey aided in running into and through all those chapters and fadeless lines of Army blue.

And so it was that, in line of duty and by circumstances, he figured in some quite exceptional events, both of professional importance and of historic consequence; he contacted every kind of plains and mountain Indian this country knows; he was in forty Indian fights before he was ten years in the saddle; he participated in three of the greatest Indian campaigns of later history and was in their respective severest engagements. The first was at Washita River, Indian Territory, in 1868. The foe were Cheyennes, Arapahoes and Kiowas, led respectively by Chiefs Black Kettle, Little Raven and Satanta.

The second campaign referred to culminated in Little Big Horn River, Montana, when the gallant General George A. Custer and 265 officers and men of the fearless and feared Seventh Cavalry were victims of Chief Gall and his swarming Sioux. General (then First Lieutenant) Godfrey was in Major Benteen's command, was in the party first on the battle-field and first personally examined the slain commander, who had been shot in the head and heart, but not mutilated in any way. During the long survival of that battle, he was frequently called on or referred to for related opinion, version or judgment, both by individuals and by the War Department, all of which entailed a large, though willingly borne, burden of correspondence.

The third battle was at Bear Paw Mountains, Montana, in 1887, when wily Chief Joseph and his disciplined Nez Perces were defeated and captured after a 300-mile pursuit and a six-day siege. Captain Godfrey received the brevet of Major and was awarded the Congressional Medal of Honor "for most distinguished gallantry in action against hostile Nez Perces Indians at Bear Paw Mountains, Montana, September 30th, 1877, in leading his command into action, where he was severely wounded." His white horse was killed under him, and he was badly injured by the resulting fall. But he was assisted to another mount, rejoined the dismounted troops and led them until very seriously shot. Both times he saw the Indian kneel, aim and fire.

Upon his own request, he was relieved from a Board on Drill Regulations in order to join his troops in the field against hostile Sioux in the Pine Ridge Campaign, engaging in the actions at Wounded Knee and Drexel Mission, Dakota, December 29-30, 1890.

When promoted Lieutenant Colonel, 12th Cavalry, in March, 1901, he had nearly thirty-four years of service in the 7th Cavalry. He had joined that regiment upon graduation from the Military Academy in 1867 and, consequently, very soon after the regiment's organization in 1866.

He was instructor in cavalry tactics at the Military Academy from 1879 to 1883.

During September and October, 1897, he was in command of troops from Forts Apache, Arizona, and Wingate, New Mexico, to arrest Zuni Indians who in performance of tribal ceremonies had committed murder. The objective was bloodlessly attained by boldness. Despite warnings, he went alone on foot to the village, impressed his views upon the head of the tribe and returned to camp to await developments. And that procedure was wholly vindicated the next day, when those wanted were delivered at the camp.

He was in command at Fort Duchesne, Utah, from April to October, 1898. Thereafter, he was stationed successively at Huntsville, Alabama; Macon, Georgia; Havana, Pinar del Rio, and Columbia Barracks, Cuba; Fort Sam Houston, Texas; Legaspi, San Pablo, and Iloilo, P.I.; Fort Walla Walla, Wash.

He commanded the Department of the Columbia in May and June, 1904, commanded the First Brigade, Maneuver Camp, American Lake, Washington, July, 1904, and was at Fort Riley, Kansas, commanding regiment, post and School of Application for Cavalry until January, 1907. On the last date, he was promoted Brigadier General. He then commanded the Department of the Missouri until retirement for age.

The address which was published in the *Proceedings* was "The Battle of Snake Mountain," by Brigadier General Frank U. Robinson.

The Battle of Snake Mountain

By Brig. Gen. Frank U. Robinson

It is with some reluctance and misgivings that I attempt to write some of the experiences of my past life that happened thirty years ago and more, as I do so entirely from memory. One having only memory and impressions to rely upon is very apt to get things slightly mixed. More especially does the task become very difficult when one is very punctillious about stating the exact facts as they occurred, neither taking from nor adding to. Other names are connected with all that I have to say and it is far from my thoughts to do any injustice, and I can't see how it would be possible for me to do anything but justice, to those with whom I was connected at this particular time of my life. They deserve nothing but the greatest eulogy and praise. I might err in not giving them enough in a proper way.

It may be as well for me to state here that I am a retired officer of the Army, spending most of my military service in the Second Cavalry, and at the particular time of which I write I had the honor to be Second Lieutenant, Troop B, of that distinguished regiment. Captain Bates was the Captain and James N. Wheelan the First Lieutenant. Captain Bates was absent on detached service at West Point but joined later, as will appear.

In the spring of 1870, after wintering at Omaha Barracks, Nebraska, my troop was ordered into the Wind River country. We proceeded by rail to Fort Bridger, Wyoming, the Wind River being about 130 miles north of this point. Troop D, Captain Gordon commanding, was already there, as the hostiles were raiding, killing, stealing and committing other depredations. The Wind River country is that line of country lying directly east of the Wind River mountains which head up near Yellowstone Lake and extend south to the South Pass proper — Freemonts being the principal peak — and being the headwaters of the Big Wind, Little Wind, Popoagies and Sweetwater rivers. The South Pass gold mines and the little mining towns of South Pass City, Atlantic City and Miners Delight were in this belt. Altogether this was a very rich country, the river bottoms being well adapted to agriculture and surrounded by fine grazing lands, making it an ideal place for settlers and settlements. But on the east lay that vast region known as the Sioux Country, stretching far to the Missouri River, and the hostiles were continually raiding and killing the settlers, hence the necessity for troops.

While at Fort Bridger getting ready to march to the north, news came that Captain Gordon of Troop D was in trouble and had had a fight, known as the Battle of the Beaver, in which First Lieutenant Stambaugh and several men were killed. These are all the facts we could learn, but they were enough. We marched next morning and were soon on the scene, joining Gordon at his camp on Atlantic Gulch between Atlantic City and Miners Delight. These two towns were four miles apart. In the meantime Company B, Fourth Infantry, Captain Bartlett in command, had pushed on up into the valley of the Big Popoagie, about thirty miles further north — where Lander City now is — and established a fortified camp named Camp Brown after Captain Brown of the 18th Infantry who was killed at Fort Phil Kearny. As the government intended to fortify and hold this line of country, orders soon came to build a two company post. We found a suitable site close by and the post, known as Camp Stambaugh, was soon built. Troops B and D were stationed here for the following three years, scouting, fighting, and giving the settlers all the protection that two small troops of cavalry could, being almost constantly in the saddle.

In 1873 my troop was ordered to Fort Washakie on the Little Wind river, 45 miles north of Camp Stambaugh, Infantry taking our place. Here was established the Snake Indian Reservation, Washakie being the principal chief of the Snakes. Fort Washakie was established and the post was erected mostly by Company E, 13th Infantry, Captain Torrey in command. On our arrival we built the cavalry addition. Our work was greatly impeded by the constant raiding of the hostiles. About this time 20 Snake scouts, commanded by Lieutenant Young, 4th Infantry, were added to our cavalry force. Captain Bates had returned from detached service and was on duty with his troops. This was, I am quite sure, in the fall of 1873. It would take volumes to tell all about our numerous scouts and hard riding after the hostile war parties that invaded this line of country during our stay. Something had to be done to hit the hostiles in a vital part and teach them that they were not perfectly safe in their own country. Heretofore they could dash in and kill some one, steal what stock they could, and then ride hard for their own country. After putting in 75 or 100 miles they were perfectly safe. Our only chance of punishing them was to overhaul them before they could get well out of our lines. That was next to an impossibility for they would usually commit their depredations from 20 to 50 miles from our camp and, by the time we received word and got fairly on their trail, they would be well out of the country. Our force was entirely too small to go further than 60 or 75 miles into the hostile country. Our force at Fort Washakie at this time was Company E, 13th Infantry, Troop B, 2nd Cavalry, and 20 Snake scouts, a force entirely too small, situated as we were directly west of the vast Sioux country in which all the Sioux and hostile Cheyennes and Arapahoes were congregated. It is true we had at this point the Snake Indians as our allies as they were always deadly enemies of the Sioux, but they numbered, I am quite sure, not more than 300 warriors who were not fond of going very far into the Sioux country. It was resolved to make the best of what we had and give the hostiles a lesson teaching them that they could not raid into our line of country with impunity. I would state here that the fortified camp on the Big Popoagie had been abandoned but two companies of Infantry still garrisoned Camp Stambaugh. Captain Torrey, 13th Infantry, was in command of the post of Fort Washakie, which was then called Camp Brown, the designation being changed sometime later. When Captain Bates joined he took a lively interest and meant to put a stop to the hostile raids. In this I was with him "hand and glove." The First Lieutenant (Rawolle) of the troop was absent on detached service, so there were but two officers with the troop, Captain Bates and myself. Lieutenant Young, 4th Infantry, was in charge of the 20 Indian scouts who were attached to the troop. Captain Bates prevailed on Chief Washakie to keep some small parties of his warriors well out into the hostile country and if possible to get wind of and inform us of any raiding hostiles, but more especially to see if they could locate some hostile village or camp that it would be possible for us to reach and surprise. This Washakie did and had scouts well down to the Sweetwater and up toward the head of Powder River. Thus matters went on, we scouting in a small way hoping to strike some war parties before they could get in their work, until the latter part of June, 1874, when word came that Washakie's scouts had located a small village of 40 lodges of hostiles near the head of Norwood River, a small stream heading in the Powder River mountains and running northwest into the Big Horn river below Owl Creek Canyon, and about 125 miles from Fort Washakie. Having received this information and having the promise of Chief Washakie that he would go with us with a band of his warriors, Captain Torrey concurring, Captain Bates resolved to strike. All

186

was soon ready. Just as soon as it was dark enough so as not to be seen by any scouts of the enemy that might be lurking in the vicinity, our little command started from Fort Washakie the evening of July 1, 1874. It consisted of Troop B, 2nd Cavalry, 56 men, Captain Bates, Lieutenant Robinson, 20 Indian scouts under command of Lieutenant Young, acting assistant surgeon Thomas McGee, four hospital men, a pack train of ten mules with a chief packer, and about 50 Snake warriors under Chief Washakie. Captain Bates was in command. We marched all night and just as soon as the day began to break went into camp in the brush low down on the Little Wind river. Washakie, on intimation, sent out videttes to keep a bright look out during the day, to see without being seen, which the Indians understood to the letter. There are no scouts that could have performed this duty better. We lay very close during the day of July 2nd and just as soon as darkness set in were on the march, pushing at a rapid gait, mostly on the trot, across an undulating sage brush country. Our course was a little north of east. Just as the day was breaking we went into camp in the brush on a little creek which, I presume or am quite sure, was Bridger Creek, named after old Jim Bridger, the pioneer and scout of this line of country. This bivouac was, I am quite satisfied, near the old Bridger Trail leading up into Montana. Here we lay well concealed all that day, taking more precautions than on the preceding day. By this time men, horses, and mules had taken on that quiet business air that is so noticeable when all realize that something serious is at hand. Nothing of note transpiring, we were in the saddle again as darkness set in and marched at a rapid rate around the eastern point of the Owl Creek mountains. The night was clear and starlit and I noticed, by the stars, that our course was about northeast. Our Indian guides appeared to understand themselves perfectly and evidently knew every inch of the country we were passing over. We crossed over a considerable range of mountains on this night, which I judged to be an offshoot of the Powder River mountains. The trail was good and we made excellent time, not hearing a sound during the night but the clicking of the horses' hoofs as they occasionally struck a rock. Just at daylight we were entering a rather close valley beyond. Here was the place that our Indian scouts had located the village. A halt was made while our scouts went forward to reconnoiter. It was not very long before they returned with the information that the village was not where it had been located but from the very fresh signs and other indications they felt quite sure the village was not very far off. This they said was certain, as there was quite a little bunch of ponies grazing further up the valley. Every moment was precious, yes more than precious, so we just could not wait for the pack animals to close up. Bates gave the command to mount and the whole command took the broad trail and broke into a swinging gallop, keeping well close up to Captain Bates, who, accompanied by two Orderlies and Norcott the Indian interpreter, was leading. I was with the troop and Young, with the Indian scouts, just in the rear. Washakie with his warriors, except quite a number who were acting as videttes, was in the rear of the scouts. We were entering a rather close country, high hills covered with bunch grass, and deep arroyos, not very percipitous sides, and opening bottoms. To the west lay a narrow undulating sage brush plain. We had travelled in this manner for nearly an hour before day began to break in earnest, it becoming quite light except for a mist which hung about the hills. Some of the videttes, riding furiously in, caused a halt and reported that the village was right ahead but a little to our left and down a deep arroyo. Captain Bates and party went ahead to reconnoitre, leaving me in charge. The Indians under Washakie having by this time come up, commenced chanting their war chant, decking themselves in their war bonnets and feathers, and making a horrible din. I tried my best to stop them or all hope of surprising the village would be at an end. He did what he could but these Indians were so terribly excited that they could not keep still, so I resolved to push on and join Captain Bates, for now we had not a moment to lose. After proceeding a short distance I met him returning. He told me that the village was about a mile away and was a large one, many more than 40 lodges which we had expected to find. It proved afterwards that there were 112 lodges, more or less in regular order, besides numerous outside lodges that were not counted. I saw at once that the time of our lives had come and that this Fourth of July, for it was the morning of July 4, 1874, would in all probability be my last on earth. But I felt about as ready as ever I should be so did not worry. On meeting Bates we came down to a walk while he was giving the order for Lieutenant Young and the Scouts to branch off to the left and come down on the head of the village. Washakie and some of his warriors went with Young and the rest followed in our rear. We pushed down the line of hills to take or hit the village in flank. I saw at once by these dispositions that Captain Bates understood himself and the situation perfectly, and I felt satisfied that the country would hear a good account of us on that day.

It now became broad daylight so we pushed on at a gallop out to a point on the hill overlooking the village, and there it was with its long lines of lodges. As Bates and I looked at it and then at our handful of men we saw at once that we must hit them and hit them hard or our chance of getting out of the country would be slim. Our men had 80 rounds of carbine cartridges in their belts besides some in the saddle bags. We carried at that time the Springfield carbine, caliber 45, a fine little gun of its kind, excellent for short range but not of much use for over eight hundred yards. We looked for the pack mules carrying additional ammunition but none of the pack train was in sight. We did not give this a second thought then, but I assure you it came in for very serious consideration afterwards, when it appeared that all our extra ammunition had been lost during the night. Besides the carbines, our men were armed with Colt revolvers. On the other side of the village the hills were very much higher and very much more abrupt than the side we were on. A very high rocky point with many gnarled cedars growing in the crevices of the rocks was just above the lower end of the village, and some way further down was a little creek. The descent on our side was grassy and easy.

The village beneath us, about six hundred yards away, had not yet taken the alarm, so we dismounted to fight on foot. Leaving every fourth man as horse holder, the horses were placed in charge of Sergeant Fuller. Our gallant Surgeon McGee was on hand with plenty of first aid to the wounded and was directed to hold himself in the rear. All this did not take more than two minutes. Then Captain Bates, with only thirty-two men in line and about twenty Indians in the rear, led us down the hill at a double time to the attack. We had gone but a short distance when, seeing such a hot time ahead of us, Bates and I and many of the men threw away our blouses, for we preferred to meet it in blue shirts. After making about half the distance and directing our course to hit the village about midway in the flank, we heard yells and the sharp crack of many rifles at the upper end of the village, showing that Young and the scouts had opened fire. We then doubled our pace and rushed into the village in close skirmish order. When partly down the hill our Indians had halted and by this time had commenced firing over our heads, but we did not fire a shot until we were close to the first tepees, although the enemy had opened fire on us some little time before. Then we came to a halt and the battle opened in earnest. It was almost a perfect surprise. If it had not been we certainly could not have cleaned them up as we did. There was a wide ravine, running down through the center of the village, into which the Indians crowded and were running down to

188

escape at the lower end. Many pushed across and gained the rocks on the other side and opened a deadly fire on us from this quarter. Now the fight became deadly. Yells, cries, and curses rang out far above the incessant rattle of the carbines and the sharp crack of the Winchesters with which the enemy was mostly armed. Part of the time it was hand to hand and in some instances the Indians and our men were wrestling for the same gun. This lasted for about twenty-five minutes, when we were complete masters of the village. In the meantime the firing had ceased at the upper end of the village. Lieutenant Young had fallen badly wounded and I understood one of the Indians was killed and some others wounded. They had fallen back carrying the Lieutenant with them and were up at a point some distance above the upper end of the village. We then had time to look at our losses and found we had only two men killed and eight wounded, which was astonishing considering the way the bullets had been flying. As fast as men were hit they were taken to the rear and the men taking them would bring back the ammunition from the saddle bags. I would say here that after the fight was over we only had an average of seven rounds of ammunition per man, this owing to the serious loss of the ammunition mules which I mentioned before. The enemy lost, as near as we could count, about 60 killed in the village. There were 17 dead in the main elbow of the ravine.

Surgeon McGee, who did not think he had work enough in the rear, pushed into the village. As he was dressing a wounded man an Indian, gun in hand, rushed from one of the lodges close by and was taking aim at one of our men. The doctor dropped his bandages, seized the man's carbine and shot the Indian dead, then returning to his work as if nothing had happened. I also noticed Captain Bates killing an Indian with his revolver. I had the honor of doing the same thing during the fight. All being over, Captain Bates gave the order to fall back to the horses and, without disturbing any of the lodges, we gained the hill and found the horses near where we left them. The enemy still held the high point of rocks before spoken of. As our ammunition was at its lowest ebb, and having accomplished much more than we dared to hope for and having eight wounded men to look after, we concluded it would be foolish to cross over and attempt to drive the Indians from their very strong position. It would be little or nothing gained and would very much jeopardize our chances of getting out of the country without having serious trouble, so we decided to start on the return march to Fort Washakie. Our Indians rounded up three hundred and fifty horses and ponies which we took with us. There must have been 1,200 to 1,400 head of stock belonging to this village, as we could see their herders, as the attack was about to be made, driving off large bunches. Those we captured were grazing on the upper side and were cut off from the main herd. By this time it was nearly eleven o'clock and the wounded were suffering a great deal. We got them on their horses and, detailing men to hold them from falling off, commence our long slow march back. This was the 4th of July and it was very hot even for this mountain region. The wounded men suffered terribly but we marched steadily all day, halting often to give them a drink of water.

Captain Bates directed me, with ten of the men who were holding horses and were not in the heat of the fight, as the rear guard.

We were returning by an entirely different route from the one taken on our advance, and it was much shorter. This day we were marching over a sage brush plain with rolling hills.

The enemy had somewhat recovered themselves and were following us in quite a force, but I would hold the rising ground long enough to let the column gain the hill far in advance. As soon as it had disappeared I would take the gallop and hold that point in the same manner. I am quite sure the Indians were as bad off for ammunition as we, for they did not offer to come close nor attempt to fire a single shot, and besides they had been so roughly handled that they evidently had no stomach for more. Yet I believe they had been reinforced in the meantime by some band in the vicinity. Of course I gave them no chance to get in on us. Thus the day wore on and just as the sun was setting the column halted at a little creek near the eastern end of the Owl Creek mountains, far to the north. I joined with the rear guard and, as we were making coffee, could see the enemy watching us from the far hills.

The wounded were all doing remarkably well, except one man by the name of French who had his left eye shot out, and from the nature of the wound I thought it a little less than wonderful that he was alive, to say nothing of his being cheerful. The day had been very hot and the night set in cold. After about two hours' rest we resumed the march and pushed on over the east end of the Owl Creek mountains, crossing down near the head of Badwater Creek, arriving here a little after daylight in the morning, thence down the Badwater to Big Wind river, arriving about ten A.M. After posting our pickets we bivouacked and prepared to take a little rest. I need not add that the whole command was completely tired out. Two days and nights constantly in the saddle, except when fighting, with but little to eat in the meantime, had done its work. After lying down all were like dead men. I would add here that Captain Bates, the night before, sent two noncommissioned officers, mounted on fresh Indian stock, forward into the post notifying Captain Torrey of the fight and requesting him to send out ambulances as far as possible for the wounded men. This he did at once and they met us that same evening at the Big Wind river about thirty miles from the post.

We slept about four hours when all were awakened, made some coffee, saddled, and moved on up the river to the big bend, where quite a number of settlers, who had pushed down to help us, were waiting. Here we met the ambulances for the wounded. The next day we marched into the Fort and our troubles were over for the time being, for other raids and scouts were soon to interest us.

The Battle of Snake Mountain, by which this fight is known, had been fought and won. Of the officers engaged, Lieutenant Robert H. Young, 4th Infantry, and Surgeon McGee deserve much praise for their gallant conduct throughout. As to the men, with two or three exceptions, their conduct was most gallant and meritorious. No command could have behaved better. The village of hostiles which we attacked was mostly made up of Arapahoes, under Chief Black Coal, some Cheyennes, and also what was known at that time as Dog Soldiers — discontents from many tribes who joined for rapine and plunder. It appeared that this village was a head center for these raiders who raided not only along our line of country but along the Union Pacific railroad as well. This whipping that they received almost entirely broke that sort of thing up. It showed them they were not even safe in their own country. Their base was destroyed, as was also their confidence in finding a safe retreat after their bloody raids were over.

In all my experience on the Frontier, which covered many years, I will say that the Battle of Snake Mountain, not because I was in it, was one of the most gallant and spirited little fights that ever occurred in the West.

Too much praise cannot be given to Captain Bates, not only for his gallantry in the fight and for the ability shown in handling the little campaign from the start to finish, but for striking this deadly blow to these hostiles and, in a great measure, completely breaking up their bloody raids. He deserves well of his country and the hearty thanks of the settlers in the Wind River country even to the present day.

NOTE: The above was written by General Robinson in July, 1907.

1934-1935

There are no records of any of the papers being delivered at either of these two meetings, and certainly none were printed in the *Proceedings.*

1936

The 28 Companions and their 3 guests met once again for dinner at the Army Navy Club. Most of the discussions were impromptu. Lieutenant Colonel Robert H. Fletcher spoke off the cuff on the work of the Historical Section, Army War College. General Kerr, Mr. Ghent and several other Companions joined in a discussion relative to claims put forward from time to time by persons purporting to be survivors of the Custer Massacre. It is regretful their observations were not recorded for posterity as this kind of fraud has been going on since the battle had been fought and their contributions to the list of frauds would have been interesting.

One major paper was read before the group. It was Colonel Fiebeger's personal experiences in General Crook's Campaign in Mexico in 1883.

General Crook's Campaign in Old Mexico in 1883
Events Leading up to it and Personal Experiences in the Campaign

By G. J. Fiebeger, *Colonel, U.S.A., Retired*

The Apaches are the various tribes of Indians whom we found occupying what are now the states of New Mexico and Arizona when our commissioners entered this area after the Mexican War to mark the new boundary between the United States and Mexico. In this area and the adjacent Mexican Provinces of Chihuahua and Sonora the Apaches had been waging ceaseless war with the Mexicans for generations, a war so ruthless that the Mexicans had offered large rewards for Apache scalps.

The Apaches were divided into many separate tribes, the principal of whom were the Mescaleros and Warm Springs of New Mexico, the Chiricahuas of southern Arizona, and the White Mountains, Tontos, Mohaves, Pinals and Hualpis of central Arizona. The Navahoes and Moquis of northern Arizona were of the same great family.

Warfare between the Apaches and the Americans who invaded the territory which the Indians considered their own began in the 1860's and ended only in 1886 when Geronimo finally surrendered and the Chiricahuas were transported to Florida. It was a war in which there were many examples of great daring and not a few of base treachery on both sides. On the part of the Americans its worst phases were the work of border ruffians.

In this war as in most Indian wars it was the duty of the Army to protect the settlers and force the roving bands of Apaches to move to and remain on the reservations assigned to them by the government. Here they were under the Indian Bureau of the Interior Department whose agents were to give them the supplies furnished by the government, and to have full control of them. Because of the great mobility of the Apaches, the work of the Army fell mainly on the cavalry, which was handicapped by having to operate in a sparsely settled country of almost waterless desert or rugged mountains, and further by the Apaches' thorough knowledge of the country, and the fact that if hard pressed the Indians could seek refuge in Old Mexico where our troops were not authorized to follow.

As an adversary the Apache was not to be despised. He was brave and fearless. He was capable of great physical exertion, and carried no load of any kind as he could live on the country. As a scout he was unexcelled. He carefully reconnoitered his objective, be it ranch, wagon train, or body of troops, and attacked only an inferior force and that by surprise. If pursued by a force not too great he sought to draw it into an ambush, usually in the mountains where he could command the ground and compel the cavalry to dismount and fight an unseen foe. The Apaches, if in danger of being dislodged, did not retreat in a body but scattered like so many quail leaving no trail to be followed. Their losses were usually small. The very fact that they raided in small bodies made their pursuit the more difficult. They were however so ceaselessly pursued that one tribe after another finally consented to go and remain on its reservation, but here they were too often cheated out of their government supplies by contractors with the connivance of the agents until, outraged by injustice, they again took to the warpath.

When on the warpath the Apaches were absolutely merciless, killing men, women and children, and submitting their prisoners to the most horrible tortures. It was this that turned every citizen of New Mexico and Arizona, as well as most Army officers, against them. The Apaches developed some famous raiders; Mangus Colorado, Cochise, Victorio and Geronimo are the best known.

General Crook was an Ohio farm boy who went to West Point where he was graduated in 1852. As a lieutenant of the Fourth Infantry he was soon in service against the Rogue River Indians of Northern California and Oregon, who belong to the same family as the Apaches, and here he remained until the Civil War. He entered that war in 1861 as a colonel of Ohio volunteers, was in McClellan's campaign in West Virginia, was a cavalry leader in the Army of the Cumberland, commanded an army corps under Sheridan in the Shenandoah, and was at Appomatox in command of the cavalry of the Army of the Potomac, a brevet major general of the United States Army. After the war, as lieutenant colonel of the Twenty-First Infantry, he was engaged in operations in Idaho until called to Arizona in 1871 to pacify that territory.

For a man who had spent so many years in Indian warfare and among the pioneers of the Northwest his outlook on the Indian question was unusual. He was more interested in improving their condition than in fighting them. Perhaps because his favorite recreations were hunting and fishing, he could sympathize with a people who found their game preserves and means of livelihood more and more restricted with the coming of the white men. For their own protection he realized that they must be made to see that they must submit to living on reservations. He also appreciated that life on the reservations would not satisfy them unless they could become interested in farming and stock raising. He hoped that the government would in time grant them the same rights in the courts and as citizens that it had given to the negro.

When he came to Arizona in 1871, the population of the territory consisted of about ten thousand whites, mostly Mexicans, and about thirty thousand Indians, a large part of them peaceable. The life of the whites was made unpleasant by various bands of roving Apaches who raided ranches, small settlements, wagon trains and stage lines in their ruthless way. The United States forces consisted of two small regiments of cavalry and one of infantry, controlled by a headquarters in California. About all the scattered troops could do was to wait until an outrage was reported, then go in pursuit of the marauders, who were rarely overtaken unless the troops ran into a prepared ambush.

Crook established his headquarters in Arizona and began his operations by forming a small column at the head of which he visited all the posts and Indian reservations to make himself familiar with conditions and with the terrain. He informed the Indians of his plans. Within a reasonable time all Indians must return to the reservations assigned them to be counted and issued a tag, so that thereafter any raiders would be known. This was for the protection of those peaceably inclined.

Crook did not expect that his orders would be complied with by all the bands off the reservations. He learned that most of the hostile bands were in a rough rugged country known as the Tonto Basin in which they felt safe. He determined to convince them they were safe nowhere outside the reservation. For this purpose he organized a number of

194

columns which were to enter this region simultaneously from different directions. Each column had its Indian scouts taken from trusted tribes, and a pack train which could operate in the roughest country. Operations were begun late in 1872, and in 1873 there was peace in the territory and Crook was promoted from lieutenant colonel to brigadier general, an unusual promotion at that time. The great San Carlos Indian reservation had not then been organized by the Indian Bureau, so Crook placed the subdued tribes on a temporary reservation, supplied them with tools and encouraged them to begin farming, offering to purchase their products for the army. He organized a paid company of Indian scouts for the preservation of order, and Indian courts for the trial of minor offenses among themselves. General Crook had complete control of the Apaches of central Arizona until the latter part of 1874 when Agent John Clum took charge of the San Carlos Indian Reservation, a tract of land in eastern Arizona some sixty miles wide and eighty miles deep. The central Arizona tribes were peaceful and he had no difficulty in organizing a police force similar to Crook's scouts and continuing the use of Crook's Indian courts.

In the spring of 1875 Crook was sent to command the Department of the Platte to operate against the Sioux.

There was however in Arizona one tribe that had been excluded from Crook's authority. This was the Chiricahua tribe in southeastern Arizona. When Crook first arrived in Arizona a commission was engaged in making a treaty with this tribe, and assigned it a reservation in southeastern Arizona in the Chiricahua Mountains. This was satisfactory to the Chief Cochise. But shortly thereafter the Indian Bureau decided to move the tribe to the Mescalero Reservation in New Mexico. The Indians rebelled; Cochise took to the warpath in 1872 and harried New Mexico. After some time General Howard made a treaty with Cochise giving his tribe the old reservation. Cochise died in 1875 and left two sons as his successors. The Chiricahuas now began new depredations and in 1876 the Indian Bureau decided to move the entire tribe to the San Carlos Reservation. About half the tribe under the sons of Cochise complied with the order and made the move, escorted by Agent Clum's police, but the other half under Geronimo, who now assumed leadership, withdrew into Mexico. Geronimo soon had under his command not only disgruntled Chiricahuas but deserters from other New Mexican tribes. Outrages by this band continued.

Early in 1877 Lieutenant Henley reported that Geronimo and his men were encamped near the Indian reservation of Ojo Caliente in southwestern New Mexico. The Indian Bureau directed Agent Clum to take his Indian police and if possible arrest Geronimo and take his tribe to San Carlos. With one hundred Indian police Clum reached the reservation and was fortunately able to conceal eighty of his men in one of the buildings without their presence being discovered. With the remainder in plain sight he sent word to Geronimo inviting him to a conference. Geronimo came with six of his subchiefs and suddenly found himself surrounded by a hundred aimed rifles. The seven were placed in irons and, with the entire tribe, were taken to the San Carlos Reservation. Shortly thereafter, in the summer of 1877, Clum resigned, and Geronimo was given his liberty.

For the revolts now to be described the conditions on the Indian reservation were no doubt partly responsible. For a short time General Chaffee, then a captain, was acting agent, but he found himself unable to cope with the dishonest contractors with their political backing, and with the Indian Bureau. He was relieved at his own request. Of conditions under his successor a Federal Grand Jury said in 1882: "For several years the people of the territory have been gradually arriving at the conclusion that the management

195

of the Indian reservations in Arizona was a fraud on the government, but never until the present investigations . . . could a proper idea be formed of the fraud and villainy which was constantly practiced in violation of law and in defiance of public justice. Fraud, peculation, larceny, etc., seems to be the rule of action. In the meantime the Indians are neglected, half fed, discontented and turbulent, until at last with the vigilant eye peculiar to the savage, the Indians observe the manner the government through its agent complies with its sacred obligations." The presence of the turbulent Chiricahuas on the reservation was a further disturbing element.

Outbreaks began in August, 1881. A medicine man was inciting the Indians on the San Carlos Reservation and the agent directed his police to arrest him. Two attempts were made but both were frustrated by the Indians. Then the troops were ordered to make the arrest. Encouraged by other Indians, a company of Indian scouts mutinied and the troops were fired upon. In this engagement one officer and several men were killed, as was also the medicine man. An attempt of the Indians to raid Fort Apache was repulsed, and shortly thereafter the mutinous scouts were tried by court martial and some were executed.

A short time later some of the Chiricahuas killed the chief of police and made off for Mexico. In the following year the rest of the Chiricahuas started for Mexico, and soon thereafter a band of San Carlos Indians were off on a raid in the Tonto Basin. This band was speedily overtaken and severely punished in the battle of the Big Dry Wash; the remnants fled to the reservation. The Chiricahuas en route for Mexico were fighting a rearguard action near the border against the pursuing troops when their old men and women, whom they had sent on ahead, ran into a Mexican regiment and suffered severe losses.

It was at this time that General Crook was ordered back to Arizona.

On June thirtieth of that year I reported as engineer officer of the Department of Arizona and later took part in a scout over the Mogollon Mesa in which the battle of Big Dry Wash had been fought. When I returned to headquarters at Prescott, General Crook had arrived.

General Crook had no difficulty in restoring order and gaining the confidence of the Indians of central Arizona who had known him before. This he did by visiting the San Carlos Reservation without escort and talking to the principal men of the different tribes and listening to their grievances. This was done in the autumn of 1882. The problem of the Chiricahuas, and the renegades of other New Mexican tribes who were with them, was a different matter; he had never met them. They could not be left in the Sierra Madre Mountains to raid at will on both sides of the border. He proposed to deal with them as he had with those of central Arizona. His first move was, as before, to convince them that their stronghold was not impenetrable by invading it with a strong force.

This was possible if the Mexican military and civil authorities would take a liberal view of a recent international agreement which allowed the troops of either country in close pursuit of Indians to follow across the boundary. General Crook could not count on a "close" pursuit. Furthermore he intended his invading force to consist mainly of loyal Indian scouts and it was important that the Mexicans keep out of the area during his operations lest there be unfortunate clashes such as that in which Captain Crawford later lost his life. Another point was to secure a guide who could lead a column into the Sierra Madre Mountains, which had not been penetrated by white men or by our Indian scouts. It was this problem which was the first to be solved. In the spring of 1883 the Chiricahua chief Chatto made a rapid raid through Arizona to the San Carlos Reservation and back through

New Mexico with twenty-six Indians, killing many persons and capturing livestock, with the loss of only a single man. In this band was a White Mountain Apache who had married a Chiricahua squaw and thus became a Chiricahua. This squaw was killed by the Mexicans in the encounter previously mentioned, and her husband again became a White Mountain and did not return with Chatto. He offered to guide an expedition into Mexico, and as he was intelligent and vouched for by the leading men of his tribe his services were accepted.

It was now necessary to confer with the Mexican officials, and at this point I entered the picture as assistant aide to General Crook. His chief aide was Captain John Bourke who had been with him since 1872. Just a few words about these two men. As a soldier, General Crook was of the type of General Grant — reserved, modest, reticent, self-reliant. He was courageous both morally and physically, a woodsman of the type of Daniel Boone who could read the terrain like an open book. He indulged in neither tobacco nor liquor. Rarely seen in uniform, in campaign he wore a canvas suit, a rather worn white helmet, and rode a mule with a shotgun or rifle attached to the pommel.

Bourke, in his serious moods, was an indefatigable student of Indian customs and language, and wrote valuable treatises on them, as well as a complete and entertaining account of all of General Crook's military operations after he became his aide. In his lighter moods he was the best story teller in the Army. He could imitate an Irishman, Dutchman, Mexican or Jew, and had an unlimited list of stories about the queer characters he encountered in his life in the west. Never cracking a smile himself, night after night he left the mess at Whipple Barracks in peals of laughter as he told a story each evening after finishing his dinner. He was invaluable to General Crook in entertaining his guests, meeting reporters, and making records of events.

Our trip took us first to Tucson whose inhabitants insisted on giving the general a reception. About all I remember of that is that a young lady with whom I was dancing asked me for a glass of water. My quest was in vain — plenty of champagne but no water.

From Tucson we went by rail to Hermosillo, the capital of the Mexican province of Sonora where the general was met by the governor of Sonora and the generals of the zone and district. We were taken to the governor's mansion, which in true Castilian style was vacated by the governor and turned over to General Crook. That night the general was entertained by the governor at an elaborate dinner in a French hotel nearby. I remember that we had innumerable courses of Mexican dishes and that we smoked cigarettes after each course. My neighbor on my left informed me that the gentleman on my right was a cousin of General Torres and was to be the next governor of Sonora, and that the President had sent him, the speaker, from Mexico City to see that Torres was duly elected the following Sunday.

The next day while the general was arranging matters with the Mexican generals, Bourke and I were taken to see one of their beautiful estates. That evening when we took the train we found a special car attached filled with roses and oranges.

From Sonora we went to Albuquerque, New Mexico, where General Crook had a conference with General Mackenzie of that department. Then on to El Paso and down to Chihuahua, the capital of the Mexican province of that name. I gathered later that General Terrasas of Chihuahua was not so enthusiastic over Crook's plans as the Sonora generals, since we almost ran into some of his troops in the Sierra Madres.

All the preliminaries being arranged, the expedition was organized at Willcox, Arizona, on the Southern Pacific railroad. It consisted of Captain Chaffee's troop of cavalry, about two hundred Indian scouts under Captain Crawford, and five splendidly equipped pack trains. In addition there were six troops of cavalry with wagon trains to form a base near the boundary. At Willcox the scouts indulged in their usual dances day and night, while the medicine men made medicine to assure success and sold trinkets to the scouts to protect tham from all sorts of dangers. The overland trains used to stop here to let the passengers see the sights. One day an elderly gentleman hailed one of our officers and said his wife had heard so much about the Arizona bad men that she wanted to see one. Lieutenant Gatewood was as tough a looking specimen as we had, so he was pointed out. The gentleman went up to Gatewood and asked him if he would have a glass of champagne with his wife and himself while the train was waiting. Gatewood readily consented, but when he appeared later smoking a fine cigar he remarked: "I don't remember ever meeting that man before."

On April 23, 1883, Captain Crawford gave the command "Ukashe" to his scouts and we were off for the border. In small squads the scouts formed a long skirmish line as we were marching across a desert devoid of obstructions. Two incidents I remember of this march to the border. One day I was riding along behind the scouts when I saw a black bear loping along their front from one flank to the other. Not a gun was raised as the bear is held in reverence by the Apaches. One day the mules of one of the pack trains saw a bunch of burros some five hundred yards to one side of the trail. At once the whole train galloped across the intervening ground and drew up in a circle about the burros with ears cocked to the front. It was an amusing sight. The language of the packers I leave to your imagination.

We were five days in reaching the border in the southeastern corner of Arizona. Not a ranch did we pass as it was not safe to live along that route. At the boundary the last preparations were made. We were to cross into Mexico on the first day of May with supplies to last sixty days. With General Crook we were to mess with one of the pack trains, and Bourke and I were allowed one pack mule to carry out bedding, etc. One change of flannel shirts and underclothes was allowed. We were to do our own laundry work. The outfit for the Indians consisted of a loin cloth, shirt, drawers and moccasins. About the head was a red flannel band to distinguish our men from the hostiles. Each carried a rifle and ammunition belt; to the belt were attached the sheaths for knife, awl and tweezers, and a personal tag.

The first day we camped about noon in some high grass. Our man brought up our bedding and unrolled it not far from the cook's fire. Bourke was lying on his back with his hands under his head and I was on my side looking at him when a big rattlesnake crawled slowly across the blankets near our feet and went off towards the cook's fire. I gave the alarm; it circled around the fire and started down a hole under a mesquite bush when a packer grabbed it by the tail, pulled it out and killed it. It was the largest snake any of us had ever seen.

We followed down a small stream and on the sixth day reached the village of Bavispe. It is mentioned in accounts of the Jesuits some three hundred years earlier, yet in 1883 it had no other connection with the outside world than a mule trail. That night Bourke turned out the village orchestra and managed to teach it to play some semblance of the Mexican air "La Paloma." The following day we passed through two other small villages.

We were now at the foot of the Sierra Madres where the trail led up into the mountains. The guide insisted that the mountains must be entered by a night march lest the column be discovered by some roving Chiricahua. What occurred on the unknown mountain trail when we stopped about midnight with mules and horses wandering around loose I leave to your imagination; we did not get much rest. The next day we had no doubt we were on the right trail for it was strewn with the skeletons of cattle and horses who had been too worn out to climb and had been slaughtered along the way. The trail ran along the side of a steep mountain and several mules rolled down the slope. Curiously enough all were recovered in spite of their unexpected descent, for the mule is tough. That day I saw a mule exercise his reasoning powers. I was riding in rear of the mule carrying our bedding rolls, which bulged out on either side. At one point of the trail he stopped and his ears pointed forward. Close to the trail on the upper side was a stout tree. He looked at this tree for a moment and then turned out of the trail and made his way up the slope and around it.

For the next five days we were in a very rugged region, following the general course of the Bavispe River towards its source. One day as we rode along a ridge a black-tailed deer ran along the column so close that one could almost touch it. Of course no one was allowed to use a rifle now that we were in the mountains. It was during these days that I had my first Apache sweat bath. We were encamped on the river bank and the Indians had made a kind of tent of blankets thrown over a skeleton of poles. Stones were heated in a fire and put in a pile in the center of the tent. Using towels as loin clothes, Bourke and I took our places in the circle around the stones. The opening was closed and an Indian poured water on the stones. As the steam arose we all began to sing in true Apache style. When we were thoroughly covered with perspiration the blanket was pulled aside and we all jumped into the river. I noted the modesty of the Apache who never takes off his loin cloth in the presence of others.

During this week we saw many evidences of some older civilization. There were many terraced slopes, evidently gardens, cliff dwellings, etc. On the top of one isolated mountain I saw two parallel stone walls enclosing an eliptical space. One day as I was standing in the high grass viewing a cave dwelling I heard a buzz and looking down saw a rattler with his rattles vibrating going through between my feet. I did not pursue him.

On the sixth day in the mountains word was sent back that evidences of the Chiricahuas had been discovered. Every Apache now discarded his shirt and drawers. On the seventh day Crawford sent back word that his scouts had found a Chiricahua rancheria, and he asked the trains to stop. Crawford planned to surround the rancheria during the night and attack in the morning, but some of his young scouts saw a hostile leading a horse to water and could not resist the temptation of a pot shot. At once there was a fusillade and the enemy fled back into the mountains. That night the scouts returned with the plunder of the rancheria and I noticed one scout with a small baby on his shoulder. I can testify that no nurse could take better care of a baby than did that Indian scout during the following days, until it was claimed by its mother. The rancheria was that of the tribes of Chatto and Chihuahua. The attack was unexpected by our scouts and I doubt if many hostiles were killed; none were taken prisoner.

We moved on into the mountains for the next three days, during which we saw Chiricahua signal fires on the mountains and squaws came in to say the bands wanted to surrender. I think General Crook sent word that he would deal only with the chiefs. As I was sitting in camp on the third day I heard a commotion, and looking up I saw an Indian on a white horse galloping towards our camp and waving a blanket. It was the handsome chief Chihuahua, who drew up right in front of me. He had come in to surrender, and soon his tribe began to straggle in.

199

I think that Chihuahua informed General Crook that Geronimo was on a raid in the Mexican province of Chihuahua and was expected back in a few days, and suggested that we move on to a camp on the trail to Chihuahua. We did so, and camped in a beautiful pine forest at the foot of a high isolated peak. It was now the twentieth of May. That morning I decided to climb the peak to take some observations, but one of my classmates, Lieutenant Mackey, who was with the scouts, asked me to wait until the afternoon and he would go with me. While we were at luncheon we heard a shout, and looking at the peak we saw it was covered with figures. It was Geronimo and his band inspecting our camp. I think probably Chihuahua explained the situation to them and they asked permission to enter the camp. This being given, they straggled in. Crook was sitting at the middle of a log apparently taking little interest in the proceedings when Geronimo came up behind him and seated himself at the end of the log, facing in the opposite direction. Crook never looked at him. Geronimo began the conversation, and Crook sent for his interpreter. Bourke and I were sitting nearby but not close enough to hear all that was said as both spoke in low tones, and we noted long intervals between the remarks. I presume Geronimo asked why we were there, and Crook informed him that we were there to show the Chiricahuas that they were no longer safe in their stronghold and it was up to them to decide whether they would return to the reservation or fight it out. Chatto and Chihuahua had already decided to go back with him. It was not an easy decision for Geronimo to make, for when Clum had carried him back in irons he told him he was to be tried for murder, and his record had been pretty bad since. He had never seen Crook before and was not certain of his protection. Furthermore he had been a raider all his life and he did not enjoy the restrictions of the reservation.

That night the White Mountain scouts who were best acquainted with the Chiricahuas asked if the two tribes might have a peace dance. By the light of the log fire and to the accompaniment of tom-toms they kept it up all night. General Crook and Bourke and myself had our blankets in plain sight of the dance and not far away. The situation seemed a little weird to me.

Whatever Geronimo thought about it, in the next few days the tribes came in one after the other, and a week later we started back with nearly four hundred men, women and children. During those days I wandered about the camp and saw many interesting phases of Indian life, but it would take too long to go into this.

On May twenty-eighth we began our return journey, this time under the guidance of the Chiricahuas, and on the Chihuahua slope of the Sierra Madres instead of the Sonora slope by which we entered. It was a much easier trail. As we crossed the divide we saw a tree with the inscription "The Eleventh Battalion of Chihuahua camped here on May 21." This was a day after Geronimo appeared on the peak. These Mexican troops had pursued him to the mountains and then fortunately turned back. The only incidents of the return trip were that we started a prairie fire in the plains of Chihuahua, and that we passed over the battlefield where the Mexicans had encountered the Chiricahuas the preceding year.

We reached our base camp on June fifteenth. Here my connection with the expedition ceased, and I did not see the Indians on their march to San Carlos. I have no doubt there were many discussions among the Chiricahua chiefs on their way to the border as to the advisability of the movement to the reservation. They remembered what it had been under Agent Riffany. They crossed in various groups at different times, with Geronimo himself, came in, but eventually all were there.

I am sure that the expedition accomplished just what Crook planned. He believed that if he were given police control of the reservation he could effect the same results with the Chiricahuas that he had with the other Apaches. This power was first given and later in part withdrawn. The Indian Bureau would not cooperate, and in January, 1885, Crook asked to be relieved. This however was not granted.

In May, 1885, Geronimo, with about one hundred and twenty-five men, women and children, left once more for the Sierra Madres, leaving behind some three hundred and fifty of the tribe who would not join him. Perhaps the various chiefs of the deserting band were too wedded to their roving life to settle down on the reservation at this time. That Crook had won the confidence of three hundred and fifty of the tribe to the extent of enlisting many of them as scouts to pursue Geronimo was no slight victory for him. It is not impossible that the others might also have been won had he been properly supported.

The pursuit of Geronimo was resumed by Crook, and carried on under him until April, 1886, and resulted in the surrender of eighty men, women, and children under Chihuahua. The terms offered them by Crook were disapproved, and he asked to be relieved. He was succeeded by General Miles. The authorities in Washington, probably urged on by the people of Arizona, are now so exasperated by the Chiricahuas that Miles was ordered to arrest the entire tribe, those living peaceably on the reservation as well as those he might capture, and send them all to Florida. So when Geronimo finally surrendered in September, he and his companions were sent to join his people in Florida. With him into exile were sent the two loyal Chiricahua scouts who had located him for Lieutenant Gatewood and so helped bring about his surrender.

The change from their native mountains to the damp lowlands of Florida proved so disastrous to the health of the Apaches that, at the urgent plea of the Indian Rights Association, the government moved them to Alabama after about three years, and later to Oklahoma where Geronimo died. In 1907 the remaining members of the tribe, about two hundred and fifty in all, were sent to the Mescalero Reservation in New Mexico.

1937

By now the years had begun to take their toll; only 19 Companions with 6 guests attended the meeting. Each year's ritual Necrology Ceremony lasted longer and longer as there were more names to be added and remembered.

General Brainard was to have been the principal speaker but he was absent for some unexplained reason, so the program had to be altered somewhat. General Rhodes read a letter through the courtesy of Major General Peter E. Traub concerning the Modoc War and written by a participant therein. General McIver read two letters, received through the courtesy of Major Henry H. Steelhammer, Swedish Army. Both presentations were printed in the *Proceedings.* The one contribution which did not find inclusion was the letter read and commented upon by Colonel Corson concerning an action in the Seminole War which occurred one hundred years previous to the meeting.

True Extract Copy of Letter
Read by General Rhodes

Camp in the Lava Bed.—50 yards from Capt.
Jackson's Camp — South Shore Tule Lake, Cal.

April 29th, 1873.

My dear ————:

Your letter, dated, first, March 14th and mailed March 25th, was received this morning, after wandering about as you will see from a comparison of dates, for more than a month.

You make the remark in your letter that I must be leading a very rough life. You never guessed so closely to the truth in your life. I am leading as rough a life as it is possible for one to lead.

I have been in this country now five months; with very slight prospect of getting out for at least six months to come. During that time I have marched a couple of hundred miles on foot and three or four times as many on horseback. I have fought and marched for thirty-three consecutive hours, without anything to eat and without an overcoat, when the weather was intensely cold. I have been in the saddle twenty-four consecutive hours, during which I had nothing to eat, and during the same week, I was obliged to go the same length of time without food and to pass the night in a dirty little log cabin in the heart of the Modoc country with nothing to cover me but my overcoat, — afraid to build a fire on account of the Indians and the thermometer indicating the freezing point.

I never spent such an intensely miserable night, and hope most sincerely that it may never fall to my lot again. I nearly froze to death and my sleep was anything but a peaceful one. In the middle of the night I was awakened by what I supposed to be Indians at the door, It did not require any remarkable length of time for me to rush to the door and draw my revolvers. I was exceedingly relieved to find, instead of Modocs, a few sneaking coyotes or prairie wolves, which I drove away with no difficulty as they are the most cowardly animals on the face of the earth; and finally I have fought for three days sleeping under one blanket and on three sharp rocks, vainly endeavoring to distribute myself comfortably but with a success not worthy of mention.

We have been in this delectable place (the promised land I call it — the name induced by the closeness of resemblance of its features to the descriptions I have read of that country, — with one slight difference, scarcely worth chronicling, (I give it up I can't spell it, you know what I mean) that, instead of flowing with milk and honey, — as that land is represented to be, — this flows with rattlesnakes and scorpions —) just exactly two weeks, as shown by the Farmers' and Mechanics' Almanac, and a year and a half as indicted by the appearance of my regiment. I inadvertently looked into a ten-cent mirror hanging against a rock where an officer had been indulging in a shave the other day and was just on the point of saying, "Go away, poor fellow, I haven't anything for you and besides it's against my principles to encourage beggars," when it suddenly occured to me that I was looking at my own image. I believe if I were to walk through the streets of Pottsville, or any other town, I would be arrested in ten minutes for vagrancy, and fined ten dollars and cost.

I live in a den of rocks, — which I have had constructed on the most scientific principles as regards ventilation. It is covered with a tent-fly as a protection against the rain, — a function which it does not perform entirely to my satisfaction or comfort, on account of sundry holes, the result of long service. I am very comfortable considering (?), I have plenty of blankets and a nice bed of tules, — a species of white bull-rush which grows luxuriantly on the shores of the lake. I frequently awake however, with an unpleasant sensation of having a rattlesnake or a scorpion for a bed-fellow. There are so many around that it is more than probable that some adventurous fellow will, one of these nights, make his way into one of our beds. One of the enlisted men of the command had been bitten by a scorpion. I understand that the latter insect, very much like a crab in appearance, but with a long tail, is not dangerous, although the sting is very painful. It is not quite warm enough for the snakes to come out in full force, but if we remain here any length of time I think from all that I have heard, we will be perfectly overrun with them. A pleasant prospect, isn't it?

You have, undoubtedly ere this reaches you, read accounts in the daily papers of our last fight with the Modocs and the massacre of the last detachment sent out against them on the 26th. All the accounts of our doings here that I have seen have been very much exaggerated, and, in many instances, statements have been made which have no foundation on fact. It may interest you to read a true narrative, by an eye witness and participant. I must make it very brief, touching only the most salient points — for it is a subject to which I care not to advert oftener than is necessary.

Before the death of General Canby, everything indicated a peaceful settlement of this difficulty, and all of us immediately interested, were looking forward with anticipations of pleasure to our march toward home where we could enjoy the comforts, if not the luxuries of civilization. The Indians were in the habit of visiting the camp where General Canby had his headquarters daily and it was currently reported that Captain Jack, the Chief of the insurgent tribe, had said in Council that he was tired of fighting and wanted peace; that he knew — being a man of sense — that if he did not accede to the demands of the Peace Commission, war would ensue, and although he felt confident that his warriors could kill many of our soldiers before they were exterminated, he was aware that we could bring more, and, eventually they would all be killed; it was a mere question of time. Such were the reports that were circulating and knowing as we did, that the Peace Commissioners had authority, in the event of the Indians not being willing to accede to any other stipulations, to give them a reservation on Lost River, — the second from which they had been ejected, and for which they were contending.

We all felt confident that the war was practically at an end. Alas for human conjecture! But not withstanding this confidence, the authorities deemed it prudent, and necessary, in case there should be trouble, to have a sufficient force in readiness to move immediately and compel them into submission. With this object in view there were assembled in camp on the west side of the Lava Bed, about three miles from the stronghold, three companies Artillery, two companies Infantry and two troops and a detachment of Cavalry. The Artillery being provided with four Cohorn or twenty-four pounder mortars. On the east side, under command of Col. E. C. Mason, (whose Adjutant I am) we had three Companies of Infantry, of my regiment, two troops of Cavalry, and a section of Howitzers — 12-pounder guns. Our camp was on a high rock, which in the first fight on the 17th of January, we named "Hospital Rock," it having served as a hospital during the day. Up to this time the negotiations had been carried on through the agency of squaws, and a few settlers who had the entree of Jack's

206

camp, but, upon no occasion, had the Peace Commission had an interview with the leading, representative men of the band.

Gen. Canby had accidentally met Jack, while on a reconnaissance to look at their position. I witnessed the interview. Nothing was achieved by this meeting, and it is the only one between any of the Comission and Jack.

After the troops had moved into their respective positions on either side of the Modocs — which was done without opposition on the part of the Indians, these negotiations were still continued, and Indians were allowed to come into camp at will, where they were loaded with presents, in order to gain their confidence and allay their suspicions, — Indians being naturally treacherous, — they are always suspicious of the motives of the Whites.

The day before the murder of Gen. Canby, Capt. Jack sent in word by a rascal by the name of "Boston Charley" that the Commissioners had lied enough and that they, the Indians, had lied enough and that tomorrow at noon they would meet the Commission about three-quarters of a mile from Gen. Canby's camp, at a spot where a tent had been erected for such purpose and would talk "Truth."

Before going out, Riddle — the interpreter — who had been advised by his wife — a Modoc squaw — of the intention of the Indians, called all the Commissioners into Gen. Gillem's tent, and entreated them not to go; that the Indians meant treachery, and that, if they persisted in going in the face of his warning, they would undoubtedly be killed; and called upon Gen. Gillem to wash his hands of the whole affair. There seemed to be a fatality about the whole matter. It may seem strange to you, that notwithstanding this impressive warning, they should conclude to go out. The fact is, they had no confidence in Riddle. It was supposed that he was working in the interest of the Indians, and on previous occasion he had made a statement, substantially of the same nature, in reference to the Modocs' attacking a wagon-train, which, owing to some accident, did not prove to be true. He was immediately set down as a "liar." He was getting, I think five dollars per day for his services as interpreter, and it was thought that he was using every means in his power to thwart the Commission and to prolong the war as long as possible for the sake of obtaining his paltry five dollars. Gen. Canby did not feel perfectly safe for he requested Capt. Adams, the Signal Officer at that camp, to ask me (I am Signal Officer on our side) to keep a look out, with the glass, in the direction of the strong-hold so that I could warn them in case anything unusual was noticed. I complied with his directions, although it was impossible for me to see any movement of the Indians toward the place where the Council was to meet on account of a ridge which intervened between them and me. Nothing occurred until about noon when several Modocs, bearing a white flag, were seen approaching our camp. Lt. Sherwood, of my Regiment, who was officer of the day, was sent out to see what they wanted. Lt. Boyle, 21st, requested permission to accompany him, which was granted. I ran down from the signal station to go with them, but found that I could not overtake them by walking and did not think a sight of the Indians, several of whom I had previously seen, would compensate for the effort of running, necessary to catch up with them, so I gave it up. It was the intention of the Commanding Officer that they should not go beyond the most extreme picket post, an injunction which they either did not hear or did not heed, for they went several hundred yards beyond. When they came up within twenty yards of the Indians, it suddenly occurred to Lt. Sherwood that they looked rather treacherous. He stopped and told them to come and meet him — which they refused to do. He asked them then whether they wanted to "talk." They said No. He told them that he had nothing to say to them and that they should go to their home and he would go to his, and turned around and walked off. He had not gone many steps, when the Indians fired upon him and Lt. Boyle. They both ran but Lt. Sherwood was shot in the arm, and in an instant afterward, in the thigh — the bone being very much shattered. He of course dropped. Lt. Boyle got away unhurt but pretty badly frightened as you may imagine. The picket then began to fire, which deterred the Indians from following up. In a moment afterward the troops went out and brought Lt. Sherwood in. His wounds, however, were of such a nature that he died two days after.

When I heard the first shot I knew what it portended. I immediately ran to the signal station and flagged a message to Gen. Gillem, advising him of what had happened and telling him how necessary it was that he should get Gen. Canby and the Commissioners back immediately. Some time elapsed between the receipt of my message and the firing upon the Council tent but it seems that they could not get troops out in time to save them. When the companies reached the Council tent, they found Gen. Canby stripped and shot in three places and stabbed behind the ear. Dr. Thomas shot twice and partly divested of his clothes. Mr. Meacham wounded several times, with part of this clothing gone, but not dead. He has since gone to his home and is in a fair way to recover. Mr. Dyar, the fourth Commissioner, escaped without hurt. It was a terrible thing, and has cast a gloom over the officers and men which will not be dispelled for many a day — and has forced us into the alternative — the only one — of exterminating the Modocs, and I fear, in fact I know, that many an officer and many a man will fall before we can bring this war to a termination. This occurred on the 11th of April.

We were waiting for the arrival of a company of Warm Spring Indians, on their way to our camp, and hourly expected, before we should make the attack. They arrived at Col. Mason's camp on the 13th and on the 14th at midnight, we moved on our side toward the stronghold within seven hundred yards of which we reached before daylight without a shot being fired. We threw up breastworks of stone, which we had ample time to do before daylight, in which position we remained the following day without any accident occurring. It was our intention to take the Indians by gradual approaches, completely surrounding them, cut them off from water, and in fact to have them completely at our mercy. It was generally understood before the movement was commenced on the other side that they would do the same thing; that is, advance as close as they could to the Modoc position the first night, throw up barricades, remain there until the next night, move forward again — in fact to do exactly what we did. The plan, however, was not carried out, and as a result, a great loss of life ensued, and we on this side were the first in the works. This was at the end of the second day. On the third day, (no junction having been made between the extremities of the two lines as agreed upon) we were ordered to charge, which we did so effectually (and the result might have been foreseen by anyone with ordinary intelligence) that we drove the Indians out of a place, which was in reality ours, if we had been properly maneuvered, to one more strong, three miles further to the south, where they now are. As bold and defiant as their almost invincible position warrants their being. We had two men wounded, one a Warm Spring Indian, through the calf of the leg, and the other, a Cavalry-man, in the right breast, — both very slight wounds, while on the other side, as was to be expected from our experience on the 17th January — charging in daylight, they lost seven killed, and from fifteen to eighteen wounded. There are contradictory statements — I have never ascertained the exact number. The loss they sustained in comparison with ours shows the foolishness of attacking these Indians in daylight in a position where they have every advantage of cover besides the advantage of a thorough knowledge of the ground; and the wisdom of the plan we adopted. There are, however, some men who have no sufficient intelligence to plan an engagement or to generalize from past experience, and whose egotism will not permit them to be advised by others endowed with greater ability.

I think our failure was owing entirely to bad management. I think if there had been concert of action on both sides, if those on the east side had moved at night instead of in the daytime and an effort had been made to surround the position, the Indians would not have gone off, and we would not be here today in this desolate hole, with every prospect of remaining for many, many months. For I must confess that I see no way of bringing this war to a successful termination, either without, or with, a great sacrifice of human life. We can drive them from any position they may take, but from the nature of the country, rough and broken-up in the extreme, we cannot well surround them; for as soon as they see our tactics — and they are not lacking in intelligence I can assure you — they scatter out, each Indian for himself and will not allow themselves to be surrounded. They can glide among those rocks like snakes, and it is impossible to catch them, and by drawing them from any position they may hold, we gain nothing, — for the Lava Bed includes a hundred and fifty square miles of the roughest ground to be found anywhere on the face of the globe I think, and they can retreat from one place to another equally as strong, and keep it up ad finitum. We can't starve them, for the country surrounding the Lava Beds abounds with cattle and however perfect our system of vigilance, they can get all they want. They have abundance of ammunition, and are by this time all armed with our improved breech-loading Springfield rifle, which they have taken from our dead. They can always keep up their supply of cartridges by going over the lines we have occupied in an engagement — so many being lost by our men. If we move against them at all, it must be with our whole force. The experiment was made the other day, and a most senseless one it was, as we all knew; but we were not the commanding officer and therefore had no voice in the matter. You have probably heard ere this of the terrible massacre of Major Thomas' command, which went out on the 26th to see if a trail could be found, over which mortars and howitzers could be packed. There was no reason in the world for sending troops out for this purpose. We have, as I have already stated, a company of Indian Scouts, enlisted for just this kind of duty. However, Maj. Thomas, 4th Artillery, was sent. Of course he had no alternative but to go. He had about sixty-five men. He got very close to the Indian camp without receiving a shot. He had completed his reconnaissance; had ascertained as far as he could the nature of the country and the approaches to Jack's place, and was about returning, when the Indians opened fire upon him. They were in a perfect cul-de-sac and completely surrounded and at the mercy of the Indians. At the first fire, the troops were so demoralized that the officers could do nothing with them. Captain Wright was ordered with his company, to take possession of a bluff, which would secure effectually their retreat, but Captain Wright was severely wounded on the way to the height, and his company, with one or two exceptions deserted him and fled like a pack of sheep; then the slaughter began. Four of the five officers accompanying the expedition were killed and the other dangerously wounded and now lies in a very critical state, — Lt. Harris of Philadelphia. Not an officer escaped; even the surgeon, Dr. Samig, was wounded twice, while dressing the wounds of an enlisted man. Twenty-four men were killed on the spot and twenty-one wounded and missing, and four officers killed and two severely wounded.

It was a horrible thing. The tragedy began at half-past ten and the troops did not get out until after dark. it was so intensely dark that night that they were unable to find the killed and wounded, although they were within eighty yards of them all night. Conceive if you can the suffering, the terrible anxiety of the wounded that night, when they heard our troops throwing up breastworks and thought they were Indians preparing to slaughter them in their entirely defenseless position in the morning. Those who went out — I was not among the number — say it was a most horrible sight. Dead and wounded, officers and men, in one confused heap. Almost all were shot several times — Major Thomas, four times, Captain Wright, three, — Lt. Howe had his skull crushed frightfully and Lt. Cranston and five men have not been found. Many of the bodies were stripped of their clothing. One wounded man — wounded in the arms, both forearms broken, in the back and the heel, kept all the Indians from the wounded men, and prevented them from mutilating the bodies of the officers. A Brave Man! and deserving of substantial notice by the government. All the wounded are in the hospital on the other side and oh what a horrible sight it is to see them in all their agony. I never fully realized what a horrible thing war is, until I came out on this trip. I want no more Indian fighting of this kind in mine. It is bad enough in Arizona where a troop of cavalry can surprise an Indian camp, kill fifty or sixty and not lose a man. In fighting there the danger is not much greater than in deer hunting. But among these rocks every one must look out for himself, officers and men, and the officers stand the worst chance of all. The Indians have been allowed to visit our camp until they have become thoroughly acquainted with all the officers, and of course where they can make a selection in an engagement, they will pick off the officers first.

We have all adopted the precaution of discarding all insignia of rank and it would be a difficult matter to tell us from enlisted men. I wear a private's uniform, no straps or stripes, and a white broad-brimmed hat. I have discarded boots and taken to government gun boats. Altogether, I feel ragged and happy. I doubt if you would consent to dance the German with me in my present garb or even to admit me into your house.

Your sincere friend.

Signed— H. E. W. Moore.

True exact copy from the original letter:
Augusta, Georgia.   Signed — Peter E. Traub,
January 12, 1937.   Major General, U.S. Army, Retired.

Recorder's Note: The author of the foregoing letter was Harry De Witt Moore, who, at the time the letter was written was a Second Lieutenant, 21st U.S. Infantry. he was a native of Pennsylvania and a Military Academy graduate of the Class of 1872. He was promoted to be First Lieutenant July 19th, 1876, and was drowned May 10th, 1878, at Fort Klamath, Oregon, aged 29 years.

Copy of Original Documents Loaned by Companion Major Henry H. Steelhammer, Swedish Army

Cimarron Canon, N.M.,
October 15, 1879.

Actg. Ass't Adj't General,
District of New Mexico,
Sante Fe, N.M.

Sir:

I have the honor to report that Doctor Thomas — under instructions of the Commissioner of Indian Affairs, the import of which are known to you — arrived here on the morning of the 13th instant. After about fifty Indians had collected in my camp a council was held resulting in a reluctant and somewhat equivocal consent on the part of the Indians to remove to the Aibquiu Agency. During the evening the principal Indian Chiefs revisited my camp and told me that they had reconsidered the matter and would not go to Abiquiu. Moreover they would not accompany Dr. Thomas anywhere as they knew him to be a bad man and had no confidence in him, etc. In justice to Dr. Thomas, whose character, I am sure, is above all reproach, I would say that it seems more than probable, from the constantly increasing hatred manifested by the Indians towards him, that some enemy of the Doctor has been at work undermining his influence.

The Indians make the following objection to their being removed to Abiquiu: Dislike to Dr. Thomas — no grass at the proposed Agency — scarcity of water — severity of winter, and distrust of the present agent at Abiquiu.

Yesterday Dr. Thomas had another talk with the Indians when they positively refused to be moved by him to Tierra Maria. They were then asked if they were willing to go to Fort Union and be fed by the military. They did not seem willing to agree to that proposition either. The Chiefs told me subsequently that they would willingly go with me to Union on the condition of being fed provided they were allowed to locate sufficiently far from the post to allow a necessary supply of grass and water for their stock. I gave them the promise that if the government ordered their removal to Union, there to be the wards of the Military, proper attention would be paid to the grass and water question and that I would recommend that they be located somewhere on the Ocate. The Indians seemed so well pleased with this that, should their removal to Union be ordered, I trust no serious objection to such an arrangement may exist particularly as I suppose that the stay of the Indians in the vicinity of Union will only be temporary.

It seems to me that the Indians refusal to go to Aibquiu is, at the present time, rather fortunate. Would it have been well to bring them so much nearer the Utes? Might not the influence and pressure of the latter have strongly tempted the Apaches to unite with them?

The Indians here, with full knowledge of what is going on in the Ute country, are behaving well. They have molested no one since my arrival and, with or without rations for them, I am satisifed that I can keep them quiet until the Ute fight is over. May I ask what is gained by a temporary removal of the Indians from this place to one only forty or fifty miles from here? Some sort of reservation has to be selected for them anyway next spring. They are reasonably contented and quiet now and would be more so were they supplied with rations. In justice to the Indians they should be given something to eat. They deserve it, if for nothing else for refusing to go to Tierra Maria which refusal, in my opinion, is conclusive evidence that the Jicarilla Apaches intend to remain at peace.

I am Sir, Very respectfully

Your obdt. srvt.

(Signed) Charles Steelhammer

Capt. 15th Infantry.

Fort Stanton, N.M.

Feb. 25, 1880.

Dear Captain (Steelhammer)

I read your letter of yesterday with great interest and hope you will succeed in securing Victorio's surrender. If success does crown your efforts keep the prisoners under guard or in charge of your Company at the Agency. It would not be policy to send them here for we could not guard them and our weakness would be exposed. Arms and ponies might be sent here but not the Indians themselves. As in all you do I cannot but command your discretion and I am very glad and am sure General Hatch will be also that you are on the spot to attend to these matters. I cannot understand why Conline did not carry out your instructions. He will have to explain. I want him to come in now. That force is not doing much good now and needs rest and recuperation. If he communicates with you again and there is no emergency preventing direct him to return here.

Please deliver enclosure to McGunnegle when he arrives. It is important he should run in here to have a power of attorney acknowledged before the Clerk of the Court without delay and if possible I would like you to let him come.

Yours truly,

(Signed) P. T. Swaine

(Lieut. Col., Commanding Regiment.)

I do not expect to be able to get off before March 15th and may have to stay a day or two latter.

Recorder's Note: The foregoing letters were read at the annual dinner and are printed in this report for the purpose of illustrating some of the problems and difficulties confronting officers on frontier duty.

1938

When the 20 Companions and their 8 guests pushed their chairs away from the dinner tables and settled back to listen to General Rhode's address, it was felt by all that this country was heading for another war — one which was brewing in Europe. Although these old soldiers were alert and aware of this eventuality, their immediate interests were on a subject of an action which had transpired over sixty years previously.

General Rhodes gave a condensed version of his article on Chief Joseph and the Nez Perce War of 1877, and the complete article was printed in the *Proceedings*.

Following his address, General S. W. Miller, a member of the 5th U.S. Infantry after his graduation from the Military Academy in 1879, related some of his experiences in the final campaign against Chief Joseph. These were not included in the *Proceedings*.

213

Chief Joseph and the Nez Perces Campaign of 1877. An Epic of the American Indian

Foreword

This little story of a great military leader who happened, also, to be a great Indian, has been prepared by a military man to accentuate and bring in relief, if possible, the extraordinary military genius as both tactician and strategist in which an unlettered, untutored red man, hitherto totally inexperienced in the art and science of war, was richly endowed by nature.

If the story will also give to its readers, for the first time perhaps, a new conception of the remarkable human qualities of charity, courtesy, hospitality, possessed in an unusual degree by one combining outstanding qualities as an orator, legislator, executive, judge or his chosen people, as he led them in an anabasis which though brief, deserves to take its place in history, — then its object will have been more than happily accomplished.
Washington, D.C. July, 1937.   C.D.R.

Prologue

When, in the years 1804-05, the pioneer explorers of the American Northwest reached the locality now forming the junction of Idaho, Oregon, and Montana, they encountered an Indian tribe known as the Chopunnish or Niampu, later and more commly called the Nez Perces (Pierce Noses), although at the time and later, the tribe had discarded nose-piercing for ornamental purposes.[1] They were not an agricultural people, but seemed to subsist mainly upon fish, roots, and berries — with occasional dashes into the buffalo country. This mode of living required the periodic moving for short distances, of their simple villages in search of food.

The explorers[2] found these native red-men stout, portly, good-looking, amiable, with the women small, handsome, and possessing fine features. They were fond of displaying buffalo or elk-skin robes, decorated with feathers, beads, and sea-shells, or similar ornaments hung in their hair which usually fell to the front in two queues. They also liked to ornament their skins with white, green, or light blue pigments, all found within their own tribal territory.

In winter, these Nez Perces wore short tunics of dressed skins and long ornamental leggings and moccasins, with occasionally plaits of twisted grass about the necks. They seemed to have few amusements; life for them was painful and laborious. In summer, fishing for salmon and collecting their winter store of edible roots took up all their time; in spring, crossing the Continental Divide to the head waters of the Missouri River, to traffic in buffalo robes and skins. In this they appeared to have frequent encounters with their Indian enemies,

---

1. Encyclopedia Britannica, Vol. IX, p. 248.
2. History of the Lewis and Clark Exp. (1902), p. 186.

but it also served to give the Nez Perces considerable knowledge of a terrain, rough and mountainous, which, many years later, was to be the scene of a series of short but strategic marches and tactical engagements between these untutored warriors and the trained soldiers of the government.

In the year 1856, several of the northwestern Indian[3] tribes, — notably the Coeur d'Alenes, the Palouses, and the Spokanes, went on the warpath, — and almost inevitable happening by reason of the ever-increasing influx of white settlers; and required the disciplinary action of a punitive expedition under Colonel George Wright, to restore order and bring about peace. But during this restless period the Nez Perces continued traditionally friendly to the settlers in the face of many provocative incidents, contemptuous of the prior rights of the Indians to the land of their forefathers. However, in the year 1860, traces of gold were reported in Idaho, and three years later the Territory of Idaho was officially organized, including until 1864 what is now Montana, and until 1868, a part of Wyoming. This occasioned renewed friction.

But it is a matter of history that in spite of the great rush westward of adventurers and seekers after gold, the Nez Perces consistently showed marked kindness and hospitality towards the whites. This dated from the time of the famed Lewis and Clark Expedition in 1804-05, when the Americans left with the Nez Perces their animals and other property while they descended the Columbia River. In after years it was the truthful boast of these Indians that in nearly one hundred years of intercourse with a superior race, no white man had ever been killed by a Nez Perces.[4]

At the same time, conditions for the Indians grew steadily worse. With this settling up of the great Northwest, the building by the whites of houses and the planting of farms, the Nez Perces could not but suspect that in the course of time the day might come when the white man would crowd them off from time immemorial they had regarded as "their country." And about this time, the records show that the great tribal chieftain of the Nez Perces, Old Chief Joseph, warned his people against trading with the greedy white men.

In consequence, about the year 1865, Governor Stevens, of Oregon, invited them to a joint council, with a view to delimiting the country of the Nez Perces, so that all might live in peace.[5] At the conference, Old Chief Joseph bluntly refused any agreement whatever, on this score; maintaining logically from the native viewpoint, that no man owned any part of the earth. Though urged to consent to the new treaty, both by Governor Stevens and by the American missionary, who had most influenced the tribe towards civilized living,[6] the old patriarch left the council chamber in silent resentment. With his opposition removed, other Nez Perces chieftains duly signed the treaty, and Governor Stevens rewarded the signers with presents of blankets and other tokens of good will.[7] This agreement, made, it was claimed without full tribal authority, practically signed away nearly all the Nez Perces country (the "Wallowa," "Winding Water Country"), and the government subsequently claimed that the so-called purchase included all the Indian lands outside the Lapwai Indian Reservation. However, the Nez Perces continued to live as before on their tribal lands for a number of

3. Encyclopedia Britannica, Vol. XIV, p. 279 (History of Idaho).
4. Serving the Republic (General Nelson A. Miles), Harpers', 1911.
5. North Western Fights and Fighters (Brady), p. 52.
6. Rev. Henry H. Spaulding.
7. Brady, *ante,* p. 52.

difficult years, when again the encroachments of the white settlers began to crowd the Indians within the bounds originally set up as marking their country, by Old Chief Joseph. History shows that at this crucial period, the ancient leader was fast becoming both feeble and blind, and in no condition to resist the rapacious demands of the white settlers. Here, his son, Young Chief Joseph enters the picture and took his revered father's place in council. When the government agents again ordered the Nez Perces to move with all their belongings to the Lapwai Reservation, Young Joseph respectfully but firmly declined, in a dignified oration which pointed out that here his forefathers were born, here they had lived and had died, and that the tribe would never leave what they regarded as their home. Soon after, Old Chief Joseph died.

For a while all continued quiet in the Nez Perces country. Then, with new discoveries of gold in the mountains of the Indian country, native ponies were stolen, their cattle was driven off, and, as Young Joseph is said to have declared, the white men were doing things to provoke an Indian war.

Early in the year, 1877, the government issued orders through its military commanders that all Indians of the Nez Perces tribe must move to the Lapwai Reservation. At a great council, called by General Oliver O. Howard, the Indians again refused to comply and the meeting broke up without tangible result. But negotiations continued, and in the end, rather than provoke a war for which Young Chief Joseph felt that his people were almost totally unprepared, he reluctantly consented to the tribal movement, for which General Howard allowed thirty days. Said Joseph, "We are not strong enough. Let us take what the white men offer and have peace."[8]

Again there was great tribal unrest, with Joseph attempting to restrain the hot-heads. And, in time, the danger of resistance to the government's final mandate seemed past. Then, suddenly, a young Nez Perces, whose father had been killed by white settlers five years before, went on the warpath with several other reckless braves, and killed four white settlers without provocation. At the same time, one of the tribal chiefs, Tu-hull-hil-sote, who had been imprisoned by General Howard, began organizing a war party. And thus, in spite of every effort by Young Joseph, — not yet the strong and trusted leader of his people that came in after years, — the bloody Nez Perces War of the year 1877 began.

White Bird Canyon

On June 16 of that year the tribal warriors immediately available and numbering but sixty braves, moved under command of Joseph to White Bird Canyon, Idaho. Although the young chief had hitherto been distinguished for his wisdom and eloquence, and had never as yet been in battle, he was implicitly accepted in this great crisis, as the tribal military leader.

It was Joseph's plan of campaign to assemble the somewhat scattered clans of the Nez Perces, and initiate a rapid movement into the so-called buffalo country on the eastern slope of the Bitter Root Mountains, where it was hoped the tribe might escape or evade pursuit, following the killing of whites by young hot-heads. It is not at all certain that this early in the maneuvers Joseph had as his ultimate objective escaping into Canada, as had Sitting Bull with several thousand of his Sioux. That possible solution of his problem seems to have come later. At this time, rather, Joseph seems to have had in mind the possibility of inducing the government to negotiating a new treaty, allowing the Nez Perces to return to their native

---

8. Chief Joseph (Fee), p. 115.

lands. At the same time, research shows that after murders and pillaging by his young men, the leader's native sagacity warned him of little probability of a reversal of governmental policy.

On June 15, Colonel David Perry, with certain troops of the First U.S. Cavalry left Fort Lapwai in pursuit of the recalcitrant Indians, and after some delay at Cottonwood waiting for delayed pack-trains, prepared to attack the marauding Nez Perces at White Bird Canyon.

Chief Joseph's scouts had promptly apprised him of the white soldiers' approach, and with that natural aptitude as a tactician that he displayed throughout the war, he made deliberate preparations for battle. All women, children, and camp equipage was sent across the swift-flowing Salmon River, and a trusted sub-chief, Mox-Mox was designated to look after the Indians' vast pony herd, and supply reserve mounts to the firing line if and when it became necessary.[9]

Perry's troops, including some armed citizens who had joined his force, made their descent into the Canyon in a very vulnerable military formation — history says, "Column of Fours," although it is far more likely that the narrow trails required an even greater elongated approach. This column had the usual point, support, and reserve of the books on tactics; and as the command advanced, they found Chief Joseph's irregular cavalry deployed in a rough skirmish line, and taking advantage of every incident of the rocky canyon walls for cover. They were not only protected from observation by the white troops, but from carbine and pistol fire.

As Joseph's riflemen began firing from their concealed positions, Perry's advance was halted in some confusion; and while the subordinate officers were deliberating as to just what their next step should be, Joseph directed Chief White Bird to execute a flank movement around Perry's left. At the same time, small squads of Nez Perces sharpshooters pressed to commanding vantage points on Perry's right. With cavalry horses unmanageable and troopers demoralized by Joseph's enveloping movements, the white troops initiated a withdrawal from the canyon which well-nigh became a rout. Men were falling momentarily; riderless horses were galloping haphazard and increasing the confusion. The Indian flanking parties pressed on in a method of warfare in which, as big game hunters, they were adept. Colonel Perry and his officers repeatedly attempted to rally the disorganized troops, but it was not until the rim of the canyon was reached, that the command was halted and assembled in a more orderly retirement, effected towards Mount Ida — closely pursued by Chief Joseph's confident and aggressive warriors to within sight of the frontier town of Gainesville.

This engagement was most disastrous for the American troops engaged. More than one-third of those engaged, including one officer, were killed and left on the field. And when Chief Joseph's Nez Perces finally withdrew, they were able to gather up for their own use great quantities of arms, ammunition, and clothing, abandoned by Perry's command in its flight.

Colonel Perry was very severely censured and criticized at the time, by the public press and even by certain of his own officers, notwithstanding every evidence of personal bravery and precautions against surprise. A Court of Inquiry found that Perry's left flank which armed volunteer citizens had been directed to hold and protect, was abandoned by them in a panic which soon spread to the main column of troops, and that Perry, after the beginning of the fearsome flight to the rear, did everything possible to collect and reorganize his men. The Court, in its finding, "did not *deem* his conduct worthy of censure."

Contemporary accounts of this battle seem to indicate that Chief Joseph rode about

9. Memorandum of Captain E. S. Farrow, U.S.A. (Northwestern Fights and Fighters: Brady, p. 119).

among his fighting men during its continuance, encouraging his men like a good commander, and directing new movements from time to time. He seemed to be everywhere at once.

White Bird Canyon stands as one of the most crushing defeats every suffered by white troops in Indian warfare,[10] being surpassed only by General Custer's ill-fated and tragic defeat on the Little Big Horn. The American force suffered a loss of sixty-nine dead; and when it is considered that fully half of Joseph's warriors were unsupplied with firearms and could rely only upon bows and arrows, this initial engagement demonstrated to a marked degree Chief Joseph's outstanding qualities as a great military leader at the early age of thirty-seven years and without previous experience in battle. With characteristic modesty Joseph subsequently explained his successs with: "The Great Spirit puts it into the heart and head of man to know how to defend himself."

Clearwater River

On July 11, 1877, General Oliver O. Howard, in charge of military operations against the defiant Nez Perces, crossed the Clearwater River with his entire command of some half a thousand men of the cavalry, a small detachment of artillery, and some mounted infantry. Chief Joseph, although greatly outnumbered, did not retreat. Confident in the advantage of position and encouraged by his marked success at White Bird Canyon, Joseph quietly waited Howard's approach. The rugged banks of the mountain stream, intersected by numerous deep ravines, furnished excellent protection for the Indians, and when Howard's advance guard of cavalry under Perry came within firing distance, Chief Joseph aggressively attacked. Followed, the second sanguinary engagement of trained, well-armed, intelligently led white soldiers with this remarkable band of fighting men, known as the Battle of Clearwater River (South Fork).

General Howard's best information as to Joseph and his Nez Perces seems to have been that the Indian encampment was near the mouth of Cottonwood Creek, with ponies grazing and lodges standing. This led him to believe that the hostiles might be surprised by a sudden advance.

Captain Trimble, whose cavalry had the extreme front, has said that as his troops advanced to the edge of the bluffs, the rest of Howard's command moved by the flank to the bluffs, where they were fiercely attacked by the enemy.[11] Meanwhile, Joseph's orders had caused careful withdrawal of all Indian stock into the valley of the Clearwater to a place of safety. Repeated assaults were made by the infantry and dismounted cavalry on the Indian position, which was established in woods on the edge of the bluffs. But each assault was repulsed by Joseph and his men, and finally the engagement became a fight at long range.

About one o'clock in the afternoon, Howard's howitzer and two Gatling guns were brought into action, but owing to the depth and rugged nature of the canyon walls, little damage to the Indians followed, except to frighten the women and children. And subsequent critical examination of Joseph's position showed three lines of Nez Perces rifle pits — one facing directly towards Howard's advance; the other two protecting the Nez Perces flanks,[12] the Indian intrechments being mostly constructed of piles of loose stones.

---

10. Chief Joseph (Fee), p. 142. Northwestern Fights and Fighters (Brady), p. 93. See also: History of the First U.S. Cavalry (Wainright), Journal, M.S.I., Vol. VXI, p. 193; and History of the Fifth U.S. Infantry, Journal, M.S.I., Vol. XV, p. 1104.
11. The Battle of Clearwater, by Major J. G. Trimble (Chap. VIII, Northwestern Fights and Fighters; Brady).
12. Chief Joseph (Fee), pp. 156 and 202.

As the troops progressed, Fee says, "The battle that now took place on the banks of a fork of the Clearwater, was of a kind unheard of before in warfare with Indians. It was a battle in which warriors fought from their own intrenchments, attacked positions held by white soldiers, stood up to and repulsed bayonet charges, and held in check and besieged a military command almost twice their number."

When the fighting became general, and Joseph had had time and opportunity to form an estimate of the military situation and Howard's disposition of troops, he detached some forty warriors to make a wide detour and flank the left of the advancing line, its centre in open order. A furious rain of bullets met the troops, and upon retiring to more sheltered terrain, the line was reinforced by additional cavalry and infantry — presumably Howard's support and reserve. In time, Howard's position assumed the form of a huge semi-circle, a mile and a half in diameter. Here the soldiers lay prone and intrenched themselves — the infantry making use of the newly invented trowel-bayonets. Meanwhile, all mounts had been led to the rear.

Time and again, as Captain Trimble has said from his own limited point of view, the Nez Perces themselves left their ponies in the timber, and charged the white lines, only to be turned back by counter-charges. Crowded out of their more advanced rifle-pits, their main line held fast and forced the troops back, although a charge by Lieutenant Humphries recovered possession of the howitzer and Gatling guns, which had been temporarily abandoned.

As night came on, the circle of United States troops gradually closed in until the opposing lines were barely six hundred yards apart — Joseph's flanking parties outflanking the troops' position over a very wide sector. Under cover of the night both sides threw up additional barricades, and sporadic firing continued until morning.

With sunrise, Joseph sent scouting parties to learn if Howard had received reinforcements, and the soldiers spent most of the morning strenghtening their lines. In the afternoon, with the arrival of an additional troop of cavalry, under Captain Jackson, guarding supplies, a general movement against Joseph's position caused his rather orderly withdrawal across Clearwater River, with an abandonment of the Indian camp. Thirteen American soldiers had been killed and twenty-two wounded. Later information placed the Nez Perces casualties at twenty-three killed and thirty wounded.

Howard's victory was one in name only, for with some five hundred and eighty troops, he was held to the defensive by about three hundred Indians, who ultimately conducted an unhurried retreat with the saving of their non-combatants, horses, and supplies. They were again practically free to resume hostile operations against their fancied oppressors, and with this new victory to his credit, Chief Joseph became the virtual War Chief of his people.

The Battle of the Big Hole River

The day following this combat at Clearwater, Howard ordered detachments of troops under Whipple and Jackson to feel out the Nez Perces position along the river bluffs, and as the troops converged upon a ferry-crossing of the stream, they were fired upon — presumably by Joseph's rear-guard which that wily tactician had instructed to delay pursuit and cover his secure retreat. In any event it had the desired effect. Howard hesitated to cross the river in the face of probable mid-stream casualties. Night came on and Howard's troops again went into camp.

Meanwhile, Joseph had skillfully eluded all pursuing detachments, and had made a new

220

camp for his considerable body of men, women, and children, — as well as horses, on the so-called Lolo Trail, near the frontier settlement of Kamiah. Subsequently, the Indian leader continued his leisurely but well-protected flight up Clark's Fork of the Columbia River and thence eastward to what is known as the Big Hole Basin. Soldiers had great difficulty following such a route over mountains split by tortuous canyons, ravines, and gullies, to say nothing of heavily wooded areas.

So that on July 25 General Howard wired the military authorities at Fort Missoula, Montana, that the Nez Perces had escaped by the Lolo Trail, and to send all available troops to either intercept Joseph or so to engage his attention that Howard's force could close in and accomplish their capture or destruction.

These instructions reached General John Gibbon, Civil War veteran, at Fort Shaw on Sun River, and he immediately ordered a concentration of troops at Missoula from Fort Benton, Camp Baker, and other points. The movement started about July 27, and, carrying limited supplies on pack-animals, Gibbon covered one hundred and fifty miles of Rocky Mountain country by August 3. On the following day, reinforced by thirty-five volunteers from the Bitter Root Valley, he reached the Big Hole River with an approximate total strength of two hundred officers and men. But to Gibbon's keen disappointment, he found that Joseph and his warriors had again eluded the white soldiers and had already crossed the Big Hole River. Meanwhile, back on the Lolo Trail, Howard's tired troops were slowly pushing onward; additional detachments were moving to intercept Joseph, and from as far distant a locality as Georgia, General Frank Wheaton was fast approaching with the entire Second U.S. Infantry. The government at Washington was much concerned with measures to intercept and punish Joseph and his tribesmen for their defiance of governmental authority.

On August 7, General Gibbon sent sixty of his mounted men on a secret night march across the mountains, to strike the hidden Nez Perces camp, and if possible to stampede the Indian pony herds. By this time, rumors had it that Joseph's objective was safety across the border to Canada. Gibbon, with the main body of troops, went into camp at Ross' Hole, at the foot of the Continental Divide, — near the headwaters of the Bitter Root River. The next day, August 8, Gibbon and his troops accomplished a difficult crossing of the Anaconda mountain range, only to learn from couriers sent back from Gibbon's reconnoitering detachments that the latter had arrived too late to surprise Chief Joseph's camp. Joseph had already moved on, but not far. Burdened as he was with much impedimenta, it was his policy to conserve his strength. His scouts had kept him accurately informed, not only of Gibbon's prospective arrival on the scene, but of Howard's progress with cavalry, infantry, and artillery across the Clearwater on July 26, and arrival at the mouth of the Lolo Trail on the 30th[13] The going was slow for Howard's troops, and the Nez Perces had kept just out of reach. And yet, over this same Lolo Trail, obstructed as it was with fallen rocks and trees, Chief Joseph, with remarkable speed and mobility, found little difficulty in safely conducting some seven hundred braves, squaws, and papooses, and fifteen hundred ponies.

To go back a bit, Captain Charles C. Rawn, from Fort Missoula, had, on July 28, hastily constructed a barricade on the Lolo Trail, before which Joseph made a tactical demonstration by a thin skirmish line of Indians, while he himself led the main body of his command through canyons, trails, and passes, with the intuition of mountain people, around Captain Rawn's flank into the Bitter Root Valley.

---

13. Of the Lolo Trail, General W. T. Sherman has said: "One of the worst trails for man and beast on this continent" (Fee. *ante.* p. 173).

A noteworthy incident in connection with this strategic movement by Joseph, was that while in no way morally obligated to keep a promise that had been invalidated by circumstances, Joseph nevertheless held literally to his word and committed no depredations whatever along the Bitter Root. It seems that an envoy of Joseph's had carried word to Captain Rawn that if Joseph's band were permitted to proceed along the valley, he would spare white settlers and their farms. His request was denied by Rawn, but Joseph, the magnanimous savage, still held to the moral code. In fact, his progress was so humane that the citizens of the Valley were emboldened to actually sell Joseph much needed supplies, including guns and ammunition, used later against United States soldiers. And Captain Rawn, deserted by the American citizenry which had originally sought his protection, was forced to give up direct pursuit and to join General Gibbon's main column of troops.

The night of August 8, after his heart-breaking march across the mountains, Gibbon left a small guard in his camp, and pushed on with all speed for Joseph's camp. He reached its location about two o'clock in the morning, and found the Nez Perces' tepees pitched in a meadow on the south side of the Big Hole River. It seems rather certain, after study of all authentic information, that Chief Joseph was ignorant of Gibbon's swift approach. He was concerning himself chiefly with General Howard's much delayed pursuit, and his own warriors needed all the rest possible. One lone sentinel was on guard at the Nez Perces camp, as Gibbon's advanced scouts reconnoitered the ground.

As daylight broke early on August 9, the attack on the unsuspecting encampment was launched with a fierce cavalry charge by Gibbon's leading troops. Many Indians fell at once as they emerged from the tepees. But others, rifle in hand, retained their presence of mind and quickly sought cover in the willows outside the camp. Meanwhile, however, in the ten-minute period of the surprise attack, the troops fired at short range upon fleeing men, women and children, and many non-combatants were necessarily killed and wounded.

For a few minutes panic seized the Indian camp, but this soon passed away, and as the sun arose and the unprotected position of Gibbon's men was better observed, the Nez Perces fired upon them with deadly accuracy from improvised shelter, and the soldiers' losses were heavy, although within twenty minutes following the initial attack, Gibbon's troops were in complete possession of Joseph's camp.

But the Indians clung tenaciously to the willows and river bluffs, and within a short time Joseph had succeeded in rallying them and personally led a counter-charge to regain possession of the burning tepees. There followed a hand-to-hand fight which was most serious in its effects upon both sides. As its height Chief Joseph, in the thick of personal combat, realized the indecisive nature of the engagement, — greatly outnumbered as the Indians were, and ordered an immediate retreat to the shelter of the willow thickets, from which the Indians gradually withdrew to higher ground. Chief Joseph undoubtedly must have realized that his fighting men were at their best where their mobility, and natural aptitude for utilizing the advantages of the rough mountain terrain, could be taken advantage of. Accordingly, under cover of long-range rifle fire from a covering detachment which had earlier mounted ponies and seized strong points along the hills, the main body of Nez Perces stubbornly intrenched themselves anew, and were not to be ousted. Repeatedly, Gibbon's soldiers in two lines, back-to-back, charged the willow thickets on either side of the Indian camp; the Nez Perces kept their morale and held possession.

General Gibbon's losses in killed and wounded were most severe. He himself had been shot in the leg. So that in due time, the old Civil War veteran ordered a retirement, — first to the banks of the stream, then by wading to the farther side, and up through additional willow thickets to higher ground. And, in this retreat under fire, the troops must needs carrying their wounded. It was a sorry ending to what had seemed primarily to be a brilliant victory.

And now a new danger threatened the American troops, due to the far-seeing leadership and exceptional military initiative of Chief Joseph. Gibbon soon learned that the new and better protected positions he now sought for his troops, were being out-flanked by Nez Perces sharpshooters, refusing to be dislodged except at riflepoint. And as the day wore on, the tired soldiers found themselves slowly forced up the slope of the hills, and all but surrounded. The fighting continued all day; several officers were killed and wounded, and Joseph even resorted to setting the grass afire to dislodge the soldiers and to mask his own flanking movements. His mobility reached a climax with an attack upon Gibbon's wagon-train, held in rear of the American lines, including the capture of a howitzer and the seizure of several thousand rounds of small-arms ammunition by the Indians. This state of affairs continued all of the following day, with inconsequential results, and the night of this second day Chief Joseph, feeling no doubt that he had gained a moral victory, wisely ordered a withdrawal.

The Nez Perces left eighty-three (some authorities say eighty-nine) dead on the field, of which about thirty were warriors. Near by lay the bodies of thirty-three officers or soldiers, while in Gibbon's camp his surgeons attended some forty wounded, some of them dangerously.

After the end of the Nez Perces war, Chief Joseph's only comment upon the killing of Indian non-combatants was: "The Nez Perces never make war on women and children . . . . we would feel ashamed to do so cowardly an act."

Major General Hugh L. Scott, U.S.A., himself a brilliant soldier and student of military history, has this to say of this engagement at Big Hole River and Chief Joseph's final withdrawal: "They (the Nez Perces) would have killed the entire command (Gibbon's), corraled as it was, away from water, if General Howard, following their trail, had not raised the siege. The Nez Perces had enough to think about with General Howard on their trail, and they did not wish to encounter any more troops in their front, with the risk of being caught between two forces.[14]

Camas Meadows

Generally speaking, within the next few weeks, the retreating Chief Joseph and his brilliant fighting men, were followed by General Howard's command through the country now known as the Yellowstone National Park, and out along Clark's Fort, a tributary of the Yellowstone River. And now, a new and entirely fresh aggregation of American troops were injected into the desperate effort of the American government to intercept Joseph before crossing the international boundary.

On August 3, General Nelson A. Miles, commanding the District of the Yellowstone, judging wisely that the Nez Perces would elude the troops in western Montana, and would endeavor to reach the so-called Judith Basin, ordered detachments of the Second and the Seventh U.S. Cavalry Regiments to try and intercept Joseph. And a week later, he ordered additional troops of the Seventh Cavalry under General Sturgis, to Judith Gap, the pass through which the Nez Perces subsequently marched. Neither body of troops succeeded in stopping Joseph, and they joined the command of General Howard as he came up from the

14. Some Memories of a Soldier (Major Gen. Hugh L. Scott), p. 65.

south.

Meanwhile, after taking the honors at Big Hole River, Chief Joseph had crossed the Bitter Root Mountains and was again in Idaho, making his way eastward towards Camas Meadows, and eventually to enter the Yellowstone region by way of Teacher's Pass. At or near Camas Meadows, Joseph succeeded in securing some two hundred and fifty fresh mounts, an important factor in his fatiguing march. Howard and his forces followed, and on August 20 camped only fifteen miles from the Nez Perces camp, — as reported to Howard by his scouts of the friendly Bannock tribe. He was very confident of soon overtaking the hostiles, and seems in no way to have had any inkling of the unexpected maneuver which Joseph was about to execute.

On the other hand, as aggressive in his military plans as he had ever been, Chief Joseph is said to have openly declared in council that "he was tired of being trailed by the white soldiers." He knew at this time of Howard's detachment of Lieutenant Bacon and some forty cavalrymen to occupy Teacher's Pass, before the Indians reached that point; and, like the skillful general that he was, Joseph resolved to strike his enemies hard when the blow was least expected.

On the night of August 20 Joseph took some forty or fifty of his mounted warriors, and with military precision in "column of fours," advanced towards Howard's camp. The soldier sentry at the camp, believing the Nez Perces to be Lieutenant Bacon's returning detachment, was slow in giving the alarm, and dashing forward, the daring Indians were successful in completely stampeding Howard's important pack-train, and in driving the animals off under cover of a furious fire upon the soldiers' camp by the mounted Indians.[15]

All was confusion in the surprised camp, but finally, saddling hastily any horses that came to hand in the darkness, several troops of cavalry were soon in pursuit of the elusive Nez Perces. Soon after dawn, some seventy-five of the mules were reported as recovered, but the pursuing troops in their rash eagerness, fell into a trap. Joseph, with his usual cunning, drew them towards his main line of riflemen, lying dismounted in lava beds, while enveloping lines of Indians attacked on both flanks. General Howard, with reinforcements, eventually came to the relief of the hard-pressed troops, and Joseph with his fighting men successfully withdrew.

Howard found himself without a pack train, and quite crippled in any future effort to follow Joseph. So he returned with his command to his former camp with his casualties three dead and six wounded.

This midnight surprise attack by Joseph was a humiliating disaster for Howard, acknowledged brilliant leader in many great battles of the Civil War. For just as he had confidently made all preparations to overtake and destroy Joseph and his men, the latter, impersonating his own troopers, entered his camp, killed his men, and escaped scot free with all of his pack animals.

Canyon Creek

Promptly, General Howard made haste to resume persuit of the fast moving Nez Perces, and counted on Lieutenant Bacon and his troop preventing Joseph's escape into Wyoming. But the Indians eluded Bacon, and, strange to say, actually encountered a party of tourists whom Joseph spared, — although two men of the party were killed attempting to escape. He crossed the Yellowstone River and by a tortuous route entered densely wooded country.

---

15. Fee, *ante*, p. 204.

General Howard, guessing Joseph's general objective, followed by a shorter march to Baronet's Bridge, which he found destroyed by the Nez Perces. A temporary structure over the Yellowstone, it was soon repaired.

Meanwhile, General Sturgis, with his troops of the Seventh U.S. Cavalry, had moved so that Chief Joseph and his marauding band were between him and Howard's command. Here, again, Joseph resorted to strategy. Pretending flight along the Stinking Water River, he drew Sturgis and his force in hot pursuit. This done, Joseph avoided Sturgis by a forced march through dense forests and passed over the Yellowstone between the two bodies of American troops. Howard joined Sturgis, and both commands halted and went into camp.

Joseph had again slipped away from his pursuers. The worst of the mountain country, which in many ways had been his salvation, was now behind him. Before him and his devoted assemblage of men, women, and children, lay a straight route to Canada and to safety.

But Sturgis, furious at having been tricked, took up the pursuit with comparatively fresh mounts; and on September 13 came up with Joseph near Canyon Creek, Montana. Preceded by Crow scouts, Sturgis made a race to precede Joseph to the canyon's entrance. But Joseph had guessed his purpose, and had taken the precaution to post an advance detachment of Indian sharpshooters on the bluffs lining either side of the canyon, while Joseph with his main body redoubled his efforts to reach protective cover. Fire from Joseph's riflemen checked the onrush of Seventh Cavalry troops, while a small, mounted, rear-guard detachment which was covering Joseph's retirement, brought supporting white troops to halt through fire from the backs of their ponies. Hard fighting from cover followed, but by nightfall Joseph had again succeeded in retiring in good order, and effecting his escape.

The Seventh Cavalry lost five killed and eleven wounded; the Indians, sixteen killed and an unknown number wounded.[16] But Sturgis had crippled Joseph in one way, — the capture of several hundred ponies.

Bear Paw

With Joseph's new escape from his pursuers, couriers were hastily dispatched eastward by both Generals Howard and Sturgis to notify General Nelson A. Miles at Fort Keogh on the Yellowstone of the new and unexpected turn of events, and suggesting that immediate steps be taken to intercept the Nez Perces before they might reach the Canadian border.

In keeping with this plan, both Howard and Sturgis deliberately slowed up pursuit, knowing from past experience that the Indians would do likewise; and that encumbered as they were with impedimenta, they would probably content themselves with keeping at a fixed distance from their pursuers. This view proved correct.

Miles received the news on September 17 on Tongue River, and learned that Joseph had crossed the Yellowstone five days before at a point one hundred and fifty miles west of its intersection with Tongue River. Of the chase which Miles was about to make, Major General Hugh L. Scott has said: "Then Colonel of the Fifth Infantry, commanding the District of the Yellowstone, his (Miles') capture of the Nez Perces was one of the most brilliant feats of arms ever accomplished by the American Army, considering the immense distance he had to travel through primeval country."[17]

Miles had at his disposal about three hundred and eighty-three men, — a battalion of the

---

16. Fee gives the losses: Seventh Cavalry, 7 killed, 11 wounded: Indians, 21 killed.
17. Some Memories of a Soldier (Major Gen. H. L. Scott), pp. 65-66.

Fifth U.S. Infantry, mounted on captured Indian ponies, two battalions of cavalry, the Second and the Seventh, one Hotchkiss gun, one pack-train and escort of the Fifth Infantry, one 12-pounder Napoleon gun, one small detachment of white scouts, together with thirty Cheyenne scouts, and a wagon and a pack-train carrying abundant supplies of food and ammunition.

Early in the morning of September 18, 1877, this force began its march along the north bank of the Yellowstone in an effort to quickly reach the Missouri River and intercept Joseph before he might possibly effect a junction with Sitting Bull and his band of exiled Sioux Indians in Canada.

Many days behind the Nez Perces, Sturgis' command was following the Mussellshell River towards the Missouri, while Howard, delayed by an enforced wait for supplies, was also following the Mussellshell. Soon, the two commands joined forces.

On his fourth day out of Fort Keogh, with a forced march of some fifty-two miles the last twenty-four hours, General Miles was able to encamp six miles from the Mussellshell. His scouts, covering a broad front twenty miles ahead of the main body of troops, were seeking out every possible trace of the fleeing Nez Perces. On the evening of September 23 Miles was nearing the Missouri River.

Meanwhile, Chief Joseph was speeding northward close to the Big Snowy Mountains, past the Moccasin Mountains, and on to the Missouri River. At Cow Island, September 23, Joseph crossed the great river at a point which was the head of low-water navigation for steamers.

Here at Cow Island stood a stockade fort and a freight warehouse, guarded by an Army non-commissioned officer and twelve soldiers. Joseph attacked without hesitation. Three soldiers were killed, and the way being clear, the Nez Perces moved on through what is now known as the Bad Lands. But the leader knew that he must have supplies, so he took possession of a wagon-train and fully replenished his stock of stores. His most formidable obstacle now, the broad and treacherous Missouri River, was behind him, and he seems to have felt rather confident that he and his Nez Perces would reach Canada in safety.

General Miles, meanwhile, planned to strike Joseph before he could effect a crossing. So, on September 24 — the same day that Joseph burned the captured wagon-train, Miles sent a battalion of cavalry under Captain Taylor, across the Missouri by steamer, to attempt to prevent the Nez Perces from crossing at any of the ferries above the mouth of the Mussellshell River. At this time, it would seem from recorded memoranda, that Miles believed the Indians from fifty to seventy-five miles south of the Missouri. So that the Army commander was filled with astonishment to learn that the Nez Perces had already crossed the Missouri, some seventy or eighty miles to the west.

Fortunately for Miles, he had barely time to signal with his Napoleon gun and recall to his assistance a departing river steamer — the last of the navigable season, and ferry his troops to the north side of the Missouri.

As soon as safely across the wide river, Miles made all possible speed northwestward along the north slopes of the Little Rockies in the general direction of Bear Paw Mountains. To facilitate the movement, he left his wagon-train behind and subsisted through pack-transportation only. For scouts had informed him that like the wise commander that he was, Chief Joseph had halted near the Bear Paws to rest, reorganize, and refresh his command.

The Little Rocky Mountains run northeast and southwest for about fifty miles; the Bear Paw Mountains farther north, run approximately east and west. Miles believed from his scouts' reports that Joseph aimed to cross a divide between the two mountain ranges, which would give him free access to the level country northwestward. So, the Army commander marched in such a way as to be concealed from observation by the Little Rockies to the west, while his active Indian scouts were able to observe Joseph's movements from the higher peaks. The entire force had strict orders to avoid the firing of guns.

Meanwhile, in the Judith Basin, General Howard had begun to send back to their permanent stations many of his tired and worn troops, while General Sturgis, practically out of the chase, had halted on the banks of the Missouri. Thereafter, General Miles must needs operate without supporting troops.

Filled with eagerness to get into action, Miles was finally, on September 29 and 30, fully apprised by the scouts of discovery of Joseph's trail and location. The Nez Perces, protected in part from observation by the Little Rockies, had decided to go into camp at Snake Creek on the north slope of the Bear Paws. Extreme cold weather had set in, the hunting was good, and the tribal squaws began drying buffalo meat for the winter. Apparently now realizing that General Miles' command was within easy marching distance, Joseph had decided to remain here for the time being. He had many wounded, and his fighting men as well as the ponies had well-nigh reached the limit of their endurance. In fact, it would seem that the Nez Perces felt themselves now secure, and with little or no intimate knowledge of local topography, Joseph may even have surmised that he and his people had actually crossed the international boundary into Canada.[18]

This, it seems now, was the most serious error of Joseph's long and skillfully conducted *trek* towards the north. For the Canadian border still lay a day's journey distant, — probably forty miles, and it now seems certain that had Joseph thrown out a broad circle of scouts, as he had wisely done in traversing the Yellowstone Park region, he might easily have slipped away from General Miles' fast approaching troops, and the remnant of Howard's command some six days' journey to the rear.

The Nez Perces camp on Snake Creek had been selected with a view to easy defense if attacked. The creek beds and coulees were protected by high bluffs which would furnish natural cover for riflemen.

On the night of September 29, Miles sent an experienced scout, Jack Mails, to reconnoiter the east slopes of the Bear Paws. Miles wished to be absolutely certain that the Indians' trail had stopped somewhere in those rugged hills. And after finally turning southwest, Mails' scouting party came upon Joseph's long-looked for encampment, early in the morning of the 30th. Miles was promptly notified, and his estimate was that the hostile camp was only eight miles away. His plan of attack was formulated without delay.

Captain Hale, with the Seventh Cavalry troops, were immediately deployed and ordered to advance and ultimately charge into the southern end of Joseph's camp. Captain Tyler, with the troops of the Second Cavalry and some thirty Cheyenne scouts, were sent by a somewhat circuitous rout to stampede Joseph's pony herd at the north end of his camp. The companies of the Fifth Infantry, mounted on ponies, and the pack-trains, formed a reserve under Captain Snyder, which Miles held for a short time to the left of Joseph's camp, and then

18. Chief Joseph is reported to have said, after the battle of Bear Paw Mountains: "When . . . . Bear Coat (General Miles) and his soldiers came in sight and stampeded our horses, I knew I had made a mistake by not crossing into the country of the Red Coats. Also, in not keeping the country scouted in my rear." This statement may or may not prove that Joseph realized that he had not yet reached Canada.

moved forward.

There is no possible doubt at this late day, after study of all available data, that Joseph and his Indian soldiers were surprised, and it would seem that the earliest intimation that the camp had of the near proximity of troops, was when a Nez Perces youth saw the Cheyenne scouts and gave the alarm. This occured about eight o'clock in the morning.

With his usual calm judgment in great emergencies such as the present one, Joseph issued prompt and decisive orders moving all the Indian women and children out of immediate danger. Under cover of the fire of his quickly organized defense squads at strong points in the creek bottom, over a hundred ponies were loaded quickly with camp equipage, and within half an hour from the initial attack by the Cheyenne scouts, were rushed to safety under escort of some sixty Nez Perces braves.

The weather was fine but quite cold.[19] The leading cavalry charge on the camp covered some four miles of rolling country, the troopers cheering, swinging their carbines, and apparently anticipating little resistance. And as the long irregular line approached the camp, the canter of the horses changed to a gallop, and finally to a headlong charge.

It was awaited by some one hundred and twenty-five Indian riflemen, in hiding along the bluffs. And as the troopers came within effective firing distance (some accounts say as close as one hundred yards), the Winchesters of the Nez Perces opened fiercely and the losses among the charging troops was serious. At the end of five minutes of charging and counter-charging, with some hand-to-hand encounters, the line of soldiers withdrew, leaving on the field the bodies of their leader, Captain Hale, and of Lieutenant Biddle, one of his subordinates, together with fourteen others, besides a large number of wounded, helpless between the lines for hours. Fifty-three of one hundred and fifteen men had been killed or wounded. Troop K lost over sixty per cent.

Meanwhile the troops of the Second Cavalry, not engaged in this frontal attack on the camp, had made a successful contact with the Indian pony herd, and had driven off nearly eight hundred horses, which were brought to a sheltered spot in rear of the American lines. And as this was taking place, the mounted infantry under Snyder had moved forward, had swung to the right, and, dismounted, went forward across the last ridge in a skirmish line, their ponies on lariat. And as the infantry charged, the accurate fire from the Indian riflemen met them and they faltered and finally ran for cover. Snyder fell, desperately wounded. To attempt to retrieve the failure of these charges, the howitzer detachment was ordered forward to a commanding ridge, but it was abandoned temporarily, as one soldier and two of the mules were killed by the Indian fire.

Every effort of this rather tragic morning failed to dislodge the well-protected Nez Perces, and in the early afternoon General Miles determined upon a simultaneous attack from several sides. This was carried out, but again the troops were forced back with severe losses. By three o'clock, Carter's Company of the Fifth Infantry, having lost over thirty-five per cent, General Miles concluded that it was impracticable to force surrender of the hostile camp and decided upon a siege to starve the Indians out.[20] Five inches of snow lay upon the ground and additional snow fell throughout the night. Miles' trained and well-equipped troops had been brought to a halt. Sitting Bull, with over two thousand recalcitrant Sioux was but one day's

---

19. Several accounts state that the morning of September 30th was stormy and inclement but this is disproved by a marginal note in the handwriting of Gen. E. S. Godfrey, that it was "fine but cold."
20. Personal Recollections of General Nelson A. Miles, p. 273.

march northward in Canada, and could he be induced to join forces with Chief Joseph, General Miles' position would have been critical. But Sitting Bull had had enough fighting, and he declined to reinforce Joseph and his besieged Nez Perces.

By October 1 the temperature had dropped below freezing point, and the Indians were still manfully and skillfully occupying their strong defensive positions. Thereupon, Miles determined upon a conference, and sent a flag of truce to Joseph suggesting that they meet between the lines and talk things over. The latter consented, and soon after, rode to the centre. Joseph was asked to surrender. His reply was that he and his people were quite willing to return to their ancestral homes on the Wallowa, if it could be arranged. General Miles retorted that the surrender must be unconditional, to which Joseph shook his head. This ended the conference, and the two leaders returned to their respective lincs.

Miles' wagon-train arrived, and with it the 12-pounder Napoleon, which immediately opened fire upon Joseph's camp, but with little or no effect, owing to its well-protected position. And by October 3, General Howard, with a small escort, joined Miles, but refrained from assuming command of the troops.

On October 4, after prolonged negotiations with General Miles, and unwilling to abandon his women and children in a last minute effort to escape into Canada, Chief Joseph surrendered. Miles promised to spare the lives of all Nez Perces and to send them back to their government reservation, — a solemn promise which, through no fault of General Miles, the government at Washington failed to carry out.

Miles went into battle with three hundred and eighty-three men. Two officers, twenty-three men, and two Cheyenne scouts had been killed, and five officers and fourty-four men had been wounded, some mortally. Three Nez Perces chiefs, two head men, seventeen warriors, and six squaws were killed in the five days' battle. Seventy-nine warriors surrendered, — forty-six of them wounded, together with one hundred and eighty-four women and one hundred and forty-seven children. [21]

For Joseph and his devoted followers, surrender was to mean broken promises, ill-treatment, and ultimate exile from the land of their forefathers.

One detachment of the band which had escaped capture were treacherously set upon and killed by a band of Assiniboines. Another was completely wiped out within a few days by the fierce Blackfeet.

On October 7 Miles started his return journey to Fort Keogh with his four hundred and eighteen prisoners, and by the 15th had reached the army post. Two weeks later he received orders from General Sheridan to embark the Nez Perces for Bismarck, North Dakota, and General Sherman wrote him: "They should never again be allowed to return to Oregon or to Lapwai." Miles protested: "I acted on what I supposed was the original design of the government to place the Indians on their own reservation, and so informed them, and also sent assurance to the war parties that were then out, and those who had escaped, that they would be taken to Tongue River and retained for a time, and sent across the mountains as soon as the weather permitted in the spring. They cheerfully complied. By subsequent orders they have been removed to Fort Lincoln and Leavenworth."

At Fort Leavenworth, the Nez Perces passed the winter of 1877-78, where incipient

---

21. Fee, *ante.* p. 263. General Miles says also in his Recollections: "Those were surrendered with Chief Joseph and those taken outside the camp numbered more than four hundred. There were killed, twenty-six in all, and forty-six wounded."

malaria and typhoid followed them. In July, 1878, a third move by the government, carried them to Baxter Springs, Indian Territory, where many died, and where all longed again for return to the mountains of the Wallowa country. For seven long years General Miles continued urging that his promises to Joseph be recognized by the government and that the Nez Perces be returned to Lapwai. But it was not until 1883-84 that the remnants of the once proud and prosperous tribe were finally brought back to the northwest, and that Joseph and his band took up their abode on the banks of the Nespelem River, a short distance above its junction with the Columbia.

Epilogue

Physically, Chief Joseph was distinguished by his striking facial features and his figure. Tall, straight as an arrow, he was wonderfully handsome, with lines modelled after chiselled marble.[22]

While he spoke little or no English, and made no pretense of embracing religious doctrines, there can be little doubt but that the touch of humanity that ever marked his military campaign, had its inception in childhood impressions as well as teachers from American missionaries. Reverend Henry H. Spaulding, who lived among the Nez Perces for some eleven years and who baptized Old Joseph, Chief Joseph's father, must have been largely responsible for this. Joseph, in his "Own Story"[23] has stated that, "Reverend Mr. Spaulding talked spirit-law. He won the affections of our people because he spoke good things to them."

And among Chief Joseph's ancestors there existed a rough code of morals or commandments, handed down from father to son: "Treat all men as they treat us." "Never be first to break a bargain." "It's a disgrace to tell a lie; speak only the truth." "It's a shame for one man to take from another, his wife or property, without paying for same." "The Great Spirit sees and hears all things . . . . he never forgets, and he will give every man a spirit home according to his deserts."[24]

In addition to these rules of conduct, Joseph is quoted as having said: "Look twice at a two-faced man." "Cursed be the hand that scalps the reputation of the dead." "The eye tells what the tongue will hide." "Firewater courage ends in trembling fear." "Big name often stands on small legs." "The finest fur may cover the toughest meat."[25]

But though humane in his heart-of-hearts, truthful, and just in his dealings, Chief Joseph's religion remained that of his untutored forefathers. It is related that in his later years he would occasionally on Sundays be joined by a few of his leading men, and in his deep, rich voice would pray to the Great Spriit. But the white man's religion never displaced with Joseph the faith of his ancestors.

These last-mentioned qualities of Christian hospitality and kindness were exemplified to a marked degree as early as the years 1804-05, when the Nez Perces met and extended a generous welcome to the members of the Lewis and Clark Expedition; and notably gave the best of care to the Expedition's live-stock and camp equipment, while the leaders and their men made the epochal descent to the Pacific Ocean by way of the Columbia River.

As a fighting man, Joseph was one of the rare, natural leaders in combat that, once in

22. New York Times, Sept. 24, 1904.
23. North American Review, April, 1879.
24. Northwestern Fights and Fighters (Brady), p. 50.
25. Fee, *ante,* p. 301.

centuries, are developed by processes of evolution from among savage and unlettered peoples.

Among American Indians of all racial classifications, he must certainly be held as the "Napoleon" of them all. For over eighteen hundred miles, Joseph had led his people during a period of one hundred and twelve days, through the wildest country known in the United States, carrying with him women and children with all tribal possessions, defending themselves in battle with educated, trained officers and soldiers, and subsisting themselves in large part on what they found in the country. In this historic flight from those whom they regarded as their persecutors, the Nez Perces crossed the Rocky Mountain range five times, the Bitter Roots and the Bear Paws once each.

In his letter to his superiors, asking that the Indians be returned to their old reservation, General Miles had this to say of the exceptional military as well as the humanitarian qualities of the Indians: "The Nez Perces are the boldest men and the best marksmen of any Indians I have ever encountered, and Chief Joseph is a man of more sagacity and intelligence than any Indian I have ever met; he counselled against the war and against the usual cruelties practiced by Indians, and is far more humane than such Indians as Crazy Horse and Sitting Bull." And again, "Chief Joseph was the highest type of Indian I have ever known, — very handsome, kind and brave. He was quite an orator and the idol of his people."

In the sixteen separate engagements in which Joseph participated with his Nez Perces, research shows that the most remarkable features of this Indian General's leadership were the constant use of rifle-pits and hasty intrechments; the formulation in almost every instance of a "plan of attack," with designated supports and reserves; the very intelligent selection of his camps with a view to easy and natural defense; his skillful feinting attacks from, quite usually, a frontal position with a thin line of mounted skirmishers, while his main attack aimed to envelop the white soldiers' flanks or even extend to his rear; his keen appreciation of the value of strong points occupied by sharpshooters, either for a diversion of attention from his main attack or in delaying action during withdrawals; his use of false marches to draw his enemies aside, while with wonderful natural mobility, his main body, with non-combatants and impedimenta, slipped away unmolested; his occasional use of the modern "smoke screen" to mask his own movements as well as to confuse the operations of his adversaries; his correct tactical use of "points" and supporting troops in advance and rear guards for his marching columns.

Added to all this, the natural logistics with which he maintained his supply service is in itself marvelous, not only living off the country through hunting, fishing, and preserving food supplies through curing and drying while constantly on a perilous tactical march, but when opportunity offered, of actually attacking and capturing his enemies' wagon-trains, laden with rich supplies of food and ammunition.

At the close of the campaign against the Nez Perces, General William T. Sherman wrote of them: "Thus has terminated one of the most extraordinary Indian wars of which there is any record. The Indians, throughout, displayed a courage and skill that elicited universal praise. They abstained from scalping, let captive women go free, did not commit indiscriminate murders on peaceful families (which is usual) and fought with almost scientific skill, using advance and rear guards, skirmish lines, and field fortifications."

Chief Joseph fell dead September 21, 1904. Some have said that he died of a broken heart. Be that as it may, from the day that the old warrior said, "From where the sun now stands I fight no more against the whites," he kept to his word. What a shame and pity that it took many, many years for the people of the United States to come to a realization that in its dealings with Joseph and his band of patriots, — as in many other instances in its relations with the red men, — the government at Washington failed to keep *its* word.

CHARLES D. RHODES,
Major General, U.S. Army, Retired

THE WAR WITH THE NEZ PERCES (1877), HEITMAN'S REGISTER, VOL. 2. P. 443. COMPILED FROM WAR DEPARTMENT RECORDS.

Dates of Engagements and Organizations engaged.

1877
June 17. White Bird Canyon, Idaho — Troops F and H, 1st Cavalry.
July 1. Clearwater River, Idaho — Troops E and L, 1st Cavalry.
July 3. Near Craig's Mountain — Detachment Troop L, 1st Cavalry.
July 3-5. Cottonwood Ranch — Troops E, F, and L, and citizens.
July 11-12. Clearwater, South Fork — Troops B, E, F, H, L, 1st Cav.; Cos. B, C, D, E, H, I, 21st Inf.; Bats. A, D, E, G, 4th Art.
July 17. Weippe, Oro Fino Creek — Dets. B, E, H, L, 1st Cav., and Indian Scouts.
July 21. Belle Fouche, Dakota — Dets. A, D, E, G, I, K, 3rd Cav.
Aug. 9-10. Big Hole Basin, Mont. — Detachment Troop L, 2nd Cav.; Cos. A, D, F, G, I, K, and dets.; Cos. B and E, 7th Infantry.
Aug. 20. Camas Meadows, Idaho — Troops B, C, I, K, 1st Cav.; Troop L, 2nd Cavalry; Det. Bat. E, 4th Artillery; Company H, 8th Inf.
Sept. 13. Canyon Creek, Mont. — Troop K and Dets. C and I, 1st Cav.; Troops F, G, H, I, L, M, 7th Cav.; Det. Bat. E, 4th Artillery.
Sept. 23. Cow Island, Mont. — Det. Co. B, 7th Infantry.
Sept. 30. Snake or Eagle Creek, near Bear Paw Mountains, Mont. — Troops F, G, H, 2nd Cavalry; Troops A, D, K, 7th Cavalry; Cos. B, F, G, I, K, and det. D, 5th Infantry; Indian Scouts.

1939

There were ten more names read before the assembled 17 Companions and 6 guests this year — names which were to be remembered during the Necrology Ceremony.

Only one address was made, and it was delivered by Mr. Samuel J. Flickinger, Assistant Chief Council, Bureau of Indian Affairs, Department of Interior. He spoke on the Indian problem under civil administration and on the recently adopted policy of the Federal Government toward the American Indian.

Address of Mr. Samuel J. Flickinger, Assistant Chief Council, Office of Indian Affairs, Department of the Interior

THE AMERICAN INDIAN

Commander Rhodes and members of the Order of Indian Wars of the United States:

I appreciate, deeply, the privilege accorded me this evening. Your kind expressions extended to the Honorable John Collier, Commissioner of Indian Affairs, in the resolution adopted this evening by your organization will be conveyed by me to Mr. Collier. I am sure he would like very much to have been here in person if other previous engagements had not prevented. I extend to you his greetings.

When General Kerr invited me to address your distinguished Order I was filled with considerable timidity, realizing that your organization is composed of officers of the United States Army, who actually engaged in battle with Indian tribes during the period when the urge to press deeper and deeper into the western territory was prevalent. This timidity was accelerated as General Kerr briefly related the procedure followed at your annual dinners as having distinguished members describe different Indian campaigns. You can imagine my relief when the General informed me it was the desire in inviting me to speak on this occasion to obtain information of the Indian problem under civil administration and of the more recent adopted policy of the Federal Government toward the American Indian.

At the time of Columbus it has been estimated by some historians there were approximately 350,000 Indians in the area which is now the United States. Other have estimated this number reached 900,000. At the present time there are approximately 372,000 Indians within the United States, including about 30,000 Indians and natives residing in Alaska. This latter figure constitutes about one-half of the total population of that territory.

Principal States Where Located

The State of Oklahoma has far more Indians residing within its boundaries than any other state. There are about 96,000. Arizona ranks second in the order with approximately 46,000 Indians. Third in order is New Mexico with over 35,000 Indians.

The State of South Dakota is next in line with over 27,000 Indians and California follows closely with approximately 24,000 Indians.

The other five states with over 10,000 Indians each, in the order given are Montana, Minnesota, Washington, Wisconsin, and North Dakota.

Of the enrolled or registered Indians at some 250 reservations and jurisdictions, over 60 per cent are full-bloods. The mixed-bloods consist of less than 40 per cent of the total.

Authority

The Constitution of the United States, Article 1, Section 8, vests in the Congress of the United States the power, among other things to regulate commerce with foreign nations, and

235

among the several states *and with the Indian tribes.*

Among the duties imposed upon the War Department when it was created on August 7, 1789, was that of handling Indian Affairs, the holder of which was subject to the Secretary of War and the President of the United States in the direction and management of all Indian affairs and of all matters arising out of Indian relations.

At that time due to the treatment meted out to the Indians by some of the white pioneers, the Indian in general had come to mistrust most of the whites in all of their actions and he felt that the only way he could protect himself and his hunting grounds from the invading whites was by force. This situation led to the belief that most of the Indians were savage and war-like, and accordingly, it was necessary to use force at all times to protect the white pioneers from the Indians residing within the territory such pioneers were invading. It was natural therefore for Congress to continue the control of Indian matters under the military department of the Government.

At this point I am reminded of a statement referred to by General Kerr with respect to whether or not the affair on the Little Big Horn which resulted in the death of General Custer and the members of his army was a massacre or a battle. It appears that some have said when the Indians were victorious in a fight leaving very few, if any, of the whites particularly alive, that was a massacre, but when the whites were victorious leaving very few, if any, of the Indians alive, that was a battle. A discussion on this point could well lead into many ramifications and differences of opinion. The decision of that question I will leave to future discussions by those best qualified in military affairs and confine my talk to the non-military course pursued by the Government in its treatment of these people.

Congress by an Act of March 3, 1849, created the Department of the Interior in which the Bureau of Indian Affairs was transferred. By this Act the control of Indian matters passed from the military to the civil branch of the Government.

Sections 441 and 463 of the Revised Statutes of the United States provide that the Secretary of the Interior is charged with the supervision of public business relating to the Indians and that the Commissioner of Indian Affairs under his direction and agreeable to such regulations as the President of the United States may prescribe shall have the management of all Indian affairs and all matters arising out of Indian relations.

Since the transfer of the civil authorities of the Federal Government took place, innumerable acts of Congress have been passed until at the present time the Indian Bureau finds itself meshed in a maze of laws, some of which are archaic.

Many Problems Confronted the Authorities

Originally the Indians roamed over the vast territory embraced within this country without restraint, except as one tribe may have encroached upon another. Rapidly increased population caused expansion over the entire area of the country and resulted in restricting the areas over which the several tribes of Indians roamed. Treaties were entered into with different Indian tribes by representatives of the United States, many of which were ratified by Congress wherein provisions were made defining specific reservations for the particular tribe or tribes to reside upon. In many instances these treaty reservations were subsequently reduced in size by further treaties or by acts of Congress to meet the demands of the encroaching white race. Often the best part of the Indian reservation was thus taken from the Indians to provide farming areas for the whites.

The right of occupancy of areas by Indian tribes was recognized in a degree by the

United States. The treaties in diminishing the areas over which the Indians formerly roamed and confining them to specific diminished reservations naturally created new problems. The reduced or diminished area of a reservation to which a particular tribe or tribes of Indians were confined under treaty or act of Congress was known as the diminished reservation while the area formerly occupied by such tribe or tribes which was relinquished to the United States by the Indians became known as the ceded reservation.

Congress on March 3, 1871 (R.S. 2079) decreed that therafter no more treaties would be entered into with any Indian tribe but that future business, such as had been transacted through the treaties, would be taken care of through agreements, so that after that date, instead of having representatives of the United States appointed to negotiate treaties with the Indian tribes, agreements in proper cases would be entered into. Some Indian reservations were created by Acts of Congress while others were created by Executive Orders of the President.

The Indian reservations were held in common by all the members of the particular tribe or tribes residing thereon. In some instances treaties provided for the allotment of the lands embraced within the reservation to the individual members of the particular tribe or tribes residing thereon. Some of the treaties specifically provided that certain chief or chiefs should have set aside for his or their use a particular number of acres of land.

General Allotment Act

On February 8, 1887 (24 Stat. 388) Congress enacted what is known as the General Allotment Act. This Act provided for the allotment of lands of the reservations to the individual members and the issuance of patents to the Indians which recited that the United States would hold the land so allotted to the individual Indians in trust for a period of 25 years at which time a fee patent would be issued to the allottees for their allotted lands free of all encumbrances. This Act was amended on several occasions to take care of needs which became apparent as time went on. The original legislation provided that upon the issuance of the original patent the Indians would become citizens of the United States. Subsequently by amendment the right of citizenship was deferred until after the fee patent had been issued. This change was due largely to misunderstanding as to the real legal significance. At that time it was the belief that wardship and citizenship were incompatible. This theory, however, was exploded by the Supreme Court of the United States in the case of Brader v. James, reported in 286 U.S. 88, wherein the Court held that the granting of citizenship to the Indians was not inconsistent with the right of Congress to continue to exercise its authority restricting the alienation of lands by the Indians under legislation adequate to that end. In the case of U.S. v. Noble 237 U.S. 84, the Court said, "Guardianship of the United States continues notwithstanding the citizenship conferred on the individual Indian allottees."

The Indians were not aliens and could not be naturalized under the general naturalization laws dealing with the naturalization of aliens. They could only became citizens of the United States by specific act of Congress. That body by the Act of June 2, 1924 (43 Stat. 253) provided "That all non-citizened Indians born within the territorial limits of the United States be, and they are hereby declared to be citizens of the United States; provided that the granting of such citizenship shall not in any manner impair or otherwise affect the right of any Indian to tribal or other property." Thus it will be seen that all Indians born within the territorial limits of the United States are now citizens of the United

States.

While on this subject it may be well to point out that most of the Indians have the right of suffrage in the particular state in which they reside. Some states, however, such as Arizona and California prevent the Indians, who are wards of the United States, from voting by providing that certain persons, naming those under guardianship, are not eligible to vote. In the State of Arizona the statutes specifically name Indians as being excluded. The constitutionality of such legislation has not been determined definitely.

Under the General Allotment Act and amendments thereto the reservations were divided into individual allotments, the Indian becoming a restricted owner of that part of the reservation allotted to him.

The guardianship of the United States over the Indian has to do largely with the Indian's land or matters arising by reason of the land. Title 25, U.S.C. Section 175 requires the United States Attorneys within the several states to represent the Indians in all suits and law and equity. This law has been interpreted by the Department of Justice to apply principally to cases involving or growing out of the Indian trust property. Recently that Department has been more liberal in its interpretation of this law and has handled a great variety of cases for and on behalf of the Indians looking to and protecting their interests even when the action did not affect trust or restricted property.

Criminal Laws

In the absence of Congressional enactment courts are without jurisdiction to try an alleged offense committed by one Indian against another on his person or property within Indian country or an Indian reservation. The Supreme Court of the United States on December 17, 1883, in the case of Ex Parte Crow Dog held that the First District Court of Dakota was without jurisdiction to find or try the indictment against Crow Dog, a Sioux Indian, who had been convicted by that Court for the murder of an Indian of the Brule Sioux band; that the conviction and sentence were void and the imprisonment illegal, because as stated by the Court,

"To give to the clauses in the treaty of 1868 and the agreement of 1877 effect, so as to uphold the jurisdiction exercised in this case, would be to reverse in this instance the general policy of the government towards the Indians, as declared in many statutes and treaties, and recognized in many decisions of this court, from the beginning to the present time. To justify such a departure, in such a case, requires a clear expression of the intention of Congress, and that we have not been able to find." (Ex Parte Crow Dog, 109 U.S. 556-572.)

The decision in the Crow Dog case resulted in Congress enacting on March 3, 1885 (23 Stat. 385) what is commonly referred to as the Seven Major Indian Crimes Act. This legislation provided that:

"That immediately upon and after the date of the passage of this act all Indians, committing against the person or property of another Indian or other person any of the following crimes, namely, murder, manslaughter, rape, assault with intent to kill, arson, burglary, and larceny within any Territory of the United States, and either within or without an Indian reservation, shall be subject therefor to the laws of such Territory relating to said crimes, and shall be tried therefor in the same courts and in the same manner and shall be subject to the same penalties as are all other persons charged with the commission of said crimes, respectively; and the said courts are hereby given jurisdiction in all such cases; and all such Indians committing any of the above crimes against the person or property of another Indian or other person within the boundaries of any State of the United States, and within the limits of any Indian reservation, shall be subject to the same laws, tried in the same courts and in the same manner, and subject to the same penalties as are all other persons committing any of the above crimes within the exclusive jurisdiction of the United States."

There was added to this list by the Act of March 3, 1909, (35 Stat. 1151), "assault with dangerous weapon" and by the Act of June 28, 1932 (47 Stat. 336) incest and robbery were added. Any of these crimes, therefore, committed by an Indian against another Indian or his property on an Indian reservation is subject to suit in the Federal courts since the Federal courts are the tribunals having jurisdiction when crimes are committed on property within the exclusive jurisdiction of the United States.

Land

In 1887 the total area of Indian land within their reservation was approximately 137,000,000 acres. The General Allotment Act of 1887 was passed in furtherance of the policy to break up Indian community land holdings by allotting them and creating individual property ownership, with the view of thus absorbing the Indians to the general population. In most instances while the carrying out of the policy changed the mode and method of living of the Indians by making them individual land owners and attempting to make them agriculturalists, limited funds of the individual Indians and with very litte and woefully inadequate appropriations to aid them in accomplishing this change resulted largely in failure of the purpose. No provision was made to provide credit to those Indians who desired to progress and owing to the inability to pledge their property as credit, outside credit was usually not available to them. School, health, medical and dental aid, and other necessary assistance was limited by sufficient appropriations by Congress with the result that the Indians in the main were unable to cope successfully with the changed conditions they found themselves in.

The death rate of the Indian was high. Many of the allotments made to individual Indians was never utilized by the individuals themselves. Upon the death of the allottee in many instances years lapsed before definite determination of the ownership to the deceased allottee's land was made. The State courts in some instances assumed to take jurisdiction in determining heirs of deceased Indians. By the Act of June 25, 1910, Congress vested in the Secretary of the Interior the exclusive power to ascertain and determine the legal heirs of deceased Indians to their or restricted property. The 1910 Act was amended in 1913 (February 14, 37 Stat. 678-679) by vesting in the Secretary of the Interior the power to approve Indian wills.

Many allotments after the death of the allottee and the death of successive heirs passed into ownership of many individual Indian heirs. For example a 40-acre tract of land may have as many as 200 heirs making it virtually impracticable to utilize the land. Each heir's share being exceedingly small many of the heirs will not bother with it, so often beneficial use of the land is not made. This situation complicates exceedingly the administration of the land.

This complicated situation in the past plus the desire of non-Indians to acquire good farm land belonging to the Indians resulted in the sale of many of these allotments to non-Indians. This desire of the white man also resulted in many instances in the further extinguishment of the Indian title to his land. After the allotments had been made to the

239

individual Indians residing on a reservation, acts of Congress were passed providing for the disposal of the so-called surplus Indian lands. The unallotted lands were appraised and thrown open to entry to non-Indians at the appraised price. The Indians receiving the value placed on the lands less cost of administration. Through these several mediums much of the large area, approximately 137,000,000 acres of Indian land, passed rapidly out of Indian ownership.

From 1887 the year in which the General Allotment Act was passed up to 1932, the average yearly diminution of Indian title in lands was 2,000,000 acres. In 1933 there remained 29,481,685 acres in tribal Indian ownership and about 19,000,000 acres of Indian lands allotted to the individual Indians were still in a trust status held by the United States for the individual Indian allottees or their heirs, or a total approximating 49,000,000 acres. At this rate of disposition of Indian lands only a few years separated the time when all Indians would be landless, and to think, at one time this entire country was theirs.

Reorganization Act — New Policy

A new Governmental policy was established by Congress by the passage of June 18, 1934 (47 Stat. 984) of an Act known as the Reorganization Act or the Wheeler-Howard Act. This legislation provided for the setting up of self-government and for self-determination by the Indians themselves. The Indians of a particular reservation voted on whether or not the provisions of the Act should be rejected. Some 189 Indian tribes voted to retain the provisions of the Act and some 78 tribes voted to reject the Act. The tribes of Oklahoma by amendment of June 26, 1936, are entitled to some of the benefits of the Act as are the tribes of Alaska who were granted such benefits by the amendment of May 1, 1936. Constitutions and By-laws have been adopted by many and charters granted pursuant to Section 16 and 17 of that Act. Under this new system of policy group organization is encouraged; credit supplied to Indian tribes and Indian co-operatives.

There has been a decline in the acreage of Indian lands leased to whites and an increase in the use of lands by Indians. Plans for land, range, timber and soil conservation have been carried on, the latter in cooperation with the Soil Conservation Service. The Indians have been granted fundamental rights enjoyed by white citizens; power of the Indian Bureau over Indians (tribal funds, civic authority) restricted. Social Security Administration, Civilian Conservation Corporation, Works Progress Administration, State Board of Education, and state welfare agencies have cooperated. The right of Indians to their own language, ceremonies, arts and traditions have been respected and encouraged. Certain so-called gag and sedition laws repealed. System of justice for Indians recognized and safeguarded from official control of Indian courts whose jurisdiction has been carefully defined. The Indian Bureau fosters the right to negotiate through representatives of the Indians' own choosing. Increased medical, dental and health activities of the Bureau have resulted in the decrease in the Indian death rate to 13.7 per thousand in 1936; whereas the average rate in the United States is 11.5. Nine new hospitals have been built; twenty have been remodeled or enlarged and one is under construction. Many boarding schools were closed or reduced in size and personnel improved; others developed as centers for older children or children from broken or problem homes; seventy-four new community day schools have been opened, enrolling 5,000 children. 6,430 more children have been enrolled in public schools with the cooperation of the states in Indian education. The total number of Indian pupils in schools is 65,000. Arts and Crafts Board was created to raise the workmanship, establish authenticity, and provide markets for Indian arts and crafts.

J.dian employment in regular and emergency services have greatly increased, for example, Indians in Washington Office have increased from 11 in 1933 to 83 in 1937. On April 1, 1938, a total of 3,916 Indians were employed in the Service of whom 3,627 were regular employees and 389 emergency workers employed for six months or more. The total number of the regular personnel is about 6,000.

Between March, 1933, and December, 1937, the total of the Indian land holdings increased approximately 2,780,000 acres. The Reorganization Act authorized an appropriation of $2,000,000 a year for land purchase. There has been acquired 246,110 acres as of December 1, 1937, for Indian use. During the same period an additional 349,207 acres was added to Indian reservations, under the authority of the Indian Reorganization Act conferring upon the Secretary of the Interior power to restore lands which had been opened to homestead entry as surplus Indian lands whenever such lands are still held by the Federal Government and their restoration is not contrary to public policy. Special legislation enacted accounts for the addition of another 1,203,808 acres to the Indian domain. An additional area of approximately a million acres has been included in submarginal land purchases for use by the Indians.

Under the Reorganization Act $4,000,000 has already been appropriated for loans to incorporate Indian tribes. These credit funds are being expended almost entirely for capital investment in the form of agricultural machinery, farm buildings and other improvements, livestock, sawmills, and fishing equipment.

In addition to the advancements made by the Indians it will not be amiss to give you some idea of a few of the projects carried on by and for the Indians. Approximately 45,000,000 acres of Indian lands are now in forest and range; timber land approximating 6,000,000 acres, and woodland 8,000,000 acres. The estimated volume board feet of timber is 33,000,000,000 with an estimated value of $90,000,000. Timber production and sales for the fiscal year, 1938, amounted to over 426,000,000 feet with a gross income of $1,175,000. The range area approximates 40,000,000 acres which produced a total income to the Indians for the same period of approximately $1,420,000. There are two principal sawmill operations carried on, one on the Menominee Reservation, Wisconsin, and the other on the Red Lake Reservation, Minnesota. During the year the Menominee Mills manufactured 18,000,000 feet of lumber and shipped approximately 15,000,000 board feet. At the Red Lake Mills approximately 7,000,000 feet was manufactured and approximately 4,000,000 feet were sold.

Irrigation

There are approximately 1,200,000 acres of Indian lands with Indian irrigation projects of which about 800,000 acres are under completed works. The cost of constructing irrigation works has amounted to $54,000,000. About $46,000,000 more will be required to complete the projects. The largest single structure on any of the reservations projects is the Coolidge Dam in Arizona across the Gila River. Electric power is generated as an incident to irrigation at this dam.

Another enterprise carried on is the cattle industry. For the fiscal year, 1937, the Indians received a total income in the cattle operations of approximately $2,000,000 sheep and goat operations brought in an additional 1,500,000. There are about 21,000 Indians who own cattle.

On the Flathead Reservation in Montana a license for the development of a hydro-electric power project on the Flathead River within the Flathead Indian Reservation was granted by the Federal Power Commission with the consent and cooperation of the Department under conditions which will ultimately net $175,000 annually to the Flathead Indians.

The Act of April 16, 1934, authorized the Secretary of the Interior to make contracts with states for social service to Indians. Under this Act contracts have been made with the states of California, Washington, and Minnesota for the education of Indian children in public schools. In the field of public health a similar basis of cooperation has been established in the states of Minnesota, Wisconsin, North Carolina, and Oklahoma.

The lack of opportunities for higher learning for Indians was partially remedied by a provision of the Indian Reorganization Act setting up a special loan fund for the collegiate, professional and vocational education of Indian youths in college in their own choice.

In the field of health, increased efforts towards the control of tuberculosis, trachoma, and other diseases endemic within the Indian country have resulted in lowering the Indian death rate as heretofore indicated. The following figures tell an interesting story of the Bureau's health efforts and accomplishments:

There are:

80	General hospitals
14	Tuberculosis sanatoria
3,043	Beds and 367 bassinets for general hospitals
1,494	Beds for tuberculosis patients
51,270	(approx.) Patients treated last year
4,088	Tuberculosis cases treated last year in hospitals and sanatoria
3,893	Indian babies born in general hospitals
416,822	Treatments given in out-patient clinics
27,000	Patients given 48,700 dental treatments by a personnel of:
17	Dentists
167	Full-time physicians
99	Part-time physicians
114	Field nurses
352	Staff nurses
76	Head nurses
18	Chief nurses
1,932	Total health personnel.

There are many other activities of the Indian Service which could be dwelt on at length if time permitted. Before closing it may be well to point out that the Indians have been subject to special legislation by Congress. The general rule of law which construe same favorably to the sovereign does not maintain in cases affecting Indians. The laws are construed in favor of the Indian and against the sovereign.

The state law insofar as the Indians and their trust property within the state are concerned, are without force or effect unless Congress enacts law authorizing their application. Crimes by Indians against other Indians are governed by the so-called Indian Major Crimes Act which I have referred to. Prior to their enactment neither the Federal nor the State courts had jurisdiction of such offenses. Now the Federal courts have exclusive jurisdiction in any offenses committed which are covered by that Act. Other offenses not cognizable by the Federal courts are controlled and subject to trial in the Indian court of the particular tribe.

No doubt you have wondered about the many mistakes made by the Federal Government in handling the affairs of the Indians and how the Indians may obtain redress if any was forthcoming. The Indians through their attorneys employed for such purposes present to Congress their grievances and if meritorious succeed in having enacted into law what are known as jurisdictional acts. These acts authorize the particular tribe of Indians to go into the United States Court of Claims and sue the United States for such alleged wrongs with the right to have the Supreme Court of the United States finally pass upon the case. Some 160 suits by different tribes of Indians have been prosecuted in this way. During 1938 two sizable judgments were rendered by the Supreme Court of the United States in favor of the Indians, namely the Shoshone Indians in the State of Wyoming, approximating $6,000,000, and the Klamath Indians, in the State of Oregon, approximating $5,000,000.

Many Indians have distinguished themselves. They have served in Congress and State legislatures. A former vice-president of the United States, Charles Curtis, was a Kaw Indian. The famous humorist, the late Will Rogers, was a Cherokee. Last, but by far not least, some 17,000 Indians served the good old U.S.A. in the World War.

1940

General Rhodes read a paper contributed by the Past-Commander, Colonel Morgan, at this year's meeting of 17 Companions and 8 guests. The paper dealt with a fight with the Apaches in 1882. Following the paper's presentation, pertinent remarks — unfortunately unrecorded, but reported as having been made — were made by Dr. McPherson, General Roberts and Mr. Ghent.

Before General Rhodes read the paper, an interesting discussion was had and a resolution was made. The report of it is included here.

General Kean brought to the attention of the Board a radio address by the Honorable John Collier, Commissioner of Indian Affairs, printed in the Washington *Evening Star* of December 5, 1939, in which Mr. Collier made certain derogatory statements with reference to the conduct of the 7th U.S. Cavalry at the fight with Big Foot's band of Sioux Indians at Wounded Knee Creek, S.D., December 29, 1890.

After the discussion, in which the Order had access to General E. D. Scott's splendid reference to the fight and the involvement in combat of the children and squaws, the Commander was authorized and directed to bring the matter to the attention of the War Department and the Recorder was authorized and directed to bring the matter to the attention of the present Commanding Officer of the 7th Cavalry.

The following letter to The Adjutant General of the Army and his reply thereto are published for the information of the membership. The letter to the Commanding Officer, 7th Cavalry, and his acknowledgment, together with a copy of the newspaper account of Mr. Collier's address, are on file with the Order's records and available for reference.

"December 22, 1939.

Subject: Misstatements made in a Radio Address by a Public Official to the Discredit of Officers and Enlisted Men of the Army.

To: The Adjutant General of the Army.

1. The Council of the Order of Indian Wars of the United States has requested the undersigned, as Commander of the Order, to bring to your attention the following facts: — On December 4th John Collier, Commissioner of Indian Affairs, made an address which was broadcasted over a nation-wide network and published in the Washington *Evening Star* of December 5th, thus insuring the widest publicity. A copy of the printed address, with the objectionable paragraphs marked. by heavy lines, is

245

inclosed. These statements refer to the conduct of two squadrons of the 7th U.S. Cavalry at the fight with Big Foot's band of Sioux Indians at Wounded Knee Creek, S.D., on December 29, 1890.

2. Mr. Collier stated in substance that at the time and place above mentioned, a regiment of United States soldiers massacred a great number of Sioux Indians: —

(a) For reasons not yet fully and formally established.

(b) That the Indians had gathered for purposes essentially peaceable.

(c) That after shooting down the men, the soldiers turned their guns upon the women 'who were standing by a flag of truce.'

(d) That children who escaped and hid were called under a promise of safety, surrounded by the soldiers and then butchered.

(e) No mention was made of such essential facts as that the Indians began the conflict by an attack, at a signal, upon the soldiers, with repeating Winchester rifles which they had concealed under their blankets; also that the women and children became involved in the fire by the act of the Indians themselves in retreating to the camp where the former were and mingling with them. The heavy loss in killed and wounded of the soldiers is not alluded to, nor does he mention the Ghost Shirt movement by which the Indians hoped to exterminate the whites.

3. The entire picture presented to the public by Collier was that of a premeditated and unprovoked massacre of innocent Indians with the intentional killing of women and children.

4. Fortunately for the truth of history and the reputations of the officers and men involved, all of the statements indicated in (a), (b), (c) and (d) above, have been shown to be untrue by facts fully and formally established by official investigation and the depositions of responsible eye-witnesses.

5. The President of the United States, within a week after this fight, ordered a full investigation of its occurrence by an impartial Board. The whole question was again investigated only a year ago by a Congressional Committee in hearings on a bill to give pensions to the Indian survivors and to the families of the slain in that fight. The evidence of the Indian's responsibility for the conflict settled that claim in the negative.

6. The testimony of many army officers who were present, of the Surgeon, Colonel John Van R. Hoff, of Father Francis J. Craft, S. J., who was

stabbed by an Indian, and of other responsible witnesses is on record and available.

7. The mass of evidence proves conclusively that none of the statements made in the exparte account of Commissioner John Collier are credible and that they could have been accepted only by ignoring the well established facts and accepting fully the statements of interested Indians. This mass of credible evidence is accessible to any seeker after historical truth. A fully documented article reviewing it was published as recently as the January-February issue of this year of the *Cavalry Journal.*

8. The leading purpose of the Order of Indian Wars is to collect and preserve for history a true record of the incidents which make up the long story of the conflicts between the settlers of our Country and its aboriginal inhabitants. To permit much perverted statements as those under discussion to go unchallenged would be inconsistent with this worthy objective. The council of the Order of Indian Wars requests, therefore, through me its Commander, that the War Department take the proper steps to refute the aspersions cast by Mr. Collier, an official of the Government, in the most public manner, on the brave officers and men of the Army, eighteen of whom received the Congressional Medal of Honor 'for acts performed at Wounded Knee Creek.'

(Signed)   GEORGE H. MORGAN,

*Colonel, U.S.A., Ret.,
Commander."*

"1st Ind.

War Dept., A. G. O., January 10, 1940. To: Colonel George H. Morgan, U.S.A., Ret., care of Mrs. D. C. Cabell, Aberdeen Proving Ground, Maryland.

1. It is a rule of the War Department to refrain from participation in controversial discussions arising from time to time in connection with comment by radio or public speakers, or with respect to artciles appearing in the press, where the activities of the Army or its personnel are criticized. So closely is this rule adhered to that the Department does not feel justified either in affirming statements found to be correct or denying those which are erroneous. Any other course of action would inevitably involve the Department in controversy from which no advantage could possibly accrue.

2. In accordance with that policy it is deemed inadvisable for the War Department to issue any statement or comment with respect to the radio address mentioned in this instance. However, there is inclosed a copy of the Hearings before the Subcommittee on Indian Affairs, House of Representatives, 75th Congress, 3d Session, On H. R. 2535, a bill relating to the

so-called Wounded Knee Massacre. As will be seen on pages 4 to 7 of this this document, the Acting Secretary of War submitted a report to the Acting Director, Bureau of the Budget, on June 3, 1936, setting forth the views of the War Department and facts disclosed by the records here conconcerning the Wounded Knee Affair, in connection with a similar bill H.R. 1178, introduced in the 74th Congress.

By order of the Secretary of War:

(signed)

Wm. C. Rose,
Adjutant General. "

2 inclosures.
1 Incl. Added.

L. Bjorklund

The Fight at the Big Dry Wash in the Mogollon Mountains, Arizona, July 17, 1882, With Renegade Apache Scouts From the San Carlos Indian Reservation

The big San Carlos Reservation was flanked on the north by the command at Fort Apache, on the south by those of Forts Grant and Thomas, and on the west by the command at Whipple Barracks. At the time of this outbreak Fort Verde was abandoned as a garrisoned post.

The Third Cavalry had just arrived in the territory from Wyoming, and excepting the older officers, were entirely ignorant of the country. It was distributed among the Posts of Apache, Thomas and Whipple Barracks. The squadron of Cavalry stationed in camp at Whipple Barracks consisted of two troops each of the Third and Sixth Regiments, commanded by Captain Gerald Russell, First Lieutenant George F. Chase, Captains Adna Chaffee and Wallace. I was the usual "Poo Bah" of the times: Adjutant, Quartermaster, Ordnance Officer, etc. Major J. W. Mason, Third Cavalry, in command.

After a long march through the western part of the territory, an interesting episode on the trip being the fact that frequently we were compelled to pay for water (at one place near the head of Chino Valley it was fifty cents a head), we went into a permanent camp on Granite Creek near the Post of Whipple Barracks. Captain Chaffee's troop had been sent to Wild Rye on the western slope of the Sierra Aucha nearer the western edge of the San Carlos Reservation, now possibly covered by the water backed up by the Roosevelt Dam.

One Sunday evening Major Mason was called to the Commanding General's office. He took me along to care for the details. We were informed that a band of renegade scouts had broken out from the Reservation and started north through the Tonto Basin country. We were ordered to pursue them. When asked how much time would be necessary to break our rather comfortable camp the General was informed that we could get away at noon the following day.

As the noon call sounded we marched past the cheering Infantry of the garrison, taking the eastward route towards old Fort Verde and camping that night at Cedar Springs, getting into Verde the next day.

The civilian pack train, hired to supplement our one pack train, not appearing, I was directed to put on our (McNight's) train absolute necessities and to bring up the rest of the supplies with Simon's train, for which I was to remain behind with my acting Quartermaster Sergeant, George Niles of K Troop, Third Cavalry.

Early the next morning the three troops and pack train pulled out, and much against my will I was compelled to remain behind.

The belated Simon's train came in after noon, and as the pack loads had been all arranged, I ordered them to pack at once as I thought we might make Stoneman's Grade by night, fifteen or sixteen miles. The Packmaster explained that he had just taken charge of the train, that it was completely out of condition and every aparejo had to be restuffed, etc. There was an outfit of Mexicans, only one of whom, the Cargadero and Chief Packer, knew how to pack. I gave him futile orders to get ready as soon as possible. He was not ready at night-fall and then ordering him to be ready to start at dawn the next day, worn out by my troubles, the Sergeant and I retired to one of the abandoned houses on the Post, had supper and went to sleep.

I was awakened by the sun pouring into my eyes through the uncurtained window, and leaping up called to the Sergeant to make the coffee. I then ran over to the corral where I expected to get some articles always left behind by an outfit breaking camp. To my disgust I found the entire train asleep.

With the Sergeant and myself, four packers in all with the full fifty mule train, we managed to finally start about noon and make Stoneman's Grade at dusk. I was doing the rear packing, when, the train halting, I rode up to see what new trouble had developed. It was merely that the cook leading the bell mare had lost the trail of the three troops and pack train. Hearing frogs, a sign of water, went into camp.

Next day I arose about three o'clock, aroused the camp and looked for the trail. It hardly seems credible, but it was not visible even in daylight on the hard, dry "malpais" covering the surface of the ground. I rode directly east about three miles and then taking a circle, finally found the plain trail on more reasonable ground. Then I took myself rather seriously as a tracker.

Starting as soon as practicable we found that the trail was over what I subsequently learned was called "hard scrabble" and it was properly designated. Just before arriving at Strawberry Valley, my estimated goal for the day, we had to cross a canyon which must have been 600 or 700 feet deep. When I rode to the rim I thought it hardly possible to get the train through, but the trail certainly went down there. It took us seven hours to pass the canyon and it was nightfall when, worn out, we arrived in Strawberry Valley. As soon as we had had supper we hit the hay.

I was awakened about early dawn, three o'clock probably, by the Sergeant announcing that the Chief Packer had deserted! Reason — supposed that I had worked him too hard. I was just getting off some remarks about it, when a fine looking cowboy rode up on a good horse and we passed the time of day. I asked him if he knew the diamond hitch. He replied that he did. I asked him if he wanted a job. He queried as to its nature. I replied, "Chief Packer of the train." He accepted and soon after we were off. Later I became very well acquainted with this Arizonian, by name of John Hicks. He had a small bunch of cattle on the Mogollons and physically was a fine specimen. He was a fortunate find for me.

Wrangling along until about ten o'clock, I got fairly impatient with the slowness of my progress and was quite sure that things could not go all right at the front without the Adjutant, Quartermaster, Ordnance Officer and Chief of Scouts, especially the last, my latest title, so explaining to Sergeant Niles and the new Packmaster that the chase was probably approaching us, I directed them to pull into Round Valley and await orders. I started off for the front riding the excellent saddle mule and leading my horse. After about fifteen miles of this I was concluding that, although a saddle mule was good for work about a pack train, it was little use in a man's hurry. I swapped saddles and tying the mule by the wayside, with some belated information to the Sergeant, I pushed on.

When challenged at Wild Rye the Camp was abed, but I got some feed for man and beast and at the invitation of my generous K. O. rolled in with him. My bedding was with the train at Round Valley, I hoped.

The Commanding Officer told me that Captain Chaffee had been directed to get onto the trail of the renegades with the scouts and had left Wild Rye early that morning. Thus he and my command were still a day away.

The next day we surmounted the Sierra Aucha and made camp after about twenty-five miles. Our bivouac was probably where Chaffee had camped. Later a scout came in from Chaffee with dispatches. While we were climbing the western slope of the Aucha the entire outfit was demoralized by a nest of wasps. The Commanding Officer and Staff missed it but the leading troop did not. There were several casualties — stings!

That evening I asked for and obtained permission to join the advance under Captain Chaffee. Therefore, next morning at daybreak I started, accompanied by the scout from Chaffee's troops.

With a short halt at noon on a beautiful branch of the Tonto Creek for lunch, bread and coffee and how good it was! we rode until about four o'clock. We ran into the train at the rear of Major Evans' command from Apache. On the difficult trail it took me until nearly eight o'clock when the column halted for the night.

Just before I had met Lieut. Tommy Cruse, who was working the pack train, I had passed a burning house which heartened me, because it indicated that the renegades were not too far ahead. Therefore when Major Evans' scouts told him that the renegades were several days ahead and could not be caught, I butted in with a minority report. Lieut. George L. Converse, a classmate, was in command of one of the troops and was my host for supper and bed. He told me that his troop would be in the advance the next day and for me to beg Captain Chaffee to go a bit slow and he would be along right shortly. I did so and he came, I am sorry to report, because he received during the engagement a severe wound which compelled his retirement.

Ordering the scout with me to be prepared to start at three thirty A.M., he reported that his bronco had not been up since he laid down on reaching the halting place. Telling him in the morning that he should come along as fast as possible, I left camp on time. The episode of the horse of the west playing out before the superior horse of the east, settled in my mind the relative value of the two brands.

A little bit of map work might be illuminating at this point. At the north of the Tonto Basin appears a high wall of rock, The Rim Rock. It is explained that at some prehistoric time the land south of the line sank some 2,000 feet. I do not remember the extent of this drop, but from the Cibicu on the east to the East Fork of the Verde it was impossible for animals to climb this sheer rock, therefore, as soon as a trail trend was ascertained one knew where the outcome would be in case the trailmakers had animals. Close to the Rim Rock where the trail ran, and it was now definitely fixed for the East Fork, the country was badly broken. One was continually either going into a deep gulch or climbing out. I rode rapidly over the short flat between two canyons I heard a deep voice giving the command, "Prepare to mount." I have frequently wondered how many miles I covered in the three days from Strawberry Valley. Thinking my horse should be tired, as soon as I was introduced to my command I got a saddle mule, and my horse, which seemed to have a drawing power over mules, promptly kicked half the train down the next hill when they too persistently and unanimously tried to get next to him.

On the trail to reach the advance, there were, besides the burning houses, the too numerous sights of the passage of the war party, dead men, cows and calves horribly mutilated. One could never understand the reason for this, a general destruction. Wherever they bivouaced there was a fortification. It was partly due to the fact they had taken many horses from the looted ranches, that we caught up with them as quickly as we did. Even foot Indians, as are Apaches, will not walk if they can ride. Towards the last, the poor, sore-footed animals they rode could not be urged very far. From General Springs it was only about twelve miles to the Big Dry Wash and we passed at least two fortifications in that short distance, indicating two marches at least.

I found that my company of Indian Scouts consisted of a Chief of Scouts, Al Sieber, an old Arizonian and soldier of the Civil War; a First Sergeant; a Chief, and twenty Indians. When ready for the day's work, one Indian was detailed to lead the troop and packs, a distasteful duty if one could judge by his expression. The Chief of Scouts and the First Sergeant also were at the head of the marching column. At a wave of his arms, much like our signal for "as skirmishers," the rest of the Indians, at a run, formed a fanlike cover for the column. One or two on the right flank managed to get up the cliff-like "Rim." During the morning Lieut. George Dodd, with his scouts from Apache, joined the advance and I presume that Lieut. Converse was not far behind because he came up soon after we struck the hostiles.

When, after a very hard climb, I reached the top edge of the Rim Rock near a place called General Springs, I found the entire outfits of Scouts in conference. They gave me more guff about the impossibility of our being able to catch the hostiles, but they were compelled to go on.

Passing within a few miles of the marks of the hostiles' enforced rest, we were as eager as hounds after a fox, and sure enough about twelve miles out from the Rim Rock, our Indians began to get excited about our poor soldiering, and to shed some of the scanty clothing they had.

We dismounted and, under the care of our Indian aides, crawled into position. I judged that the enemy was not aware of our proximity. Although they had the usual fortification, they were trying to move the horses up the side gully in which they had probably passed the night.

We found ourselves on the south side of the so-called Big Dry Wash at a point where the "Old Moqui Trail" crosses it by means of two side gullies happening to meet from the opposite sides of the vast canyon.

After the firing began the enemy hustled their captured horses up the side canyon and, diving to cover, the action was on. Somewhere the enemy had obtained an English Express rifle. It was in the hands of a competent marksman and when fired sounded like a cannon in the confined area. As I remember it, the Indians' position was quite four hundred yards from ours on the brink of the canyon. Sieber and I lay behind a large rock in front of one another, behind which the Scout, First Sergeant and the column leader were disposed. Sieber played the old trick of exposing his hat on the end of a stick, and the Indian marksmen made quite good practice on it. Whenever a shot would spatter on the rock behind us, the Sergeant and the scout would unite in the one English word I ever heard them get off — "Damn!"

I requested permission of Captain Chaffee to take the scouts to the rear of the enemy's position to get the horses, but he refused, saying that they would leave me. Finally he directed me to take eighteen of his men, get over the "Wash" to the east and gain the mesa across the "Wash" to the east of the enemy's position. By this time a portion, at least, of the Fort Apache command had arrived on the ground.

We had a very difficult problem getting into the bottom of the "Wash" but once there it was safe enough running across to the opposite side where we were able to gain the top.

The country at this place was like a beautiful pine covered park. The pine cones and needles covering the surface prevented the growth of much underbrush, and the trees were magnificent. The top of the Canyon was formed by a perpendicular ledge of rock probably seven or eight feet high. To surmount this with as small a loss as possible, I directed each man to select his tree and at my command everyone was to get his place on the top of the mesa. Where we were, the edge of the canyon had a curve, which I did not notice. The consequence was that when, seeing the last man disappear over the edge, I made my run to the tree immediately in front of me; to my surprise I found five or six men had chosen the same shelter. In those days one must remember that a good tree was a protection against the lead bullet of that date. The Indians in our front would not expose themselves, therefore their bullets struck the tree at least three feet from the ground and we were quite safe as I dropped behind my wall of men. They had different ideas as to the direction of the hostile fire and were not all on the safe side of the tree. The idea seemed to strike them all at once, and with the same teamwork which got them there they, as a man, jumped up and disappeared behind the shelter of the canyon wall. To get over my surprise, I drew up closer to the tree, which was not the largest in the vicinity, and received a second surprise. An Indian, dressed in his "G" string and a few feathers, jumped from behind his tree a few paces to my front and began a war dance, supposing that he had driven off his foes. At that distance I could not miss him and he did not move after falling. Then to find out where my army was, I hated to waste the time crawling back a safe way, and finally made a dash for it. Getting back safely I was relieved to find the men were all where we had been before the advance to the trees, shepherded by the good scout, Al Sieber.

Again explaining the more practicable method of advance by pointing out to each man his personal tree, we then made a successful conquest of the top of the canyon. Passing the dead Indian, my Chief and his companion Apache scout both made "coups" and both were cussed by Sieber who claimed the credit for their new Commanding Officer, a proper introduction to those people. They followed me closely until I got too near the enemy. My troubles were due to the fact that I did not belong to the troop; the men did not know me or my methods, etc. About that time Lieut. West of Chaffee's troop appeared and I asked him to take command of the detachment. I then began a series of independent maneuvers which had some effect until, heedlessly exposing myself quite in the manner of the young Indian of the earlier part of the day, I was so severely wounded that I was unable to move and was so near the enemy that my friends could not assist me until after dark. A soldier, whom I had passed while getting my forward position, remained with me until darkness when I was carried across the canyon.

Probably about the time I was crossing the canyon, Lieut. Converse was very seriously wounded while leading his troop into position on the west side of the enemy's position. The tragedy was that he was compelled to retire from active duty before he had had a chance to show his great capabilities as a soldier, which he undoubtedly had.

Although I gave Major Evans' message to Captain Chaffee, I believe that he would have made the attack with his small troop, although a company of Indians forty-two strong and not counting the good fighters, the squaws, is a serious problem. General Crook told me that we should have been whipped.

Our loss was one man killed and seven, I believe, wounded. Our man was buried on the field beneath a beautiful pine. The Indian dead were left on the field where, some years later, I saw their whitened bones. The place has been dubbed "The Battle Field" by the settlers in

253

the vicinity. The wild country is, of course, no more. The Tonto Basin is a beauty spot and the Rim Rock must take its place as a wonder of Arizona with the Grand Canyon, Fossil Forest, Sun Set Butte and Natural Bridge near Strawberry Valley. The Apaches, in this last fight, lost more heavily than in any previous or later encounter. As he did not assume command, Major Evans gave the entire credit to Captain Chaffee for his initiative. The squadron from Whipple Barracks got in about three A.M. and that from Fort Thomas at some time the next morning.

When one passes over the present concrete roads at forty miles or more an hour, and remembers our safe if sure progress encumbered with either the necessary wagon or pack trains at a maximum of four miles in the not so long past days of our youth, the movement of the world, I shall not presume to call it progress, is exemplified.

The menace of the western Apache is now replaced by that of the "Eastern Gun-Toter and Hi-Jacker," not forgetting the "Hit-and-Run" driver.

The conservatives of the 80's should look back with longing to the days when, if one kept his eyes open, he might have some guarantee of keeping his block on its proper pedestal. Sanitarily the wide open ranges were healthier than can be the purlieus of the congested centers of the new and dangerous civilization.

The contrast in efficiency between our regular pack trains and the civilian ones it was necessary to hire for emergencies, was so great that, when in the 80's just before the Garza trouble on the lower Rio Grande, for economy's sake the Army was required to dispose of its mule transportation, we knew that we had lost a valuable asset to our efficiency. However, due to the construction of the transcontinental railroads, the Indian question was practically settled and the Army merged into its new life of schooling, and there was "no more use for the Cavalry."

GEORGE H. MORGAN,
Late 2d Lieut., 3d Cavalry.

1941

Although this was not to be the final meeting of the Order of Indian Wars, it was the last meeting in which a major address was given and printed in the *Proceedings*. But first, the 15 Companions and 6 guests observed the Necrology Ceremony in which eleven more illustrious old soldiers were remembered for their part in our country's history.

General Kerr read Colonel Morgan's paper on life on an Indian Reservation in the eighties. It was faithfully reprinted in the year's *Proceedings*.

Before adjourning after the presentation of the paper, there was a short general discussion after which Chief Bigman, a Crow Indian, gave a short talk about the Crows and their relations with the whites. Then he and Chief Hawk gave a demonstration of Indian sign language. This concluded the program, and in retrospect, it is remarkable that as many members of the various Indian fighting armies could and did meet. The date was April 12, 1941.

Before they were to meet in session again — and none knew the next meeting was to be the last — the United States was to enter into World War II after an attack on Pearl Harbor, Hawaii. The end of an era had been long in coming. The Indian fighter was no longer the subject of hero worship by the young, of admiration by the middle-aged and of envy by his few peers. The remaining Order of Indian Wars membership — by virtue of a sneak attack — became *ancient* history, and no longer *just* history. They — the few who were still alive then — were soon to suffer the humiliation of becoming anachronisms within their own lifetime. America was now mobilizing for a struggle which would make all struggles in the past almost insignificant. Our heroes of the past were now to become lost in the present and almost forgotten in the future. It was an unfitting death of an image so long loved, admired and respected by Americans.

Army Life on an Indian Reservation in the 80's

I graduated from the U.S. Military Academy on June 12th in the Class of 1880 and, made suddenly rich by the pay of a Lieutenant for the 18 days of that month, I passed a very happy and carefree three and a half months before being finally compelled to start for my assigned station with my regiment, the 3rd Cavalry, Troop K, Captain Gerald Russell. Every older officer kindly enquired about my assignment. When I informed them to what troop I was assigned, they gave me to understand that my Captain was an Army character. This did not off-set my enthusiasm for my chosen arm of the service as I had already encountered such characters at the Academy and also in the service when I was a child.

At last I did make my way slowly to the post where my troop was stationed. It was formerly named Camp Brown, Wyoming, but the name had been lately changed to that of Fort Washakie. The Paymaster who paid by advance mileage did not know where it was and, as on his book appeared the railroad station of Washakie on the Union Pacific Railroad, it has always been my idea that Uncle Sam owes me the mileage from that station to the post, a goodly distance.

However, I finally arrived at Fort Fred Steele, a station of the regiment a few miles east of Rawlins, with an exhausted treasury. I wasted several days trying to find out which of my friends there might be able to loan me the necessary amount to get me to Washakie when, much to my relief, an ambulance from Washakie rolled in, with Captain Wessels of the regiment going on recruiting service. He brought an order from the Commanding Officer of Fort Washakie, Major Mason, 3rd Cavalry, that Lieutenant Morgan should return the transportation to Washakie.

Everything about that trip was interesting and exciting to the shavetail and is as vivid now as it probably was then. But it had little to do with the subject of this paper as I don't think that I saw an Indian until we actually entered the boundaries of the great Indian Reservation of the Wind River section.

When I reported, Troop K was out on duty escorting a surveying party in the north of Wyoming. I was placed in charge of the small detachment of troops which remained at Fort Washakie. A few days later the Commanding Officer made me, as was customary in those days, his "General Staff." I was Adjutant, Commissary, Quartermaster and Ordnance officer. This naturally brought me in touch with all the doings of headquarters and, as the reason for the existence of the post was the policing of the great reservation, it gave me very good facilities for studying and learning much about the Indians concentrated there.

I think it is a fact that the Indians' best friends were the soldiers who were at times required to punish them. Personally I had many good friends among them and, although one may lose all sympathy for them when they make war in their peculiar way, they undoubtedly are a great and fine race. They have never been enslaved.

On the Wind River Indian Reservation at that time were settled two distinct tribes. The Shoshones and the Northern Snake Indians, related more or less to the Utes, and the remnant of the great Arapahoe Nation. Both tribes, of course, were Plains Indians or otherwise known as Horse Indians. They had little to do with each other, were indeed not very

257

friendly and decidedly different in their customs and manners. The Shoshones had been friendly with the white man for a long time and were, in their way, quite well off as Indian wealth goes. The Arapahoes had quite recently been on the war path and were consequently poor in comparison. The Shoshones had skin covered tepees and large herds of ponies. Most of them were able to have several wives and, led by a very remarkable Chief by the name of Washakie, were quiet and peaceful, and in an emergency stayed on the reservation when urged to go out by their relations, the Utes. They had a musical language, of which we made use in our slang. On the other hand, the Arapahoe tongue, a series of grunts, was terrible. It was so unwieldy that the Arapahoes themselves usually contacted each other with the universal sign language, of which they were the experts of all the tribes. Of this I was assured by a Ute trader whom I met one day while on a hunting trip. I have seen two of them sitting on opposite sides of a small fire exchanging thoughts without a single word. On the request of Captain Clark, 2nd Cavalry, it took me all of one winter to ascertain the names of the subordinate families in which that small tribe was divided.

The Arapahoes had a real head chief, "Little Wolf," and one they designated as an Agency Chief, "because he was a good beggar," "Black Coal." Little Wolf was a fine character while, according to the white soldiers' notions, Black Coal was not.

The Indians on the reservation were given a week's rations, quite a liberal one, every Saturday. They at once began to feast and I judge that by Tuesday, or at the latest Wednesday, the rations were gone. Until the following Saturday they then either lived on the little game and fish obtainable, or starved. Then, much as we liked them or were amused by them generally, our friends, the Indians, were rather a nuisance.

Occasionally we had one at dinner with us at the mess. They would watch carefully our methods and procedure and endeavor to copy them. Although they were lavish feeders at home, as our guests they would never take more than their host.

To them it appeared to be bad medicine to tell their names. However, one would readily give, if there was another standing by, the friend's English name, especially if it was, as it frequently happened to be, a ludicrous one. One young Indian was my companion on hunts and hikes and to try him, after we had become "blood brothers," I asked him for his name. He knew little English and I am now sure that he gave me his correct name, "Left Wrist." It was so odd that I did not catch it at the time. Years later, in the roster of the Arapahoe Indian Scouts, I noticed one named "Left Wrist." At the time I thought his name was "Cheyenne" as the sign for that tribe was about what he gave me.

Chasing horse thieves with him and a younger brother as scouts, we arrived at the west end of the Sioux Pass and there went into camp. As our trail went into the pass, all understood that after a rest that was where we were going. Early next morning when I stirred I saw Left Wrist, on the top of a small peak near camp and with his face toward the east, praying. His brother was missing and, when my friend came down for breakfast, I asked him where the boy was. I was told that he had gone back home because we were entering into bad medicine country. When I demanded if he was also intending to desert, he bravely said, "No, I go where you go," and so he did, but I required him to join blankets with me so that I was sure of him. We amateur trailers were too apt to make errors. On that trip it happened that a horse, belonging to the thieves, had a footprint just like that of my own horse, except that the rear hind shoe had a crack in it. When the pursued party split up, our pack train followed that trail and I, going without blankets and food for nearly a day, followed the other party.

The Doctor at Fort Washakie, in the pursuit of knowledge, and two of us youngsters in the pursuit of fun, asked and obtain from Little Wolf, who was also the Medicine Man of his tribe, permission to enter the sweat house with him and a sick Indian. The wick-i-up was about eight feet in diameter and perhaps four feet high. It was covered with robes and canvas to exclude air. A hole was dug in the center and a lot of smooth stones were heated at an outdoor fire and then piled in the center hole. A bucket of water and a gourd were supplied as we entered naked. Little Wolf then dashed water on the red hot stones and we had a Russian Bath. The wick-i-up was so contracted that one was compelled to turn his naked hide constantly to avoid being burned by the heated stones. Soon the steam became so thick that it was difficult to breathe. The squaws outside laughed, put more blankets on the outside and trod on our fingers when we tried to raise the edge of the canvas. Making him think it was the proper thing to sit up, we bedeviled the medico as long as possible. It finally got too hot for us and we burst forth and made for the river. The Chief, a brother of Black Coal, had formed on the shortest way to the cold water, a double line of squaws and children through which we had to pass. All of this was very amusing to the bystanders, especially to our young chief.

Some time later I rode into his camp and was informed that he was taking a siesta. I demanded that he be awakened and, as he threw back the tepee opening, I saw that he was naked, except for the blanket. I dismounted at once and, telling the kid to hold the horse, advanced to him. He was about my size, but heavier, and I supposed that I could handle him only by surprise. As he came up and held out his hand to shake, I suddenly grasped him around the middle and, exerting all my strength, threw him down and rolled him out of the protecting blanket. He made a break for his tepee and, amid the easy laughter of everybody, he disappeared. He would not speak to me for a month but eventually got over his peeve.

A regular accompaniment of the Saturday Issue was the horse races. The Indians were great jockies and had wonderful ponies and race horses. It happened that I obtained a mount that was bit faster than anything they had. Seventeen years later, in 1898, I met in Washington a delegation of the Indians from the Wind River Reservation. Knowing whom I was to meet, I had little difficulty in recognizing the individuals. Young Dick Washakie was the most familiar one so I walked directly up to him and, as he looked rather at a loss for he had never seen me in civilian clothes before, I said, "How Dick, don't you remember me?" At once he turned to old Sharp Nose, who appeared to be blind, and stated, "He is the young chief who owned 'Tope-she-beth'," the name they called my horse. Perhaps he never knew my name but, horseman as he was, he remembered the great racer.

It is a curious thing that our horses did not like the Indians. When, with a small outfit and a "running guard" was most economical, I was compelled to take my turn, I would hold my horse near and go to sleep if necessary. A snort from him would bring to my attention anything he didn't like. During one of my hunts I met a tribe enroute to a new camp. They were probably also on a hunt. Although it was early, about eight o'clock in the morning, several of the bucks who knew me turned to ride along. One of them, an especially talkative chap, rode up too near me. I warned him that he was bad medicine to my horse. The others laughed at this but paid no attention. Although I was somewhat on my guard, suddenly my horse turned sideways and, unfortunately for the Indian, planted both heels on the side of the man's leg. The pony was turned completely over. When I found the Indian was not seriously injured, I joined in the laughter of his fellow Indians. They are rather given to practical joking and this passed off for a joke.

A few miles father on we came to their last camp. It was deserted except for one travois outfit. A little girl, not more than nine or ten years of age, was busy getting ready to start.

259

It was before the days of the kodak, but what a picture she made! She was very capable and had apparently rigged the whole thing up. The pony was a fine one, the travois quite complete, and the load was composed of three or four cute papooses with not a yell in the bunch. I stopped to watch her go about her work. She did not even look up until everything was ready and then she started off to join the tribe which was about a mile ahead.

As rations were issued only to those present, on Issue Day the families would squat down together. One day, while I was enjoying this scene, a cur dog, and there were many, sneaked from a neighboring family party and grabbed a bone a small boy had laid down for a moment. When the little tad, not a day over three years of age, saw the theft, his little face became perfectly distorted with rage and he grabbed the nearest stone and let it fly at the cur, but it hit a squaw instead. She joined in the laughter at the baby's rage. I have never seen an Indian boy punished by a squaw.

A renegade Ute, with his wife and ponies, came to the reservation to induce the Shoshones to go on the war path. In attempting to arrest him, he was killed and the Arapahoes, who had been our informers, brought in the herd of horses. I gave them a fine pony for their work. They then wished to know what was to become of the other ponies. They were informed, of course, that they belonged to the widow. Although she was no chicken and not too good looking, she took a week to decide as to who should be the new owner of the ponies. That was one occasion when an Indian woman had her will. We never did know much about their marriage customs. A good squaw was worth about five ponies.

A fine character among the Arapahoes, (they could not pronouce the letter "R" and called themselves, in English, "Napahoes"), named Sharp Nose, was made a corporal of scouts by General Sheridan, commanding the Division of the Missouri. This gave him Corporal's pay and allowances; also pay and forage for two ponies. The Interior Department had furnished him with a wagon. I told him that he should drive in and load up as much wood as he needed and whenever he needed it. When he was thus "taken on" he was a poor, old man with but one wife and one tepee covered with Interior Department white cotton cloth. I did not see him for some time, but one day I rode down to call on him. He had accumulated four more wives and with them most of their relatives I judged, and here was the nucleus of a good sized addition to the tribe. Like the Moros, a chief had as many followers as he could support.

Some time later I had occasion to guard three separate trails. Placing Sharp Nose on one, I started my vigil. It was a bright, cold night in December and, to escape some of the wind and also to hear better, I laid flat on the ground. I heard a horse travelling in the vicinity of the poor, old Sharp Nose and, riding over there, found him dead to the world with an empty whiskey bottle by his side. I called in the other men and just left him there. However, he did not freeze, but we were not so friendly afterwards.

Attached to their necks each Indian carried a small bag in which were most of their valuables and medicine. With great pride one showed me a paper, written by Captain John Bourke, an Aide to General George Crook. This paper stated that the bearer was about the most unmitigated rascal in the Arapahoe nation and that anyone reading this trusted him at his own peril, or words to that effect. The statement was possibly true, but the trusting way it was handed out made it very impressive. Captain Bourke's writings gave a very vivid account of the use of General Crook and other leaders of this era, made of the friendly Indians in the campaigns conducted by them.

The following incident may illustrate the apparent childishness of the Indian character.

I was given six men and ordered to capture a hostile Ute, reported to be in the Shoshone encampment. Proceeding there, the quarry was found in a log hut built for the Indians but not generally used by them. He escaped from this hut and ran into a tepee on the edge of the village. I was personally chasing the man when the young son of Chief Washakie, named "Dick" by us, and heading about twenty companions, rode between me and my man. I asked him what he meant by it. He replied, "You no catch Ute Jack. He heap medicine man." I replied, "You watch my smoke. Give me your rope." When he, apparently without thought, handed me his lasso, I asked him to give me the ropes of his followers. This he at once ordered and wonderingly watched me tie the several lines together. Then I dismounted three men and we proceeded to pull down the tepee which covered the refugee. Apparently the minds of Dick Washakie and his men were at once changed from that of being opposed to us, to being with us on the man hunt. To make sure that the Ute was harmless, it was finally necessary to pull over another tepee in which he had made his defense. Two of the Shoshone warriors, on their ponies, swept it over by use of a long rope I had obtained from the Indian Agent. The Ute was buried where he died and the next day there was not a tepee in the vicinity. The tribe had moved.

After citing another incident, this rambling effort shall close. On the Fourth of July, 1881, a wild-eyed cowboy rode into the post and, indicating how hard he had ridden, his horse promptly dropped dead as he dismounted. His story was that the Indians had broken out on the north of the Owl Creek mountains and he gave harrowing details of his narrow escape. We had just finished firing the National Salute, and, after allowing the men time to get their dinner, Troop H, Lieut. Jordan and twenty scouts from each of the two tribes, left the post at 2:00 P.M. and made the distance, about 100 miles, early the next morning. Jordan found that the scare was due to a practical joke played upon the cowboy, a shavetail, by his comrades doing the Indian act.

A couple of days after the party left, old Chief Washakie came to the post and said there had been a fight and that a chief had been badly wounded. As his son Dick was in command of the Shoshone contingent of Jordan's party, we were both, of course, anxious to get reliable news of the expedition. I knew that we could not expect any word for at least a week, but was agreeably surprised to see the column return intact about five days later. This matter off our minds, I busied myself in hunting down the reason for Washakie's report. Nearly a month later it was discovered. A squaw-man, who could read some, was giving the newspaper account of the shooting of President Garfield, to some of the Indians. He translated the President's name as "Big Chief." This, old Washakie at once decided, was his son and on the old man's report I feared it was Lieutenant Jordan, 3rd Cavalry. So it might seem that the allegedly wonderful reports of communication between widely separated Indian outfits were subject to the same weaknesses that our telegraph and radio messages have.

During the World War there were many Indians who enlisted and served with great honor in our Army. The old blanket Indian can never change; his sons can and have. Many have accepted the benefits of civilization and are workers and leaders among their people. Like many of us, they enjoy living an out-of-door life, hunting and fishing, but I hope and believe that they can take a great part in the future of our country.

GEORGE H. MORGAN,
Late Lieut., 3rd U.S. Cavalry.

APPENDIX A

Order of Indian Wars of the United States Proceedings of the Annual Meeting April 11, 1942

The annual business meeting was held at the Army and Navy Club, Washington, D.C., April 11, 1942. Due to uncertain conditions, the Board decided it would be inadvisable to hold the annual dinner this year.

The Commander called the meeting to order at four o'clock. Roll call and the reading of the minutes of the last meeting were ordered dispensed with and the following Companions recorded as present: Brig. Gen. Fred S. Foltz, William J. Ghent, Maj. Gen. Grote Hutcheson, Brig. Gen. James T. Kerr, Brig. Gen. Geo. W. McIver, Lt. Col. Henry S. Merrick, Col. Guy S. Norvell, Brig. Gen. Chas. D. Roberts and Donald McP. Whiting.

The Commander read the following statement and then turned over to the Recorder the business of conducting the meeting:

"Now that the hour has come for the annual meeting of the Order, I have the feeling of wishing to express my welcome to the members who are here present. Your attendance is a prospect of the continuation of the existence of our honorable Society from the time it was first organized many years ago.

"There is one important matter to which I wish to call your attention. At the Board meeting on January 8th of the present year, it was decided that a business meeting be held on April 11, 1942. At the same meeting a Nominating Committee, Gen. Brainard, Gen. Foltz and Col. Norvell, was appointed. Among those nominated to take office April 11, 1942, was Dr. Dorsey M. McPherson to become the Commander in the place of the present Commander. In accordance with the established rule, Dr. McPherson was elect to the office of Commander. However, on March 2, 1942, death came to him. Owing to the death of the Commander-elect, a vacancy exists in that office. Under the provisions of Article X of the Constitution the Board is empowered to name a member to fill this vacancy.

"After the death of Dr. McPherson in Washington, being conscious of his long service and distinction as a member of the Order, I attended his funeral service. At the same time I sent a communication to his widow expressing to her the regret for his death on the part of the Order.

"The Recorder will now please read the reports of officers and Committees."

Report of Recorder & Treasurer

The Investigating Committee approved the following nominations for Junior membership under the Junior Foundation Fund: — Accepted: — Charles L. Gandy, Jr., James M. Hartshorne, 2nd., Douglas S. Parker, Glaes G. M. Steelhammer, Jon A. Steelhammer and Joseph T. Whitaker. Not yet accepted: — Philip S. Grant, Edmund S. Kopmeier and Fred

V. D. Siefke.

The Investigating Committee confirmed the following Junior Companions as Hereditary: — Accepted: — Mathew A. Baxter, Van Santvoord Bowen, Thomas Q. Donaldson, 3rd., Lewis A. Greene, Edward G. McCleave, Jr., George R. Nichols, 3rd., Alexander M. Patch, 3d, and Dave W. Rockwell. Withdrew: — Swift McKinney and J. F. Reynolds Scott, Jr. Not yet accepted: — James P. S. Halloran, Henry D. Packard and John H. Stutesman, Jr.

Status of Junior Companions formerly confirmed as Hereditary: — Withdrew: — Joseph N. Green, Jr. and Kent Packard, Jr. Not yet accepted: — Chas. McGhee Baxter, Jr., George B. Foster, Sewell T. Kauffman, Edward C. Nicholson and John W. Scott. Formally suspended at this meeting for failure to accept membership or answer correspondence: — Edward L. Bingham, Wm. P. Kauffman, Philip W. Long, Chas. G. O'Connor, Alan W. Rockwell and Eugene O. Spencer.

George R. Nichols, 3d. is the only Companion to subscribe to life membership since the last annual meeting.

The following Companions were formally suspended for non-payment of dues: — Sidney V. Bingham, Davis B. McCoy, Girard L. McEntee, Jr., Chas. M. O'Connor, Jr., Cornelius C. Smith, Jr., Allen L. Story and Fred S. Strong, 3d. These Companions, as well as those indicated above as having been suspended for failure to accept membership, may apply for reinstatement under Artcile XIII of the Constitution.

The following resignations were considered and acted upon as follows: — Alexander M. Patch, 3d., accepted. Carl F. McKinney, Jr., action deferred pending outcome of further correspondence.

The following deaths, not previously reported, are recorded at this meeting: — James H. Cook, Edward F. Corson, 3d., Chas. A. Dempsey, Guy J. Fountain, Robert N. Getty, George W. Goode, Herbert L. Harries, Dorsey M. McPherson, P. Tecumseh Sherman, William H. Somervell and John C. F. Tillson.

Present membership: — Honorary 6, Associate 1, Original 42, Hereditary 179, Junior 35, Total 263. This is a decrease of 22 since the last annual meeting.

The following action of the Board as its meeting on January 8, 1942, was confirmed. Generals Foltz, Kerr, McIver and Roberts and Colonel Norvell were present.

"A business meeting be held April 11, 1942, in lieu of the usual annual meeting and dinner.

"Plan of reorganization of the Missouri-Pacific Railroad accepted.

"Continuation of Gen. Wood and Col. Ahern as members without further payment of dues.

"Renewal of Mr. Robert B. Parker's suggestion for a ten dollar life membership fee not favorably considered, and previous action adhered to.

"Publication of the following in connection with the arrow presented to the Order at the last annual meeting on behalf of Mrs. Francis R. Hagner: —

'The Indian arrow presented to the Order at the last annual meeting on behalf of Mrs. Francis R. Hagner, was one of a quiver full picked up by Dr. Dorsey M. McPherson on a battlefield in the San Andres mountains immediately following the defeat and rout of Victorio's band of Indians. Dr. McPherson had given this arrow to Dr. Hagner to add to his collection of Indian trophies.'

"Suggestion of Col. Wm. M. Wilder that membership cards be issued was not favorably considered.

"Suggestion that the Historian select from the Order's file an article suitable for publication in the annual report was approved."

Financial statement for the year ended Dec. 31, 1941

Receipts:

Cash:

Balance, January 1, 1941:

General fund	............................$	320. 64	
Junior fund	....	65. 50	
Junior fund income	....	65. 69	
			$ 451.83
Dues	....................................$	353. 50	
Initiation fees	....	5. 00	
Initiation fees (by transfer)	....	40. 00	
Interest and dividends	....	158. 10	
Junior foundation fund	....	37. 97	
Junior fund income	....	20. 00	
Stocks and bonds redeemed	....	500. 00	
Annual meeting and dinner	....	54. 50	
Miscellaneous	....	6. 09	
		$1,175.16	
			$1,626.99

Stocks and bonds:

Balance, January 1, 1941:

General fund	...........................$6,016. 14		
Junior fund	.... 1,155. 00		
		$7,171.14	
Adjustment to par value:			
General fund	............................$	133. 86	
Junior fund	....	20. 00	
		153.86	
			$7,325.00
			$8,951.99

Disbursements:

Cash:

Clerk hire	...............................$	300. 00	
Postage	....	46. 18	

Printing and stationery	73. 70		
Junior fund income (by transfer)	40. 00		
Annual meeting and dinner	41. 18		
Miscellaneous	31. 69		
		$ 532.75	

Balances, December 31, 1941:

General fund	$ 945. 08		
Junior fund	103. 47		
Junior fund income	45. 69		
		1,094.24	
			$1,626.99

Stocks and bonds:

Sold and redeemed:

General fund	$ 500. 00		
Junior fund	55. 00		
		$ 555.00	

Balances, December 31, 1941:

General fund	$5,650. 00		
Junior fund	1,120. 00		
		$6,770.00	
			$8,951.99

(Signed) Charles D. Roberts, Recorder and Treasurer.

Report of Auditing Committee

The Committee checked the books of the Treasurer and verified the cash in bank and the stocks and bonds on hand as of December 31, 1941, and found same correct.

(Signed) J. T. Kerr and Guy S. Norvell, Committee.

Report of Nominating Committee

The Committee nominated the following to take officer as of April 11, 1942. Col. Norvell, a member of the Committee, was not present when the nominations were made. Commander, Dr. Dorsey M. McPherson; Senior Vice-Commander, Lt. Col. Julian M. Cabell; Junior Vice-Commander, Maj. Gen. Chas. D. Rhodes,; Historian, Brig. Gen. G. W. McIver; Chaplain, Dr. Alexander Leo; Recorder and Treasurer, Brig. Gen. Chas. D. Roberts; Council: — Col. Robert H. Fletcher, Brig. Gen. Fred S. Foltz, Maj. Gen. Guy V. Henry, Brig. Gen. J. R. Kean, Brig. Gen. J. T. Kerr, Col. Geo. H. Morgan and Col. Guy S. Norvell.

(Signed) D. L. Brainard and Fred S. Foltz, Committee.

The Recorder certified all nominees as having been duly elected to their respective offices. However, owing to the death of the Commander-elect, the Board made the following changes: — Col. Cabell in place of Dr. McPherson as Commander. Gen. Rhodes in place of Col. Cabell as Senior Vice-Commander. Gen. Henry in place of Gen. Rhodes as Junior Vice-Commander. Lt. Col. Henry S. Merrick in place of Gen. Henry as Member of the Council.

These changes were confirmed by the members present at the annual meeting. All officers-elect, who were present, were duly installed.

Report of Historian

The following papers are gratefully acknowledged and have been filed with the Order's records in the Historical Section, Army War College. The books will be held temporarily in the files of the Order. From Col. Edgar Erskine Hume, A sketch of the official career of Col. Edward P. Vollum. From Mrs. David S. Rumbough, Report of Gen. D. S. Stanley on the expedition to the Yellowstone River, 1872. From Gen. Thos. Cruse, a copy of his book, Apache Days and After. From Col. Wm. A. Graham, a copy of his book, The Story of the Little Big Horn.

(Signed) Charles D. Rhodes, Historian.

The reports of officers and committees and the action taken were formally approved and confirmed.

New Business

Application of George Willcox McIver, Jr., for Hereditary membership was read and approved. The formality of sending the application to the Investigating Committee was ordered dispensed with.

Mr. Donald McP. Whiting, grandson of Dr. McPherson, addressed the meeting, and in his remarks concerning his grandfather's association with the Order, told of Dr. McPherson's deep appreciation of the honor bestowed upon him through his nomination and election to the highest office.

The following resolution, based upon the remarks of Major General Grote Hutcheson and concerning the devotion to and interest in the Order manifested by the late Dr. Dorsey M. McPherson, was proposed by Brigadier General James T. Kerr and duly adopted:

"Be it resolved by the Order of Indian Wars of the United States in annual meeting assembled, that in the death, since our last annual meeting, of our Commander-elect, Dr. Dorsey M. McPherson, we feel a very real loss of one who was sincerely interested in the welfare of the Order. He was for many years an officer and scrupulously attended the meetings unless unavoidably prevented. He took an active part in formulating the policies of the Order. His high sense of integrity, his strong Christian character, and his genial personality endeared him to all those with whom he was closely associated. His passing is not only a great loss to his family, but to the Order and to all who knew him and were associated with him.

Be it further resolved that this resolution be printed in the annual report and a copy furnished the widow of Dr. McPherson".

There being no further business, the meeting adjourned.

APPROVED:

G. W. McIver, Commander.
Charles D. Roberts, Recorder.

Recorder's Note: — After the annual meeting the Board decided, in view of present conditions, the fact that many members are in the armed forces and not likely to receive the annual report, and the necessity for conserving funds and paper, the annual report of the business meeting be mimeographed and the article selected by the Historian for publication be not published.

APPENDIX B

The Membership Rolls

From the first year until the last the membership was an impressive one. There were officers who actually fought on the western frontier and there were offsprings of offsprings who proudly vied for membership in this society. So, for the purpose of historical geneology of the society, herewith is the total listing of the membership as it existed over the years and as of 1942:

Charter Originals

Baird, George W.—Brigadier General
Bernard, Reuben F.—Brigadier General
Capron, Allyn—Captain
Cloud, J. W.—Brigadier General

Conrad, C. H.—Major
Hathaway, Forest H.—Brigadier General
Irwin, B. J. D.—Brigadier General

As there are, and will be at all times, men eminent for their abilities and patriotism whose personal interests are manifested by their researches, investigations, and reports, and whose views or efforts shall be or may have been directed to the accomplishment of the objects of the Society, or men who have rendered, in civil capacity, direct and exceptional service with troops in conflicts, battles, or in actual field service against hostile Indians, such men shall be eligible as Honorary or Associate Companions as the Official Board shall determine in each case.

Honorary

Brininstool, Earl A.
Burleson, Hon. Albert S.
Camp, Walter M.
Ghent, William Jr.
Graham, William A.—Colonel
Grinnell, Dr. George B.

Heye, George G.
Hodge, Dr. Frederick W.
Irwin, George LeR.—Brigadier General
Leo, Rev. Alexander
Neihardt, Dr. John G.

Associates

Barnes, Will C.
Cook, James H.
Daly, Henry W.—Lieutenant

Mazzanovich, Anton
Ostrander, Alson B.
Ross, Simon P.—Colonel

Commissioned officers and honorably discharged commissioned officers of the U.S. Army, Navy and Marine Corps, and of State and Territorial Military Organizations, and Acting Assistant Surgeons, U.S. Army, of the Caucasian race, who have been or who hereafter may be engaged in the service of the United States in any military grade whatsoever, in conflicts, battles or actual field service against hostile Indians within the jurisdiction of the United States, or whose service was under the authority or by the approval of the United States or any State or Territory in any Indian War or Campaign, or in connection with, or in the zone of any active Indian hostilities in any of the States or Territories of the United States. Those becoming Companions under any of the foregoing qualifications shall be designated as

Original Companions.

Ahern, George P.—Major
Albee, George E.—Captain
Alden, Charles H.—Colonel
Aleshire, James B.—Major General
Alvord, Benjamin—Brigadier General
Andrews, George—Brigadier General
Andrews, James M.—Colonel N. G.
Andrus, Edwin P.—Colonel
Averill, Nathan K.—Colonel
Ayer, Edward E.—Major
Bailey, Harry L.—Lieutenant Colonel
Bailey, Hobart K.—Colonel
Baird, William—Lieutenant Colonel
Baker, Chauncey B.—Colonel
Baker, David J.—Colonel
Baldwin, Frank D.—Major General
Barry, Michael H.—Lieutenant Colonel
Barry, Thomas H.—Major General
Barth, Charles H.—Brigadier General
Bates, Alfred E.—Major General
Baxter, George W.—Lieutenant
Beach, John—Brigadier General
Beach, William D.—Brigadier General
Bentley, Edwin—Colonel
Biddle, John—Brigadier General
Biddle, William S. Jr.—Major
Bingham, Gonzales S.—Colonel
Birmingham, Henry P.—Colonel
Bisbee, William H.—Brigadier General
Bishop, Hoel S.—Colonel
Bliss, Zenas R.—Major General
Blocksom, August P.—Brigadier General
Bloom, Jacob E.—Major
Bomus, Peter S.—Colonel
Booth, Charles A.—Colonel
Borden, George P.—Brigadier General
Bowen, Edgar C.—Captain
Bowen, William H. C.—Colonel
Braden, Charles—Lieutenant
Brainard, David L.—Brigadier General
Brett, Lloyd M.—Brigadier General
Brewer, Edwin P.—Colonel
Brown, William C.—Brigadier General
Bryan, Will C.—Captain

Budd, Otho W.—Captain
Buffington, Abraham P.—Colonel
Burbank, James B.—Brigadier General
Burkard, Oscar—Major
Burkhardt, Samuel Jr.—Colonel
Burnett, George R.—Lieutenant
Burt, Andrew S.—Brigadier General
Burton, George H.—Brigadier General
Byron, Joseph C.—Major
Cabell, DeRosey C.—Colonel
Cabell, Julian M.—Major
Campbell, Lafayette E.—Lieutenant Colonel
Carrington, Frank DeL.—Major
Carter, Robert G.—Captain
Casey, Thomas L.—Colonel
Cecil, Charles N.—Major
Chase, George F.—Brigadier General
Clay, Thomas J.—Lieutenant
Cloman, Sydney A.—Lieutenant Colonel
Cockey, Dr. Melchoir G.
Conline, John—Major
Converse, George L.—Colonel
Coolidge, Charles A.—Major
Corbusier, William H.—Colonel
Crowder, Enoch H.—Major General
Crozier, William—Major General
Cruse, Thomas—Brigadier General
Cusick, Cornelius C.—Captain
Dalton, Albert C.—Brigadier General
Dapray, John A.—Colonel
Dashiell, William R.—Colonel
Davis, Britton—Major N.G.
Davis, Charles L.—Brigadier General
Davis, George B.—Major General
Davis, George W.—Major General
Davis, Henry W.—Captain
Davis, Milton F.—Colonel
Davis, Thomas F.—Brigadier General
DeCouvey, Ferdinand E.—Major
DeFrees, Thomas M.—Captain
Dempsey, Charles A.—Colonel
Dempsey, William W.—Captain
Dickman, Joseph T.—Major General
Dimmick, Eugene D.—Brigadier General

274

Dodd, George A.—Brigadier General
Donaldson, Thomas Q.—Brigadier General
Dorst, Joseph H.—Colonel
Dravo, Edward E.—Colonel
Duggan, Walter T.—Brigadier General
Dykman, William N.—Lieutenant
Eagan, Charles P.—Brigadier General
Edgerly, Winfield Scott—Brigadier General
Elliott, Charles P.—Major
Emmet, Robert T.—Colonel
Evans, Robert K.—Brigadier General
Ewers, Ezra P.—Brigadier General
Ewing, Charles B.—Major
Farrow, Edward S.—Colonel O.R.C.
Feibeger, Gustav J.—Colonel
Fletcher, Robert H.—Captain
Foltz, Fred S.—Colonel
Forbes, Theodore F.—Brigadier General
Forbush, William C.—Colonel
Foster, Herbert S.—Colonel
Fountain, Samuel W.—Brigadier General
Fowler, Joshua L.—Major
Freeman, H. B.—Brigadier General
Fuller, Ezra B.—Colonel
Galbraith, Jacob G.—Colonel
Gale, George H. G.—Colonel
Gandy, Charles M.—Colonel
Gardener, Cornelius—Colonel
Gardner, William H.—Lieutenant Colonel
Garlington, Ernest E.—Brigadier General
Garrard, Joseph—Colonel
Gaston, Joseph A.—Colonel
Gerhardt, Charles—Colonel
Getty, Robert N.—Colonel
Girard, Alfred C.—Brigadier General
Girard, Joseph B.—Colonel
Glennan, James D.—Brigadier General
Godfrey, Edward S.—Brigadier General
Godwin, Edward A.—Brigadier General
Goldman, H. J.—Colonel
Goode, George W.—Colonel
Gordon, Davis S.—Brigadier General
Grant, Frederick D.—Major General
Greene, Lewis D.—Lieutenant Colonel
Grumley, Edward I.—Major
Guilfoyle, John F.—Colonel

Hale, Harry C.—Major General
Hall, William P.—Brigadier General
Hardaway, Benhamin F.—Lieutenant Col.
Hardin, Charles B.—Major
Hardin, Edward E.—Lieutenant Colonel
Harries, George H.—Major General
Hartman, John D. L.—Colonel
Harvey, Philip F.—Colonel
Hasson, Patrick—Captain
Hatfield, Charles A. P.—Colonel
Healy, James J.—Colonel N.G.
Hein, Otto L.—Lieutenant Colonel
Heyl, Charles H.—Colonel
Hodgson, Fred G.—Colonel
Holbrook, Willard A.—Major General
Hooton, Mott—Brigadier General
Howland, Carver—Major
Humphrey, Charles F.—Major General
Hunter, Edward—Colonel
Hunter, George K.—Colonel
Hutcheson, Grote—Major General
Ives, Francis J.—Major
Jarvis, Nathan S.—Captain
Jerome, Lovell H.—Colonel
Jones, Edward N. Jr.—Colonel
Kean, Jeff R.—Colonel
Kell, William H.—Lieutenant Colonel
Kelly, Luther S.—Captain
Kerr, James T.—Brigadier General
Kimball, William A.—Captain
King, Charles—Lieutenant Colonel
King, Joseph H.—Captain
Kingsbury, Henry P.—Colonel
Kneedler, William L.—Major
Knight, John T.—Brigadier General
Koehler, Lewis M.—Colonel
Kress, John A.—Brigadier General
LaGarde, Louis A.—Colonel
Landis, J. F. Reynolds—Colonel
Larned, Charles W.—Colonel
Lee, Jesse M.—Major General
Lemley, Henry R.—Major
Lewis, Thomas J.—Colonel
Liggett, Hunter—Major General
Lockwood, John A.—Colonel
Long, Oscar F.—Brigadier General

Lyon, Henry G.—Captain
McBlain, John F.—Captain
McCaleb, Thomas S.—Major
McCarthy, Daniel E.—Colonel
McClernand, Edward J.—Brigadier General
McDonald, Isaiah H.—Lieutenant
McDonald, John—Major
McDonald, John B.—Brigadier General
McGinniss, John R.—Brigadier General
McIver, George W.—Colonel
McPherson, Dr. Dorsey M.
Macomb, Augustus C.—Colonel
Maghee, Dr. Thomas G.
Mallory, John S.—Brigadier General
Mann, William A.—Brigadier General
Marshall, Francis C.—Colonel
Martin, William F.—Colonel
Matile, Leon A.—Brigadier General
Maus, Louis M.—Colonel
Maus, Marion P.—Brigadier General
Meade, Peter F.—Captain
Mercer, William A.—Colonel
Merrill, Elijah H.—Colonel
Michler, Francis—Lieutenant Colonel
Miles, Nelson A.—Lieutenant General
Miller, Crosby P.—Brigadier General
Miller, Samuel W.—Colonel
Miller, William A.—Major
Miller, William H.—Colonel
Mills, Albert L.—Major General
Mills, Anson—Brigadier General
Mills, Stephen C.—Colonel
Morgan, George H.—Colonel
Morris, Edward R.—Lieutenant Colonel
Morris, Hon. William E.
Muir, Charles H.—Major General
Mulhall, S. J.—Captain
Neifert, William W.—Major O.R.C.
Nichols, Maury—Lieutenant Colonel
Nicholson, William J.—Brigadier General
Noble, Robert H.—Captain
Oakes, James—Colonel
O'Connell, John J.—Brigadier General
Oliver, Robert S.—Brigadier General
Ovenshine, Samuel—Brigadier General
Owen, William O.—Colonel

Parker, James—Brigadier General
Parker, Percy—Colonel Mass. N.G.
Parker, Dr. William T.
Parkhurst, Charles D.—Colonel
Patch, Alexander M. Sr.—Captain
Patzki, Julius H.—Lieutenant Colonel
Paxton, Robert G.—Colonel
Penrose, George H.—Colonel
Perry, Alexander W.—Captain
Perry, John A.—Captain
Pershing, John J.—General
Phisterer, Fred—Captain
Piper, Alex R.—Captain
Pitcher, John—Lieutenant Colonel
Pitcher, William L.—Colonel
Pond, G. E.—Colonel
Poole, DeWitt C.—Colonel
Pope. J. W.—Brigadier General
Pratt, Richard H.—Brigadier General
Rathgeber, George H.—Major
Ray, Patrick H.—Brigadier General
Reade, Philip—Brigadier General
Reed, Hugh T.—Captain
Rhodes, Charles D.—Brigadier General
Rice, Sedgwick—Colonel
Richardson, Wilds P.—Colonel
Roach, Hampton M.—Lieutenant
Robinson, Daniel—Major
Robinson, William W.—Brigadier General
Roe, Charles F.—Major General NYNG
Roe, Fayette W.—Captain
Roudiez, Leon S.—Colonel
Ruhlen, George—Colonel
Russell, Frank W.—Lieutenant
Ryan, James A.—Major
Schuyler, Walter S.—Brigadier General
Scott, Hugh L.—Major General
Seyburn, Stephen Y.—Captain
Sheridan, Michael—Brigadier General
Sherwood, Wallace—Major N.G.
Shunk, William A.—Colonel
Simpson, John—Brigadier General
Skinner, John O.—Major
Slavens, Thomas H.—Brigadier General
Slocum, Hubert J.—Colonel
Slocum, S. L. H.—Lieutenant Colonel

Smiley, Samuel E.—Colonel
Smith, Abiel L.—Brigadier General
Smith, Cornelius C.—Colonel
Smith, Frederick A.—Brigadier General
Smith, George R.—Brigadier General
Spencer, Eugene J.—Colonel
Squiers, Hubert G.—Captain
Stanton, W. S.—Colonel
Starr, Charles G.—Lieutenant Colonel
Stedman, C. A.—Colonel
Steele, Matthew F.—Lieutenant Colonel
Stolbrand, Vasa E.—Colonel
Strong, Fred S.—Brigadier General
Sumner, Samuel S.—Major General
Swift, Eben—Brigadier General
Taylor, Charles W.—Colonel
Thornburgh, Robert M.—Colonel
Tiernon, John L.—Brigadier General
Tillson, John C. F.—Colonel
Tompkins, S. R. H.—Colonel
Town, Francis L.—Colonel
Traub, Pete E.—Colonel
Trippe, Percy E.—Colonel
Tyson, Hon. Lawrence D.
Varnum, Charles A.—Colonel
Vestal, Solomon P.—Colonel
Wagner, Arthur L.—Colonel

Walcutt, Charles C. Jr.—Colonel
Walker, Edgar S.—Colonel
Walsh, Robert D.—Colonel
Walton, J. M.—Lieutenant
Waltz, Millard F.—Colonel
Ward, Fred K.—Brigadier General
Waterman, John C.—Colonel
Webster, John McA.—Major
Weigel, William—Major General
West, Frank—Colonel
Wetmore, William B.—Major NYNG
Wey, Peter W.—Captain
Wheeler, Homer W.—Colonel
Wheeler, William H.—Captain
Wilcox, Timothy E.—Brigadier General
Wilder, Wilbur E.—Brigadier General
Winn, Frank L.—Major General
Winne, Robert L.—Captain
Wood, Leonard—Major General
Wood, William T.—Colonel
Wotherspoon, William W.—Major General
Wren, William C.—Major
Wright, Walter K.—Colonel
Wygant, Henry S.—Colonel
Yeatman, Richard T.—Brigadier General
Young, Samuel B.—Lieutenant General

The male descendants of Original Companions and the male descendants of those eligible for membership as Original Companions, such descendants having attained the age of twenty-one years, shall be eligible for membership and shall, when duly elected, be designated as Hereditary Companions. Commissioned officers of the Army, Navy and Marine Corps of the United States, Commissioned officers of the National Guard and persons holding commissions in the Officers' Reserve Corps, descendants of honorably discharged enlisted men who had the qualifications requisite for eligibility for membership as Original Companions save that of having been commissioned, are also eligible and may be elected as Hereditary Companions.

Hereditary Companions

Aleshire, Joseph P.—Major
Anders, Frank L.—Captain O.R.C.
Andrew, Henry H.—Colonel N.G.
Andrews, James M. IV
Andrus, Clift
Andrus, Cowles
Arnold, Allen

Baird, John A.—Major
Baker, John P. III
Baldwin, Theodore A. Jr.—Colonel
Baldwin, Theodore A. III—Lieutenant
Banning, Kendall—Lieutenant Colonel
Banning, William C.
Barth, Charles H. Jr.—Lieutenant

Baxter, Charles McG. Jr.
Benton, James W.
Bernard, Thomas P.—Lieutenant Colonel
Biddle, William S. III—Lieutenant
Biggs, Dr. Montgomery H.
Billings, Frank—Brigadier General O.R.C.
Bingham, Edward L.
Bingham, Sidney V.—Major
Bingham, Sidney V. Jr.
Bisbee, Eugene S.
Bisbee, William Haymond—Colonel
Bowen, Edgar C. Jr.
Brennen, Russel H.—Major
Brown, Franklin Q.—Colonel
Bryan, Charles S.—Colonel
Bryan, John K.—Lieutenant
Budd, Otho W. Jr.
Burrage, Russell Jr.
Butler, William J.—Major O.R.C.
Byron, Joseph W.—Major
Cantacuzene, Prince Michael
Capron, Paul A.—Major U.S.M.C.
Carlton, Schuyler C.
Carr, Clark M. Jr.
Cecil, Charles C.
Chandler, George M.—Captain
Chase, William B.
Clark, Dwight
Connor, Forbes B.
Conrad, Casper H. Jr.—Colonel
Converse, George L. Jr.—Major
Converse, George L. III
Corson, Edward F.—Lieutenant O.R.C.
Corson, Edward F. Jr.
Coyle, John P.
Craighead, Alexander McC.
Crossett, Edward D.
Crossman, J. Heron Jr.
Cruse, Fred T.—Major
Cruse, Frederick T. Jr.
Cruse, James H.
Danielson, Ole W.
Davis, Dudley—Major O.R.C.
Davis, Fellowes
Davis, William G.
Deming, Edwin W.—Captain

Donaldson, Thomas Q. Jr.—Lieutenant
Dooley, Oscar E.
Dorst, James A.—Major
Douglas, Henry B.
Dravo, Charles A.—Colonel
DuBarry, William H.—Lieutenant O.R.C.
Dunlap, Alexander M.
Dunn, Jared I.
Dykman, Jackson A.
Earle, Dr. Baylis H.
Edward, George W.
Edwards, Warren H. D.
Ely, Charles T.
Evans, Hornsby—Captain
Evans, Robert Wilson
Ewing, John F.—Lieutenant
Farrow, Edward S. Jr.
Farrow, Vernon R.
Farrow, William H.
Finley, Thomas D.—Major
Fletcher, Robert H. Jr.—Major
Foster, Archibald McG.
Foster, Francis A.
Foster, George B.
Foster, Volney W.
Fountain, Guy J.
Garlington, Creswell—Major
Gatewood, Charles B.—Major
Gerhard, Dr. Arthur H.
Gerhard, Arthur H. Jr.
Gilpin, McGhee T.
Goddard, Calvin H.—Major O.R.C.
Godfrey, David E.—Captain
Godfrey, Dr. Edward S. Jr.
Godfrey, Russell
Goldman, Alfred M.—Captain
Grant, Francis C.
Grant, Ulysses S. III—Lieutenant Colonel
Grant, Water S.—Lieutenant Colonel
Grant, Walter S. Jr.
Greene, Douglas T.—Major
Greene, Joseph N. Jr.
Greene, Lawrence V.
Greene, Michael J. L.
Greenough, Charles E.—Major O.R.C.
Greve, Charles T.

Guthrie, Bayard
Haering, Roy W.—Lieutenant
Hagner, Dr. Francis R.
Hagner, Randall H. Jr.
Halloran, George M.—Major
Hancock, John M.
Hancock, Stoddard P.
Hardaway, Benjamin F. Jr.
Hardin, Donald C.—Lieutenant
Harries, Herbert L.—Captain
Hedges, Edgar—Captain
Hein, Herbert R.—Lt. Commander U.S.N.
Helm, William F.
Henderson, Virgil J.
Henry, Guy V.—Colonel
Henry, William S.
Hentz, Albert G.—Lieutenant Colonel
Herrick, Samuel
Herron, James E.
Hochberg, Max—Captain
Hofer, Edward J.
Hoffman, Floyd H.—Lieutenant
Hogle, John R.
Holbrook, Willard A. Jr.—Lieutenant
Horton, William E.—Brigadier General
Howard, Chancey O.—Captain N.G.
Howard, Harry S.
Hume, Edgar E.—Major
Hunt, Henry J.—Colonel
Henry, Henry J. Jr.—Lieutenant
Hunter, George B.—Lieutenant Colonel
Hunter, George B. Jr.
Hunter, Russell H.
Hussey, Albert S.
Hutchins, Walter Stilson
Jones, Edward N. III—Lieutenant
Kauffman, Andrew H.
Kauffman, R. King
Kauffman, Sewell T.
Kauffman, William P.
Kenyon, Jacob M.—Colonel
Kerr, James D.
King, Albion S.
King, Charles III
King, Harry L.—Lieutenant Colonel
King, Rufus—Commander U.S.N.

Knox, Dudley W.
Kresse, Clarence C.—Lt. Commander U.S.N.
LaGarde, Richard D.—Captain
Larned, John H.—Lieutenant Colonel
Larned, Paul A.—Major
Lemley, Rowan P.—Major
Leonard, Laurence
Lewis, Gibson
Lines, Harvey K.—Captain
Long, John D.—Colonel
Long, Philip W.
Loomis, Franklin A.
Lull, Charles E. T.—Lieutenant Colonel
Lyne, Harry Jr.
McCowan, Robert J. F.
McCoy, Davis B.
McCoy, John G.—Captain
McDonald, Robert D.—Colonel O.R.C.
McEntee, Ducat
McEntee, Girard L. Jr.
McEwan, John A.
McEwan, Robert H.
McGarry, William R.
McIver, Alexander—Captain
McIver, George W. Jr.
McIver, Renwick S.—Commander U.S.N.
McKinney, Carl F. Jr.
Macy, Edward W.—Major
Magruder, Charles A.
Magruder, David L. Jr.
Major, Ralph H. Jr.
Mauck, Frederico F.
Mauck, Herbert S.
Merchant, Marvin H.
Merrick, Henry S.—Lieutenant Colonel
Merrill, John H.—Colonel
Millis, Wade—Lieutenant Colonel O.R.C.
Modisette, Welton M. Jr.
Moffett, Clemens—Captain O.R.C.
Morton, Charles E.—Colonel
Morton, Emmet C.—Major
Morton, Emmet C. Jr.
Murphy, James P.—Captain
Naylor, Emmett H.—Major O.R.C.
Newell, John E.
Nichols, Frank B.

Nicholson, Edward C.
Norvell, Guy S.
O'Connor, Charles G.
O'Connor, Charles M. Jr.—Major
O'Connor, Edwin—Major
Ord, J. Garesche—Major
Packard, Kent
Packard, Kent Jr.
Parker, Courtlandt—Major
Parker, Robert B.
Parker, Robert B. Jr.
Parkhurst, George C.—Captain
Patch, Alexander M. III
Patch, Joseph D.—Major
Patterson, Robert
Pemberton, Ralph
Phelps, Fred C.—Major
Pierce, Arthur J.
Piper, Alexander Ross Jr.
Pleasanton, Eugene S.—Major
Poultney, Arthur E.
Powell, Graham H.
Rafferty, William A.—Major
Read, Burton Y.—Major
Read, George W. Jr.—Lieutenant
Reber, Miles—Lieutenant
Reeve, Charles McG.—Brigadier General
Richards, John B.—Lieutenant Colonel
Richardson, Malbon G.—Lt. Colonel
Roberts, Charles D.—Brigadier General
Rockwell, Alan W.
Rockwell, Charles K.—Captain O.R.C.
Rockwell, Stuart W.
Romeyn, Charles A.—Colonel
Root, William F. S.
Ross, Edward H.
Roth, Edward Jr.—Major
Roth, Edward III
Ruhlen, George IV
Rumbough, David S.—Captain
Rumbough, Joseph W.—Major
Russell, George M.—Lieutenant Colonel
Russell, Walter H.

Russell, William W.
Ryan, Reginald T.
Safford, Ralph K.
Scott, J. F. Reynolds—Captain
Scott, John W.
Scott, Lewis M.—Major O.R.C.
Scott, Richard C. Jr.
Seyburn, Wesson
Shaw, Quincey Adams Jr.—Captain
Sherman, P. Tecumseh
Slocum, Hubert J. Jr.
Slocum, Myles S.
Somervell, William H.
Spencer, Eugene O.
Spencer, Eugene T.
Stanley, Joseph W.—Captain
Steever, Edgar Z. III—Colonel
Story, Allen L.—Lieutenant
Strauss, Elliott B.—Ensign U.S.N.
Strong, Fred S. III
Sweitzer, Charles McG.
Sweitzer, Nelson B.
Sweitzer, Nelson B. Jr.
Swift, Eben IV
Taylor, Herbert E.—Major
Tompkins, David D.—Lieutenant Colonel
Townsend, J. Henry—Captain N.G.
Ulio, James A.—Major
VanVoohees, Albert B.
Vincent, Dr. Thomas N.
Vollum, Paul E.
VonKummer, Samuel M.
Walsh, Robert LeG.—Major
Wells, Rush S.—Colonel
West, Arthur K.
Whiteside, Warren W.
Whiting, Donald M.
Wickman, Clarence H.—Captain
Wilder, William M.—Colonel
Wilson, George F. Jr.
Yates, George L.
Zimmerman, Charles B.—Major
Zoll, Allen A.

AND

Steelhammer, Henry H.—Captain Swedish Army

Original and Hereditary Companions may propose for membership as Junior Companions a minor who fulfills as to descent, direct or collateral, the qualifications, except as to age, for membership as Hereditary Companion as set forth in this Article. Upon such Junior Companion becoming of age, if deemed worthy by the Investigating Committee, he shall become automatically an Hereditary Companion for life, with all the privileges pertaining thereto.

Junior Companions

Ahern, Philip E. Jr.
Anders, Franklin Q.
Barlow, J. Woodman Bryan
Barlow, Raymond C. Jr.
Baxter, Mathew A.
Berg, Frederick W.
Bowen, Van Santvoord
Brown, Dudley B. W.
Bryan, John K. Jr.
Byron, Joseph Rice
Chase, George F. McC.
Corson, Joseph K.
Coyle, Lawrence T.
Donaldson, David R.
Donaldson, John W.
Donaldson, Thomas Q. III
Douglas, Henry B. II
Eynon, William J. II
Fountain, Guy J. Jr.
Fountain, Warren L.
Gandy, Charles L.
Garlington, Creswell Jr.
Gilpin, Kenneth N. Jr.
Godfrey, Edward S. III
Godfrey, Macdonald
Grant, Philip S.
Greene, Douglass
Greene, Lewis A.
Griswold, George M.
Halloran, James P. S.
Hardin, Donald C. Jr.
Hartman, George F.
Hartshorne, James M. II
Huffman, Forbes B.
Hume, Edgar E. Jr.
Kauffman, Andrew H. Jr.
Kauffman, George A. Jr.

Kauffman, R. King Jr.
Kerr, James D. Jr.
King, Charles Jr.
Kopmeier, Edmund S.
McCleave, Edward G. Jr.
McEwan, Oswald B.
McIver, George W. III
McKinney, Swift
Mauck, Frederick T.
Mauck, Ward L.
Newell, John E. III
Nichols, George R. III
Packard, Henry D.
Parker, Courtlandt Jr.
Parker, Douglas S.
Parker, James Jr.
Patch, Alexander M. Jr.
Rockwell, David W.
Rumbough, Joseph W. Jr.
Scott, David
Scott, J. F. Reynolds Jr.
Scott, Peter D.
Scott, Loxley R.
Siefke, Fred V. D.
Smith, Cornelius C. Jr.
Spencer, James T.
Stearns, Carle W.
Steelhammer, Charles
Steelhammer, Claes G. H.
Steelhammer, Jon A.
Stutesman, John H. Jr.
Sutton, Charles Zook Jr.
Taylor, Reuben C. Jr.
Trippe, Richard E. Jr.
Whitaker, Joseph T.
Yeiser, William C.

281

INDEX

285

286